A THOUSAND
MAY FALL

ALSO BY BRIAN MATTHEW JORDAN

The War Went On: Reconsidering the Lives of Civil War Veterans
(edited with Evan C. Rothera)

Marching Home: Union Veterans and Their Unending Civil War

A THOUSAND MAY FALL

Life, Death, and Survival in the Union Army

BRIAN MATTHEW JORDAN

Liveright Publishing Corporation

A Division of W. W. Norton & Company

Independent Publishers Since 1923

For information about permission to reproduce selections from this book, write to
Permissions, Liveright Publishing Corporation, a division of
W. W. Norton & Company, Inc., 500 Fifth Avenue, New York, NY 10110

For information about special discounts for bulk purchases, please contact
W. W. Norton Special Sales at specialsales@wwnorton.com or 800-233-4830

Manufacturing by Lake Book Manufacturing
Production manager: Julia Druskin

Library of Congress Cataloging-in-Publication Data

Names: Jordan, Brian Matthew, 1986– author.
Title: A thousand may fall : life, death, and survival in the Union Army /
Brian Matthew Jordan.
Description: First edition. | New York : Liveright Publishing Corporation, A division of
W. W. Norton & Company, 2021. | Includes bibliographical references and index.
Identifiers: LCCN 2020041255 | ISBN 9781631495144 (hardcover) |
ISBN 9781631495151 (epub)
Subjects: LCSH: United States. Army. Ohio Infantry Regiment, 107th (1862–1865)
| Ohio—History—Civil War, 1861–1865—Regimental histories. | United States—
History—Civil War, 1861–1865—Participation, German. | United States—History—Civil
War, 1861–1865—Participation, German American. | United States—History—Civil War,
1861–1865—Participation, Immigrant. | German American soldiers—Ohio—History—
19th century. | Immigrants—Ohio—History—19th century. | United States—History—
Civil War, 1861–1865—Regimental histories—Ohio. | United States—History—Civil
War, 1861–1865—Regimental histories.
Classification: LCC E525.5 107th .J67 2021 | DDC 973.7/471—dc23
LC record available at https://lccn.loc.gov/2020041255

Liveright Publishing Corporation, 500 Fifth Avenue, New York, N.Y. 10110
www.wwnorton.com

W. W. Norton & Company Ltd., 15 Carlisle Street, London W1D 3BS

For My Dad
and
For the 107th Ohio Volunteer Infantry (1862–1865)

You will not fear the terror
of night, nor the arrow that flies by day,
nor the pestilence that stalks in the darkness,
nor the plague that destroys at midday.
A thousand may fall at your side,
ten thousand at your right hand,
but it will not come near you.
—*Psalm 91*

CONTENTS

A THOUSAND
MAY FALL

Ohio in the Civil War

PROLOGUE

FROM THEIR POSITION on the campus of the Adams County Almshouse—a trio of buildings that sat in a neat row along Gettysburg's northern edge—the Ohioans surveyed the wide, flat plain that extended between the Carlisle Road and the Harrisburg Pike. To the west, a sequence of sturdy ridges creased the ground, and an unfinished railroad trace gashed into the earth. Stone fences and stands of timber supplied the Union soldiers deployed there with a measure of protection; units huddled behind fence rails, beneath the crown of Oak Ridge, and in the fingers of the McPherson's Woods. But out here north of town there was no cover, no shelter, no refuge to be found. As they looked to their front on this warm July afternoon, the men spied only the slight earthen knob that locals called Blocher's Knoll. War makes a habit of promoting otherwise unremarkable ripples in the ground to sudden significance, and in that respect, this day would be no different. Atop the forlorn rise, a precocious division commander unlimbered four Napoleon guns, shook out a skirmish line, and planted a tiny brigade—stretching the thin blue ribbon coiled around Gettysburg just about as far as it would stretch.

Shot and shell soon winged overhead—the first portent of enemy soldiers massing for an assault. After what seemed a lifetime, the 107th Ohio Volunteer Infantry was nodded toward the knoll to brace the beleaguered Union line. They advanced with heavy steps and knotted throats, some inserting one last cheekful of tobacco. To be sure, such a daunting errand might have given any troops pause. But it was a distinct dread that flooded the Ohioans. Exactly two months before, at the battle of Chancellorsville, the men had been among the first troops crushed under the weight of "Stonewall" Jackson's flank attack—a daring maneuver that delivered twenty-six thousand rebels to a federal line that derelict commanders had left dangling dangerously in the air. In mere minutes, Jackson's howling rebels added more than half of the regiment to the Civil War's ever-lengthening register of killed, wounded, missing, and captured. Now, on this first July afternoon of the war's third summer—once more deployed on the right flank of a threadbare Union line—it seemed as though the past was repeating itself.[1]

The prospect of still more death and suffering unnerved the men, but no more than the likelihood of another embarrassing defeat. For the last six weeks, the northern press had defamed the Ohioans and their comrades in the Army of the Potomac's Eleventh Corps as lily-livered cowards, consuming column inches with mocking editorials. A thrashing as thorough as the one the Yankee army took at Chancellorsville demanded a scapegoat, and hasty correspondents found one in the regiments that extended the federal line along the Orange Turnpike. "Threats, entreaties, and orders of commanders," the *Daily National Intelligencer* harrumphed from Washington, D.C., "were of no avail . . . Thousands of these cowards threw down their guns and soon streamed down the road toward headquarters." Even their comrades within the army joined in the insults. "Every man [in the Eleventh Corps]," one federal captain indignantly snorted, "ought to be hauled off the face of the Earth."[2]

With some clever wordsmithing, other Union regiments might have transformed that disastrous rout into a defiant stand, marveling at their ability to squeeze off even one round from such a hopeless position. They might have turned for support to Henry Lee Scott's *Military Dictionary*, the well-thumbed soldier's primer that insisted there were "no troops with sufficient *sang-froid* and self-possession" to resist the "ball and grape" of a flank attack. But the 107th Ohio failed in that effort. As an ethnically German regiment amply stocked with immigrant soldiers—nearly seven in ten were foreign-born—its men battled ethnic stereotypes no less than the rebels. "You have no concept at all," one soldier protested, "how deep Know Nothingism is rooted in all layers of American society." Indeed, nativism was so woven into the fabric of Civil War America that an official field manual advised Union medical officers to regard all German soldiers as potential malingerers. "It has happened me to observe a larger number feigning and fewer wounded amongst the Germans than the Americans or Irish," its author wrote. "I say this whilst remembering the devotion of the German race to national unity and liberty, and their attachment to their adopted country; but they love ease and money not less—many of them more."[3]

So it was that on a battlefield teeming with ten thousand men, the 107th Ohio felt uniquely abandoned—and entirely alone.

MUSKETRY SMOKE lazed on the horizon as Augustus Vignos's company hastened toward the knoll. All his life, the twenty-four-year-old captain had longed to become a soldier. As a youngster in Louisville, Ohio, a small farming community tucked in the state's northeastern corner, he had drilled a company of neighborhood boys armed with wooden muskets on the square anchored by his father's humming tavern and livery stable. His father's protests prevented him from enlisting when the war broke out in April 1861, but nothing—not even his "weak" vision, the consequence of a risky childhood operation to correct crossed eyes—could keep him from the war for very long. That September, Augustus mustered into Company I of the 19th Ohio Volunteer Infantry as a musician. Thickly mustached and sporting a tuft of fringe beneath his lip, he looked every bit the part. After several weeks of training at Camp Dennison, perched in the leafy hills north of Cincinnati, his regiment was packed off to Kentucky for an unforgiving winter. Those who survived were rewarded only with a tiresome, foot-blistering march into Tennessee. War makes a habit of that, too. By April 6, 1862, when he climbed aboard an overcrowded river steamer bound for Pittsburg Landing, his fife was no longer chirping martial tunes.[4]

The boat carried Augustus and his comrades through a drenching rain, but delivered them to a dismal scene. Dead bodies littered the ground as far as the eye could see. Twisted and swollen, they betrayed the calamity that had been visited upon Grant's army on the first day at Shiloh. Augustus hooked through the human debris, reaching after dark the place where his regiment would rest upon arms, wring out their socks, and await the renewal of battle. They went in at five o'clock the next morning, halting at the edge of a field, holding the right of their brigade. An enemy battery nestled in the woods opposite belched an impersonal greeting; from the brambles that knotted the surrounding acres came the crackle of small-arms fire. Though uncovered and outgunned for much of the day, the men stood "like soldiers." It was the same tale up and down the federal lines that day.[5]

Reveling in Grant's uncanny ability to wrest victory from the jaws of defeat, northern newspapers failed to fully convey the human agonies of Shiloh and its aftermath. In fact, as northerners exulted over the headlines, typhoid fever delivered Augustus to a congested army hospital. (Bivouacking in raw mud for more than a week after fighting a battle, as it turned out, was hardly conducive to good health.) By an odd quirk of fate, back in Louisville—more than six hundred miles away—the same disease had afflicted his father. Augustus slowly regained his strength, but by the time he returned to Ohio bearing a medical discharge, his father had already succumbed to the illness. Whether at the front or at home, it seemed that Augustus Vignos could not escape the pall of death.

The Shiloh veteran was still recovering—from his own grief no less than the typhoid—when Seraphim Meyer called on him late that summer. The prominent lawyer from nearby Canton had been

tapped as the colonel of a new volunteer infantry regiment, at once
a reward for his fidelity to the Democratic Party and an opportunity
to appeal to northeastern Ohio's large ethnically German population.
Meyer had no military experience, and he needed recruits. Augustus
Vignos could supply both. His late father's handsome brick tavern
still throbbed with activity, and he "knew all the roads and trails" and
most of the travelers "within a radius of forty miles." Already restless
and eager for another chance at soldiering, Vignos went to work. By
September, he had recruited more than seventy men for Company H
of the 107th Ohio Volunteer Infantry.[6]

BACK IN GETTYSBURG, as Captain Vignos steadied his men from
Stark County atop Blocher's Knoll, Second Lieutenant George Billow
braced neighboring Company I for the fight. Born in Hesse-Darmstadt
in 1833, Billow was eleven when he emigrated to the United States
with his parents and seven siblings. They formed the tail end of the
Auswanderung, the migration of self-sufficient farmers, shop owners,
and artisans—according to one historian, "people who had something
to lose, and who were losing it"—across the Atlantic. Buoyant reports
from the growing population of ethnically German immigrants in the
United States (the German population would swell to some 1.3 million by the eve of the Civil War) helped to revive dreams dashed by
the soaring land prices and dwindling harvests at home. While later
waves of German immigration delivered prominent political refugees
and veterans of the failed democratic revolutions of 1848 to American
shores, the *Auswanderer* embarked for the United States not "to build
something new," but to "conserve something old."[7]

For the Billows, that "something old" was sowing their own land
and reaping their own harvests. They left Hesse-Darmstadt ("notwithstanding the noble air of its spacious mansions," the English novelist
Frances Trollope remarked, it appeared to be "a city whose glory has
passed away") for a farm near Sandusky, Ohio, not far from the shores
of Lake Erie. George tilled the fields until the age of seventeen, when
he was apprenticed to wagoner Ambrose Ochs—himself a recent Ger-

man immigrant—in nearby Fremont. The "low wages and long days," as one carriage maker remembered, made most boys "long for the time when [their] apprentice days would be over." After perfecting his craft in Cleveland, he trekked south, along the towpath of the Ohio & Erie Canal, to Akron; there, he rived hickory spokes for two buggy manufacturers and started a family. By 1860, he had struck out on his own, establishing a profitable wagon-making concern.[8]

Not unlike Augustus Vignos, George Billow felt called to serve as war rent the nation. "Inspired by a stern sense of loyalty," the Republican enlisted as a private in the 107th Ohio on August 7, 1862. His unruly hair notwithstanding, Billow cut a soldierly profile with his square jaw and prominent nose. Together with fellow Akronites Richard Feederle and William Bechtel, he manned a recruiting office in Adam Krohle's leather goods store at the foot of Howard Street. "As they are all active, energetic, and patriotic," the *Summit County Beacon* observed, "we doubt not they will speedily fill up a company, in this vicinity, for that splendid regiment."[9]

Fresh recruits gather at the corner of Howard and Market Streets in Akron during the Civil War. *Samuel Lane Collection, Summit Memory*

The editor was prescient, for scores of German-speaking immigrants seized the opportunity "to enter the service of their adopted country in a regiment composed of their own countrymen" over the next three weeks. Those men joined the nearly two hundred thousand German immigrants who donned federal blue during the Civil War. Though accounting for no more than five percent of the U.S. population, German-Americans constituted more than ten percent of the Union armies. Today, even devoted students of Civil War history maintain only the dimmest memories of their service. Yet German immigrants proved—beyond even the fabled Irish, the fighting sons of Erin—to be the "most overrepresented" cohort among Lincoln's legions. This was especially the case across the Midwest, which had experienced a surge in German immigration in the decade prior to the war. In part, the blistering condemnation of the Germans after Chancellorsville serves as an index of their size and visibility as a cohort in the Union army.[10]

Most German immigrants fought in native-born regiments, or else in "mixed" outfits that fielded three to five companies of foreign-born volunteers. But with nearly seventy percent of the men on its muster rolls non-native, the 107th Ohio numbered itself among just thirty Union regiments deemed "ethnically German"—the fifth of six mustered from the Buckeye State. Among the thirty-five hundred regiments that fought in the Union armies, it was at once ordinary and unique. Its ranks weathered the human ordeal of war even as language, identity, and popular perceptions of their loyalties set them apart. They were men betwixt and between, men who belonged but did not.[11]

Some historians have supposed that German regiments "were little more than an extension of traditional German associations and clubs," and that "the organizing of German regiments had little if anything to do with the lofty goals of preserving the Union or the abolition of slavery." Recovering fewer "expressions of patriotism" among ethnically German soldiers, these scholars conclude that many "did not know 'what they were fighting for'—aside from the pay, their own survival, and perhaps vague hopes of recognition and advancement in American society." Doubtless this was the case for many ethnic soldiers (including the not insignificant number drawn from *Turnverein*, German clubs that promoted physical vigor and masculine culture through gymnastics). But we should pause before ascribing "more mundane goals" or merely mercenary motives to immigrant soldiers. When the men of the 107th Ohio foregrounded their suffering and rehearsed their sacrifices, they revealed more about their culture than their ideological commitments.[12]

IT WOULD BE difficult to imagine a worse position than the one the 107th Ohio had been ordered to assume in Gettysburg that afternoon. After spilling onto Blocher's Knoll, they formed a line that faced north and east, holding the tip of a sharp salient that would soon invite a fierce enemy musketry fire. Holding the line in Company A were two sons of Navarre, a tiny collection of grist mills and dry goods stores tucked in a curl of the Tuscarawas River—one of many villages that owed its existence to the Ohio & Erie Canal. The canal measured time in Navarre, and both Alfred Rider and William Siffert were reared on romanticized tales of the days before the "artificial river," which exported bushels of wheat and delivered the fires of spiritual reform. Even decades after the war, local histories wrote elegiacally of Alfred's father, Jacob, the "good pioneer" and strapping yeoman farmer who, axe in hand, helped to plant a new settlement in "the wilderness." Similar notice was paid to William's father, Joseph, a farmer and miller whose wagon first trundled to Stark County within a decade of Ohio's statehood.[13]

The Riders were among the most prominent families in Navarre. Jacob made a comfortable living manufacturing harnesses and saddles; throughout the 1850s, the outspoken Democrat was also elected to several terms as a township trustee. In 1860, however, "Father Rider" laid aside partisan fidelities and cast his ballot for Abraham Lincoln and the Republican ticket. The demands of southern Democrats at the party's convention in Charleston—including calls for a federal slave code, a constitutional amendment protecting slavery in perpetuity, and the reopening of the transatlantic slave trade—left him "thoroughly disgusted." While his personal feelings about African-Americans are irretrievable—in the nineteenth century, opposition to slavery hardly implied a ready embrace of racial equality—he could not abide the thought that the Union might be sacrificed to the self-interest of "aristocratic" slaveholders.[14]

Rider was not unique among Ohio's ethnically German population. Throughout the 1850s, violence, aggressiveness, and political discord prompted more than a few northerners to abandon the studied neglect with which they had regarded slavery during the age of the early republic. Rejecting the old consensus view that chattel slavery was a "necessary evil," white southern slaveholders—reaping the boggling windfalls of the cotton boom, and alarmed by a new, more vocal abolitionism—demonstrated that they had enough vigor, creativity, and determination to plant their prized institution anywhere. Slave renditions and gag rules, ballot box swindles and activist court decisions conspired to persuade many northerners that the "Slave Power" posed a real threat—not only to the Union, but to the very idea of self-government. The new Republican Party quickly tallied support from Whig and Democratic voters whose old parties collapsed under the weight of events. "Between 1856 and 1860," one historian contends, many "German working people" rallied to the Republican banner. Appeals to the promise of "free labor" and republican liberty were persuasive enough to overcome both the new party's nativism and the "distance" some wary immigrants kept from antislavery crusaders. In Cleveland, for instance, "nearly half" of the city's German population cast ballots for Lincoln. The returns were still more impressive in Cincinnati, where the ethnic wards cushioned Republican margins at the polls.[15]

Jacob Rider thus expressed few if any reservations when his twenty-three-year-old son Alfred enlisted in the 107th Ohio in July 1862. A few weeks later, Alfred's boyhood "chum," eighteen-year-old William O. Siffert, joined him. As one of the youngest soldiers in Company A,

William, with his coal-black eyes and mane of matching hair, quickly "won his way into the hearts of the officers and privates," one comrade recalled. Since casualty reports regularly crowded newspaper columns by the war's second summer, the boys had some indication of what they could expect. They could also rely on a firsthand account from the front: earlier that year, William's older brother, Alfred, suspended his studies at Otterbein College and mustered into the ranks of the 76th Ohio Volunteer Infantry. That spring, Alfred would have plied his family with tales of what he saw at Shiloh—the same fight in which Vignos experienced his baptism by fire. Even so, as Alfred and William reached for their cartridge boxes atop the knoll, that rude schoolhouse at Navarre's edge must have seemed a world away.[16]

GIVEN THEIR newfound political allegiances, it was hardly surprising that Rider and Siffert were among the regiment's first and most enthusiastic volunteers. But hardly anyone would have expected Christian Rieker and John Brunny to respond to the steady drumbeats beckoning young men to war. Rieker and Brunny were both sons of Zoar, a pacifist, communitarian society nestled in the chestnut- and hickory-shaded Tuscarawas Valley, no more than fifteen miles south and just slightly east of Navarre. Almost a half-century before, a quest for religious freedom and spiritual "re-birth" delivered an earnest band of Württemberg Separatists to northeastern Ohio. Adhering to Radical Pietism, these men and women had chafed under the eighteenth-century "rationalism" of the Lutheran Church. Embracing the Holy Scriptures as the only true "measure and guide" of their lives, the Separatists withdrew from all "ecclesiastical connections and constitutions," refusing to doff their hats, bend their knees, or uncover their heads for anyone. "True Christian life," they held, demanded neither ceremony nor sectarianism. Anticipating Christ's return, the Separatists withheld their children from the "schools of Babylon" and rejected the military service required by the state. "We cannot serve the state as soldiers," they explained, "because a Christian cannot murder his enemy, much less his friend."[17]

The Separatists became the object of taunts that quickly devolved into tyranny. The state levied steep fines on parents who refused to send their children to the state-run school. Those who could not pay were "imprisoned indefinitely, suffering the ill effects of bad food, vermin, stench, hard labor, and lack of heat." The children of those jailed were packed off to orphanages. Ironically, these humiliations merely reinforced the unique bond that welded the Separatist community together.[18]

Unable to find any refuge from oppression in the Fatherland, the Separatists set sail for America. In August 1817, just three months after their crammed ship nudged its way into the English Channel, the Separatists offloaded onto the docks of Philadelphia. There they met a German Moravian land broker whose bargain price on a 5,500-acre tract in northeastern Ohio proved irresistible. That autumn, they zagged their way through spinneys of forest and over chains of hills, arriving just before Christmas at the "little place" they called Zoar. While one of the earliest arrivals recalled planting "a wretched settlement of log huts" in a "trackless wilderness," his reminiscence (not unlike the cloying boosterism of local histories) rendered invisible the Delaware people who had long seeded the soil.[19]

Zoar quickly grew beyond a collection of log huts and into a bustling community. In April 1819, having survived the vicissitudes of an Ohio winter, the refugees inked Articles of Association for the Society of Separatists of Zoar. Disclaiming all ownership in property, the Zoarites joined the host of communitarian experiments and "backwoods utopias" that dotted the landscape of mid-nineteenth-century America. Even so, the Zoarites tracked national political developments with some interest and readily identified slavery as the source of the deepening sectional rift. Sympathies with the cause of emancipation—one of the Separatists regarded slavery as "a blot of shame" that "cannot be allowed to stay"—collided with their pacifism, especially as the shock and violence of the war moved the conflict in new, more revolutionary directions. Bloodletting on such a massive scale demanded deeper meaning, which at least some Civil War Americans divined in slavery's fitful demise. Still, most Zoarites proved stubbornly resistant to war fever as it romped across the nation. In fact, after considering the war's means and ends, many renewed their commitment to pacifism.[20]

Master tinner John Brunny and his friend the blacksmith Christian Rieker, however, would not be among them. In late August 1862, the duo of twenty-year-olds, together with ten of their neighbors, announced that they would enlist in the 107th Ohio. The eldest of the seven children born to Zoar's shoemaker, Brunny would join the regiment's band—a natural fit, considering how music dominated the Zoar soundscape (the village boasted an orchestra, chorus, and brass ensemble). Rieker, whose hazel eyes and auburn hair were offset by a thick mustache, set aside his hammer and anvil and attached himself to Company I. "We know that it is contrary to the Principles of the Separatists to go to war," they declared, "but now, in this present crisis, in order to contend for freedom and human rights, we feel it our duty to unite our forces with those who, at the first call, sacrifice all . . . in order to contend on behalf of those who cannot fight for posterity and for a free home." While society elders resolved that even a crusade against slavery could not justify a resort to arms, these men clearly perceived something of their own struggles in the war. Slavery was simply a more extreme variety of the tyranny that their ancestors had escaped a generation before. Southern planters denied enslaved men, women, and children their freedom, but they also menaced white liberty— making a mockery of democratic institutions and promising to plant slavery even where the founders had declared "free soil" for "free men." For lads like Brunny and Rieker who believed in the dignity of labor and subscribed to a millennial vision of personal, social, and societal reform, slavery was a curse.[21]

Still, their clear-eyed statement of purpose concealed gnawing doubts. Initiation into military service is an agonizing transition for anyone, but the bawdiness and debauchery of army life must have seemed especially far removed from their spiritual haven on the Tuscarawas.[22] The duo wondered how—or even if—those back home would sustain and remember them through the war. Could those who opposed war support those who waged it? Rieker's anxieties on this question were especially pronounced. He kept up a constant correspondence with his sister, Mary: "Don't forget me," he implored, "and I'll not forget you. Thus we'll be good siblings." Appeals for homespun shirts, stockings, and mittens were frequent, for these items would supply material evidence that the connection between the battlefield and the home front was not yet broken. Zoarites devotedly forwarded crates brimming with supplies and provisions to the front. The connection must have seemed tenuous, though, when just a week after the 107th Ohio rushed out to Blocher's Knoll, two dozen Zoarites declared themselves to be "conscientious objectors." Among them was John Rieker, Christian's half-brother.[23]

IN ALL LIKELIHOOD the men spent little more than an hour atop Blocher's Knoll, but it felt like a lifetime. The rebel skirmish line appeared first, probably about two o'clock. Then, a gray and butternut line "charged through" Rock Creek, which coiled its way around the base of the knoll. The rebels surged up and over the lazy creek's steep banks to overwhelm the Ohioans. As they choked on the fumes of the musketry smoke that now enveloped the field, the heat became almost unbearable. Enemy bullets began to tally casualties. Years later, one meticulous Union veteran endeavored to catalogue the range of sensations experienced by soldiers when wounded. "When felt at all," he concluded, "bullets through the flesh usually produce a burning sensation more or less acute."

> When bones are broken, stinging accompanies the burning. When bones are hit but not broken, there is a numbing sensation in the whole region involved in the shock, followed very soon by severe and sometimes intense pain. When muscles and tendons are involved there is a tugging sensation, sometimes very slight, and shell-wounds produce feelings similar

to those by bullets, more or less exaggerated, according to the size of the missile and the degree of velocity.

More than a few injured men "alternated between a desire either cry like a baby or swear like a pirate." Among them were Siffert and Vignos. A spent Minié ball clipped the former's right leg, while an enemy shell struck the latter's right arm. Two days later, a foul-smelling discharge from Vignos's wound signaled gangrene, necessitating amputation.[24]

Though the Ohioans stubbornly held their ground, they could not withstand the "terrible" enfilading fire forever. Their line buckled and then collapsed as men broke for the rear, the yowling rebels extending an already lengthy casualty list by bagging knots of prisoners. Among them was Christian Rieker, who would be packed off to a dank Richmond prison pen for the next four months. The chaotic retreat surged through the congested streets of Gettysburg, delivering the regiment to its new perch behind a squat stone fence at the base of Cemetery Hill. There, the next day, George Billow, Alfred Rider, and John Brunny—who by some minor miracle eluded capture and survived the fight unscathed—would have another chance to prove their mettle. But for now, at least, it seemed that providence was once more smiling on the cause of the Confederacy—and that misfortune was their lot as a regiment.[25]

VIGNOS, BILLOW, Rider, Siffert, Rieker, and Brunny—like the rest of the men in the 107th Ohio, and like most of the troops who shouldered government-issued muskets between 1861 and 1865—were volunteers, not professional soldiers. They were ordinary men who took part in an extraordinary war. Although they fought alongside a few of the Civil War's most renowned units and in several of its most studied battles, today their graves are weeded over and their sacrifices long forgotten. Although Private Henry Finkenbiner of the 107th earned the Medal of Honor for his daring performance in a late war skirmish, few others achieved any lasting distinction. Even in northeastern Ohio, few remember the regiment. Its entry in the otherwise exacting *Encyclopedia of Cleveland History*, for example, misreports both the unit's battle record and casualty statistics.[26]

But therein lies their significance: mocking all pretenses and resisting empty generalizations, the men of the 107th Ohio allow us to retrieve something of the war as it was actually lived, felt, and experienced. Throughout the nation's bloodiest conflict, they whipsawed between hope and heartbreak, duty and dereliction, cynicism and conviction. With little fanfare, they shivered in squalls of snow at Brooke's Station and flagged under the fevers of Folly Island. They swatted at gluttonous mosquitoes in camp and navigated treacherous roads on the march. They battled treasonous rebels at the front and then exchanged taunts with contemptuous civilians back home. They knew the taste of victory, but more often felt the ache of defeat. When they returned north, they tended to the errands of memory—and to the noiseless agonies of the many sick, wounded, and disabled men among them. They did not wage the Civil War; rather, they endured it.[27]

For generations, scholars have drawn two very different portraits of Billy Yank. Some have depicted him as steel-jawed, sure-footed, and self-restrained, motivated by patriotism and a keen sense of what was at stake in the contest. The escalating demands of the war paid him remarkably little trouble; if anything, experiences under fire or in proximity to slavery only magnified his convictions. Even as these gilded histories exaggerated his courage, pluck, and determination, however, other writers foregrounded the Union soldier's anguish, misery, and woe. In these accounts, the natural, physical, and psychological deprivations of war exhausted the youthful idealism that first inspired the Yankee soldier to enlist. On bloodstained battlefields he confronted the stark divide between the glittering war he imagined and the horrific war he fought.[28]

Both views have revealed some important truths about Civil War soldiers and their service. But in their rush to esteem or to pity, these divergent perspectives have effaced the raw, lived realities of the conflict: the murk and the muck of life in camp or on the march; the not insignificant demands of carrying on, standing guard, or putting one foot in front of the other; the satisfaction of having suffered, sacrificed, and somehow survived. Historians have dutifully mapped the war's military campaigns, but they have only just begun to chart the war's human topography. Historians are well acquainted with the conflict as an event, but they know much less about the conflict as an experience. Reassured by its results—the end of slavery in America and the preservation of the Union—it can be easy to forget that for the people who lived it and for the soldiers who fought it, the war's outcome was never certain. "War is a curious affair," one Connecticut volunteer who fought alongside the 107th Ohio at both Chancellorsville and Gettysburg mused. "It has more crooks and turns than the City of Boston, with not half as sensible endings. War is a something we must put up with . . . we have got to face it point blank."[29]

This book attempts that work. It rummages around snowy winter camps, trundles along dusty roads on thirst-inducing marches, and prowls along distant picket lines in palmetto-choked swamps. It follows Vignos, Billow, Rider, Siffert, Rieker, Brunny, and their comrades as they attempted to do what they understood to be their duty. Confronted with impossible circumstances, they sometimes faltered, often struggled to maintain order, and not infrequently wondered whether the war was worth it after all. They gained hope before misplacing it again, living within the war's juxtapositions. Eager to attest that they had battled no less manfully than native-born regiments, they drew meaning from their misfortunes and refined their understanding of manhood, duty, and service—drawing on lessons learned during the failed democratic revolutions of 1848.[30]

Indeed, some fathomed the war as a new theater in that old struggle. Secession had dismembered the Union—the shield of the democratic liberties they had crossed an ocean to enjoy. Among those who connected the rebellion in the United States to the revolutions back home, many identified slavery as the source of discord: a cancer on the republic that mocked the principle of self-government and needed to be rooted out. "A German has only to be a German," Frederick Douglass famously quipped months before John Brown's raid on Harper's Ferry, "to be utterly opposed to slavery." Yet the 107th Ohio in no way teemed with abolitionists, reflecting instead the sharp political divisions that fractured the German-American population. The Democratic Party, with its earnest appeals to popular sovereignty and local rule, remained popular among the *Auswanderung*. The many Democrats who stocked the regiment's ranks fought primarily to preserve the Union as a province for white men. These men believed that nativism, not slavery, posed the real threat to their liberty. While some soldiers embraced a more capacious understanding of the war, many Democrats maintained their dutiful skepticism about the necessity of emancipation.[31]

In the late nineteenth century, the local booster and historian William Henry Perrin succinctly captured the Janus-faced nature of the 107th Ohio's service. "No Ohio regiment," he declared, "furnishes a more terrible record of its slaughter, or one of more distinguished gallantry." There was substance to his claim. The men could point to an intrepid performance in a little-known raid through the heart of South Carolina—a campaign that, in the conflict's waning days, finally brought the war to the cradle of secession. And yet throughout nearly three years of service, 589 of the regiment's 1,080 men were killed, wounded, or reported missing. Some analysts contend that a unit becomes "combat ineffective" when it suffers losses in excess of thirty percent of its strength. Astoundingly, the 107th Ohio was decimated five times over; even those fortunate enough to survive returned home to tend to an imposing litany of ailments, including chronic diarrhea, ague, fever, chills, gangrene, consumption, constipation, dysentery, liver trouble, deafness, blindness, shortness of breath, fluttering of the heart, nervousness, and insanity.[32]

Importantly, the regiment's veterans also counted among their maladies the bitter sting of nativism. The raw memories of Chancellorsville endured. "Although numerous essays have since been written about that terrible conflict and disaster, exonerating the 11th Corps," one ethnically German veteran bemoaned at the century's end, "yet the stigma still remains and very frequently the phrase is heard, '*I fights mit Sigel and runs mit Howard.*" This old soldier lamented nothing more than having to "hear slurs thrown even by men who call themselves Comrades—and Comrades too of the G.A.R." Importantly, while survivors of the 107th Ohio joined Grand Army of the Republic posts, marched in parades, and even attended soldiers' reunions, their experiences would prevent them from full participation in the hypermasculine veteran culture that sentimentalized the war.[33]

ONE VETERAN of the 107th Ohio was Jacob Smith. Throughout the war, as an ambulance wagon driver, he twisted through knots of woods and navigated rutted roads to deliver scores of wounded comrades to makeshift hospitals. The physically exhausting and emotionally demanding labor exacted a heavy toll. By the early twentieth century, he was prematurely grizzled and crooked with rheumatism. Still, he took up his pen and began to compose a regimental history. The labor-intensive project was made more difficult by the 107th Ohio's shoddy record keeping. Eight brittle volumes—several missing their leather covers, each caked in ruddy grime—only sporadically documented special orders and communications. Following their rout at the battle of Chancellorsville, several dazed companies did not file morning reports for many months. "The Regimental Books and Papers of the 107th Ohio," one brigade inspector scolded that December, "are very incomplete and badly kept . . . in some cases the[y] are blotted and defaced and exhibit so many manifest errors that new ones should be required . . . and records and accounts commenced anew."[34]

To fill in the gaps, Smith mined the 128 volumes of the *Official Records of the War of the Rebellion*, published by the War Department, and made ample use of wartime letters and diaries, copies of which his comrades dutifully supplied. Sifting through conflicting testimony was no simple chore. "In writing a history of this kind," Smith explained, "there is a material difference in many respects, between the movements and work accomplished by a troop or regiment of soldiers, [and] that of a single individual belonging to that organization."[35]

The enormous intellectual challenge aside, Smith relished the opportunity "to wander back through the mazes of memory." He understood implicitly the importance of his work. The war had passed into history not as a wrenching, liminal experience, but instead as a confident, hushed epic. Cloying romances, brawny monuments, and misty-eyed reunions effaced the confusion and doubt of lived realities. He knew that his efforts would ensure that "something about the toils, dangers, labor and hardships" endured by his comrades would find its way into print.[36]

This book shares Smith's aim. Tracking a single regiment shifts our angle of vision, allowing us to measure the Civil War on a more intimate, human scale. By getting onto the ground, we can distinguish more clearly just what the conflict demanded of the generation that fought it. What follows is a messy tale of pride and pain, courage and cowardice, loyalty and betrayal, life and death—a narrative that embraces the war's complexities, ponders its contingencies, and challenges its chronologies. It provides, in the end, a more inclusive and unflinching account of how the Union was saved—and by whom.

CHAPTER 1

"WE FEEL IT OUR DUTY"

August and September 1862

THE REPORT of a cannon interrupted an otherwise quiet summer evening in Cleveland's Public Square on July 31, 1862. The blast heralded not another battle, but rather the commencement of a recruitment rally for a new, three-year infantry regiment to be raised from the Buckeye State. That evening, just off the spacious, amply shaded square, hundreds crowded into National Hall, the handsome four-story building where, almost a decade before, Phineas Taylor Barnum, "as attractive as his circus," rehearsed "the evils of intemperance." More recently, in the frenzied wake of the rebel attack on Fort Sumter, "the colored people of Cleveland" had thronged the civic forum, determining to "organize military companies to assist in putting down the rebellion." Ohio's then-governor, William Dennison, had rejected their offer before really considering it, and so it was with no small irony that this latest assembly gaveled to order. Earlier that day, the telegraphs at the offices of the *Daily Cleveland Leader* impatiently clicked with reports that the rebels were reinforcing the maze of works they had coiled around Richmond—news that raised concerns about federal manpower levels. "Only by active and rapid enlistments" could a dreaded draft be avoided. "The ranks must be filled," the paper insisted, "and that speedily."[1]

The editorial hardly meant to imply that Ohioans wanted for voluntarism. Already, the nation's third most populous state (only New York and neighboring Pennsylvania boasted more residents) had outfitted some one hundred infantry regiments, thirteen independent batteries, and six cavalry outfits for Lincoln's armies. The state had exceeded its quota in each of the five calls for troops made since the war began—meeting the first demand within days. By July 1862, it had supplied nearly 155,000 able-bodied men to the Union war effort. But Ohio's supply of manpower was not limitless. Indeed, in some respects, it was a marvel that Ohio had placed itself on a war footing at all. The state's antebellum militia had existed only on paper, and though Columbus boasted a handsome new arsenal building with thick, masonry walls, its prized holdings amounted to "a few boxes of smooth-bore muskets" and "a few brass six-pounder fieldpieces, worn out from firing salutes."[2]

Recruitment was further complicated by Ohio's schizophrenic politics. Tucked in the state's northeastern corner and anchored by Cleveland, the Western Reserve—a neat grid of steepled town greens that paid homage to New England—was a citadel of abolitionism and reliably Republican. The abolitionist John Brown, whose raid on the federal armory and arsenal at Harper's Ferry, Virginia, had pushed the nation to the precipice of war, passed his formative years there. Not surprisingly, Republicans also performed well in areas where the Whigs, their ideological forebears, had promoted industrial growth and commercial development. The canals that gouged into the earth, together with the web of macadamized roads that spiraled in every direction, endured as monuments to the promise of "free labor." But elsewhere—especially in the state's rural counties and along the Ohio

River—the Democrats were carried to victory by the votes of racist whites and native-born southerners.[3]

When the war broke out, many Ohioans set aside their political differences and rallied to the flag; that accord, however, failed to survive the war's first trying summer. When the quick victory that some Ohioans anticipated proved stubbornly elusive, doubt yielded to despair, and despair to outright defeatism. Then, in the spring of 1862, Ohio regiments suffered devastating losses in the Shenandoah Valley and—as Augustus Vignos could attest—at Shiloh. "Thousands of our people now regard with dampened spirit and sad silence the condition of our country," lamented Ohio congressman Samuel Sullivan Cox, an outspoken critic of President Lincoln, on the floor of the U.S. House of Representatives. Across the state, Democratic newspapers sighed as they tallied the war's multiplying costs.[4]

The most intractable opponents of the war, like Cox, became known as Copperheads. Republicans felt the name of a venomous snake fitting for men treacherous and disloyal, but the Copperheads—in a display of their brazen effrontery—literally wore the label as a badge of honor, taunting their detractors by fixing copper cents to their lapels. True to their old Jacksonian moorings, the Copperheads were jealously protective of local self-rule and adhered to a strict constructionism. As the war for the Union demanded ever more of men, the federal treasury, and the Constitution, they sharpened their initial skepticism about the conflict into a barbed critique of the Lincoln administration. The confiscation acts and a steady drumbeat of emancipation measures enacted by the Republican Congress in the early months of the war, however, lent a real coherence and new sense of urgency to their arguments. After all, the tips of the Copperheads' arrows were poisoned with a virulent white supremacism. "If slavery is bad," Cox supposed, "an unrestrained black population, only double what we now have, partly subservient, partly slothful, partly criminal, and all disadvantageous and ruinous, will be far worse." Such rhetoric threatened to sabotage enlistment efforts. In Canton, a bespectacled former congressman named Edson Baldwin Olds did his best to discourage would-be volunteers.[5]

Not all Democrats were Copperheads, though Republicans often made it seem that way, distinguishing between treason and loyalty in a blizzard of broadsides and editorials. ("When you compromise with treason," one Republican explained to a Cleveland assembly in late July, "you become traitors.") In fact, William Dennison's successor as governor, the newly inaugurated David Tod, a portly Youngstown railroad executive and coal industry attorney who had served three presidents as the U.S. minister to Brazil, was a War Democrat. Like others of his political stripe, Tod attempted to track between Republican radicalism and Democratic defeatism. He emerged as an early if unlikely advocate of prosecuting the war as vigorously as possible, buoyed by the expectation that a "hard" war might crush out the southern rebellion before northern radicals turned it into a revolution.[6]

Such a vision of the war demanded well-stocked armies, and this work fell squarely on the governor's shoulders. During the Civil War, the federal government left to individual states the task of raising and recruiting, arming and provisioning, drilling and coordinating regiments. Once readied for the front, these locally harvested outfits were packed, three to five at a time, into larger bodies called brigades. Brigades were then collected into divisions, with the divisions assembled into army corps. Commanded by a colonel and comprising one thousand men (ten companies of one hundred men each), the regiment was the essential element of a Civil War army. Men developed fanatical loyalty to their units; indeed, the bonds of comradeship were "almost mystical," sustaining the rank and file through trials and hardships on and off the battlefield. "More than any other unit," writes one historian, the regiment "was a self-aware community."[7]

Ethnic regiments, or outfits that derived more than half their strength from non-native volunteers, were especially self-aware. By the summer of 1862, Ohio had already fielded four ethnically German units. In fact, the 9th Ohio Volunteers, a German outfit that sprang from Cincinnati's ethnic wards, was the state's very first three-year infantry regiment. Rallying at the Turner Hall, it mustered into service within days of Fort Sumter. "Although the blessings of our free institutions have been enjoyed longer by native-born than by adopted citizens," the men declared in an index of their steely resolve, "the adopted shall rise all in a body, united to defend the Union and protect the Star-Spangled Banner." Motivated by the success of the 9th, three more ethnically German regiments from the Buckeye State—the 28th, 37th, and 106th Ohio—soon slung cartridge boxes over their shoulders and trudged dutifully to the front.[8]

Shared language, heritage, and culture proved a powerful adhesive for German regiments. Each of Ohio's German regiments likewise brimmed with recruits who were eager to fight *mit* Franz Sigel, the rev-

FRANZ SIGEL.
MAJ. GEN'L U.S.A.

A veteran of the failed democratic revolutions of 1848, Franz Sigel inspired legions of German immigrants—including some volunteers for the 107th Ohio—to shoulder muskets in defense of the Union. *Library of Congress*

olutionary émigré turned Union major general. Revered for his "passionate devotion" to the democratic revolutions that pulsed through Europe in 1848—the failed crusade that drove him into exile, first in Switzerland, later in England, and ultimately in the United States—Sigel commanded the almost fanatical devotion of German immigrants. Sigel kept the promise of radical social equality alive. His very presence persuaded German-Americans that even in these turbulent times, the United States was the "last best hope of Earth." That men continued to find him inspiring was a tribute to their idealism, for apart from his able choreography of the federal artillery at Pea Ridge that March, Sigel's record on the battlefield was exceptionally bleak.[9]

Hoping to harness some of that idealism, Tod authorized the formation of still another ethnically German unit in the summer of 1862. Ohio adjutant general Charles Hill affixed his looping signature to "General Order No. 21," which called for the new unit to be stocked with men from "that part of the state lying north of the National Road." Headquartered in Cleveland, the "German Citizens' Military Committee" would coordinate the ambitious recruiting effort, canvassing ten northeastern counties for volunteers. In a circular widely reprinted in local newspapers, the committee's secretary, Charles Arnold, saluted the honor and bravery of Germans who had already donned Union blue, electrifying memories of their wartime exploits—from the streets of St. Louis, where immigrant soldiers twisted through riotous mobs after bagging a secessionist militia, to the Shenandoah Valley, where they confronted the legend of "Stonewall" Jackson. "Your country again calls upon you," Arnold implored, "to rush to the rescue of your gallant comrades and countrymen already in the field." To this patriotic appeal, the committee added the temptation of "one month's pay in advance," promising the first wave of enlistees an additional $100 bounty.[10]

NATIONAL HALL was already jammed when fifty-one-year-old Edward Hessenmueller took the stage at the recruitment rally. Stocky, short-statured, and fringed with a gnome-like beard, the immigrant served as Cleveland's justice of the peace and published its first German-language newspaper. Though "an ardent, consistent Democrat in politics," he had rallied to the Union cause. Hessenmueller had perhaps hinted at that stance before the war when, only a few months into his term as federal commissioner for northern Ohio, he abruptly resigned, citing his belief that the Fugitive Slave Act was "morally wrong."[11]

Hessenmueller called the meeting to order and introduced Seraphim Meyer, the man Governor Tod had tapped to lead the new regiment. Flooded with emotion and possessing a freshly inked colonel's commission, Meyer was exhausted, having delivered a twilight lecture to a war meeting in Canton—some sixty miles south of Cleveland—the previous evening. Still, his "short and patriotic" remarks had an electric effect on the crowd. No one recorded his words that evening, but the once dutiful Democrat likely touted his willingness to sunder "all party ties" and take a "stand for the Union." It was that resolve—not any previous military experience—that recommended him for the colonelcy.

Born in 1815 in Bourbach-le-Bas, a steepled hamlet tucked in the rugged folds of northeastern France, the eighth and final child of Jacob and Maria Anna Meyer immigrated with his family to the United States at the age of twelve. They settled in the unassuming village of Kendal, Ohio, in 1828, the same year that mule teams began tugging barges along the nearby Ohio & Erie Canal. The Meyers quickly relocated to Canton, then a mostly uninspiring town about a dozen miles east of the canal bed (not until Cornelius Aultman opened his reaper manufactory within its limits on the eve of the war would the city even hint at its later eminence).[12]

A diligent student fluent in three languages, Meyer was admitted to the bar and began practicing law at twenty-three. Soon the gifted attorney began using the oratorical skills he had honed before juries on the political stump. In 1844, at a German "mass meeting" in Massillon, Meyer enthralled the crowd with his roast of the perennial Whig presidential candidate Henry Clay—a "powerful address" that exceeded an hour. Four years later, in a telling measure of his effectiveness, the *Ohio Repository* fashioned him "the demagogue stumper," chiding Meyer for peddling "falsehoods" in an effort to rally immigrants behind Lewis Cass. (Although the rotund Michigander lost the election, he edged Zachary Taylor in Ohio.) Meyer's political star only continued to climb. As early as the mid-1850s, Democrats included him on lists of "aspirants for the Senate." And with top billing on the Ohio Democratic ticket, Meyer stood ready, in the event of a Douglas win, to cast one of the state's twenty-three electoral votes for the "Little Giant" in 1860.[13]

Meyer, of course, would not have the opportunity to cast that vote. Republican Abraham Lincoln carried Ohio (together with seventeen other states) and triumphed over a crowded general election field to win the presidency. Predicting that the election of a "Black Republican" would yield to race war, and further persuaded of the political impotence they long dreaded, southerners ratified secession ordnances and commenced a treasonous rebellion on behalf of chattel slavery and white supremacy. Hostilities, however, did not begin until the wee hours of April 12, 1861, when more than forty rebel mortars trained their fire on Fort Sumter, the squat pentagon of brick and stone that stood sentinel over Charleston harbor. If at first many clung to the forlorn hope that the news from South Carolina was a hoax, its confirmation sent an epidemic of war fever throughout the northern states. Volunteers rushed to respond to the president's call for seventy-five thousand troops. "Where is the paltry scoundrel who dares to talk of party when our flag is insulted?" one speaker demanded to know at a pro-Union demonstration in Canton.[14]

It was with the zealotry of a convert that Seraphim Meyer asked the same question. Following the lead of Stephen A. Douglas, he rallied to the cause of the Union: "the duty that we owe to ourselves, to our posterity, and to the friends of constitutional liberty and self-government throughout the world." In mid-May, Meyer took the stage at a war meeting in Stark County, professing with trademark vim his "undisguised love of Union, hatred of traitors," and "hope and longing for speedy and ample retribution." He said nothing about slavery but, encouraged by an earsplitting ovation from his old political foes, censured ex-president James Buchanan for failing to respond decisively when an impetuous troop of Citadel cadets opened fire on the *Star of the West,* the civilian steamer that made an attempt to resupply the Charleston garrison in January.

While the oration earned predictably glowing reviews from Republicans, the scorned *Stark County Democrat* did its best to defang Meyer. Recalling his support for a "peaceable separation" of states, as well as his advice to fellow Democrats, who needed "to organize and arm themselves for self defence against abolition tyranny and mobocracy," the paper regarded Meyer as a craven political opportunist. "In this country it is every man's right to change his mind," the *Democrat*'s editor Archibald McGregor irreverently concluded. "We sincerely hope Mr. Meyer . . . is happy in the embrace of those who have always heretofore denounced him as 'a heartless Jesuit.' "[15]

Meyer was remarkably unfazed. Throughout the spring, as a member of the Military Committee of Stark County, he crisscrossed Ohio's Seventeenth Congressional District to recruit fresh volunteers. Among those who responded to Meyer's patriotic appeals were three of his sons, Turenne, Marcus, and Edward, as well as a son-in-law, John Lang. "We doubt if the State of Ohio contains a man who has placed upon the altar of his country an offering of such profound significance," the *Stark County Republican* hyped. A month before the armies engaged each other in a major battle, with some local Democrats insisting piously that the war promised only "ruin and bankruptcy," the prosecutor who temporarily set aside his Farmers' and Mechanics' Block law practice had understandably earned the affection of the *Republican.* In late June, the paper yielded several columns to a letter from Turenne, who offered a stirring account of his activities in western Virginia. Near Philippi, several companies of his 14th Ohio Volunteers exchanged fire with the enemy, chased the rebels through the woods, and then plundered their wagons and supply trains. "They broke and ran in every conceivable direction," the regiment's historian exulted decades later.[16]

Just weeks later, eager to see his son—as well as something of the war—Seraphim Meyer set out for the hills of western Virginia. Promising news from the front lines kept alive—at least for the moment—delusions of a short war. On July 11, 1861, blue-coated Hoosiers and Ohioans, paying little heed to a cold, intermittent rain, twisted through knots of spruce and climbed the rugged spine of Rich Mountain, an eminence just west of Beverly that commanded the dramatic Tygart Valley River. Perched on the mountain's summit, Brigadier General William Starke Rosecrans's soggy troops waged a brisk battle that resulted in a Confederate defeat. Only two days later, the retreating rebels again met with misfortune at a curl in the Cheat River, where their commander, Brigadier General Robert Selden Garnett, was killed.

Upon his return to Ohio, before an applauding crowd of some two thousand Cantonites, Meyer narrated, with "vivid description," as well as "anecdote, mournful and mirthful," his excursion to the seat of the war. In a speech of two hours, he reassured his neighbors that the Union soldiers were conducting the war within strict limits; he saluted the reverence for "personal rights and private property" that pervaded the federal ranks. "It is said we have among us those who call this a war of abolition, of extermination," he roared. "None but traitors can cherish such sentiments!"[17]

Indeed, the address was as much an indictment of "foul plotters" and "domestic traitors" as it was a tribute to the patriotism of Union volunteers. "Whilst rebellion is boldly raising its head, and its armed cohorts are threatening the very capital of the union," Turenne echoed in a letter published in the *Stark County Republican* a few weeks later: "there are traitors . . . who are making every effort, no matter how base, to thwart and paralyze the measures of the Government, no matter how necessary or appropriate." Already, Seraphim Meyer was learning that the war demanded vigilance on the home front no less than on the battlefield.[18]

THROUGHOUT AUGUST, men widely known and well regarded in their communities recruited troops for the 107th Ohio. War opponents, meanwhile, did their best to dampen new enlistments. One "sympathizer with treason," reproving the war effort "in the most unmeasured terms," posted himself outside of the unit's recruitment depot on Cleveland's East Side. Farther south, where Augustus Vignos and his fellow recruiters Peter Sisterhen, Samuel Surburg, and Jacob Hose canvassed Louisville, Navarre, and Massillon, the *Staats Zeitung*, a Democratic weekly serving the German population, did its best to discourage new recruits. In nearby East Liberty, three Copperheads attempted to disband a recruitment meeting. Rather remarkably, after spending a night in the local lockup, they "concluded the quickest and safest way out of the dilemma" was to enlist. They fought "side by side" until Gettysburg, where two fell dead and one was mortally wounded.[19]

Such provocations aside, the *Daily Cleveland Herald* could report in early August that the 107th Ohio was "filling up more rapidly than the most sanguine anticipated." In Akron, George Billow stocked Company I, which soon included Christian Rieker, John Brunny, and the Zoar delegation. Barnet Steiner rummaged neighboring Stark County for recruits. He found an enthusiastic young volunteer in Mahlon Slutz, his old Sunday School pupil. Not yet eighteen, Slutz could not enlist without first obtaining his father's consent, which was given only reluctantly. "If nothing will do you but go to the army," he sighed, "I want you to go with Barry Steiner." Four-score miles away in Sandusky, on the shores of Lake Erie, August Dewaldt crowed that his Company B had reached "its maximum number" in record time.

The volunteers tallied many reasons for marching off to war—so many, in fact, that their motivations mock any neat categorization. Reports that the regiment would "reinforce" Sigel "acted like a charm, and aroused great enthusiasm." Jacob Lichty was one enlistee who spoiled for a fight with the enemy. "If they want to try Gen. Sigel's Bully Dutch," he taunted, "let 'em pitch in." Some men desired to follow in the martial footsteps of revered ancestors. James Ellwood's maternal grandfather had shouldered a musket in both the Revolution and the War of 1812; now, the thirty-two-year-old Tuscarawas County

The Civil War was fought by volunteers, not professional soldiers. Only many tedious hours of drill could ready these citizen-warriors for the battlefield. *National Archives*

farmer joined his brother and two brothers-in-law in the service of his country. For others, pecuniary incentives appealed more powerfully than patriotism. Debt-saddled farmers and day laborers could hardly resist the promise of steady pay. Fritz Nussbaum, a twenty-year-old, sandy-haired farmer who mustered into Company C, recalled that some men refused to take the oath until they received their bounties. Among them was Rieker. "If we do not receive what was promised us," he explained to his sister back in Zoar, "we shall not go forth." Many more could not clearly articulate what it was that compelled them to enlist; instead, with a sense of adventure and no small uncertainty, they assembled in Cleveland for instruction and drill.[20]

IT WAS AT Camp Cleveland, a bustling new training complex situated on some thirty acres immediately south of the city, where Colonel Meyer first beheld the regiment. The 994 men who assembled there represented virtually every walk of life. Among the recruits were stonecutters and shoemakers, butchers and blacksmiths, tailors and tinsmiths, carpenters and clockmakers, porters and peddlers, masons and millers, weavers and watchmakers. Ranging in age from fifteen to fifty, nearly seven in ten were foreign-born. Alongside Vignos, Billow, Rider, Siffert, Rieker, and Brunny were men like Jacob Bise, the Prussian bookbinder from Tiffin; Arnold Streum, the sandy-haired laborer from New Philadelphia; and Philip Wang, the Baden harness maker who enlisted as a first sergeant in Louisville. They hailed from a dozen Ohio counties, from the shores of Lake Erie to the banks of the Tuscarawas, from the docks of Cleveland to the farms of Wooster.

Newly commissioned as the regimental surgeon, Charles Hartman conducted perhaps the most careful survey of the new enlistees, assessing the fitness of each volunteer for the demands of military service. Exiled after the defeat of the democratic revolutions he had embraced with "zeal" as a medical student in Cologne, Hartman settled in Cleveland and began to practice medicine. Though a capable physician who maintained a general practice, he was best known as a talented orator who had relinquished nothing of his youthful idealism. Throughout the 1850s he dazzled audiences by connecting the struggles of his youth to the ongoing battle against slavery. Hartman's was one of the most energetic voices in the new Republican Party, addressing a gathering of the Fifth Ward Frémont Club at Cleveland's Turner's Hall in September 1856. The doctor's speeches were "so involving and exciting," one observer remarked, "that it was thought that each spoken word must be escorted with a droplet of blood from the heart."[21]

Just as he linked his own revolutionary past with America's stormy present, so too did Hartman connect physical might and intellectual vigor. Though it was sure to visit "human distress" upon the men, Hartman relished the war as a chance to "seal with deeds what we have praised with words." Whatever his assessment of the new recruits, he believed that the impending weeks of drill and training in the ways of army discipline could only have a salubrious effect.[22]

REVEILLE SOUNDED before dawn each morning at Camp Cleveland. The men bounded from their barracks and onto the dress parade for an hour of drill before breakfast. After roll call, they drilled from seven o'clock to ten o'clock. The volunteers enjoyed free time until four o'clock in the afternoon, when they commenced three more hours of drill. Only many hours of practice could ready these raw recruits for the battlefield. While tedious tactical manuals needed to be studied and committed to memory, training in the Civil War depended on physical conditioning above all else. Officers incessantly drilled their men and then drilled them some more, aiming to program soldiers to move, march, and maneuver as mechanically as possible. A tempest of commands—*halt, right dress, forward, steady there*—could be heard each day as the various regiments took to the parade grounds. Slowly, men acquired new definitions for words like line, column, wheel, and square. Though "acquiring the trade of a soldier" was, as one Union veteran later put it, "prodigious labor," Fritz Nussbaum appeared not to mind. "I like soldiering very well," he explained.

If Nussbaum and his new comrades did not object to the monotony of drill, however, they did gripe about living conditions in the camp, whose thirty barracks were still under construction when the regiment arrived for its mustering in. "Constructed with unplaned pine boards," the long, narrow, low-slung buildings—three for each company—were anything but commodious. A volunteer from a neighboring regiment who used his knapsack as a pillow compared the camp's tower of bunks to "apple bins in a cellar." "By day we are cheerful," Christian Rieker advised his sister Mary. "By night," he added, dripping with contempt, "we lie down on our feather beds." Private John Flory remembered that he "slept very well" his first night in camp, though the eighteen-year-old farmer from Wooster "thought in the morning that Uncle Sam had purdy hard [beds]." After passing several restive nights on "hard" planks, Nussbaum took matters into his own hands. The resourceful soldier "slipt through the [guard]" and "went after some straw." "I got a very good bed now," he boasted. But the crude accommodations continued to elicit complaints from many of his exhausted comrades.

Nor did the cuisine earn positive reviews from the nearly 2,900 Ohioans who had filed into the camp by the end of August. "Meat, vegetables and soup are brought in from the cook shanty in the large camp kettle in which they are cooked and laded out upon the plates," explained Charles Clark of the 125th Ohio, another regiment that mustered in at the camp. "Coffee comes in the same kind of a kettle, and we dip in with our tin cups. So much for the government fare." Private Flory offered a characteristically polite evaluation of the camp coffee in his diary: "We had sugar to put in it," he wrote. Happily, hungry recruits could maintain a steady diet of "pies, cakes, fruit, and delicacies," which were offered up by the many local women who visited the camp. "We think we are fortune's favorites," confessed one young artillerist when asked about the donated fare.[23]

While weeks spent in Camp Cleveland tutored new soldiers in the inadequacies and improvisations of army life, they also imparted some important lessons about the support of loyal citizens, whose patriotic hymns would be too often drowned out by the clamor of the Copperheads in the coming months. When word leaked that officials had made no provision to provide the men of the 107th with blankets upon their arrival at the barracks (tens of thousands of newly mustering troops easily overwhelmed government resources), leaders in Cleveland's First Ward "appointed a committee to call upon the citizens" for donations of "blankets or old quilts." "It is proposed that our patriotic housewives make a little sacrifice, and each send one or two blankets," one of their appeals commenced, "for our gallant fellows have all left comfortable beds at home and they are beginning to feel the effects of the cool nights." Headquartered in a simple storefront at No. 95 Bank Street, the Soldiers' Aid Society forwarded the donated bedding, in addition to several crates of medical supplies requested by Surgeon Hartman. Patriotic civilians likewise hosted picnics for the troops, presented Captain Dewaldt "with a beautiful revolver, sash and shoulder straps," and supplied ministers to conduct religious services, including several in the German language, within the camp.[24]

Despite its discomforts, most veterans remembered Camp Cleveland rather fondly. The place brimmed with activity; in myriad ways, the training complex blended seamlessly into the rhythms of the city. Each day, scores of local men, women, and children prowled about the camp's tree-studded, barracks-lined thoroughfares, inspecting the boys and their new quarters. "Calls were constantly being made by the relatives of volunteers," a soldier in the newly arrived 124th Ohio recalled, "and visits were constantly being solicited and made to the old homes." Temperance crusaders extracted pledges from the volunteers and local merchants hawked their discounted wares. Jacob Smith, who maintained a daily "outline diary" of his service, recalled that his comrades in the 107th "had considerable sport" with these enterprising "Wusht peddlers." Such gaiety seemed to overshadow the "school of the soldier."

Two examples of mirth making loomed large in later memory. In early September, while still adjusting to life in the camp, the regiment seized its first rebel flag. A mischievous pupil at the Cleveland Institute, a nearby preparatory school administered by Ransom Humiston, decided to taunt the troops with the rag of secession. The Stars and Bars had been used in a "tableau" staged at the Institute the previous term. Before long, a company from the 107th summoned the priggish Humiston who, before disciplining his charge, demanded the offending banner and "delivered it over to the soldiers . . . as their first trophy."

A few days later, the jocund troops paraded downtown to the thirteenth annual Ohio State Fair. There they inspected the goats, pigs, cattle, horses, and sheep ("Rob Roy," an eighteen- hundred-pound Clydesdale, earned "top prize") as well as the many "examples of sign painting, marble works, wood graining, hair work" and "ornamental penmanship" exhibited in Fine Arts Hall. Most likely they also took time to gape at the "mechanical implements," among them the New York firm Mallory & Sanford's premium-winning "flax dressing machine." One prescient local newspaper editor forecasted a terrific demand for such devices after the war, once soldiers impeded by "disabling wounds" and "constitutions broken and enfeebled by disease" returned home.[25]

Before long, finding it difficult to maintain good health and order within the camp, exasperated officers implored the basket brigades and civilian interlopers to suspend their visits. These "good intentions," the camp officials intoned, "are mistaken kindnesses." "If the friends of the troops in Camp Cleveland wish to see the men become good soldiers and retain their health, they will forbear for the future visiting them."[26]

ON THE EVE of the First World War, American infantrymen submitted to sixteen weeks of training designed to tutor them in the ways of modern trench warfare. Training programs involved weapons demonstrations, combat simulations, and illustrated lectures during the Second World War; nonetheless, the chronic demand for fresh troops halved their length. Marine Eugene Sledge received two months of infantry training at California's Camp Elliott before shipping off to Peleliu and Okinawa. The average grunt who went to war in the jungles of Vietnam submitted to twenty punishing weeks of training that reinforced his new identity as a soldier. In the Civil War, however, Billy Yank wanted for a sustained, "standardized system of training" that could prepare him for the rigors of war. The 107th Ohio trained for no more than three weeks—and much of that time without weapons. Even once the men were outfitted with rifled muskets, they found their Austrian-manufactured, muzzle-loading weapons inconsistent or inoperable. "Broken" tubes, jammed locks, and crooked ramrods invited no little protest.[27]

Indeed, it seemed to Jacob Smith as though they had "scarcely entered the school of military instruction" when, on September 21, the men received orders to "proceed at once" to Covington, Kentucky—a bustling collection of saw, iron, and steel mills on the Ohio River that anchored the makeshift defense of Cincinnati. It was no matter that many of the troops could not yet load or discharge their weapons; they were needed at the front. As the 107th filed out of Camp Cleveland for the last time, the gunners of Captain Joseph Shields's 19th Ohio Battery tugged the lanyards of their twelve-pounder Napoleons and fired a salute.[28]

BY THE FALL of 1862, the Queen City resembled a large barracks. "All day," the *Cincinnati Commercial* rasped in September, "the city resounded with the measured tread of armed men and fatigue parties. The din of the drum and the piercing notes of the fife were constantly heard, far and near, and at some points there was hardly an intermission in the solemn tramp of regiments and companies." For the second time in as many months, Ohio's largest city—an important rail hub and thriving river town that also hosted a key supply depot for the Union armies—was bracing for a Confederate invasion. In July, the dreaded General John Hunt Morgan looped through Kentucky on a pounding raid that carried his mounted rebels within sixty miles of Cincinnati. Now, Confederate general Edmund Kirby Smith's Army of East Tennessee pounded through the Bluegrass State. After notching a newsworthy victory at Richmond, Kentucky, on August 30 and securing Lexington on September 2, Smith aimed a detail commanded by General Henry Heth toward the Ohio River.[29]

With only a thin ribbon of troops on hand to defend the city, Governor Tod "urged all men of military age who had guns to go at once to Cincinnati." For nearly two weeks, tens of thousands of citizen conscripts restlessly awaited the rebels, mounding spades of earth into a maze of fortifications. The governor, fretting about the "unsettled State of Affairs," also had defenses prepared farther east, at Ironton, Portsmouth, Gallipolis, and Marietta. The crisis came to an abrupt and anticlimactic end on September 11, however, when the invaders, both overconfident and underprepared, curled back into central Kentucky. Tod announced the news in a statement to the press, exhaling as he applauded the "gallant conduct" that had shielded Cincinnati from a "dissolute and desperate army." Yet the governor's eloquent proclamation was unable to quiet the city's misgivings. Accordingly, Tod directed the state's newest regiments to file into the vacant works coiled around Covington. Following a brief stop in Columbus (including a formal review by the governor, who described the 107th as the "best looking regiment . . . yet"), the troops enjoyed a "sumptuous supper" at the Soldier's Rest in Cincinnati. After their repast, the men received orders to tramp across the lone pontoon bridge that spanned the Ohio.³⁰

Colonel Meyer erupted in anger. Wanting essential supplies, functional weapons, and adequate training, his regiment was in no condition for the frontlines. The colonel marched determinedly down Third Street to the Burnet House—the sprawling and stately, dome-crowned hotel that housed the headquarters of Major General Horatio Wright's Department of the Ohio—to register his objection to any forward movement. Major Nathaniel McLean, the Cincinnati native and West Point graduate who now served as Wright's chief of staff, received the indignant colonel. Meyer asked to see the commanding general at once. Refusing to communicate his grievances through McLean as protocol demanded, he instead nudged his way beyond the chief of staff and stormed brazenly into Wright's office, veiled in a thick fog of cigar smoke.³¹

The startled general, who just one month before had earned the second star on his shoulder boards, demanded to know the reason for the officer's audacity. Meyer responded by reciting his grievances in "highly disrespectful" and "insubordinate" tones. Until his troops possessed everything they needed, the impudent colonel asserted, they would "not go into the field." His patience all but expended, Wright ordered Meyer placed under arrest. Further betraying the levity with which he regarded military order and discipline, Meyer mocked his fate.

"All right, general, its all right, I'm under arrest general," he began, promising that he would "report his being arrested to his particular friends, the Secretary of War and the Governor of Ohio." "I report myself to you now under arrest, do what you please; I'm under arrest General, its all right." So utterly bizarre was the exchange that more than a few officers at department headquarters supposed Meyer to be "under the influence of intoxicating liquors"—an allegation that Meyer steadfastly denied. "If I am psychologist enough to judge the matter," the colonel protested, "I would say ... it was the fruit of two sleeping nights, full of anxiety, passed on board rail cars ... combined with the effects of constantly recurring disappointments, added to the discontent [and] increasing clamors of the regiment." Whatever the case, it would not be the last time that charges of drunkenness dogged him.[32]

THE 107TH OHIO pressed into Kentucky later that evening. Notwithstanding Colonel Meyer's protests, many were eager to experience their baptism of fire. In *Camps and Campaigns*, regimental historian Jacob Smith noted that the 107th spent their first night beyond Ohio's borders "in a yard surrounding a nice residence." This seemingly trivial detail assumes significance only when one considers the orders issued to the regiment that week by their new division commander, Brigadier General Henry Moses Judah. "Soldiers must be kept in their camps," the West Pointer and brevetted Mexican War veteran instructed, "and upon no pretense whatsoever, permitted to visit the houses of citizens in their vicinity. Any Officers or Soldiers who shall hereafter interfere with, take, or injure any property of any private citizen ... shall be punished to the extent of the law."

Among the rank and file, the urge to pillage and plunder was born of the hardships and material inadequacies of army life. Deprivations real and imagined could threaten morale; disillusionment spread like an epidemic when expectations failed to align with realities.[33]

Having anticipated a war of drums and bugles, John Brunny succumbed first. Shortly after his arrival at Camp Cleveland, Colonel Meyer had tasked the Zoar bugler with organizing the regimental band—an assignment he undertook with great zeal. Dozens of new recruits either "proved to be or claimed to be musicians." Among them was twenty-two-year-old William Huy, a German immigrant who lived in Brooklyn Township.[34]

But the martial airs would not survive the regiment's first march.

In the first letter he penned from the front, tucked in an envelope addressed to a chum in Zoar, a chastened John Brunny plumbed the depths of doubt and despair. "Because I have always valued you as a good friend," he began, "I also consider it my duty to portray . . . the first significant march that we took." Ordered to relinquish its position outside Covington and slide into the artillery-studded works to the southwest, the 107th Ohio moved out on the morning of September 23 for Camp Judah. "At first, things moved forward," Brunny explained, "accompanied by song." But before long, as the men pressed along a bone-dry road, "a massive dust cloud" choked the air and obscured everything "not three steps" before them. "Thirst also set in, as we had no water with us," he continued, "and the great heat caused by our heavy packs increased the weakness of our human powers to such an extent that after only three miles, dozens were looking to the fence corners from which they were immediately driven off by the officers." Not a few among them, Brunny recalled, attempted in vain to quench their thirst by "scoop[ing] up water" from "dirty puddles."[35]

Another mile delivered the men to the camp of the 102nd Ohio— and a brief reprieve from the thankless march. Once assured that their "intended destination" was merely a "quarter of a mile away, the soldiers "set out courageously again." Yet another mile later, near-mutiny erupted in the ranks. "Despite the captain's cursing," Brunny remembered, "most lost courage and again broke." Blinking between dismay and disbelief, he described the "whole rows [of men] lying exhausted along the road." "Several fell down unconscious on the slope of the hill, overcome by sunstroke, from which one soon died," he added. By the time Brunny finally reached the regiment's new camp, sitting atop "a hill crowned by cannons and foals" and affording splendid views of Cincinnati, "scarcely half" of his new comrades had arrived. Only then did they realize that the entire day's eight-mile march had been an object lesson in absurdity. "The place where we now are located is barely two miles away from our previous camp," Brunny explained to his friend in Zoar, "and could have been reached in one hour." It was, he tartly surmised, "an exemplary masterpiece of stupidity and inability on the part of our leaders."[36]

John Brunny's introduction to the war exposed the stark gap between the romance and reality of war. The soldier was no doubt pleased when the regiment received its instructions to report at once to Ohio's Camp Delaware, "to be there more completely equipped, and receive more ample military instruction." With the rebel enemy defeated in Maryland and stumbling in Kentucky, an attempt on the Cincinnati defenses now seemed improbable. And so the troops dutifully trundled back across the pontoon bridge, before long to board locomotives bound for their camp on the Olentangy. While they had yet to see an enemy soldier, many of the themes that would come to define their civil war were already in full view. Mustered from communities riven by the conflict, affronted by hostile environments, and afflicted by recurring spells of cynicism and doubt, the 107th Ohio would battle much more than the southern rebels during the next three years.[37]

CHAPTER 2

"TO CRUSH OUT THE . . . UNGODLY REBELLION"

October to December 1862

IN AN OCTOBER LETTER to a friend back at home in Akron, a shamefaced George Billow reported that the 107th had returned to Ohio "without seeing even a skirmish." "When we left Cleveland [for Kentucky]," he protested, "we certainly expected to see an engagement quite soon." Frustrated, Billow hastened to add that his regiment had been "twice ordered into our entrenchments, in anticipation" of an attempt on their position. "At one time there were 500 Cavalry within three miles of our camp," he explained, "but they did not venture an attack." The captain's defensive note laid bare the dread of inadequacy and self-consciousness that already afflicted the young regiment. Impatient for action after only a few marches and deprived of a coveted opportunity to prove their mettle, the men were instead moored at Camp Delaware for three tedious weeks of drill. Not until the men snapped to attention "in apple pie order," Adjutant General Charles

Hill directed, would the 107th Ohio move on to their much-hyped appointment with General Sigel.[1]

Situated on "a fine piece of bottom land" a score of miles north of the state capital and a mile south of its namesake city, Camp Delaware was a new point of rendezvous for Ohio's ever-lengthening roster of volunteers. "Every accommodation necessary for the comfort and convenience of camp were to be had there," explained one enlisted man from Company D, supposing that the camp was the finest such proving ground in the state. Skirted by meadows and ripe orchards, "cider presses and hen-roosts," Camp Delaware's location lent itself to frequent "foraging expeditions" (only partially in jest, locals "talked of forming a home guard" to spare the bounty of their fields). Not only did two natural springs babble up from the ground, but the Olentangy River meandered lazily through the camp, affording the troops "pure, cool, and sparkling" water "in abundance." The availability of fresh, potable water made all the difference—especially for regimental comrades battling vexing spells of chronic diarrhea, fever, aches, or vertigo in the camp hospital. "Water," the enlisted man advised, "is the first thing for comfort."[2]

Still, proper hygiene and satisfied stomachs could only do so much to maintain good morale. Even as the men deloused and cleansed their dirt-begrimed skin, washed uniforms caked in dust, and enjoyed the sumptuous bounty of an Ohio harvest, stern reminders of the war's stark realities would soon challenge their strength as a regiment.[3]

NOT LONG AFTER arriving at Camp Delaware, the men of the 107th Ohio received word of the major announcement that President Lincoln made on September 22. Five days after a grisly showdown at Sharpsburg flushed the rebels from the Maryland countryside, the president announced that he would issue an emancipation proclamation. On January 1, 1863, the more than three million persons enslaved in areas of open rebellion would be declared free. Enslaved persons held in bondage in the border states or in areas under federal military occupation, however, would be exempt from the proclamation. In this preliminary announcement, Lincoln offered no hint of outfitting black men in blue uniforms—what would prove to be the most far-reaching effect of his final proclamation.[4]

Predictably, in a regiment teeming with obedient Democrats, many men greeted news of the preliminary emancipation proclamation with scorn and derision. "Some of the officers and a good many of the troops condemned the president," Jacob Smith recalled. At least a few of the troops may have refused to wage a crusade to end slavery. Daniel Cramer, Levi Lash, and James Parks deserted only days after the news from Washington, D.C., reached them at Camp Delaware. Dutiful sentinels returned the trio to the regiment one week later, although Lash absconded again before October's end. Yet there were still plenty in the ranks who cheered the announcement. Smith, for instance, deemed the president's action long overdue, while George Billow exclaimed that the time had arrived to tear slavery out by the root. "With few exceptions," he insisted, "the boys and especially the Akron Company" shared his sentiments. Even so, many of the proclamation's supporters embraced the measure not as a test of principle, but rather as a matter of pragmatism. Though they professed slavery to be "the real issue" underlying the conflict, emancipation seemed the most expedient way to finish off the wicked rebellion and "the work we had obliged ourselves to do."[5]

Ending the conflict was likely fresh on their minds, as the war first revealed to the regiment its capacity for human death and suffering that week. Scores of convalescing soldiers crowded into Camp Delaware's hospital, reeling from gastrointestinal ailments and illnesses they blamed on Kentucky's "miserable water." Two enlisted men succumbed to "camp fever" in short order. "Yesterday we buried a man," Christian Rieker reported matter-of-factly in a letter to his sister. "He died in the hospital and his father came and got him." On October 26, thirty-one-year-old First Lieutenant George Shambs, a private and unpretentious Mansfield tobacconist, left behind his young bride and their two children—including a five-year-old daughter and namesake son born just three weeks prior. Clara Shambs, alerted days before of her husband's flagging condition, was dashing off to Delaware when the soldier expired. "While his loss is mourned by the regiment," one comrade observed somberly, "only a mother as she beheld her two fatherless children could deeply feel the anguish of mind at the loss of her support and stay." Indeed, the twenty-three-year-old widow was obliged to move eighty miles north to Cleveland, where her brother-in-law worked as the city's police clerk and she would begin a new life "keeping house."[6]

Even as it mourned and then buried its first casualties, negative press dogged the regiment. Rumors, after all, were the boon trade of nineteenth-century newspaper editors. With great satisfaction, Colonel Meyer's arch nemesis, Archibald McGregor's *Stark County Democrat*, passed along a report of the colonel's arrest in Cincinnati. The next day, the *Summit County Beacon*, published in Akron, announced that it was in possession of a letter railing against the "drunkenness" that supposedly prevailed among "some" of the 107th's officers. Clearly, the charges stung. Writing under the pseudonym "Billy Bell," George Billow responded to the allegations in a forcefully argued message. " 'People who live in glass houses should never throw stones,' " he advised. "Could you hear the eulogies bestowed upon this regiment, and particularly the officers by the people of Delaware and vicinity, for its orderly, civil, and moral conduct," he added, "you would certain deem such letters as you have received unjust and wholly without foundation."[7]

But the reports did have "foundation," despite embellished claims that a "majority" of the officer corps was habitually intoxicated. On October 17, only days before Billow's retort appeared on the *Beacon's* front page, Corporal Gerhard Schreiber from Company B was "reduced to the ranks" for "insubordination and intemperance." It was little wonder that when the men of the regiment received instructions to fold up tents, they were keen to bid Camp Delaware farewell. "I would have never thought that I would spend a birthday, or this twenty first one under these circumstances," Rieker marveled. "How long I shall still live or shall spend in this situation," he added stoically, "is something that I do not know."[8]

GOVERNOR TOD's orders finally arrived around eight o'clock on Wednesday evening, October the 29th. The next morning, the men obediently stowed "three days rations in haversacks" and climbed aboard hissing locomotives bound for Washington. Because the train would make a brief stop in Canton, the Stark County companies delighted in the thought of a moment's reunion with family and friends as the engine made its way north. The soldiers were crestfallen however, when they arrived at a mostly deserted depot. "The word of our passing through," one enlisted man later lamented, had not arrived "in time." Still others were undeterred; their proximity to home convinced them to take French leave. Privates Charles Kastner, Henry Klingaman, and Thomas Beck deserted Company H and made their way back to Louisville, about eight miles northwest of Canton. Directed to collect "stragglers" milling about the depot before their train pushed off, Private Joshua Budd opted to abandon the unit himself, having already collected his $27 bounty and one month's pay. Though a penitent Budd returned to Company C some ten months later, he would be hauled before a court-martial jury for his offense.[9]

With a whistle, the train pulled away from Canton and lurched toward Pittsburgh, a humming collection of furnaces, factories, and mills nestled in the foothills of western Pennsylvania. At an Iron City depot, the soldiers would board another train for the remainder of their journey to Washington. Needless to say, when the men realized that rickety pine cattle cars "without windows" would deliver them to the nation's capital, it served only to intensify their insecurities. "If we are human beings," Billow insisted, "let them treat us as such." For several hours, Colonel Meyer protested that his men were "not a drove of cattle or hogs," but to no avail. Learning of his colonel's unsuccessful appeal, the wagon maker reluctantly acquiesced. "If we are cattle," he concluded, then "let them treat us as cattle."[10]

The regiment's miserly estimate of its own worth did not improve after brief stops in Altoona, a burgeoning city in the shadow of Brush Mountain, and Harrisburg, the state's capital, crowded on the Susquehanna's eastern bank. In neither city was the much touted "generosity and hospitality of the people of Penn" on active display. Months before the national press (in the aftermath of the Gettysburg campaign) invited a minor controversy by condemning Pennsylvanians for vending "whiskey, water and bread to Union troops at exorbitant prices," Billow reported that Harrisburg merchants "generously charged double [the] value" of anything the troops "wished to purchase." Indeed, the irony was hardly lost that the troops did not receive a warm reception until their arrival in Baltimore, the border-state city where, the previous April, seething secessionist mobs hurled stones, epithets, and lead as militiamen from Massachusetts nudged through on their way to Washington. "Although she is styled the 'city of mobs' and has grossly insulted—*killed*—union soldiers," Billow considered, "she *now* knows how to appreciate them, feed them when hungry, and give them rest, when sick and weary."[11]

The morning after their memorable repast in Baltimore, the troops tramped through the streets of the nation's capital before marching across the aptly named Long Bridge, which delivered them to Arlington Heights. Though that commanding Virginia eminence afforded unrivaled views of the federal city, it was Arlington's starkly militarized landscape that made a lasting impression on the men of the 107th Ohio. "As far as the eye can reach," one of its soldiers remarked, "beautiful habitations have been leveled with the earth; oaks of the forest, felled to the ground, and fences which once environed the fertile fields, are no more to be seen." "There was nothing visible to remind us of civil life," Jacob Smith echoed, awe-inspired by the twisting miles of trenches and makeshift earthen forts. If Camp Delaware awakened the men to the war's ugly realities, then Arlington Heights impressed upon them the conflict's enormous scale. "Wherever the eyes was cast," another volunteer noted, "forts, fortifications, and camps were to be seen." The scene could not help but inspire confidence in their ability to crush the enemy. "The army of the Potomac," one enlisted man concluded, "constitutes an immense force, which if hurled with its full strength upon the Rebel Capitol would without doubt make it yield."[12]

Back at home, however, Ohioans expressed no such assurance. In the fall midterms, the Democrats picked up six Ohio seats in the U.S. House of Representatives, ensuring that the party would control fourteen of the state's nineteen seats during the Thirty-Eighth Congress. The victors were anything but discreet. One editorial pronounced the election the first shot in a "revolution" that would spare the nation from the scourge of "abolitionism." For his part, Samuel Sullivan Cox, who beat back a strong Republican challenger even after the state legislature gerrymandered his district, mocked his baffled opponents in verse:

> *Oh! Shade of the fallen; Oh! Genius sublime;*
> *Great friend of the Negro from Africa's clime*
> *Alas! How low he lies;*
> *Night suddenly came, and his day was done,*
> *His sun was set, and another sun*
> *Illumes the dusky skies.*

Ohio's *Newark Advocate* immodestly reported that the recent election results were not only "unprecedented," but also a "hopeful sign" that the people were at last ready to wrest control of the government from "the madmen now in power."[13]

Republicans refused to take stock of their humiliating defeat, dismissing the results as the predictable consequence of election laws that denied active-duty soldiers access to the ballot. In 1862, just four northern states—Ohio not among them—allowed enlisted men to exercise their suffrage rights on the front. "The elections," the *Daily Cleveland Herald* pointedly objected, "would have shown a different and more desirable result had the volunteers . . . been permitted to vote." As if to confirm the paper's conclusion, more than a few regiments dashed off prickly editorials from the front lines. "While we are absent from our homes and from our most loyal State," one company of Ohio infantrymen protested from their camp near Nashville, "a set of most traitorous thieves, who would rob our country of her glorious principles, have agreed to meet in our county, and almost upon our own doorsteps, to cry, 'Vallandigham, amen,' over the success of their black-hearted, traitorous peace and compromise ticket." The troops swore vengeance if "peace propositions" or "compromise measures" ended the war short of Union victory. "We didn't take an oath to fight against traitors in the South alone," sniffed a Buckeye eyeing the works around Vicksburg in a letter to the *Cincinnati Commercial*. "And we will willingly shoot down traitors in the North whenever they go too far in their wicked schemes." Drawn up in a wintry, snow-bound camp near Romney, Virginia, the soldiers of the 116th Ohio pledged that they "would cause to be remembered those cowardly grumblers and traitors, craven spirits, who, instead of aiding us in our noble purpose by their presence in the ranks, are at home aiding and abetting rebels by keeping up a fire in our rear."[14]

By early December, northern overtures to the rebels disquieted even a regiment amply manned with Democrats. "We do not know what to make of the present affairs," George Billow conceded. "Sometimes we have the prospect of being led forward to meet the foes of our country on the field of battle," he explained, but "again we hear propositions made for a compromise and peace." Though encouraged that the Army of the Potomac would move more aggressively under its new commander, the memorably whiskered Rhode Islander Ambrose Burnside, one Stark County soldier lamented that northerners would make a "political martyr" of Burnside's predecessor George B. McClellan, the outspoken conservative who had moored the men in place for months. It was time, the soldier insisted, for the "lordly slaveholder" to reap the "fruits of secessionism." "Let every city, village and hamlet be ... brought to ruins," he pledged, lest "the Union ... be destroyed and our Government broken up."[15]

HISTORIANS HAVE described the "seasoning" of Civil War soldiers as the acquisition of the physical immunities and psychological coping strategies necessary to negotiate both "army life and the environment of war." But as the soldier who fretted about McClellan's pending martyrdom made clear, "seasoning" also entailed the development of a more capacious and sophisticated understanding of war itself—one that grasped something of the conflict's scope and complexity. The men of the 107th Ohio began to experience this noiseless though unmistakable transformation in the fall of 1862, as they swung their "picks and spades" and muscled logs onto corduroy roads. Although they had not yet fired a volley in anger, they had seen, felt, and experienced enough of the conflict to abandon their "belief that the war was but a small matter and would soon be over." "From the face of things as they presented themselves to us," Jacob Smith later explained of those fatiguing first weeks in Virginia, "everything seemed to indicate a long and dreadful struggle . . . Now we began to realize that it required minds stored with vast personal experience and study to form anything like definite conclusions" about the course of events. "The nearer we approached the scene of conflict," he noted, "the darker the scene before us became."[16]

While "seasoning" prepared men to endure the ordeal of war, it also amplified the chasm between the home front and the battlefield. Soldiers now spoke with an authority bestowed by their inimitable experiences, sometimes taunting civilians who, they insisted, could never really understand. "The hard life of a soldier in active service," an observant editorial writer explained, "wears away timid conservation." From the 107th's new camp near Fairfax, Billow confessed his urgent desire to escort those pleading for peace "to within 20 rods of Fairfax Seminary," where they could "overlook more than 800 graves of Union soldiers, who have laid down their lives, their all, for the liberty and freedom of their country." "If they wish to see more," he continued, "let them go to the Seminary itself." Planted atop a spiny ridge only a few miles from Alexandria, the federal army had transformed the Episcopal seminary into a general hospital early in the war. Its three handsomely trimmed red brick buildings teemed with more than two thousand convalescing soldiers "of every shape and form." "Is this all to be a sacrifice to slavery?" Billow asked bluntly. "Shall the free North yield, and the Slave-holding South triumph?"[17]

These questions doubtless preoccupied the regiment as the number of men listed on the sick rolls soared. Chronic illness, disease, and other bacteria-related maladies menaced filthy, overcrowded, and poorly sited camps. Worse, as Augustus Vignos explained, the troops "were very much exposed," as their tents had not yet arrived and the regiment was "scarce of fuel." After just weeks in Virginia, the number of soldiers "sent sick" in Company C almost doubled; in Company D, the increase was nearly fivefold. Chronic diarrhea delivered Alfred Rider to a hospital near Fairfax. Surgeons nursed a fatigued Fritz Nussbaum back to health at Washington's Carver Hospital, still thronged with soldiers badly maimed in the battle at Second Manassas that August.

Yet the sick wards might have been even more crowded had it not been for regimental surgeon Charles Hartman, who admonished "all men without exceptions" to wash their feet "before and after any march." Those with "sore or swelled feet" were instructed to protect the skin with "a small piece of Linen or Cotton smoothly covered whit lard." Hartman, a beloved medical doctor who had lectured in anatomy at Cleveland Medical College and served as Cuyahoga County's coroner in the years before the war, preached the gospel of good hygiene. "A good whash of the whole upper part of the body with the coldest water obtainable," he insisted, would thwart "many" of the respiratory ailments afflicting the regiment.[18]

Still, to tramp by day in remorseless rain and snow, only to shiver by night on the cold, muddy ground, billeted in a crude, canvas tent, "was anything but enviable." Fearing they might betray their position to prowling enemy pickets, the men could not build large campfires, the oldest remedy of shivering soldiers; worse, the yowling winds snuffed out smaller fires. It was little wonder that Christian Rieker, scribbling on patriotic letterhead emblazoned with bald eagles and an arrow-studded shield of the Union, appealed to his sister for "a pair of gloves and a pair of underpants," adding that others among the Zoar recruits were in need of shirts, "stockings," and "mittens." Often, keeping warm and dry proved a task as demanding as any fatigue duty.[19]

ON DECEMBER 9, the regiment folded up its camp near Fairfax and set out for Stafford Court House, a distance of almost forty miles. "To give an adequate description of the hardships and difficulties attendant upon this march," Jacob Smith later declared, "would be simply impossible." Roads caked in thick muck not only arrested their progress—no more than six or eight wearisome miles per day—but equipped them with a convenient metaphor for the war itself. Hungry, bleary-eyed, and footsore, the regiment tracked through muddy woods and splashed across Wolf Run Shoals, enduring biting squalls of "hail, sleet, and snow." George Billow's feet became swollen with frostbite, prompting the soldier to cut away his brogans so as to apply a salve of beeswax, rosin, and tallow. Still, the men remained tethered to the threadbare hope that this march, despite its miseries, would at last deliver them to "a campaign of importance," if not "an engagement with the enemy."[20]

Pledged to the Army of the Potomac's Eleventh Corps, the 107th Ohio had some cause for cautious optimism. Only days before, the men stood shoulder to shoulder as Franz Sigel, the stout, thirty-eight-year-old major general now in command of the so-called German Corps, inspected the regiment in a formal military review. "You'd better believe that to see Gen Seigel [*sic*] and his staff, followed by his body guards in full uniform & parade, is one imposing sight worth seeing," Jacob Lichty assured his brother. "It is then that you are apt to repeat the oft repeated line, 'I fights mit Sigel.'" The general, whose sense of urgency contributed to his repute as an orator, addressed the troops in his native tongue, announcing his earnest desire "to aid General Burnside in his campaign to cross the Rappahannock and defeat Lee's army." Though he had hardly distinguished himself on the battlefield, Burnside held him in esteem—keenly aware of his peerless popularity among German-Americans. And so the men plodded along, an orphan regiment bringing up the rear of a corps held in reserve.[21]

Yet by the time the Buckeyes reached their new camp at Stafford Court House, Burnside's ambitious plans for a winter campaign had already unraveled. Under enormous political pressure to notch a victory—and thereby quiet the growing chorus of war opponents in the North before Lincoln inked the Emancipation Proclamation on January 1, 1863—the general ordered an ill-considered frontal assault on the Confederate troops. The rebels were planted atop a sharp ridge known as Marye's Heights, just south of Fredericksburg's spires. It was an impregnable position. Beginning in the late morning and continuing well into the afternoon on December 13, 1862, sheets of Confederate musketry and artillery fire shredded blue-coated regiment after blue-coated regiment, littering the fields with dead and wounded men. "Column after column," one Irishman explained, moved forward "under the murderous fire . . . in [a] vain attempt to carry those impregnable heights." "It was a terable slaughterpen to take troops into," one New Jerseyan shuddered. "And when I saw it, I never expected to get out alive."[22]

As they approached Dumfries, the mud-daubed men first detected the sounds of battle in the distance. Fredericksburg's fearsome echoes, together with subsequent newspaper columns—choked with the names of more than thirteen thousand killed, wounded, or missing federal soldiers—confirmed that it had been the regiment's good fortune to miss the lopsided fight with the Army of Northern Virginia. Ohioan William Southerton shuddered as he recalled wagons "filled with the wounded" and soldiers "hobbling" to the rear. "It was sickening," he remarked. News of the calamity was quickly translated into "every European language."

Rather than shore up flagging morale on the northern home front, Fredericksburg instead inspired another wave of recrimination and disbelief. "Our regiments were simply butchered," one editor grieved. The tragedy was "not simply or chiefly the loss of life," he continued, "but the worst of it is that the sacrifice is . . . worse than in vain." The *Stark County Democrat* bluntly asked how much longer the "useless, ruinous, debt-piling" war had to continue. ""If there is a worse place than Hell," Lincoln declared as he sized up the battle's political wreck-age, "I am in it."[23]

The thrashing left a considerable number of Burnside's soldiers restless and discouraged. "When are we going to take Richmond?" an exceptionally irritable Ohio soldier asked ten days after the bat-tle. "I want to see this infernal rebellion subdued, but it is sad to see so much suffering and loss of life and nothing accomplished." Many other troops, however, remained hopeful; the Army of the Potomac, as one of its most discerning historians has noted, hardly "lay supine in Stafford County." "The battle was severe," one Massachusetts colonel conceded before insisting, "we'll try them again." Indeed, a surprising number of soldiers supposed the battle not a humiliating defeat, but rather a remarkable display of their own gritty resolve. "It was indeed trying on our boys," one brigade commander mused, "but they stood it like men." Reflecting on the recent campaign, some men trusted that elusive victories were finally around the corner. "It is said the darkest time is just before day," one Ohioan remarked. "This is indeed a hor-rible war," confessed one Union soldier on the Rappahannock front, "and my heart almost bleeds to think of aiming the deadly blow at my fellow man." "But," he went on, "then I think of the 'Star of Liberty' that is hovering just above the Horizon, almost ready to 'sink into oblivion' . . . and I feel it my duty to endeavor to sustain a free Gov-ernment." There was a fine line between abject gloom and renewed determination. "The spirits of a raw volunteer army are very easily depressed, especially after a reverse," the *New York Times* confirmed, "and they are very easily raised."[24]

WHILE AT Stafford Court House, the 107th Ohio formally joined the 25th, 55th, and 75th Ohio—along with the 17th Connecticut Vol-unteer Infantry—in Nathaniel Collins McLean's Eleventh Corps bri-gade. The Ohio-born McLean, not quite forty-eight years old and a newly minted brigadier general, wore an epic beard and looked every bit his part. A Harvard-educated lawyer, McLean hailed from real antislavery stock; his father, John, who sat for more than three decades on the United States Supreme Court, was best known for his eloquent dissent in the 1857 *Dred Scott* case—the ugly decision that declared black men had no rights a white man was bound to respect. In May 1860 Nathaniel traveled to the Republican nominating convention in Chicago, where he hoped that his father might emerge as the nominee. Elbowing his way through the crowds of influence peddlers ("it is almost impossible to move about in the hall, without tearing off the buttons from your coat"), McLean impatiently tracked the proceedings. "The friends of Seward are moving heaven and earth for his nomination," he sighed, despairing at the senator's prospects in a general election. Nor did he deem Lincoln a worthwhile alternative. "Lincoln is I believe entirely honest and a very clever fellow," McLean confided, "with talent enough for many places, yet totally unfit in administrative capacity for President." The convention goers, of course, thought otherwise. Even though his father would not ride a dark horse to the Executive Mansion, McLean at least remained hopeful that the Republicans would prevent another slaveholder from taking up residence there.[25]

When the war broke out, Nathaniel believed that he was waging an abolition crusade. McLean received a colonel's commission in September 1861; the following summer, he led the 75th Ohio Volunteers into battle at Cross Keys in the Shenandoah Valley. While sometimes overly prudent, he proved a capable officer. Promoted to command a brigade in the Army of Virginia just weeks later, his men made an impressive stand atop Chinn Ridge during the battle of Second Bull Run. To a man, the 107th professed their faith in his leadership.[26]

Though the 25th, 55th, and 75th Ohio had "seen the elephant" in western Virginia, the men of the 17th Connecticut—like those of the 107th—eagerly awaited their first rendezvous with the enemy. Brimming with frustration, the sons of Bridgeport and New Canaan, Newtown and Danbury passed the first weeks of their enlistments marking time at Fort Marshall, "just east of Baltimore." After a successful petition from their colonel, the elegant New Englanders, trimmed with "white gloves" and "collars," received instructions to join Sigel in

November. Happy to leave the tedious and tiresome duties of trench life behind, the men set out for Stafford Court House. Their euphoria, however, would be short-lived. Tramping over the old Bull Run battlefields, littered with discarded canteens, disabled cannon, and human debris, the Nutmeggers gaped at the "marks of a hard fought battle." "One sight that made a lasting impression on me," one lieutenant wrote, "was a man's leg hanging in a bush, all withered and black." One soldier tripped over a skull, still bearing "a fine set of teeth," upon which a passerby mounted the ghoulish taunt: " 'Ruling Passion Strong in Death.' " "Manassas," still another veteran reflected, "was a revelation to us."[27]

In late December, after being advised that the Army of the Potomac would more than likely remain moored in place "for some time," the troops threw up temporary quarters. "In the course of a day," Jacob Smith claimed, the regiment erected structures that would afford partial shelter from the biting winds that squalled across Virginia. Here they would remain for the next five weeks. "Every encampment has been transformed from a dreary, fever breeding collection of shelterless tents, into a mud walled village," one writer crowed, "and the curling smoke leaps and twists and wriggles from countless chimneys into a pillar of cloud, beckoning to the cheery fires that glow beneath."[28]

Although the encamped soldiers occupied themselves by taking turns on the picket line, they ached for news from home. During their stay at Stafford, with the consent of their officers, enlisted men sometimes wandered down to the Potomac "boat landings," where they snatched up "as many newspapers" as possible. Entrepreneurial spirits then hawked them to their comrades for "ten, fifteen and sometimes twenty cents a copy." Others relied on the "regular" visits of a "newspaper merchant," or received newspapers in care packages sent from home. F. A. Wildman maintained a steady diet of "the principal weeklies" and illustrated news magazines in camp. In addition to *Harper's Weekly* and the *Sandusky Register*, he even caught up on the *Norwalk Experiment*, "that stinking organ of Jeff Davis and the Rebels." William Siffert scanned the columns of Ohio papers, anxious for news from his brother, then nudging his way through Mississippi's cypress-choked swamps with the 76th Ohio. Jacob Smith preferred the *Washington Chronicle*, a hard-to-find but reliable antidote for the "class of rebel sympathizing papers" that circulated through the camps.[29]

Letters from home were even more important than newspapers. "Please write soon so I get some news from you before we leave this place," Fritz Nussbaum instructed Cary Kauke, the young friend with whom he maintained a correspondence throughout the war, from Camp Cleveland. "Almost daily," Christian Rieker explained, "I await letters with longing." While a few lines from home temporarily satisfied a gnawing curiosity about the opinions and activities of loved ones and acquaintances, letters also reassured soldiers that they still occupied the thoughts and prayers of those behind the lines. "I was very glad to hear from you," Nussbaum explained to his young friend in mid-November 1863, "and also glad to see that you had not forgotten me yet." Desiring above all to maintain their imaginative connection with those back home, soldiers scratched out letters even when they had little "new" or interesting to report. "I doubt not, but that at least some of the readers of the *Beacon* would be pleased to hear from the 107th Ger. Reg't occasionally," George Billow wrote. Hunched over makeshift desks—sometimes just "a small piece of board" stretched across the knees—the men jealously seized free moments in camp and on the march as precious opportunities to write.[30]

Not all correspondence from home was welcome, of course. "Letters home kept the men in touch with those they left behind," one historian explains, "but they also revealed the immense distance that grew up between the worlds of civilians and soldiers." By the spring of 1863, Christian Rieker doubted whether loved ones at home would even "recognize" him. While adverse news typically traveled from the battlefield to the home front, it could also move in the opposite direction. As Rieker nursed his doubts, fear and anxiety stalked eighteen-year-old Alvin Brown, a private in Company H, who had not heard from his father in three weeks. "I thought I would write another letter to you," the soldier began. "I hope there is nothing wrong."[31]

Sometimes, letters from home initiated unwelcome political debates; to be sure, soldiers were always quick to detect the whiff of treachery or betrayal on the home front. "You may be Democrats," one soldier in the 55th Ohio snapped, "but you act very much like traitors." When another Buckeye volunteer learned that his wife attended a Democratic meeting in Uniontown, a village just north of Canton, he scolded her for keeping boorish company. "I don't like any Vallandigham meeting in mime," he explained. "I don't wish any of my folks to mix in such stuff." The warning must have gone unnoticed, for no more than two months later the soldier admonished her for "writing too much about Politics." "Let us wait until this war is over," he implored, "and then we can talk about Political affairs."[32]

Other letters bespoke the difficulties of tending romantic fires from a distance. Jacob Smith recalled the unfortunate tale of "a bright, intelligent" company cook who desired a vow of faithfulness from his sweetheart. When the soldier received what he interpreted to be a noncommittal reply, he became understandably disheartened. Shortly thereafter, he succumbed to typhoid in a Washington camp hospital. While Smith acknowledged that the disease "was working in his system prior to his receiving the letter," the malevolent agency he attributed to the young woman's missive reveals not only the importance of perceived support back home, but also the keen intuition—shared by very many soldiers—that their physical and emotional health were inextricably linked.[33]

That intuition would prove essential in the days ahead. After weeks of blister-inducing marches and many fatiguing nights passed on the picket line, all were alive with anticipation for the New Year. Tinged with unease yet brimming with excitement, they sensed that the coming months would deliver them to the war in earnest at last.

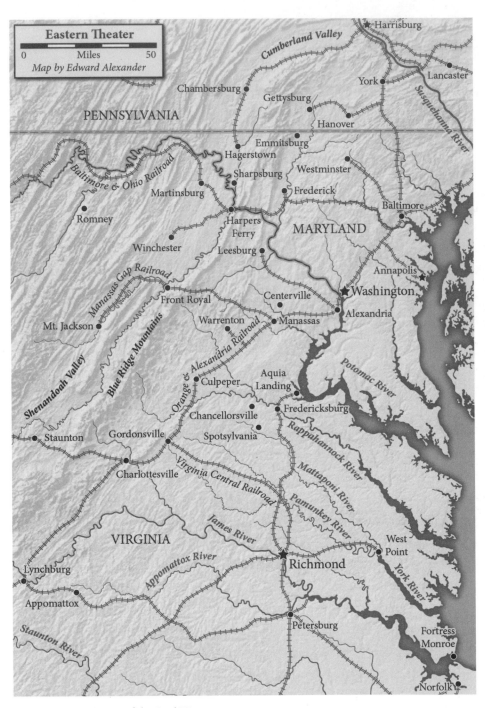

The Eastern Theater of the Civil War

CHAPTER 3

"STOP ALL FIRING IN THE REAR OF US"

January to April 1863

THE YEAR 1863 began ominously for the 107th Ohio. As anti-slavery activists in Boston and New York City celebrated the arrival of "jubilee," the Buckeyes huddled around the fresh grave of Corporal Philip Oakleaf who, on New Year's Day, succumbed to typhoid—one of many diseases that romped so destructively through the Army of the Potomac's camps that winter. Captain Barnet Steiner delivered a short but eloquent funeral sermon, seizing the moment to impress upon all "the necessity of living right, discharging every duty to the best of our ability." The war demanded physical and spiritual vigilance from its soldiers, Steiner reminded them, because death could issue its "summons" at any time. Even for a generation menaced by epidemics, communicable diseases, and deadly childhood ailments, mortality never seemed so imminent as it did during the Civil War. "Death is nothing here," poet Walt Whitman observed as he threaded his way through Falmouth, piled high with corpses awaiting burial and choked by rows of crudely marked graves. "No one makes an ado."[1]

Yet as evidenced by Steiner's simple eulogy, soldiers never became completely inured to death; nor could they brook the grim reaper's contempt for individuality. The nature of death in the Civil War—sometimes violent, often bereft of meaning, and nearly always at a distance from loved ones back home—not only invited survivor guilt, sorrow and regret; it likewise renewed the soldier's innate fear of being forgotten. Jakob Kuemmerle, one of the Zoar recruits, passed away just a few weeks later. "It was very hard for us to see him die," Christian Rieker confessed, "so far removed from family and siblings, and in such a wild, rough, unfavorable area as it is here in Virginia." Kuemmerle's hasty burial greatly distressed his old friend. "He is just lying here, only one comrade at his side in the wide, broad field, perhaps an old cotton field," Rieker protested. "I do not think it will make much difference to a dead man, but it looks quite uninhabited for those who behold it." Other soldiers wept as they watched an African-American burial detail lower lifeless bodies into a long, narrow trench.[2]

The death of a comrade tore at the fabric of a Civil War regiment, but often in a way that—however paradoxically—renewed its commitment to the struggle. Who, after all, could endure the thought that Philip Oakleaf and Jakob Kuemmerle might have died in vain? Urgently, the men needed to explain—to themselves and to their loved ones back home—the meaning of so much death and suffering. Unable to grasp anything of the relationship between death, suffering, and the progress of arms, and lacking any assurance about the war's direction, they existed in the uneasy, angst-ridden space between the war's battles. They faced each fated moment as it came. "The great question among us," an enlisted man in the 107th revealed, "is when will this war end? And how will matters stand when it is ended?" Over the next five months, bad weather and even worse roads, ever-lengthening sick rolls, and disquieting new evidence of disloyalty back home would render those questions more difficult—and thus more imperative to answer.[3]

PILLORIED BY THE PRESS, hauled before the Joint Committee on the Conduct of the War, and irked by quarrelsome subordinates, Ambrose Burnside was eager to rouse the Army of the Potomac from its post-Fredericksburg torpor. Defiantly, the burly general announced that the time was ripe "to gain that decisive victory" and, at last, "strike a great and mortal blow to the rebellion." Burnside directed his main force to march upriver, splash across the Rappahannock at Bank's Ford, and gain Lee's left flank. He hoped that the swift movement would flush the rebels from their sturdy works behind Fredericksburg, invite a battle on more favorable ground, and wring from Lee the initiative the federals lost in the ill-fated attempts on Mayre's Heights.[4]

While many soldiers dismissed Burnside's latest order out of hand ("I hope the army will go to Richmond this time or to hell, and I don't care which," one blunt Michigander growled), the rank and file of the 107th Ohio expressed a new and certain optimism. A correspondent embedded with the Eleventh Corps confessed that he could find no "evidence of demoralization," even in regiments whose sick rolls seemed to multiply by the hour. The expectation of forward action could, as one soldier explained it, have "a magical effect." "The weak grow suddenly strong, the disheartened courageous, and men who on one day would be ready to flee before an enemy, will on the next chase him with the bayonet," the *New York Times* made clear. Some in the 107th deemed a visit from the paymaster a good omen. For his part, George Billow announced that the boys were both "ready" to meet the enemy in battle and "determined not to stop short of whipping 'em out this time." "All were held in readiness to move at any notice," another volunteer echoed.[5]

Nobody predicted what happened next.

On January 20, the day the army was to move, the temperatures plummeted as biting winds squalled across Virginia. Later that evening, a doleful drizzle thickened to sleet, plastering the region's crude thoroughfares in mud. The viscous mire, which one soldier analogized to "stiff mortar," swallowed up army mules, supply wagons, limber chests, and artillery pieces to their axles, jamming the roads with "an indescribable chaos of pontoons, vehicles, and artillery." "Moving cannon and an army had to be abandoned—it was a thing impossible," George Billow sighed. "Even the cavalry horses at times stuck fast and staggered like drunken men," another soldier echoed. "The mud here in fact out-peninsulas the peninsula," marveled one incredulous veteran of McClellan's notoriously soggy campaign to capture the rebel capital. "The army, in fact, was embargoed: it was no longer a question of how to go forward—it was a question of how to get back."6

Burnside had regrettably equipped the press—and war opponents back home—with a devastating new metaphor for the army's progress in the East. The chastened troops were not just in "dead-lock," one editorial writer sneered; they were in "mud-lock." The mocking headlines were all too predictable. Appropriating the jeers of the "secesh pickets," the *New York Herald* announced that the Army of the Potomac was "stuck in the mud." Even the reliably pro-Union *Philadelphia Inquirer* conceded that recent events were "more than ordinarily unfortunate," as they had "given rise" to a traffic in "conflicting as well as false" rumors." "Every day increases the anxiety universally felt for instant, vigorous and decisive action," its editor acknowledged. "We can only hope and wait."7

Gnarled, waterlogged, and weather-beaten, the men of the Army of the Potomac limped mournfully to their campsites. Some of the 107th boys were so exhausted that they collapsed along the road and commenced a deep sleep. In the estimation of one New Yorker, the men were "about used up." "My opinion is that the army of the Potomac is about played out," advised a soldier from the 55th Ohio, who regarded the Mud March as "the greatest failure in the war." Yet even the profound disappointment of the Mud March sent no great wave of disillusionment crashing through the ranks. "The demoralization of our army is a subject of which too much has, of late, been said and written," a Maine correspondent wrote. "I don't believe it, and if I did, I would not tell of it. The boys have been abused and neglected, but you had better believe they'll fight . . . I should decidedly object to being one in any rebel force that meets that 'demoralized army' in a fair field."[8]

Overwhelmingly, the 107th Ohio's rank and file would have agreed. One volunteer informed the *Stark County Democrat* that while he overheard plenty of "growling" among his comrades, it was chiefly the result of their being "cheated out of what they call a game of ball with the rebels." While the impossibility of keeping warm and dry had "doubled" the unit's presence at the field hospital, the soldier felt "confident that our boys are good for their number." "Tired of laying around idle," he thirsted for a fight. "Let us have it now, whip or get whipped," he urged. "If rebel sympathizers in the North are basing their hopes on a speedy peace, thinking that the army will no longer fight, or are so demoralized as to be unfit and uncertain for duty," another enlisted man advised, "their hopes are vain and founded on false rumor."[9]

Shivering in camp, men expressed their faith in an all-knowing providence. "I think I see the dawn of a brighter future," one Bay State volunteer declared. "The soldiers all realize that there is a directing, commanding will now at the head of this army, with whom traitors cannot trifle. Despondency, disgust, and a deep intense feeling of homesickness are giving place in the army to confidence and a longing for the promised work." As they pondered the relationship between their circumstances and human agency, a growing number of men held that the army's fortunes depended on a higher power, not human blunder. "The fates had decreed the failure of the enterprise," Jacob Smith professed. "The sluices of Heaven opened, as it were, to prostrate the General's promising designs." The army's latest "enterprise," another observer echoed, was "balked and brought to naught by causes which mortal kin could neither have foreseen nor prevented." "Of course Gen. Burnside is not to blame for this failure," surmised the Rhode Islander Elisha Hunt Rhodes. "He could not control natural forces notwithstanding the views of certain newspapers who seem to think he could."[10]

Still, not everyone was willing to pardon Ambrose Burnside for a winter of dashed hopes and false starts, "long delays and useless marches." "All we desire is a good leader," one of the 107th Ohio's restless soldiers explained, "and we will show that the Army of the Potomac is worthy of noble deeds and that her rank and file are composed of men, true patriots, who more willingly yield their lives in defense of their rights than bow to slave aristocracy like [so many] cringing, mealy mouthed traitors at home."[11]

WITHIN A WEEK of the Mud March, that soldier got his wish. On January 26, 1863, the president removed Burnside from command and installed in his place forty-eight-year-old Joseph Hooker, an attractive man with piercing blue eyes and a sturdy jaw who carried an "erect soldierly bearing." "Anybody would feel like cheering when he rode by at the head of his staff," one of his new division commanders claimed. Born in November 1814 in Hadley, an old Puritan town perched on the Connecticut River and nestled in the hills of western Massachusetts, Hooker graduated near the middle of his West Point class of 1837. After battling through stands of cypress and Florida swamps during the Second Seminole War, he was packed off to Mexico, where he served on the staffs of five generals and fought with distinction at the battles of Monterrey and Chapultepec. Not long after personally assuring President Lincoln that he was superior to any Yankee general in the field, the pugnacious Hooker lived up to his intrepid claim—piloting a division up the Peninsula before ascending the slopes of South Mountain with the corps that would open the battle of Antietam. It was only with some hyperbole that the *New York Times* deemed Hooker "the most uniformly successful of all our officers." "He does not believe in the charm of soft persuasion," another newspaper assured. "He is not one to hang out the white rag." So it was that "every officer and private is glad that [Burnside] is removed," one enlisted man from Stark County explained.[12]

The new commanding general demanded a steely resolve and a renewed sense of purpose from his soldiers. "In the record of your achievements there is much to be proud of," Hooker insisted, "and with the blessing of God, we will contribute something to the renown of our arms and the success of our cause." As he anxiously waited for warmer weather (wisely heeding the president's advice to "beware of rashness"), Hooker implemented a number of important new policies and reforms. To ensure the "ready recognition of corps and divisions," the general directed his troops to affix corps badges to their hats. The men of the 107th Ohio pinned red felt crescents on their kepis, signaling their position in the First Division of the Eleventh Corps. Hooker upgraded the soldiers' diets, calling for "flour or soft bread" to be issued four times per week; "fresh potatoes or onions, if practicable," twice per week; and "desiccated mixed vegetables or potatoes" once per week. Hooker likewise permitted line officers to grant ten-day furloughs to men who maintained "the most excellent record for attention to all duties." To accommodate the length of their trip, men from Ohio and points farther west were eligible for fifteen-day leaves.[13]

Equally important, Hooker forbade the circulation of Democratic newspapers in the army camps. For months, the "treasonable" press had riled the men with their heavy-handed editorials. "It is manifestly impossible for the army to read these papers without feeling discouraged and homesick," one Eleventh Corps soldier explained. Accordingly, provost marshals ordered merchants hawking issues of the *New York World* "back to Aquia Creek," prohibiting the paper's sale "along the road" and at Falmouth Station. "Now we get the *Tribune* and *Post* and the Washington *Chronicle* once more," one enlisted man rejoiced, marveling at the "healthy and inspiring" effects of the loyal press on his comrades. In their letters home, soldiers appealed for "every copy of the *Atlantic, Continental, Harper's Monthly,* and *Christian Examiner*" available, explaining that such reading would "help to fix patriotic men more firmly in their purpose."[14]

In the ensuing weeks, the loyal press very likely braced the men of the 107th Ohio, as long marches and unhappy conditions once more tested their determination. No sooner had they established a winter camp (a neat row of "shanties" perched atop the "brow of a very steep bank") than they were sent packing to a new site along the Accokeek Creek, about one mile west of Brooke's Station, a tiny depot on the railroad that stretched "between Aquia and Falmouth." The Ohioans trudged through stiff winds and muddy swamps and along rutted roads, only to be greeted by sheets of sleet and ice that before long turned to snow. Absent any shelter on a night that thermometers registered subzero temperatures, with the mud beneath them congealing

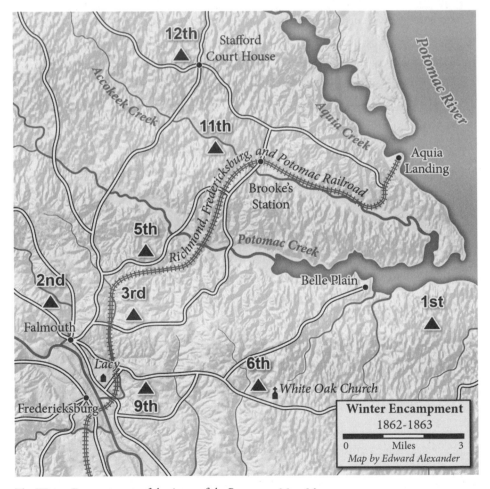

The Winter Encampments of the Army of the Potomac, 1862–1863

into "a hard frozen mass," the troops "suffered a great deal." The bone-chilling weather impressed even hearty New Englanders, including one who declared this night, "the worst I have seen since I became a member of Uncle Sam's family." Regimental historian Jacob Smith was especially blunt: "This was one of the times that we did not wish to have repeated."[15]

On February 4, their "fingers and faces" numb from the bite of the wind, men finally received orders to construct winter quarters. If welcome, these instructions—the third such in as many months—must have reinforced for many the absurdity and unpredictability of war. Forming up, heading out, falling back, digging in—the war had become a wearisome sequence of movements and motions, none of which could be readily assimilated into a larger narrative, and none of which—from the perspective of men on the ground—seemed to exert any influence on the course of the war. For some troops, bustle invited fresh skepticism about the efficacy of their leaders. It was not lost on Jacob Smith, for instance, that on the 107th Ohio's freezing trek to Brooke's Station, the regiment plodded along some of the same roads that, only weeks before, delivered them to bustling Belle Plain. "With all the marching we did, we have not done anything towards ending this war," one of the Stark County volunteers rued. Even worse, Alvin Brown suspected that as soon as the men pitched their new camp, they would once again be ordered to move.[16]

Throwing up a winter camp was hard work that began by harvesting the surrounding stands of sturdy pine, laurel, and black jack oak. Axes quickly transformed the woods into a barren, other-worldly "landscape of stumps," all the while supplying a steady tempo for the men who sawed felled trunks into logs and beams. "All the surrounding forests had disappeared," one northern correspondent remembered, "built into huts, with chimneys of sticks and mud, or burned in the stone fireplaces constructed by the soldiers." (By harvesting trees, which consume water from the soil, the men unwittingly contributed to the "mud" problem.) As he hoisted a heavy log into place on a winter hut, Anton Lang lost his balance and toppled to the ground, rupturing his right side. No longer fit for "military duties"—obliged to serve out his term as a company cook—Lang's would be among the most eloquent voices after the war reminding that the battlefield maintained no monopoly on wounds and injuries.[17]

Soon, "good substantial log huts" that afforded a partial reprieve from the gusts of winter lined the parade ground. Unlike other units that tramped across that drill field—sometimes "five hours daily when not on other duty"—the 107th Ohio adopted no such routine. "Battalion drill cannot take place," Lieutenant Colonel Charles Mueller plainly informed the regiment in late February, advising company commanders to instruct their troops in the manual of arms "whenever the weather will permit." Even men assigned to the Ambulance Corps, faced with the daunting task of learning how to wind a stretcher bearing a wounded comrade to a field hospital, drilled no more than two hours on any given day. "We don't drill any," one soldier rejoiced, "only dress parade."[18]

Consequently, the men had ample time to reflect on the war and their participation in it. They passed much of that time pondering the antiwar sentiments romping throughout much of the Midwest—especially in Ohio, where editor Edwin Cowles's pro-Lincoln *Cleveland Daily Leader* declared an open "contest between military successes and peace opponents of the war." The Copperhead movement's influence tracked the fortunes of the federal war effort. By early 1863, it had swollen in personnel, tallying new grievances and offering a more vigorous critique of the Union war effort. Encouraged by their strong showing in the midterm elections, antiwar Ohio Democrats grew increasingly shrill. Only a few weeks before the 107th Ohio set out on its wintry march to Brooke's Station, a Dayton congressman named Clement Laird Vallandigham took to the floor of the U.S. House of Representatives and commenced a blistering, one-hour tirade against the abolition "fanatics and demagogues" and their needless, costly war.[19]

"You cannot abolish slavery by the sword," Vallandigham snorted, and "still less by proclamations, though the President were to 'pro-

claim' every month." Denying that there was an "'irrepressible conflict' between slave labor and free labor," the brass-lunged second-term
congressman denounced the war as a mad abolitionist "crusade."
"From the beginning," he protested, "the war has been conducted like
a political campaign, and it has been the folly of the party in power
that they have assumed that numbers alone would win the field in a
contest not with ballots but with musket and sword." Vallandigham
seemed almost to delight in the Union armies' military reverses. "Victory," he announced, "follows the standard of the foe." "Ought this
war to continue?" he asked. "I answer, no—not a day, not an hour."[20]

The speech grabbed headlines and column inches on both sides of

Dayton congressman Clement Laird Vallandigham, a Copperhead Democrat, emerged as
the most vocal opponent of the war, earning the ire of soldiers in the field. *Library of Congress*

the Mason-Dixon Line. With keen interest, newspapers across the Confederate South tracked the proceedings in Washington, hopeful that the "peace party," now "growing in strength and boldness," offered a reliable index of northern resolve. Indeed, across Ohio, where Vallandigham made no secret of his gubernatorial ambitions, the speech reinvigorated pitched debates about the necessity of the war and the cause of emancipation. While cautious Ohio Democrats distanced themselves from Vallandigham's "formal bid to lead the peace crusade," plenty of the state's Democratic newspapers piled acclaim on the congressman's effort. The *Newark Advocate,* for example, esteemed Vallandigham's "force of reasoning," his "richness of historical illustration," and his very "depth of patriotism." From Columbus to Dayton to Cincinnati, obsequious editors paid undue tribute to the "words of wisdom" and "burning eloquence" of "the greatest living American statesman." Inspired by Vallandigham, the editor of one western Ohio newspaper reached a remarkable conclusion that winter: "He who supports the war," he announced, "is *against* the Union."[21]

As the peace movement flowered throughout the Midwest, Republicans registered their irritation. "The man who recommends and circulates, such treason, as Vallandigham's speech," the *Ripley Bee* declaimed, "does more mischief to the Union cause, than he could, by fighting against the Government." "If distrust prevails and Copperheads continue to vomit treason," one Cleveland newspaper hastened to add, "if our soldiers are slandered and our honor outraged by false and heretic doctrines by northern Rebels, then only providence can save us from national ruin." Some began to wonder what posed the greater threat to the Union—the Confederacy or Copperheadism. "Compared with Vallandigham," declared George Templeton Strong, the Manhattan attorney who served as the treasurer of the United States Sanitary Commission, "the most barbarous, brutal Mississippian now in arms against us is a demigod."[22]

Yet nowhere did opposition to Vallandigham blaze with more righteous indignation than along the north bank of the Rappahannock, in the winter quarters of the Army of the Potomac. "If they don't want us to come down here and fight," one of the regiment's enlisted men recommended, "why let them keep their mouths shut and not disturb us." "I will leave my bones to bleach on the battle field of the sunny South," he rejoined, "before I will say 'Compromise' or say 'Enough.'" "All I ask," one more Ohio volunteer echoed, unable to efface the sting of betrayal, "is for those who know nothing of war and its ravages to hold their mouths, and not discourage those who are risking their lives in an effort to restore a tottering government to its former position." "The assertion that soldiers are so tired of the war that they care not upon what terms peace is made with the Rebels," still another soldier from the Buckeye State confirmed, "is simply a notorious falsehood."[23]

In camp near Falmouth, a pair of northeastern Ohio regiments endorsed a similarly urgent set of resolutions, making public their estimation of the war's opponents back home. "While we are ready to lay down our lives in our just and holy cause," the men began, "we ask of the people at home to lay aside all partizan feeling and to act as patriots." "If men like Vallandigham . . . will join the rebel ranks and meet us face to face, on the field of battle," they continued, "we will treat them as honorable foes." "But if they continue to advocate compromises and dishonorable peace propositions, then in justice to the sacred memory of our brothers in arms . . . in vindication of all that is dear to us, we will brand them as infamous traitors."[24]

Something more than resentment for stay-at-homes stirred in those bone-chilling winter camps. Animating the response of many soldiers to the Copperheads was the conviction, steeled by sacrifice and fortified by loss, that the war *had* to be won. It was a conviction that the hissing of the peace men back home gave an unlikely and ironic boost. With every pious declaration that Lincoln was a despot and emancipation unwise, the troops measured the distance between the battlefield and home front, temporarily setting aside their own sharp political differences. "The more the Copperheads rave," Christian Schreiner insisted, "the more determined the men in the army get."

"These Democratic traitors cannot humbug me with their talk about 'habeas corpus,' 'false imprisonments,' and their mourning about 'niggers,'" insisted the Swiss-born Christian von Gunden, who shouldered a musket in Company I. "Every sane minded soldier can see that Slavery has kept the rebellion alive . . . If we can deprive the rebels of their slave labor, we take from them their commissary and quartermaster departments." The soldier believed that on this point, there was "no difference of opinion among Ohio troops in the army of the Potomac."

"Our cause is just and must prevail," one Wooster volunteer declared, "and if slavery should thereby be sacrificed, all the better; have the cause of all this bloodshed removed, and then when we get peace, we will have a permanent peace."[25]

With the weather affording a temporary respite from the rebels, many Union soldiers ached for an opportunity to confront the Copperheads back home. "Men [who] are down on the war," one enlisted man asserted, who "would treat a soldier like a dog, they are the ones I would like to see." One volunteer proposed "to send some of our weather-beaten soldiers" home, "armed with a gun and bayonet and sixty rounds of cartridges." Though eager for one of Hooker's furloughs, von Gunden vowed that he "would not take that furlough, or a discharge" if issued orders to confront the Copperheads. "Half way business is about played out," Schreiner declared. "It would indeed be a deplorable thing if civil war should break out in the North, but if it cannot be avoided in any other way than by yielding to the Copperheads and mud sill rebels, I say, 'let it come.'" Persuaded that a confrontation between furloughed soldiers and the peace men was eminent, one Stark County soldier concluded that it was "getting to be quite an exciting time."[26]

Indeed, for much of the winter, the home front became something of a battlefront. On February 28, nearly eight hundred Cantonites choked Market Street's sidewalks to hear an oration delivered by the Copperhead martyr Edson Baldwin Olds, who addressed the crowd from a rough-hewn platform erected on the grounds of Stark County's handsome brick courthouse. Once described as a "shrewd, cunning man," the bespectacled, fifty-nine-year-old former Ohio congressman possessed, in Governor Tod's estimation, "a capacity for great mischief." Just six months before, faced with allegations that his public speeches were dampening army recruitment, Olds was conducted to a holding cell within Fort Lafayette, a stout military installation perched at the entrance to New York harbor. Never charged with a crime, the Democrat secured his release and returned to Ohio, a new and most improbable political wind at his back.[27]

In Canton, Olds rehearsed many of the Copperheads' objections to the struggle; yet the veteran stump speaker punctuated his remarks with questions inviting reflection on the war's human costs. "What means that widow's moan and that orphan's wail?" he demanded to know. "Why is sadness depicted in every countenance?" When Olds concluded his oration ("adroitly sugared," in the words of the *Stark County Republican*, "with a great many pleasant things about the Union"), an especially outspoken, antiwar state legislator from central Ohio took center stage. George Converse had scarcely begun his remarks, however, when the scene devolved into bedlam.[28] Making his way through the tightly packed crowd that evening was Edward Meyer. Though at home on furlough, the young soldier was spoiling for a fight. Meyer combed the crowd for a deserter, making no secret of his object. When an on-duty deputy sheriff "refused" to aid him in the hunt, the captain offered a "fearless and emphatic expression of his opinion concerning the character of the meeting." The loud rant provoked a few "Copperhead bullies," who quickly surrounded him. Meyer attempted to ward off his attackers and was aided "by half a dozen discharged soldiers," but not before the roughs landed several blows. Others joined in the affray. In the shadow of the St. Cloud Hotel, "a large number was knocked down and bruised." "A still more vigorous engagement ensued" in front of the Stark County Treasurer's Office, as men brandished pistols and even used them as whips. Amid hisses and jeers, a "cowardly miscreant" heaved a brick that collided with a captain from the 4th Ohio. The *Stark County Republican* dripped with disgust, but couldn't resist mocking the self-proclaimed party of "law and order."[29]

Elsewhere across the state, ordinary electioneering and partisanship threatened to devolve into violence. As they organized "township clubs," Republicans and Democrats in Bucyrus suspected one another of sinister motives. "The day that sees one drop of Democratic blood [shed]," cautioned one local office holder, "that day will see your town in ashes and your streets running with blood." Perhaps in preparation for the reckoning, one Copperhead hoarded "two kegs of powder and thirty pounds of lead." In mid-March, the tiny village of Hoskinsville seized national headlines when its armed civilians foiled a deputy federal marshal's attempt to apprehend a Union army deserter. "It must seem strange to a foreign observer, having witnessed . . . the uprising of the Northern people, at the outbreak of the Southern rebellion," one correspondent remarked, "to witness the gradual change from loyalty to apathy, and from apathy to rampant treason, which the efforts of traitors in our midst have been only too successful in producing."[30]

Brimming with resentment, soldiers regarded the fire in the rear as an affront to their self-respect. "It is a very common expression among the men after hearing the condition of affairs in the North," reported an Ohio soldier who was brigaded with the 107th, "that they would like to be there for a while to poke some of the Butternuts with the same bayonet that they have used upon the enemy in the field." More than a few soldiers noted the irony that peace men, in their efforts "to weaken the arm of the army," were actually prolonging the war. "Stop all firing in the rear of us," one 107th soldier implored, "and we will attend to the foe in front."[31]

BY EARLY APRIL, Virginia had thawed and quiet army camps once more hummed with activity. The "wintry music" of wind gusts whistling "through the pine tops" gave way to the creaking of wagons and the steady tramping of men. Privates Conrad Metzler, Elias Ritz, and John Slutts returned to the regiment from their convalescence in Washington, rejuvenated and eager to fight. Soldiers inspected weapons, stocked ammunition chests, filled wagons, and shod horses. "The weather is fine now-a-days," one soldier announced, "and the roads are fast getting in good condition." On April 21, the paymaster made another welcome visit, allowing the troops to express money to needy loved ones back home. That same day, upon the request of Adjutant Peter F. Young, the 107th Ohio received a bounteous supply of new forage caps, infantry trousers, and canteens. The men expected marching orders any day.[32]

Though the winter tested the men of the 107th Ohio, it also transformed them. New "sanitary measures" and improved nutrition restored the health of the unit, once ailing and sickly, wracked with dysentery, typhoid, and diarrhea. Even Jacob Smith, whose condition flagged throughout much of the winter, announced on Easter Sunday—his twenty-third birthday—that he was "slowly improving" and would "soon be able to do full duty." It was little wonder so many of the men remembered the camp so fondly. "We had been there two months," one soldier explained, "and the place had unconsciously grown dear to us."[33]

Perhaps even more striking was the regiment's psychic renewal. Once staggered by self-doubt and insecurities, an extended opportunity to reflect on the war—and the howls of war opponents back home—steeled the 107th Ohio with a renewed sense of purpose. "Col. Meyer," one captain reported, "has by his tact, energy, and skill as an officer made the 107th one of the best regiments in the corps." "There is an army pride growing up, even now in full existence . . . that will make it irresistible," explained one enlisted man brigaded with the 107th, "and, what is very important, will place it entirely beyond the influence of Copperheadism at home." Christian Rieker could not have agreed more. "I think if we go at it again," he told his sister Mary back in Zoar, "they will get hell from us."[34]

CHAPTER 4

"COMPLETELY AND SCIENTIFICALLY FLANKED"

April to May 1863

B Y EARLY SPRING, rumor had become the official currency of the army camps. "What shall become of us, God only knows," one Eleventh Corps soldier mused. "There is any amount of what we call 'camp rumor' amongst the boys, but nothing certain." But on the last Sunday in April, suspense at last yielded to movement. From Hooker's headquarters the men received word that they would march "at day light" the next morning. "Positive marching orders for the morrow," Captain Samuel Surbrug announced in his diary. As was typical, the men had not the slightest inkling where they were headed. "What our ultimate destination is has puzzled many a head without the problem being solved," Surbrug confessed, adding, "general officers keep their plans to themselves." Nonetheless, trust in those officers, together with faith in providence, prevailed over any remaining misgivings. Confidently, the rank and file resolved that the war's final campaign had begun.[1]

That evening, as the men made preparations to move out, drum taps announced a mail call. In his capacity as regimental postmaster, Alfred Rider made his rounds. Among the letters he delivered was one "from an old democratic friend," urging its addressee "to quit murdering his southern brethren." The soldier indignantly tossed the letter into a campfire, though not before it provoked heated discussion. "What is more criminal than to incite your own soldiers to insubordination and rebellion?" one of his comrades demanded. "Behold the graves on yon hill side of our brave comrades and of southern union men who were cruelly butchered by these 'brethren' and whose bones now moulder far away from home."

So it was that on the eve of a mission certain to produce even more graves, the men of the 107th Ohio—feeling forsaken by those at home—resolved that the task of preserving "this once great, glorious and happy nation" was theirs alone.[2]

APRIL 27 DAWNED "clear & warm." With sixty rounds squeezed into their cartridge boxes and "eight days' rations" stowed in their haversacks, the men trudged up the Rappahannock. After a diligent march of thirteen miles, they bivouacked just west of Hartwood Church, the tiny, red brick Presbyterian chapel that, in February, lent its name to a sharp clash between blue- and gray-clad cavalrymen. "Sore in every muscle," the men did everything possible to lighten their loads. "Even the strongest and toughest begin to fear they will give out," one soldier explained, "and can not stand it." Before long, a trail of discarded canteens, blankets, overcoats, and knapsacks indicated the day's progress. So too did the "occasional" sight of "some poor fellow worn out by the heat," lying "helpless and uncared for by the roadside."

With precious little rest, the wearied column ("seemingly more dead than alive," in the estimation of one Ohioan) pushed farther west before dawn; a drizzly trek delivered them to Kelly's Ford by early evening. Later that night, the men forded the river; feeling their way through the darkness for nearly two miles, they established the camp that they would abandon the next morning en route to Germanna's Ford.

A dozen miles more and the troops waded the swift-flowing Rapidan River. Once more, darkness proved their only "serious opposition." William Koch "missed the ford" on this unusually dark night; after "plunging" into the river, he lost his balance and was swept away by the current. "Not much the worse for his involuntary bath," the lieutenant's frenetic attempt to reunite with the regiment ended successfully. The next morning, Koch and his sleep-deprived, blistered, and footsore comrades threaded their way along a plank road toward the ramshackle Dowdall's Tavern, the home of a Baptist preacher named Melzi Chancellor.[3]

Below the Rapidan extends a crowded forest of dogwood, "scraggy oaks, bushy firs, cedars, and junipers, all entangled with a thick, almost impenetrable undergrowth, and crisscrossed with an abundance of wild vines." Locals referred to these seventy square miles—which, for many decades before the American Revolution, fueled the region's busy iron furnaces—as "the Wilderness," an appellation as understated as it was forbidding. Hooker's chief topographical engineer thought it difficult to "conceive a more unfavorable field for the movements of a grand army." Dowdall's Tavern stood in a clearing (a rare respite from the surrounding acres of scrub) astride the worn and rutted Orange Turnpike, one of two east-west thoroughfares that stabbed through the woods, conveying travelers between the steeples of Fredericksburg and the undulating foothills of north-central Virginia. The other artery, the Orange Plank Road, surfaced with sturdy timbers, made a sharp intersection with the Turnpike just west of high ground around Dowdall's. The Eleventh Corps would pull up along the Orange Turnpike, holding the extreme right of the Union line slowly coiling itself about a crossroads in the Wilderness called Chancellorsville.[4]

THE NEW COMMANDER of the Eleventh Corps seized Melzi Chancellor's place as his headquarters. Thirty-two years old, sporting a thick beard and an empty sleeve (the latter a souvenir of the May 1862 fight at Fair Oaks, a sharp contest during McClellan's ill-fated drive toward Richmond the previous spring), Oliver Otis Howard was a priggish Mainer whose antislavery creed and teetotal ways rendered him something of a curiosity, both at West Point and in the army. Stern, erudite, and introspective—a New Englander through and through—one did not have to spend much time with Otis Howard before detecting the faint whiff of sanctimony; on occasion, however, an untamed ambition allowed his piety to yield to pragmatism.[5]

Otis Howard's ascent to command invited considerable grumbling from the German-Americans in the Eleventh Corps. He replaced Franz Sigel who, chafing under Joe Hooker's command and growing distrustful of the army brass in Washington, had tendered his resigna-

Major General Oliver Otis Howard commanded the Eleventh Corps at Chancellorsville and Gettysburg. *Library of Congress*

tion in early March. "The free-thinking element of the corps took but little stock in the ministerial reputation of the new commander," one Ohioan noted, and "felt that a representative countryman had been unjustly deprived of his command."[6]

Yet preparations for forward movement quickly drowned out these protests. It required nearly two months of toil in the shadow of Burnside's disappointments, but Joseph Hooker choreographed a truly dazzling plan. After dispatching his newly consolidated cavalry corps, now led by General George Stoneman, on a raid slicing deep into the enemy's rear, Hooker would march three infantry corps up the Rappahannock. These forty thousand men—with the Eleventh Corps in the van—would cross the river and its tributary, the Rapidan, before banking sharply east to gain the left flank of an unsuspecting and outnumbered Robert E. Lee. Hooker would distract his nemesis from the main action by directing a pair of Second Corps divisions to stalk up the Rappahannock as far as two upriver fords and in plain view of the Confederates. Hooker would also instruct two infantry corps to cross the Rappahannock a few miles downriver from Fredericksburg; there, they would stage a holding action on Lee's right. "Bold and daring," the general supposed that his stratagem—a "left jab, right punch," as one modern historian put it—would render the rebels' position indefensible. Lee would "have no other course than to flee south in full retreat." "The only element which gives me apprehension with regard to the success of this plan," Hooker assured a tetchy Lincoln, "is the weather."[7]

As the 107th Ohio shook out along the Orange Turnpike on the evening of April 30, the atmosphere at Hooker's headquarters was one of jubilation. The immodest general's gambit had succeeded, and even more splendidly than he could have imagined. "The selection of the places for crossing the Rappahannock, the maneuvers by which the army was thrown across the river, and the placing it in position for battle," the cigar-chomping General Daniel Sickles applauded, "were all conducted with perfect success, and without any considerable loss on our part." Spontaneous ovations erupted in camp upon receipt of a communiqué from army headquarters: "Our enemy must either inglo-

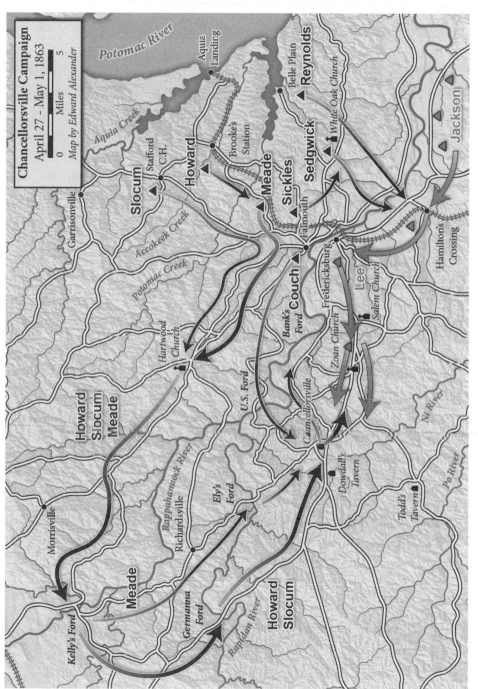

The Chancellorsville Campaign, Spring 1863

riously fly," Hooker declared, "or come out from behind his defenses and give us battle on our own ground." If the latter, he confidently predicted, "certain destruction awaits him." Given the boastful tones emanating from headquarters, it is not at all surprising that accounts of the operation left behind by the rank and file were exercises in hyperbole. "The march," one soldier reported, "was the most remarkable one of this war, or any other." "We [have] the darned rebels cornered in," reveled one Buckeye soldier in McLean's Brigade, eager for battle. The commanders of the Eleventh Corps, however, would leave nothing to chance. They forbade the men from building campfires that evening, lest distant flickers of orange or wreaths of smoke betray their position to the enemy.[8]

ROBERT E. LEE was eager for battle, too. From his purple-plumed cavalry commander James Ewell Brown Stuart on April 29 he received word that Hooker's army was maneuvering across the Rappahannock. About to find himself in the jaws of an army that outnumbered his own more than two to one, the Gray Fox blinked, but he did not flinch. Intuiting that "Fighting Joe" intended to deliver his knockout blow on the Confederate left ("the enemy in our front near Fredericksburg continued inactive"), Lee daringly divided his army to confront the threat. That evening, he ordered Major General Dick Anderson to march his division to the crossroads of Chancellorsville. Anderson and his men arrived at midnight, but the discerning general opted to button his troops on the brow of a ridge farther east, stretching lines of gray across the Orange Turnpike. On April 30, Lee directed Major General Lafayette McLaws's Georgians and South Carolinians to steady Anderson's lines. Lieutenant General Thomas Jonathan "Stonewall" Jackson's troops (with the exception of one division left to hold the works before Fredericksburg) completed the Confederate buildup on the morning of Friday, May 1.[9]

"Stonewall" Jackson would evidence his earnestness this day, moving with great speed and vigor. He assumed command of Anderson's and McLaws's soldiers, shook out a skirmish line, and ordered the gray-clad men to advance down the Orange Turnpike and Plank Road. "Cheers" erupted along the line, punctuated by the rattle of musketry and the occasional growl of artillery. Once again feeling as though they had been moored on the margins, the 107th Ohio cupped their ears and, miles away, made out the crackle of musketry fire. "Disappointment," Howard's assistant adjutant general Theodore Meysenburg recalled, "could be read on every face."[10]

BY MID-AFTERNOON Hooker's subordinates not only registered disappointment, they dripped with disgust. Unnerved by the unexpected Confederate buildup, "Fighting Joe" ordered his men to fall back to a defensive position at the Chancellorsville crossroads. "To hear from his own lips that the advantages gained by the successful marches of his lieutenants were to culminate in fighting a defensive battle in that nest of thickets," Major General Darius Couch fumed, "was too much." Foolishly, Hooker had squandered the initiative, paying little heed to his position and advantage in numbers. "I retired from his presence," Couch explained, "with the belief that my commanding general was a whipped man."[11]

The federal retreat left the rebels slack-jawed, too. After dark, once the blue lines coiled themselves in a loose arc around Chancellorsville, Lee and Jackson met at an intersection in the woods. "Seated on old cracker boxes," the generals considered the situation as smoke from a tiny "fire of twigs" curled into the air. Although no longer on the offensive, Hooker's men had "assumed a position of great natural strength," ensconced in sturdy breastworks that laced behind an "almost impenetrable" skirt of felled branches and limbs. Too, Hooker's left flank was "well anchored" on a curl in the Rappahannock. "It was evident," Lee conceded in his official report, "that a direct attack upon the enemy would be attended with great difficulty and loss."

The federal right flank, on the other hand, was a different story. "Completely in the air, with nothing to lean upon," Otis Howard's troops marked time more than two lonely miles west of Chancellorsville. "Our rear was at the mercy of the enemy," an Eleventh Corps division commander later confessed. And so for the second time in as many days, Lee rolled the dice. Dividing his forces yet again, he dispatched Jackson to steal through the woods on a looping flank march of a dozen miles. The stealthy trek would deliver twenty-six thousand Virginians, Georgians, Alabamians, Louisianans, and North Carolinians to the right and rear of the Union army—right to the men of the 107th Ohio.[12]

AT THE DIRECTION of Howard's chief engineer, the troops swung spades throughout the night of May 1, burrowing rifle pits and mounding the earth around old John Hatch's farmhouse (a modest, whitewashed log cabin flanked by two large chimneys) into hasty field works. Hatch—an old Connecticut Yankee who lived with his daughter and son-in-law, Lucy and James Talley—watched in astonishment as blue-coated swarms turned his property into a battle zone. Captain Julius Dieckmann parked the rifled guns of the 13th New York Light Artillery in an open field east of the farmhouse, while Charles Devens (the burly brigadier general who commanded the division to which McLean's Brigade had been assigned) annexed the house as his headquarters and, after reconnoitering the area, extended a picket line. Linking hands with the 17th Connecticut on their left and the 55th Ohio on their right, the 107th Ohio hunched in rifle pits just west of the Hatch house, holding a key segment of the "long, weak line" that stretched along the Orange Turnpike. The remaining Buckeye regiments in the brigade—the 25th Ohio and 75th Ohio—formed up slightly to the rear, in reserve. Meanwhile, Devens's First Brigade, under the command of Colonel Leopold von Gilsa, filed into line on the right of the 55th Ohio. Nearly perpendicular to the Ohio men, von Gilsa's rightmost regiments—Lieutenant Colonel Charles Ashby's 54th New York and Colonel Charles Glanz's 153rd Pennsylvania—faced west.[13]

The distant pop of muskets was kept up throughout the night and after daybreak, providing an odd accompaniment to what many of the

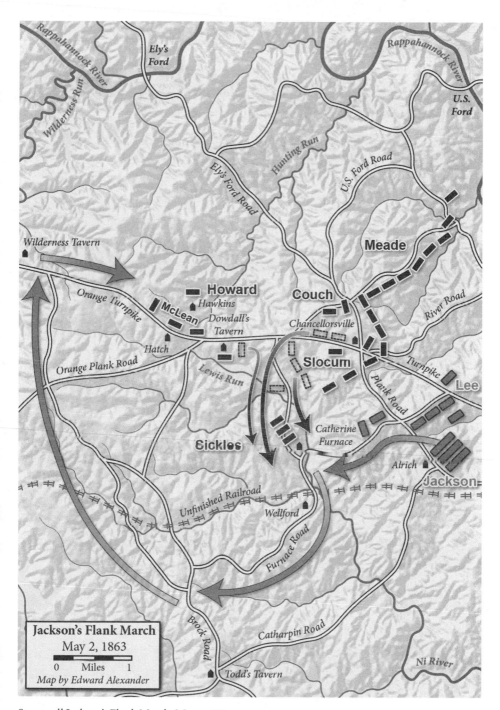

Stonewall Jackson's Flank March, May 2, 1863

soldiers described as a "beautiful" morning. "Gradually," however, the clamor "died away." By noon, "an ominous calm pervaded the whole line." It was around this time that some Eleventh Corps pickets first detected the enemy through the fingers of the pines. "In plain sight," Brigadier General Nathaniel McLean protested, "large bodies of troops with trains of some kind could be seen passing on our front." The warnings quickly multiplied. Detailed to McLean's picket line from the 17th Connecticut, William Warren "could not see much," but he "could hear artillery moving in front of us." Abe Heed, a sergeant from the 25th Ohio, dutifully informed his colonel that, "large bodies of troops had passed in our front to the right during the night."[14]

Remarkably, Charles Devens was unmoved; the thickly bearded, Harvard-educated lawyer and former Massachusetts state senator waved off McLean's initial report, unable to register even the slightest hint of concern. Just an hour later, growing increasingly uneasy, McLean returned to General Devens's headquarters with Colonel John Calvin Lee, the "first rate" commander of the 55th Ohio, and Colonel William Pitt Richardson, the Mexican War veteran who led the 25th Ohio. But the division commander had a tin ear, insisting that "the proper place" for McLean's colonels was "with their regiments." "You are more *scared* than hurt," he snarled dismissively. Hanging their heads, the men obediently returned to their worse than hopeless position, stung by the general's rebuke and aghast at his "unpardonable stupidity."[15]

Devens's fellow division commander Carl Schurz, on the other hand, *was* alarmed. The old Forty-Eighter who commanded the Eleventh Corps troops stacked north of the Orange Turnpike dashed off to Dowdall's to share the avalanche of disturbing reports with Otis Howard. Only if the southward-facing corps turned to the right and faced west, Schurz persisted, could they buy time for Hooker to rustle up much-needed reinforcements. By forming up perpendicular to the Turnpike, the outnumbered federals could at least level their muskets directly into the ranks of the oncoming rebels. But Otis Howard was frustratingly noncommittal, paying "no attention to the advice of his officers." Hopeless and forlorn, Schurz pounded back to his command and, without orders, directed two of his regiments to face west. "This was all, literally all, that was done to meet an attack from the west," Schurz recollected decades later, still raw with anger.

As the sun began to fade, painting the sky a regal auburn, anxiety seized Schurz and McLean. It is impossible to know how many among the rank and file were privy to the enemy's movements; many soldiers who "reported" knowledge of Jackson's maneuver in later years doubtless "larded their testimony with what they learned and understood only after the fact." Still, in the uneasy expressions worn by their colonels, even the most unsuspecting privates must have sensed something amiss. Colonel Robert Riley of the 75th Ohio not only announced to his men that he anticipated a fight, but also his conviction that the ensuing battle would require "every man." "If there is a man in the ranks who is not ready to die for his country," he instructed his troops, "let him come to me, and I will give him a pass to go to the rear."[16]

A PANICKED PACK of deer bounded from the woods just before six o'clock. It proved a sort of peculiar omen, for soon thereafter, "like a crash of thunder from the clear sky," a perfect storm of lead raked the Eleventh Corps line. "Fall in!" men screamed, their voices competing with the deadly trill of bullets. "Fall in!" For many decades, the men of the 107th Ohio would look back and point to this single, surreal second as the moment their lives changed forever.[17]

Barnet Steiner was prowling along the picket line when the rebels opened fire. With "wild shrieks and demonic yells," the gray-clad soldiers, advancing in their "thick, close columns," rushed "headlong" toward the federal position: a "perfect avalanche of men." Instinctively, the federal pickets scrambled for the rear. Whatever warnings were sent up that afternoon, nothing could have prepared the Eleventh Corps for the brute force of the attack. "The first note of warning that the shock had come," one Ohioan remarked, "was the shock itself." In reserve with his comrades in the 25th Ohio, Thomas Evans was warming a ration of beef when, "all at once," a "terrible musketry opened." "We were ordered in line of battle in a minute," he remembered. "Imagine our dilemma."[18]

Ensconced in their field works, the men of the 107th Ohio "could not see the enemy" at first. Bewildered, they necessarily held their fire as they dodged both "fleeing" pickets and the eager artillery shells exploding among them. The so-called "trenches," Adjutant Peter F. Young scowled, "were no protection" at all. These were among the longest and most anxious minutes of their lives. "Believe me when I tell you that I kept my eyes peeled," assured Lieutenant Fernando Suhrer, the twenty-three-year-old who assumed command of Company B just weeks before. He ducked at least three rebel projectiles that "would have caused [him] to bite the dust if [he] remained firm."[19]

As the rebels advanced "nearer and nearer," the "noise" of battle "grew truly terrific." Just to the west, the Confederates made relatively quick work of turning Colonel Leopold von Gilsa's line. "I had no regiment to cover my right flank," the Prussian army veteran protested in his official report, nor "reserves to drive back the enemy with the bayonet." Still, his New Yorkers and Pennsylvanians held on long enough to squeeze their triggers three times; even the two artillery pieces that supported von Gilsa's men from their perch on the Orange Turnpike belched several rounds into the rebel lines before limbering up and breaking for the rear, scrambling "in full flight." As one of the battle's earliest chroniclers concluded, those men "could not have fought or attempted to fight much longer than [they] did."[20]

The collapse of von Gilsa's regiments, however, subjected the Ohioans to an even more intense flanking fire. "The bullets," Christian Rieker marveled, "just whistled by my head like a real hailstorm." "Many fell on my right and on my left," the Zoar native added, "yet [the battle] did not harm me in the least." That anyone survived the storm of leaden slugs the rebels sent "whizzing through the ranks" was, in the estimation of First Lieutenant Hamilton Starkweather, a "miracle" exceeding "the limits of human comprehension." It seemed

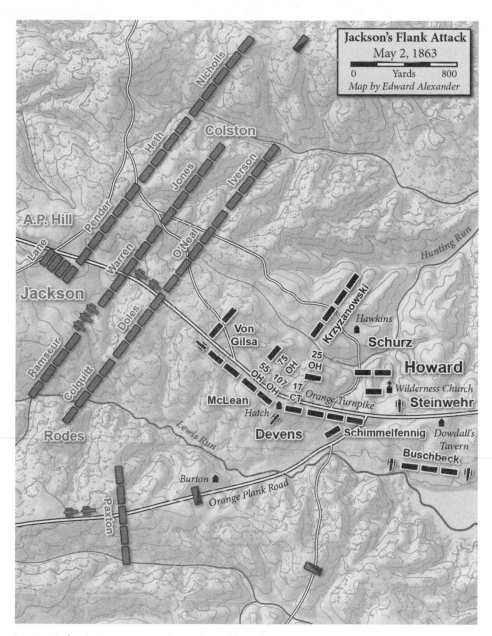

The Battle for the Orange Turnpike at Chancellorsville, May 2, 1863

"as if the population of the lower regions were turned loose to devour [our men] upon the spot," he gasped.

The 107th Ohio frantically "attempted to change front," but without success. On their right, the 55th Ohio "held for two volleys" before folding up like a jackknife; one of its soldiers conceded that the episode at the Hatch House "was the most trying experience the command ever endured." "We were completely and scientifically flanked," one emotional private poured out in a letter to his hometown newspaper. "To have longer held our position would have been suicidal madness, and we were compelled to give way."

Now totally exposed to the enemy, the 107th Ohio "stood . . . as long as a stand could be made." So eager were some soldiers to fire one more round into the enemy that, at great personal risk—their own supplies of ammunition dwindling—they knelt down to scavenge the cartridge boxes of the dead and wounded. "The 107th Ohio and 17th Connecticut made a brave stand," assured one of Thomas Evans's comrades in the 25th Ohio (as if to confirm the emphatic accounts later handed down by those regiments). "I am sure no Brigade ever stood more faithfully in the very jaws of death." Yet even this stubborn display could not overcome the enemy's superior numbers; the battle quickly "assumed the character and appearance of a massacre." Within "ten minutes," reported one Ohioan, "the ground was literally covered with the dead and dying." "Every inch of space," Justin Keeler shuddered, "was crowded with wounded." McLean's line stampeded for the rear, quickly disintegrating. Christian Rieker "sprang through" the storm "like a rabbit." James Middlebrook of the 17th Connecticut rued the retreat in a poignant letter to his wife. "We were obliged to run," he explained. "If we had remained [five] minutes longer, we should [all] have been killed or taken prisoners."[21]

Possibly, but as it was, the losses were overwhelming. In their first major combat action—their "baptism of fire"—the 107th Ohio reported at least 220 men killed, wounded, missing, or captured. "Flesh wound in right leg," "wound in the left arm," "fracture in right

side," "wound in head," "wound in right foot," "right shoulder, critical," "wounded in the thigh," "arm off," hit "by musket ball in the right
hand and also in the upper part of the right arm"—the newspapers
back home read like a ghastly index of human destruction: a sundry
catalogue of the ways battle could mangle and maim. The seemingly
endless litany of injuries occupied column inches and front pages, even
as the fate of individual men remained uncertain.

For "want of space," the *Tuscarawas Advocate* could not print the
casualty rolls. This was little consolation, of course, for anxious wives,
mothers, and sweethearts who, fearing the worst, ached for information from the front. "Since the battle," one soldier reported, "a great
many letters have been received by Co. D 107th O.V.I. soliciting information." Indeed, the first week of May demonstrated few things better than the way that the war could—at any moment—intrude on
the routines of ordinary people back home. The news that a hometown regiment had engaged in a major battle could arrest all thought
and action. "We have awfull news as far as losing life is concerned,"
reported Martha French from her home in Fairfield, Connecticut.
"You cannot think with what fear and trembling I read the names
of the killed and wounded." "I looked for a letter last night and went
down to the office," she wrote, "but came home disappointed." Whip-
sawing between uncertainty and dread, she was unable to sleep, to eat,
or to attend religious services. Private prayer became her only refuge.
"It has been a week of much anxiety with me on account of you, my
dear husband . . . I am in such suspense all the time."[22]

But, in truth, men were in no less disarray at the front. Owing to
the haste of the retreat, information about those missing or left behind
was not readily available. "About the results of the last battle at Fredericksburg," Ernst Damkoehler supposed in a letter home, "you probably will have better information than we." Individual companies
staggered about in want of organization. Christian Rieker deemed
his comrades in Company I comparatively fortunate; "we still have 52
men," he reported, explaining that "only two companies" in the entire

regiment "remain larger." "There are some," he shuddered in disbelief, "who have only 24 men." The battle had exacted an especially heavy toll among commissioned and noncommissioned officers, leaving the unit in a state of confusion and uncertainty, wanting for leadership in its most critical hour. Captain A. J. Dewaldt, the Mexican War veteran who commanded Company B, was "severely wounded" in the groin—his pledge that he would "soon be ready to give the rebs another turn" notwithstanding. Second Lieutenant John Winkler of Company C was "wounded in the right ankle"; just five weeks later, he succumbed to that injury in a makeshift hospital at Brooke's Station. "Shot through the abdomen," the regiment's beloved surgeon, Dr. Charles Hartman, was among at least one dozen Eleventh Corps surgeons mortally wounded. Enduring his last earthly moments in enemy captivity, he managed to address a heartbreaking letter to his wife, Anna, in which he explained how to secure his back pay and make an application for pension money.[23]

While attempting to rally the regiment, a bullet struck the neck of Colonel Meyer's mount. The animal bucked, spilling its rider on the ground. The Confederates instantly seized on this as an opportunity to bag another prisoner, stabbing the colonel's right wrist with a bayonet. As the rebels' prized captive was whisked to the rear, other gray-clad men eagerly swarmed the last, dazed remnants of the 107th Ohio. Not a moment later, a leaden slug smacked into the lower jaw of the colonel's son Edward, fracturing the bone in three places and ejecting the same number of teeth. The captain of Company C was left for dead on the field. Indeed, the *Defiance Democrat* lamented Edward's unfortunate demise on May 16—unaware that just days before, he had been discovered alive, in urgent need of medical care.[24]

Decades later, Edward Meyer claimed that while prostrated on the ground wounded he watched as the rebels conducted his father, together with a tiny knot of blue-coated prisoners, "away from the field." Very likely, Colonel Meyer caught a glimpse of his son, too. Added to the humiliation of enemy captivity, then, was an almost overwhelming sense of helplessness. Because for all that Colonel

Meyer knew as he readied for the wearisome journey to Richmond, his youngest son—the boy with the deep, gray eyes and the shock of dark brown hair—was dead.[25]

IT SEEMED AS THOUGH the world had stopped on the Orange Turnpike that afternoon. Men routinely confessed their inability to translate the battle into lucid or linear prose. "I cannot, will not, tell you the horrors I have seen as the effect of this last battle," a soldier from the 17th Connecticut wrote his parents. "The scene on the plank road," still another Nutmeg volunteer remembered, "was indescribable." "Oh, war! War!" exclaimed Thomas Evans. "Pen cannot describe nor tongue declaim half, nor will I attempt to say more on what I have seen." "If I were to write it all," Christian Rieker explained to his sister, "I would need almost a week in which to write." Frantic minds lurched between scenes hastily recorded and half remembered, the rush of events mocking any sense of chronology and scale. One regimental surgeon in McLean's brigade begged forgiveness, supposing that his letters would be "a poor return." "I have had so much on my mind that I could hardly direct my thoughts from pressing matters of business long enough to write a connected epistle." Jesse Spooner of the 55th Ohio commenced a narrative of the battle for his cousin, but ended rather abruptly. "I suppose you have heard all about it," he explained, "so I will not proceed to tell you anymore." For one volunteer in the 75th Ohio, the battle endured in memory not as an event with a discrete chronology, but rather as a jarring soundscape: "a fiendish yell," the "crackling hell of musketry," the "bellowing of mules," the "agonized shrieks of wounded horses." The events of that afternoon had rushed along at a furious, even dizzying pace. "There's no such thing as time on a battlefield," the enlisted man gasped.[26]

Beyond its stunning physical losses, the regiment also suffered great psychological damage. Almost immediately after the battle, Godfrey Kappel of Company I began to manifest symptoms of what some soldiers would call "nervous fever," an ailment that quickly became an "epidemic." "He is unaware of what is happening," Rieker reported in late May. "Often he wants to leave, and when one asks him to where, he says to [his home in] Zoar." Only weeks after the battle, Sergeant Charles Wimar was "reduced to the ranks," being "incapacitated by insanity." A most telling affliction—"nervous deafness"—placed at least one soldier from Company G on the sick rolls. Citing his "feeble state of health," the "perilous condition of his company," as well as the "recent trials and hardships to which the regiment was subjected in the late battles of Chancellorsville," First Lieutenant Hamilton Stark-weather resigned his commission on the spot. Corporal Franklin Bow returned to his home in Canton, where he joined the swelling ranks of army deserters. Not unlike Bow, still other soldiers wondered if their initial zeal for the war had been naïve or misguided. "If we are asked what was gained by our brave loss of men," regimental musician John Roedel insisted plainly, "the answer is no gain at all." At first, in the raw immediacy of the fight's aftermath, even those soldiers able to squint through the haze of grief saw only a fog of uncertainty. "I never believed," a still incredulous Peter F. Young later observed, "that men would fight as well for a miserable cause as the rebels did there for theirs."[27]

THOUGH HARROWING, the costly rout of the Eleventh Corps hardly spelled defeat for the Army of the Potomac. The damage inflicted by Jackson's flank march had been fairly contained, and elsewhere along the Union line, "confidence" remained the watchword. Before dawn on May 3, Hooker's line coiled about the Chancellorsville crossroads; newly reinforced, its flanks now rested on the Rappahannock. More important, the Third Corps line stabbed from the Union position so as to command the key high ground at a place called Hazel Grove.

Lee's army, on the other hand, remained divided. Even worse, it had been visited by a calamity of its own on the evening of May 2. Unwilling to yield any of his hard-won momentum to the enemy, "Stonewall" Jackson and a tiny knot of his staff officers rode out to reconnoiter another attack under the veil of darkness. Edgy rebel pickets mistook his movements for those of enemy scouts. Instinctively, their muskets rang out. Dismissing the frantic screams of Jackson's party, the rebel pickets squeezed their triggers once more. Three slugs smacked into Jackson—including one that necessitated the amputation of his left arm. To make matters worse, a "slight" wound removed Jackson's senior division commander from the fight. Command of his corps thus devolved upon J. E. B. Stuart, the cavalryman who, despite having ridden circles around the federals, lacked any experience leading long lines of infantrymen into battle.[28]

His significant advantages notwithstanding, "Fighting Joe" recoiled in fear on May 3. Sensing its "protruding line" was endangered, the army commander ordered the Third Corps to abandon its perch atop Hazel Grove. Astounded by their unexpected good fortune, the rebels eagerly unlimbered artillery atop the crown of the hill. The duel that ensued can only be described as "some of the most ferocious fighting of the war." McLean's brigade was held in reserve, but one of its soldiers noted how truly "wicked" it was to look on as men "marched up" to be "murdered." Before noon, the Army of Northern Virginia had folded up the federal line; though costly, it was a crowning achievement for Robert E. Lee. Wreathed in a thick beard, *Sacramento Daily Union* correspondent Noah Brooks vividly recalled the scene at the Executive Mansion when President Lincoln received the doleful dispatch from Joe Hooker's army. "Never, as long as I knew him," Brooks wrote, "did he seem to be so broken, so dispirited, and so ghostlike." Hooker had suffered seventeen thousand casualties in three days. "My God! My God!" the president gasped as he paced the room. "What will the country say?"[29]

FLUSH WITH AN improbable victory, the Confederates divided their many thousands of Chancellorsville prisoners ("this time," Christian Rieker quipped, "they really filled their sack") into "squads," placing each under the watchful eye of a guard. Before long, the men, among them Colonel Meyer, set out for Richmond. "Our column," one of the captives later mused, "must have seemed more like a doleful gang of condemned criminals than a body of honorably defeated soldiers."

Assailed by thirst and ravaged by hunger—issued just "one pint of meal" and "eight ounces of salt beef for three days"—the men demanded water and food, only to be informed by their imperious captors that "none" was available. The march was taxing enough, but when made on an empty stomach, it sent minds into "a sort of torpor." Uncertain of his fate and worried that he would never again see his home and family, one prisoner "went to sleep under a miserable depression of brain and heart." "I verily gave up to perish ere morning came," Thomas Evans echoed, adding he did not "expect to see half the men able to rise in the morning."

Despite their "extreme suffering," Evans and his fellow prisoners survived the night; the next day, under the eye of rebel guards, the captives resumed their grueling march. Civilians added insult to injury with their hisses and jeers. They "tantalized" us along the way, Evans recalled, "wishing us all the bad luck possible." "Kill 'em all, colonel!" one woman screeched with rage, shaking her fists defiantly. "Kill 'em

Housed in an old tobacco warehouse perched on the James River, Richmond's Libby Prison earned its reputation as a den of misery. Seraphim Meyer spent six weeks within its walls following his capture at Chancellorsville. *Library of Congress*

all right here for me!" So it was that after many decades, one prisoner confessed his inability "to forget or to ever forgive the men whose acts had brought about [such] suffering and humiliation."

At last, on May 7, "famished, filthy, and many of us ragged," the prisoners entered the city of Richmond; ironically, after such a trying journey, the captives regarded the "once dreaded" rebel capital as a "welcome place of refuge." But here too hisses and taunts greeted the men. As the "wretched looking set" wound through the steepled streets and paraded beyond the Confederate Capitol, one captive spotted Jefferson Davis, who had apparently joined a delegation of yowling spectators. Several blocks more and the men formed up before an imposing, three-story brick warehouse perched on the James; gray-clad soldiers with muskets slung over their shoulders stood sentinel outside the building. A hand-lettered sign identified the imposing structure as "Libby & Son, Ship Chandlers and Grocers," but the men would come to know it as Libby Prison.[30]

Seraphim Meyer passed a full week in that storied warehouse of misery, cramped in a "loathsome room" that one fellow inmate described as "long, low, dingy, gloomy, and suffocating." Caked in grease, dirt, and grime, the prison gave off a most offensive odor. "At least four hundred stinking pipes," one fellow inmate protested, "pollute the air most villainously." So too did smells waft upstairs from Libby Prison's ersatz morgue. As Meyer gasped for pure air, the scenes of Chancellorsville seized his mind. Grappling with the horror and anguish of that week—the toil of memory—was physically exhausting. That week, a fellow inmate and Hoosier regimental surgeon diagnosed the colonel with "prison fever." The affliction, the surgeon wrote, left him "prostrated . . . completely." After Meyer's parole at City Point, Virginia, on May 23, one of the regiment's men observed that the colonel "seemed greatly broken in health," and "never afterwards recovered his former health and vigor."[31]

WHILE SERAPHIM MEYER endured the ordeal of enemy captivity, his men endeavored to make sense of the battle. On May 6, the troops obediently trudged back to Brooke's Station, the unremitting rain a fitting accompaniment for their melancholy march. Back at the old camp north of the Rappahannock, now dotted with empty huts, the soggy men could not help but reflect on the last week's events. Returning to the place that had figured so formatively in their identity as a regiment, the men instinctively measured the distance between innocence and experience, pondering the contradictory emotions that battle had shoehorned into the surreal space of several days. Suffering demanded meaning, and defeat required explanation. Searching for both—balancing the need to make sense with the need to move on—was especially onerous work. "For one who has not been through the mill it is difficult to realize the utter exhaustion of body and mind that

Two years later, human debris still littered the Chancellorsville battlefield—a haunting reminder of Jackson's flank attack and the fight for the Orange Turnpike. *Library of Congress*

follows an arduous campaign and participation in one or two pitched battles," one veteran explained. Nothing was more wrenching than that first roll call after a battle, in which stretches of agonizing silence syncopated an anxious reading of names.[32]

On May 8, General McLean ordered his regimental commanders to "forward as soon as possible" a complete register of "killed, wounded, and missing . . . stating particularly whether the wounds are mortal, severe, or slight." As this anguished inventory got underway, the men took up their pens and commenced to write; the next few days would be an occasion for urgent self-examination and reflection. Chancellorsville tested the confidence and convictions of a few men, but many more soldiers prevailed over cynicism and despair. "Do not think I have become despondent," Christian Rieker instructed his sister. "Of course, I would rather see the war over, but not by our being beaten and the war ended in that manner." He took comfort in the rumors that "even the rebels" believed the fight a demanding one—something that the gray-clad men littering the field ("whole piles," Rieker wrote, "often five or six deep") seemed to confirm. So too did the verses of Psalm 91 reassure the volunteer from Zoar: "Just as is written in the Psalm, even if a thousand fall on your left and a thousand fall on your right, it shall not strike you, for it is God who helps you, as I myself have now seen."

Equally encouraging was the unit's performance under most trying circumstances. From now on, at least, the men would no longer have to wonder what it would be like to face the enemy. "Although the result . . . has not been what one would desire it to be," Charles Mueller conceded in his after-action report, there was no denying that the men "behaved well" under fire. With no small pride, Mueller announced that he beheld "many a deed of coolness and bravery" that afternoon. So it was that Captain Dewaldt, at home on sick furlough, was "very anxious to be with his men," whom he believed would "soon be ready to give the rebs another turn."[33]

Notwithstanding the thrashing at the Talley Farm, a watchful optimism animated the rest of the brigade, too. "I think this war will be settled before long," Francis Foote of the 17th Connecticut fore-casted. One soldier from the 55th Ohio scratched out a narrative of the battle on ornate letterhead adorned with the cheer, "Onward to Victory." "We are not discouraged, although the battle did not secure the fruits which we expected," reported one regimental surgeon. "We shall be off again in a few days." Dutifully, the *Hartford Evening Press* echoed these sentiments, declaring that there was "no cause for depression in the repulse of Hooker." "Considering the frightful storm," its optimistic editor added, "we ought perhaps to congratulate ourselves that the army got back as well as it did."[34]

Yet few other northern editors would advance this interpretation; in the disappointing wake of Chancellorsville, most preferred to pass out blame. Newspapers held the German immigrants of Howard's command almost singularly responsible for still another embarrassing reverse. Schurz's troops, they related, "almost instantly gave way." *Harper's Weekly* illustrated its account of the battle with the sketch

The northern press needed a scapegoat in the humiliating wake of Chancellorsville, and it found one in the German soldiers on the Union right. *Harper's Weekly* illustrated its account of the battle with Alfred Waud's sketch, "The Stampede of the Eleventh Corps." *Library of Congress*

artist Alfred Waud's tellingly titled, "The Stampede of the Eleventh Corps," while the *New Hampshire Sentinel* reported that, "The Germans fled past Gen. Hooker's headquarters in a panic, many of the members of Hooker's staff with pistols and sabres vainly endeavoring to stay their flight."[35]

For weeks, editorials questioning the courage and character of ethnic regiments consumed dozens of column inches. In Manhattan, where the news was heralded by a lashing "northeast storm," attorney George Templeton Strong was aghast to read of "the dastardly defection of certain German regiments which broke and ran." The press reports stung, but the ache grew worse when friends and loved ones at home began reciting the charges in letters to the front. "I saw a letter yesterday from home," Lieutenant John Winkler reported, "stating a report that our Company left the battlefield and run at the appearance of the rebels without firing a shot." In a tart epistle to the *Wooster Republican*, the Wayne County soldier explained that it was his "duty" to "inform our friends at home of the facts." "We went forth to do battle for the Union and the Constitution," Winkler wrote, "and we want to be used decently and not abused."[36]

Many of Winkler's comrades made similarly resolute appeals. "We asked to be judged by the bloody roll of killed, wounded, and missing," demanded one soldier from the 55th Ohio. "The memory of the noble men gone to their graves, and now languishing in hospitals," one correspondent from the 107th echoed, "is entitled to this plain, unvarnished statement of facts." An enlisted man from the 17th Connecticut cited not the lengthy casualty rolls, but rather the overwhelming odds faced by a brigade bereft of good leadership. "Some folks blame us for running, but what could about 11,000 men do against 30,000, and flanked at that?" he indignantly asked. "Our commanding general would not give us the order to change our line of battle." Another Nutmeg volunteer emphasized the worse than hopeless position occupied by McLean's troops. "We are called cowards and skedaddlers," he fumed, but what soldiers similarly deployed would fail to run?[37]

Still, any hope of solidarity among the men of the Eleventh Corps was dashed the day after the troops settled back into camp at Brooke's Station. Officers from three of McLean's regiments—the 25th, 55th, and 75th Ohio—appealed to General Hooker for assignment to another corps. "The unsoldierly character of the German troops" with whom their troops had been "compelled to serve," they protested, had cloaked their outfits in "unmerited disgrace." In a measure of their mettle, the petitioners even sought signatories among the native-born officers of the 107th Ohio.

The document met with the swift and sharp rebuke of the regiment. Dripping with disgust, representatives from each company—including George Billow and Augustus Vignos—met and unanimously adopted a set of resolutions, copies of which were forwarded to headquarters and transmitted to newspaper editors back home. "We consider ourselves grossly insulted," they began, arraigning the appeal to Hooker as both "unjust" and "prejudicial to the interests of our bleeding country." Such insults could only serve "to discourage these men, who have left home and its comforts to fight the battles of their adopted country, to fight for the maintenance of our Constitution and the honor of our flag."

Responding to the affront of their fellow soldiers just as they had responded to the calumny of the Copperheads back home—"we will never shrink from expressing our honest convictions," they pledged—the men once more refined their ideas about loyalty, sacrifice, and military service. Even more, they renewed their determination to fight the war—and to win it.[38]

CHAPTER 5

"HEAPING UPON US ... IGNOMINY AND SHAME"

May to July 1863

FOR THE ELEVENTH CORPS, the struggle to establish what happened along the Orange Turnpike would be as complicated as the battle itself. "If you would believe the malicious reports on the battle of Chancellorsville, the German soldiers, who were represented as forming the Eleventh Army Corps, would have fallen back on the first attack of the enemy," instructed Hugo Wesendonck, the thickly bearded liberal reformer and one-time member of the Frankfurt National Assembly who, in 1849, dodged a treason indictment by emigrating to New York City. "They would have been thrown into a disgraceful flight without firing a gun. They would have thrown away their arms and would have fled several miles, until they reached the Rappahannock, where a limit could only be set to their running by General Sickles ... Such were the reports which have been spread all over the country, and which were commented upon with many equally false additions, by a majority of the press, anxious to lay the blame for the defeat at Chancellorsville at the door of some despised foreigners."[1]

At forty-six, Wesendonck had let up nothing of his reformist zeal; throughout the 1850s he had found an outlet for his democratic yearnings within the antislavery community. Exactly one month after the fight at the Talley Farm, he stood before a restless crowd of several hundred in the basement of Manhattan's Cooper Institute. In February 1860, a reed-thin and yet clean-shaven Illinois lawyer implored an audience gathered in that very hall to "have faith that right makes might." "Neither let us be slandered from our duty by false accusations against us," Abraham Lincoln urged the crowd of fellow Republicans, "nor frightened from it by menaces of destruction to the government." Three years later, at a "vindication" meeting convened by "indignant" German-Americans "of all classes," Wesendonck conveyed that very message: "It is our duty to rebuke these calumniators," he thundered, "and to hurl these slanders back into the teeth of their fabricators."[2]

The meeting began just after eight o'clock in the evening. Draped behind the platform was an oversized map of the Chancellorsville battlefield, illustrating the various plank roads and turnpikes that stabbed through the woods. "Has credit been given to them for the manifold sacrifices they have laid upon the altar of their adopted country, in lives, property and prosperity?" he asked. "Have they been treated by our leading journals and men, as they deserve?" He was followed by still another German refugee, Friedrich Kapp, an attorney who exhibited his literary faculty not only in sharply worded editorials, but also in biographical treatments of Baron von Steuben and Johann Kalb, two immigrants whose military aid to the Continental Army during the American Revolution had proven invaluable. Drawing substantially on his authority as an historian, Kapp denounced the defamation of the Eleventh Corps as harmful to the Union cause. "I never knew a soldier," he explained, "who was willing to fight the enemy in front, when his comrades, or the people for whom he fights, stand ready to stab him from behind."[3]

Kapp's new law partner, Charles Goepp, an unapologetic Republican who had served briefly in the army, wholeheartedly concurred. "The German troops on the Potomac have at all times suffered a double share of hardships, and a double portion of delay in the receipt of their hard-earned pittance," he remonstrated. "Soldiers cannot fight under the conviction that they are predestined to be the scapegoat of the imbecility of their commanders." Without meaningful remedy, the Eleventh Corps, he predicted, would "be betrayed, and slaughtered, and broken in engagement after engagement, until not a man of it will be left in arms to bear the designation of the 'cowardly Dutchman.'" Goepp was prescient on at least one score: there would be even more misfortune ahead for the men of the 107th Ohio and the Eleventh Corps. What he mistook, however, was their remarkable ability to endure it.[4]

EARLY ON THE afternoon of May 15, nearly fifty ambulances delivered Chancellorsville's wounded to Brooke's Station. "I saw wounded men in every form," one private brigaded with the 107th explained. "Most every one that was wounded in the arms had no shirts on, and those wounded in the legs no pants on." The rebels ghoulishly stripped the bodies of the wounded; at the Talley Farm, one officer lay "naked" and "unburried" for three days. The macabre traffic continued well into the next day, providing one more opportunity for the men to reflect on battle's huge toll in human life and suffering. As the ambulance wagons navigated the rutted and corduroyed roads north of the Rappahannock, they jostled their human cargo; one enlisted man from the 17th Connecticut with a rebel ball lodged in his right shoulder reckoned that his wound "bled a pint" along the way.

Among those who endured the uncomfortable ride was Edward Meyer, who would soon thread his way back to Ohio—and recovery—on sick furlough. There, the young captain made a surreal reunion with his father, recently released from Libby Prison. The colonel was exceedingly fortunate to have secured a parole, for a once well-oiled system of prisoner exchange would soon sputter to a halt, foundering on the shoals of race. Deeming the mobilization of black soldiers

For weeks after Chancellorsville, the doleful drip of reports from the field hospitals continued. The world seemed new after their baptism of fire; now, living among the wounded, the
men struggled to make sense of it. *National Archives*

that summer as "the most execrable measure recorded in the history
of guilty man," Jefferson Davis prescribed summary execution for
any African-American his troops encountered on the field of battle.
Lincoln's threat of retaliation—and principled refusal to exchange
prisoners until the southern policy was revoked—would produce the
congested prison camps of the war's final year.[5]

A FLURRY OF movement animated the next few weeks, as the men
marched, drilled, and prowled about on picket. A blizzard of special
orders detailed men to guard mounting or various fatigue and police
duties. They stood sentinel—at division headquarters, along the railroad that coiled behind their camp, and over the quartermaster stores.
Another detail accompanied heaping baggage trains down to Aquia
Landing. Each new request or assignment merely underscored the

tremendous, daily work required to feed, equip, and maintain an army—so routine as to become invisible in wartime letters and post-war histories. Even John Brunny's band was subject to these special requests, ordered at one point to "report at division headquarters" and, at another, to provide a "brigade bugler."[6]

Amid renewed rumors that Robert E. Lee was planning another drive north, Brooke's Station also stirred with "speculation" about the fortunes of the regiment in another campaign. Most immediately, the troops wondered how they would perform under new leadership. On May 19th, the men bade farewell to their brigade commander, Nathaniel McLean, who had been detailed to Ambrose Burnside's command in the green hills of East Tennessee. "All were sorry to see him leave," one soldier reported, for "not a man in the division" disliked him. A Mainer named Adelbert Ames, who had graduated near the top of his West Point class, assumed command of the brigade. Ames, who sported an impressive walrus mustache and tuft of chin fringe, spent the early months of the war as an artillerist. He sought and received command of an infantry regiment—the 20th Maine Volunteers—in August 1862. Before earning a place on Fifth Corps commander George Meade's staff, he led the regiment later immortalized on Little Round Top into the fray at Fredericksburg.

Division commander Charles Devens likewise took leave, but tellingly, his departure invited few laments. Into his place stepped Francis Channing Barlow, the bookish, clean-shaven son of a Unitarian minister from Brooklyn. "His men at first gazed at him," Carl Schurz remarked, "wondering how such a boy could be put at the head of regiments of men." Despite his youthful appearance, the Harvard valedictorian had packed plenty of fighting into his twenty-eight years—perhaps predisposed, one of his soldiers editorialized, "to carry his virtues to excess." The previous fall—only months after an intrepid performance during the Seven Days battles around Richmond—he was wounded while threading a pair of New York regiments into the fight for Antietam's Sunken Road. Still nursing his injury, the so-called boy general would lead the Buckeyes and Nutmeggers as they hooked north—sloshing through the Potomac and then beyond the Mason-Dixon Line, into Pennsylvania.[7]

On June 12 the men broke camp at Brooke's Station for the last time. A "lively gait" delivered them to an old churchyard a dozen miles away, where they bivouacked for the evening. The next morning, the 107th Ohio resumed its tiresome work, trudging as far north as Catlett's Station on the Orange and Alexandria. Over the next two weeks, the men scarcely had an opportunity to catch their breath; they marched almost continuously, paying little heed to the blistering heat or claps of thunder. "The men cannot march much farther without at least 2 hours rest," division commander Carl Schurz protested at one point. "They have marched 8 hours without refreshments." From Catlett's Station, it was a full day's march to the old battlefields of Manassas, now one vast maze of graves; afterward, the men obediently pushed out to Centerville, a rather underwhelming collection of dwellings "marked" by the war's "ruin and desolation." Leaving Centerville, the columns started for Goose Creek, "a stream of some size" that laced its way through stands of sturdy Virginia timber ten miles south of Leesburg. Along its banks they raised a new camp. There they remained for a week before fording the mighty Potomac at Edward's Ferry.[8]

By the time the Eleventh Corps crossed into Maryland on the afternoon of June 25, the van of the Army of Northern Virginia had lurched into south-central Pennsylvania. Tethered to his Rappahannock River line for seven months, Lee was impatient to resume the offensive—not only because it would satisfy the demand of Confederate civilians for forward movement, but because the Cumberland Valley would afford him the chance to provision his men. Fortified by a steady diet of northern newspapers, the general likewise appreciated the mounting opposition to the war north of the Mason-Dixon Line; this lent him a sense of urgency similar to the one that impelled him north in the autumn of 1862. "We should neglect no honorable means of dividing and weakening our enemies," Lee reasoned in a wordy missive to Confederate president Jefferson Davis. "It seems to me that the most effectual mode of accomplishing this object, now within our reach, is to give all the encouragement we can, consistently with truth, to the rising peace party of the North." Davis hardly shared Lee's enthusiasm for a second northern invasion (the rebel chief executive was especially concerned about the fate of Vicksburg, the Confederacy's last fortified bastion on the Mississippi, which Ulysses S. Grant's forces threatened to besiege), but he nonetheless nodded his approval to Lee.[9]

Using the Blue Ridge Mountains to screen their movements, Lee's troops loped down the Shenandoah Valley. At Winchester, the gray- and butternut-clad men easily brushed aside a seven-thousand-man federal garrison commanded by Major General Robert Huston Milroy, adding one more to the town's already imposing tally of flag changes. Albert Gallatin Jenkins's mounted troops, in the van of the rebel column, splashed across the Potomac shortly thereafter. Before long, the southerners made the aims of their invasion evident. In Franklin County, near Chambersburg, Lee's men commenced "a regular slave hunt," kidnapping free blacks and threatening to "burn down every house which harbored a fugitive slave." It was "sufficient," one civilian lamented, "to settle the slavery question for every humane mind." Elsewhere, Lee's men paid little heed to a general order forbidding pillage and plunder, helping themselves to Pennsylvania's seemingly limitless bounty. With the Army of the Potomac still feeling its way north, the governor activated home-guard "emergency militia" units, so as to offer some resistance to the invaders.[10]

As panic gripped the denizens of south-central Pennsylvania, the long blue columns of Hooker's army inched north through the Maryland countryside. From Edward's Ferry it was a grueling, twenty-eight-mile march to Jefferson. The next day, after a shorter trek, the men bivouacked near Middletown, the steepled village whose buildings had been repurposed as hospitals in the grisly aftermath of Lee's last northern gambit. Here the men learned that "Fighting Joe" would lead them no longer. "We did not know much about General Meade," Jacob Smith recalled of Hooker's replacement, but the men trusted that the Fifth Corps commander—the old, "goggle-eyed snapping turtle" who led the Pennsylvania Reserve division into Antietam's bloody Cornfield and broke through the rebel lines at Fredericksburg—would give battle to Robert E. Lee.[11]

Meade wasted little time; within hours, his troops had marching orders. On June 29 the men made a "wearisome" march, checked by "droves of cattle, ammunition & supply trains, squadrons of cavalry, [and] stragglers of all sorts." They stopped to pitch tents for the evening about "a mile north" of Emmitsburg, a Maryland village nestled in the Catoctins. "The beauty and tranquility of the place," mused one Buckeye soldier, affectionately describing the town's "scrupulously-kept gardens" and "little cemetery with its methodical array of grassy graves and white crosses," contrasted sharply with "the military tumult [that] suddenly invested it." But kid gloves once more concealed the "hard hand of war." "In Virginia everything we could lay our hands on was confiscated without delay," one enlisted man explained, "but here nothing is destroyed but what is absolutely necessary, and if we want anything the farmers have they sell it at a reasonable price and all are willing to pay for it."

Intuiting that another battle was imminent, old doubts and anxieties threatened to overwhelm the confidence with which the Ohioans had addressed their critics after Chancellorsville. "Many of those who had passed through former campaigns and defeats at the hands of the enemy," one soldier related, "seemed to think that a like fate awaited us in the coming conflict." Nearby, "the solemnity which always foreruns a battle" took possession of the 17th Connecticut, "intensifying our thoughts of home, and weaving shadows of anxiety across our future." The scenes of the Talley Farm lingered, a brooding presence never to be banished. "I stood leaning against a camp stake, gazing dreamily across the hill," one of its soldiers reported, "with mind reverting to Chancellorsville and filled with anticipations of a second edition so soon to be issued." In his "sad reverie," the enlisted man was again "amid the carnage, surrounded by gleaming bayonets and staggering wounded," tormented by the "piercing cries of the mangled combatants." After a while, a comrade was able to summon him from the eerie spell.

To be sure, it was a night that few would forget. By the "calm, mellow" light of the moon—the sky, by all accounts, was exceptionally "clear," stippled with "bright glittering stars"—more than a few soldiers took the opportunity to pen letters to their friends and families back home. The earnest labor of writing concluded, they "sought the refuge of their shelter-tents." More than a few prayers went up from "sad and heavily burdened hearts." It was Tuesday, June 30, 1863, and, for more than a few, their last night on earth.[12]

ANYONE WHO PEERED at a mid-nineteenth-century map of south-central Pennsylvania quickly took note of Gettysburg. The ten thoroughfares that delivered travelers to the town stabbed in virtually every direction, offering the illusion that the Adams County seat was the "hub" of a "wagon wheel." The convergence of roads notwithstanding, neither Robert E. Lee nor George Gordon Meade planned to fight a battle there. Though rebel troops commanded by Jubal Early ransomed the town on June 26, they quickly set their sights on the much larger prize of York, still some thirty miles east. Meanwhile, Confederate cavalry began to gape at the defenses of Harrisburg, the Keystone State's capital and an important railroad junction that sprawled along the Susquehanna. For his part, Meade announced his preference for a defensive battle—and on ground of his own choosing. In a circular, he instructed his troops that they were to withdraw to a perch behind the sturdy banks of Maryland's Pipe Creek in the event of an enemy attack.[13]

But Lee could not be certain of Meade's intentions. Upon learning that the Army of the Potomac boasted an aggressive new commander, the rebel general ordered his troops, scattered in a wide arc across the Cumberland Valley, to concentrate west of Gettysburg. He would not permit Meade to attack while his men were dangerously divided, ripe for the harvest. (With this order, Lee betrayed his lofty estimate of George Gordon Meade; at Chancellorsville, after all, Lee twice—and almost mechanically—divided his forces in the face of Joe Hooker.) So it was that as the Ohioans dutifully trudged toward Emmitsburg,

Lee's men were beginning to collect at Cashtown, a tiny village at the base of South Mountain.

While waiting for the Army of Northern Virginia to reunite, on June 30 a brigade of North Carolinians felt its way west from Cashtown to Gettysburg, making the eight-mile trek under a somber drizzle. As they approached the borough of twenty-four hundred, James Johnston Pettigrew's soggy men were baffled to find federal cavalrymen trundling into town. They instinctively fell back, reporting what they had seen to headquarters. Undaunted by the report—unwilling to concede that the Army of the Potomac had pulled within striking distance in just a few days—division commander Harry Heth resolved to return the next morning with his two brigades.[14]

THE EVENING OF June 30 had been a restive one for the Eleventh Corps rank and file, but it was no less so for Oliver Otis Howard. The previous evening, the general trotted north at the urging of Major General John Fulton Reynolds, the Pennsylvanian who commanded the Army of the Potomac's First Corps. Together, in the back of the handsome tavern that Reynolds requisitioned as his headquarters, the men pored over maps and studied a "bundle of dispatches" in an effort to deduce the positions of the enemy. Howard did not begin the six-mile ride back to Emmitsburg until after eleven o'clock. Equipped with the most up-to-date intelligence about the proximity of the rebels and their likely "designs," however, he reasoned that his troops would meet the enemy the next day. He was right. The general had scarcely nodded off to sleep when a messenger conveying orders from Meade's headquarters roused him: the Eleventh Corps was to push on to Gettysburg, where it would form "in supporting distance" of the First Corps. "Meade," one student of the battle surmises, "was preparing contingency plans in case the Confederate army attacked."[15]

The next morning, after bugles sounded the notes of reveille, the men received orders to fold up their tents, shoulder their knapsacks, and prepare to march. Frank Barlow's division took the lead, availing itself of "the direct road from Emmitsburg to Gettysburg." In the words of one enlisted man in the 17th Connecticut, it was a "hard, tedious march." The road was not only well rutted (the work of Reynolds's wagons, which had trundled along earlier that morning), but likewise "obstructed all the way" by ammunition trains and limber wagons. Each thankless stride amplified the sounds of battle in the distance, thickening the lumps in their throats. "Rustic patriots" lined the route to encourage the men, though the somber, careworn expressions worn by the civilians betrayed their sense of foreboding.[16]

Howard pressed ahead of his troops and bolted into Gettysburg with his staff, eager to inspect the situation as it was developing on the ground. Hooking his way "through a lumber-room" and up two narrow flights of stairs, the general reached "a fine post of observation" atop Henry Fahnestock's dry goods store, located at the corner of Middle and Baltimore Streets, not far from the town center. Peering through a set of field glasses, Howard inspected the ridges to the west, now outlined with long lines of blue. Earlier that morning, anticipating a return visit from the rebels, a strong-jawed Kentucky-born, West Point–trained cavalry officer named John Buford planted his 2,900-man division on those ridges. For several crucial hours, his troopers delayed the enemy's advance—ensuring that when the rebels did splash across Willoughby Run, they would meet federal infantrymen. To Buford's enormous relief, Reynolds spurred onto the field just before ten o'clock, anchoring a brigade on either side of the Chambersburg Pike. Fierce combat erupted in Herbst's Woods (where a stout brigade of Midwesterners folded up a line of Tennesseans and Alabamians) and in an unfinished railroad cut (where New Yorkers and a hearty regiment from Wisconsin took advantage of the rebels' luckless position in the trench).[17]

From his perch at Fahnestock's, Howard watched with glee as Union troops bagged enemy prisoners in the railroad cut and then led them through the borough's narrow streets. But he would not relish the moment very long. Shortly after 11:30, an aide-de-camp delivered the news that a sharpshooter's bullet had felled General Reynolds early in the engagement. This left Howard "the senior officer on the field." "When the responsibility of my position flashed upon me," he confessed more than a decade later, "I was penetrated with an emotion never experienced before or since." With little time to waste, Howard summoned the men of the Eleventh Corps, now to be led by his senior division commander, Carl Schurz. The troops were still several miles south of Gettysburg when a breathless staff officer bolted toward them on horseback, demanding they "move up at double-quick."[18]

Sometime around eleven thirty, Schurz caught up with Howard atop Cemetery Hill, a commanding knob immediately south of the borough. "This high ground," one veteran remembered, afforded in nearly every direction "an unobstructed view" of the surrounding countryside. Laced with low stone walls that could function as "natural breastworks," the rise also supplied a most enviable platform for artillery. For this reason, Howard opted to steady Brigadier General Adolph von Steinwehr's division and several batteries of reserve artillery atop the eminence. Troubled by reports that the enemy was "making a movement" to gain the flank of the First Corps, however, Howard directed Schurz to conduct the remaining two divisions up to Oak Ridge, where they could lend some support to James Wadsworth's men. "Either the enemy was before us in small force, and then we had to push him with all possible vigor," Schurz reported, "or he had the principal part of his army there, and then we had to establish ourselves in a position which would enable us to maintain ourselves until the arrival of reinforcements."[19]

But first they had to advance through Gettysburg—now a perfect picture of bedlam. "The rush of artillery galloping to the front, the eager movement of infantry, the hurry-scurry of cavalry, the scamper of the terror-stricken inhabitants, the clatter of ambulances and other vehicles," one officer wrote, "constituted about as wild a sense of excitement as the tumult of war ever presents." "We went through [the town] in such a hurry we could hardly stop to get anything to eat or drink," one private lamented with anguish. By the time the men emerged from the town's tangled streets, however, rebel batteries had already lurched into position, and Robert E. Rodes had deployed his nearly eight thousand Alabamians, Georgians, and North Carolinians (the impressively mustached Virginian commanded the largest division in Lee's army) atop Oak Hill. Unable to link hands with Wadsworth's troops, the Eleventh Corps instead stretched out into a line of battle facing north, "nearly perpendicular" to the First Corps. This permitted them to keep a watchful eye on the Carlisle and Harrisburg roads, two thoroughfares that threatened to deliver still more reinforcements to the rebels.[20]

With "promptness and spirit," Brigadier General Alexander Schimmelfennig, an old Forty-Eighter and Prussian army veteran, arrayed Schurz's division "on the right of the First Corps in two lines." Barlow then assembled his troops—including the 107th Ohio—on the campus of the county almshouse, a collection of multistory brick buildings astride the Harrisburg Road that, since the 1820s, had served the local indigent and insane. From a tactical vantage point, the position was anything but desirable; unlike the men west of town, who deployed along ridgelines and behind ribbons of woods, Barlow's two brigades were assembled on an exposed, "level plain," bereft of either "natural or artificial defenses."[21]

They wouldn't remain there very long. As his men caught a much-

Gettysburg was an unassuming county seat of 2,400 when the Army of the Potomac and Army of Northern Virginia collided there in July 1863. This period photograph captures the borough from the west. *Library of Congress*

needed breath ("after we marched through Gettysburg, I dropped on the ground, like a dead person, all exhausted and very tired," an enlisted man in the 17th Connecticut confessed), Barlow spied a "small hill" in the distance. Behind the healthy stand of oak and hickory that screened its northern edge meandered lazy Rock Creek. The locals referred to the rise, located on thirty-five-year-old David Blocher's farm, as Blocher's Knoll.[22]

WHENEVER FRANK BARLOW resolved to do something, he went at it with an almost reckless zeal. The orders he received that afternoon were unambiguous: "prolong" the line of the Eleventh Corps, maintain a "connection" with Schimmelfennig's troops, and "refuse his right wing" so as to confront any potential "flanking movement by the enemy." But after surveying the surrounding ground, he was "determined to occupy the knoll" to his front. Nothing—including Schurz's commands—would dissuade him from his considered course of action. On Barlow's orders, Colonel Leopold von Gilsa obediently delivered his brigade to the knoll. Comprising two New York units and an outfit mustered from eastern Pennsylvania, the brigade now had the strength of a single, healthy regiment—yet one more devastating testament to "Stonewall" Jackson's effectiveness at Chancellorsville. The men of the 25th Ohio soon joined von Gilsa's men, providing "battery support" for the four Napoleons commanded by nineteen-year-old Lieutenant Bayard Wilkeson, which creaked into position and unlimbered at the summit. With the balance of Ames's brigade, the 107th Ohio looked on from a reserve position several hundred yards to the rear, doubtless addled by the eerie coincidence that once again, they had been dispatched to the right flank of an overextended Union line.[23]

Von Gilsa's men had no more rustled into position when three of Lieutenant Hilary Pollard Jones's Confederate batteries—each planted on a rise "about a half mile northeast of Blocher's Knoll"—erupted in earnest. "I never saw guns better served than Jones' were on this occasion," one Confederate major recollected. The shot and shell cut down trees, which meant that before they were subjected to a hail of lead, the men first had to dodge a storm of splinters. "Large shells and six-pounders passed close over our heads," one New York captain recalled, obligating officers and men to quickly master the art of stooping, dodging, and bending "low." More ominously, however, the growl of Jones's ordnance rifles announced the arrival of Major General Jubal Anderson Early's division in Gettysburg.²⁴

At two o'clock, the rattle of musketry replaced the roar of artillery. In the narrow belt of timber that skirted the "abrupt" banks of Rock Creek, von Gilsa's skirmishers squinted their eyes, squeezed their triggers, and emptied at least three volleys into the Confederate pickets. "Slowly" at first, but then with the swiftness of a "savage charge," the howling rebels sloshed through the creek, driving the Yankee skirmishers in an effort to clear the way for John Brown Gordon's brigade of six Georgia regiments—slightly more than eighteen hundred soldiers. Showered with near universal acclaim for his "soldierly bearing" (the five gunshot wounds that he received in the space of two hours at Antietam's Bloody Lane conveyed something of his poise in a fight), the thirty-one year old brigadier general trotted into the battle on a "beautiful coal-black stallion captured at Winchester." Gordon leapt from his saddle, "bareheaded, hat in hand, arms extended," urging his men forward in "a voice like a trumpet." In the estimation of one rebel enlisted man, it was "absolutely thrilling." Campbell Brown, a Confederate staff officer, enthusiastically agreed. Gordon's advance, he wrote, was "one of the most warlike & animated spectacles I ever looked on."²⁵

For von Gilsa's men, the scene was one of acute terror. Dressing ranks behind Gordon's troops—straddling the Harrisburg Road and extending the Confederate front farther to the right—were five Louisiana regiments led by Brigadier General Harry Thompson Hays, in addition to the three units packed into the Tarheel brigade commanded by Colonel Isaac Avery.

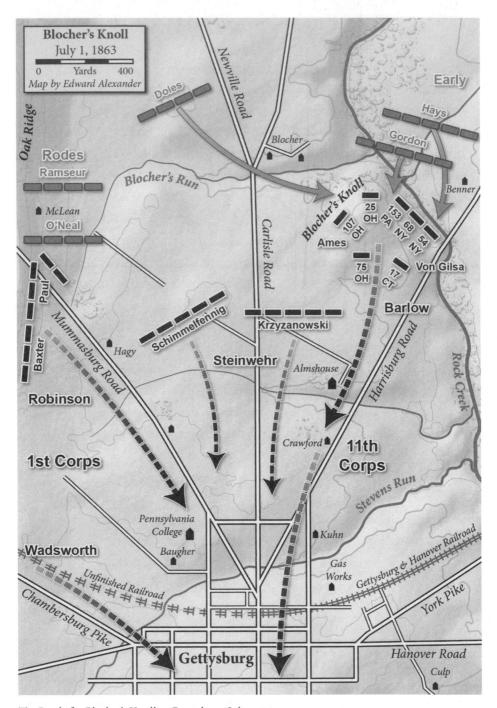

The Battle for Blocher's Knoll at Gettysburg, July 1, 1863

While significantly outgunned, von Gilsa's first line resisted the rebels with everything they had. A German-born officer from the 68th New York paced anxiously behind the skirmishers, "encouraging the men to keep cool and aim well." Though not yet paroled after a brief but unhappy sojourn in Libby Prison, one lieutenant in the 153rd Pennsylvania insisted (over the protest of his more honorable men) on entering the fight. Shortly after moving forward, he fell with a wound to the knee. "The contest," one of his regimental comrades attested, "was fierce from first to last."[26]

"Come on boys," still another Pennsylvanian implored, "let us give them what they deserve!" The words had scarcely escaped the soldier's lips when an enemy ball struck his right shoulder, knocking his musket to the ground. Though in great pain, he "worked the gun up against his other shoulder" and managed to squeeze off one more round.

By this time, in an attempt to steel von Gilsa's feeble line, Adelbert Ames had ordered the 107th Ohio up to the knoll. It was a wretched assignment. Instructed to form up on von Gilsa's left—"facing northwest"—Colonel Meyer's troops would be snared in a withering crossfire, resigned to hold the tip of a forlorn salient against all odds. (To the right of the 107th, the 25th Ohio and six companies of the 17th Connecticut would fare little better; the 17th's Lieutenant Colonel Douglas Fowler was decapitated by a shell, while Captain Wilson French was "severely wounded.") While Gordon's men blazed away at the Buckeye soldiers from the north, the four regiments of Brigadier General George Doles's Georgia brigade "splashed across Blocher's Run" and pitched into the fight from the west, announcing their arrival with a "soul-stirring rebel yell." In other words, it was Chancellorsville all over again.[27]

ALL WAS NOW "considerable confusion." In a signal of desperation, Ames personally delivered orders to each of his regiments. He found the 107th Ohio determined "to do as well as possible," but Colonel Meyer unstrung with apprehension and trammeled by emotion. "I noticed that at the whistling of shells and bullets he would crouch down upon his horse," Ames remembered, "his breast nearly touching the neck of his horse, and at the same time great fear [and] consternation was depicted in his countenance." "He appeared fearful of the bullets," one of Ames's staff officers confirmed. Ames "reproved" Meyer for his "unnecessary dodging at the sound," but the general had little time to spare—for not long after the Buckeyes pulled up to the knoll, von Gilsa's reed-thin line finally snapped. Knots of men rushed to the rear, surged beyond the almshouse buildings, and slipped into the confusion of the town. The 153rd Pennsylvania weathered the storm longer than the skirmishers of the 54th and 68th New York ("it proved to be a hot place for us," one of the Empire State men quipped), though they too gave way before long, their nerves unstrung. "The 1st Brigade," explained one Connecticut enlisted man, "broke and ran through our ranks like a flock of frightened sheep." Ignoring his own, not insignificant role in von Gilsa's defeat, Barlow was "unable to contain his disgust" for the immigrant soldiers under his command. This rendered the tribute paid the brigade by one Georgia private all the more ironic: "They were harder to drive than we had ever known them before," George Washington Nichols maintained.[28]

Yet that was little consolation for the men of the 107th Ohio, who were now totally exposed and floundering, lacking any steady leadership. As the troops braced for the rebel onslaught, Colonel Meyer "appeared beside himself" and "not at all cool," so overwhelmed by "fear" that he delivered neither "intelligible" nor "proper" commands. "Part of the regiment was faced to the left & moved off," Ames reported, while "part of it remained in its position." "In portions of the regiment," he added, "there was the greatest confusion." Cursing and screaming, "carelessly" swinging his sword "over his head," the colonel bolted for the rear, abandoning his men in the face of the enemy. If Gettysburg so convincingly resembled Chancellorsville, did the haunting memory of that battle overwhelm the colonel? Did the deployment on Blocher's Knoll prompt him to relive Edward's capture, his own wound, and his humiliating capture? Did he fear that this time, he might not be "fortunate" enough to land in Libby? That whatever luck he had enjoyed might finally run out?[29]

FEARING FOR the Ohioans' morale, Ames dispatched Captain John Marshall Brown, the quick-witted, twenty-four-year-old Mainer who served as his assistant adjutant general, to post the regiment. As it was, the situation was worse than daunting. "The pressure soon became so great and the fire of the enemy so hot and deadly," one Ohioan recalled, "that it was evident our brigade and in fact the division could not long hold its ground." Notwithstanding the despairing odds, Augustus Vignos rallied the men of Company H and was attempting to mount a charge when an enemy shell severed his right arm. General Ames, meanwhile, summoned the 75th Ohio from its reserve position and ordered its 269 men "to fix bayonets, pass to the front between the 107th and 25th Ohio, and if possible check the advance of the enemy."[30]

Years later, the 75th Ohio's colonel yet lamented the "dreadful cost" of that "fearful advance." For men who had been moored anxiously behind the lines, however, the rush to the front came as an odd sort of relief. "In all the hurry and excitement," one private in the 75th explained, "there seemed to be order and resolution." But the illusion of control quickly dissolved as the men "frantically ... gnawed paper from cartridges" and rammed leaden slugs down the barrels of their Springfield muskets. A "thick and acrid" smoke choked the battle-field, inhibiting visibility and polluting nostrils with the unpleasant "fumes" of gunpowder. "One could scarcely see the comrade beside him," one soldier protested. "Artillery and small arms rained their fire on the attackers," another soldier assured, "but the gloom and smoke made it hard to take aim." Even so, the 75th Ohio managed to momen-tarily "check" the Georgians in their "immediate front."[31]

"Fiercely," the battle continued for at least thirty minutes. "The enemy made a most obstinate resistance," John Brown Gordon con-firmed in his official report, noting that in places, "less than 50 paces" separated the combatants. "We stood our ground," Jacob Boroway asserted, "and shot ... as fast as we could." The Stark County volunteer got off three rounds before a shell knocked his gun from his hands "and broke it all to pieces." So close were the contending lines that "flag-bearers struck each other with their flag-staffs." Even so, the thick veil of smoke lent the intimate battle an eerie character, promoting a terrifying sense of isolation. "It appeared, as near as I [could] tell, that I stood there for some time all alone, no one as I could see near me," one private in the 17th Connecticut revealed. "Feelings came over me that cannot be described." The soldiers unable to see, the battle's auditory elements instead became especially prominent in their memories. The hail of bullets ploughing the knoll was so "terrific" that one private remembered "a continual *hiss* about my ears." "The way the bullets did rattle was curious," still another echoed.[32]

Before long, the Georgians had swamped "both flanks" of Ames's brigade. Reveling in their good fortune, the rebels began bagging prisoners. Mahlon Slutz's captors directed him to "a brick house about a mile north" of Gettysburg; Christian Rieker's pointed him to the rear. "I expected orders to fall back or assistance to hold on," the colonel of the 75th Ohio declared, "but neither came." Instead, the beleaguered soldiers instinctively abandoned that deadly perch to which a brigade should never have been sent, offering whatever resistance they could as they hurried to the rear. At one point, a corporal in the 17th Connecticut attempted to rally his regiment; a few of the Nutmeggers paused and began to load their weapons, but they could not take aim before the throngs of retreating men swept them up in one inexorable rush toward the almshouse.[33]

It was on the crowded campus of the almshouse that the 107th Ohio made its own attempt to stem the Georgian tide. Gripping the regimental colors, his brow knitted with contempt for the enemy, Adjutant Young stood in the middle of the road that reached into the borough. There, he collected the dazed remnants of the regiment. It was impossible to form another battle line ("the enemy," Jacob Smith noted, was "close behind in hot pursuit"), but for a few, critical moments, the harried knot of Ohioans "held the houses & outskirts of the town." Years later, John Brown Gordon paid the men an inadvertent tribute, claiming that he "never" remembered "more desperate fighting" than that which swirled "around the almshouse."[34]

Of necessity, the Ohioans joined the stampede of Union soldiers jamming the streets of the town. "We were much like a parcel of schoolboys turned loose," a soldier in the 75th Ohio recalled. By itself, the collapse of the Eleventh Corps line might have overwhelmed the borough's dense maze of streets and alleys, creating a dangerous bottleneck. But that afternoon a renewed Confederate attack west of town drove the men of the First Corps from the fresh defensive works they had fastened along the spine of Seminary Ridge. At the very moment Howard's soldiers battled their way into the borough, the First Corps men flooded the town from the west. The "two bodies of men," Howard reported matter-of-factly, "became entangled in the streets." Amid the bedlam, the commanding general ordered up Colonel Charles Coster's tiny brigade of New Yorkers and Pennsylvanians (it had been held in reserve south of town) and nodded them forward on a hopeless mission to "check" the "eager advance of the enemy." The men formed a line in a congested brickyard on the edge of town.[35]

The retreat through town was harrowing, but even more so for the ambulance detail, obliged to wind wagons heaped with their wounded and dying comrades through the "confused," gnarled masses congesting the streets. "We were not long in finding sufficient wounded soldiers to fill our wagons," Jacob Smith shuddered. Their freight testified to the intensity of the fight atop the knoll. One soldier, for instance, "had been shot through the mouth"; the musket ball entered through one of his cheeks and exited "out the other," ejecting "four or five teeth" and severing his tongue "pretty near off." His life appeared to have been saved by the "small Bible" that he carried "in a pocket over his left breast," in which still another piece of enemy lead had lodged.[36]

It made little difference to the rebels whether enemy soldiers trundled ambulances or not; either way, they were bagged as prisoners. Rounding one corner, the Confederates scooped up "more than half" of the 107th Ohio's ambulance squad. "This I think was about the only time in the service that I considered it really necessary to disobey orders," Jacob Smith recalled. And yet, he mustered the "considerable" strength required to "get along," his sense of "duty" soon delivering him to the new Union line taking shape atop Cemetery Hill.[37]

Standing atop that eminence with an aide by his side, Howard watched as ribbons of Union soldiers emerged from the town. Though the rush of so many "broken regiments" presented a doleful panorama, the general was encouraged. The retreat through town had delivered his command to the "good defensive" ground that he had spied that morning: the good defensive ground that would anchor the Army of the Potomac's position for the next forty-eight hours. If there was *any* consolation for the destruction visited on his men that afternoon, any reason for him to heave a sigh of relief, then this was it. "Rally, Boys!" he yowled. "Rally, Boys! Let us regain the name we lost at Chancellorsville."[38]

Howard's appreciation for the unfolding situation, however, was mostly beyond the reach of his men; in the ranks, the troops once again felt the familiar sting of "utter defeat." Only with "considerable effort," one of the Ohioans recalled, were officers able to rally their regiments and plant them behind the stout stone walls that rambled along the hill. When ordered to stretch a picket line out into the town, "within easy stone's throw of the rebels who were stationed in the houses," Fritz Nussbaum "positively refused to obey the order." In a telling exercise of caution, Howard posted "a strong guard of cavalry and infantry" in the rear to thwart potential deserters.

As it turned out, the afternoon's most infamous deserter turned up on Cemetery Hill. Hours after abandoning his men on Blocher's Knoll, an aide on General Howard's staff spotted Colonel Meyer "riding with his sword in his scabbard," making "no effort" to corral the "rabble of men coming back in disorder." (Earlier that afternoon, it seems that Howard had his own chance encounter with the troubled colonel. The general recalled that as his troops began spilling out of town, "a colonel passed by murmuring something in German," lacking, for the moment, "his command of English.") Yet seized with fear, "having in his whole aspect a very wilted and drooping appearance," the colonel lent his men no aid as they formed a new, northward-facing line near the base of East Cemetery Hill. When Ames finally caught up with the colonel, he placed him under arrest and commenced a verbal flogging. "Mr. Meyer," the general sniffed, "so long as I have a Sergeant left to command the Second Brigade, your services will not be required. Your place is in the rear."[39]

HUNCHED BEHIND a low stone fence, their left flank anchored on the Baltimore Pike, it would be a restive night as the questions drumming in the Ohio soldiers' ears competed with the dreadful moans of the wounded and dying. By any arithmetic, the regiment had been thrashed. Of the 458 men who entered the fight that morning, no more than 171 limped back to Cemetery Hill. The short span of their new line allowed the men to visualize their destruction. They shuddered as they glanced to the left and right. As had been the case at Chancellorsville, the battle exacted a considerable toll in captains, lieutenants, and sergeants, obliging the survivors to perform "the most arduous and exhaustive duties." In addition to Major Vignos, Lieutenant Colonel Charles Mueller had been "dangerously wounded." Captain William Fischer clung to life, as did Barnet Steiner, struck by a ball discharged from an Enfield musket. Injuries among the rank and file were no less overwhelming. "What will the morrow bring forth is now the question being asked, weighing heavily upon the hearts of our troops tonight as they lay upon their arms," one enlisted man told his diary. "Will the rebels again be successful, and must all this sacrifice of blood, lives and treasure be made in vain?" he asked. "Will not the prayers and supplications of God's people be regarded by a righteous God, and are we doomed to still further defeat?" He hoped that the next day would hazard a few answers.[40]

CHAPTER 6

"ALL THAT MORTAL[S] COULD DO"

July to August 1863

T HE SUN ROSE at a quarter past four the next morning, casting the entire battlefield in an eerie glow. "This morning was fresh, balmy, and pleasant," Jacob Smith recorded in his diary. "All the surrounding world was quiet and at rest." This made for a marked contrast with the previous evening, a cheerless coda to a day of gloom. Throughout the night, all had been bustle. While federal gunners studded Cemetery Hill with dozens of batteries—turning their perch into an imposing artillery park—infantrymen piled up fence rails and burrowed out rifle pits, determined that they would be prepared for their next encounter with the enemy. "All night long," one Confederate captain attested, "the Federals were heard chopping away and working like beavers, and when day dawned the ridge was found to be crowned with strongly built fortifications and bristling with a most formidable array of cannon."[1]

It is easy to imagine battle as a prolonged, epic affair, but as with every Civil War engagement, long and often unnerving intervals of inactivity punctuated the fighting at Gettysburg. The morning of July 2 would be another such intermission in the action as the federal lines took shape along the sturdy brow of Cemetery Ridge, curling from the thickly wooded Culp's Hill (where Henry Slocum planted his Twelfth Corps) to rock-littered Little Round Top (animated by the wigwag of a lone Union signal station). As the blue-coated soldiers rustled into place that morning, Robert E. Lee's scouts reconnoitered a Chancellorsville reprise—a massive flank attack to be delivered by Old Pete Longstreet's men. Lee intended his "Old War Horse" to launch the main attack on the federal left; meanwhile, Major General Richard Stoddart Ewell would pin the federal right in place and, "if an opportunity offered," ready an assault of his own toward Culp's Hill and Cemetery Hill.

Before long, the rebels—a few of whom had turned the borough into a sharpshooter's nest—made their presence known. From steeples, garrets, and attic windows, the skilled marksmen eagerly "pick[ed] off their prey whenever the chance afforded." But the main act was yet to come.[2]

It was not until four o'clock in the afternoon that the battle of Gettysburg roared back to life, heralded by the brisk fire of rebel batteries. This was the work of nineteen-year-old Major Joseph White Latimer, a "slight," clean-shaven former pupil of "Stonewall" Jackson known to some of his superiors as the "Young Napoleon." Atop a narrow ridge east of the town called Benner's Hill, Latimer planted his collection of fourteen guns and trained their fire on the knob that anchored the Union line. By silencing as many of the Union cannons as possible, Latimer would license Ewell to turn his "demonstration" into the battle's next set-piece action.

Latimer's guns rained shot and shell over Cemetery Hill for perhaps two hours. "The roar of the guns," one Louisianan remembered, "was continuous and deafening." Owing to their position in the shadow of the summit, the men of the 107th Ohio served mostly as spectators during the "heavy" bombardment. "For two hours we had to stand quiet, listening to the noise . . . the air around us literally full of whizzing balls," one soldier wrote. A lieutenant from the neighboring 17th Connecticut explained that, "we hugged the ground pretty close." He could not recollect a single casualty produced by the barrage in the entire brigade. Still, "men will get uneasy under a harmless shelling quicker than under a murderous fire of small arms." A "heavy artillery fire," Carl Schurz observed, "bewilders the mind of the bravest with a painful sense of helplessness as against a tremendous power." Indeed, while Latimer's shells did little physical damage to the Ohioans, their psychological and emotional toll was perhaps far more punishing than any of them cared to admit.[3]

Farther up the hill, Latimer's guns "literally ploughed up two or three yards of men, killing and wounding a dozen or more." Even so, the "quick and effective" reply of the Union gunners proved too much for the rebels. "We [were] able to shut them up," the First Corps artillerist Charles Wainwright crowed, "and actually dr[o]ve them from the field." Sometime around six o'clock, all but one of the Young Napoleon's batteries limped to the rear—the "dead horses, shattered guns, and ammunition carriages left on the field" telling the woeful tale of their abortive stand.[4]

It was a lost opportunity to be sure, but with James Longstreet's men pitching into the opposite federal flank—battling in turn for Little Round Top, Houck's Ridge, and the Wheatfield—Ewell was hardly deterred. As dusk approached, Major General Edward "Allegheny" Johnson—the forty-seven-year-old West Pointer and veteran of the Mexican War who earned his moniker in a battle atop western Virginia's Allegheny Mountain in 1861—nudged his division toward Culp's Hill. Once Johnson's troops stepped off, Jubal Early ordered up two brigades—the Old Harry Hays's Louisiana Tigers and Isaac Avery's North Carolinians—for an assault on Cemetery Hill.

On the Confederate right, Hays wheeled his twelve hundred men into three lines of battle. Despite their renown as "drunken, lawless renegades," these veterans, who had campaigned from the Seven Days to Second Manassas and Sharpsburg, "rated among Lee's most dependable soldiers." But while some of the Tigers were impatient to renew the fight, the mere sight of the "tremendous" hill gave others pause. "I felt as if my doom was sealed," recalled Lieutenant Joseph Warren Jackson of the Eighth Louisiana, "and it was with great reluctance that I started my skirmishers forward." Others masked their misgivings with swigs of "straight whiskey," dipping their tin cups into an open barrel.[5]

While confined to the makeshift hospital in the German Reformed Church on High Street, an Eleventh Corps private tending to an ugly Blocher's Knoll wound enjoyed a "grand view" of the battlefield. He watched as the Louisianans "closed up" their ranks, hunched forward, and started toward the base of the hill. "'Old Harry' shouted forward and on we went," one lieutenant recalled, "over fences, ditches, [and through] marshy fields." "We are the Louisiana Tigers!" they shrieked. Others let out the "rebel yell." Then, as the sun faded from the sky, they slammed their hammers back and prepared to fire.[6]

THAT FIRST SHEET of musketry, "so sudden and violent," startled the 107th Ohio. Early's division, having formed up behind the "very low ridge" that sprawled between Cemetery Hill and the southern edge of the town, had been "entirely concealed" from the Ohioans throughout the day. "We could not have been much more surprised if the moving column had raised up out of the ground amid the waving timothy grass of the meadow," alleged Colonel Andrew Harris, who now commanded the brigade. "We had no knowledge that we had any number of the enemy in our front."[7]

Convinced that his threadbare brigade would not hold, Harris grew weary. "I knew the weakness of my line," he conceded, "and felt the responsibility in which I was placed." Just moments before, supposing that the rebels would aim for the eastern face of Cemetery Hill, General Ames ordered the 17th Connecticut (which had anchored the right of Harris's northward-facing line) to change fronts. While the move helped to steady the regiments von Gilsa had assembled along the Brickyard Lane, it also created plenty of elbow room in the under-

Low stone fences knitted the brow of East Cemetery Hill, where the 107th Ohio engaged the Louisiana Tigers in battle on July 2, 1863—the second day of the fighting at Gettysburg. *Library of Congress*

manned 107th and 25th Ohio. Without time to plug the gap, Harris "rode along the line," offering his soldiers "all the encouragement possible." To hold *that* forlorn position, they would need it.[8]

With "furious determination," the Tigers "dashed forward." "They kept coming up the hill," one of the Ohioans marveled, "right into the flat area in front of our position." The artillery crowning the hill once more began lobbing shells and spurting deadly canister, but "most" rounds failed to find their targets—and this despite the very best efforts of the gunners to "depress" their tubes. "The artillery fired," Silas Schuler explained, "but they fired too high." In a matter of minutes, the "cursing screaming hordes" were within range. A familiar dread seized hold of the Buckeyes as they rammed charges down the barrels of their guns, took aim, and fired. The command to "shoot low"—the perennial plea of Civil War commanders—was not obeyed, however, and a hail of metal went arching over the attackers.[9]

Farther to the right, the 17th Connecticut "poured a destructive fire" into the rebels, which briefly "checked" their progress. Yet the gap opened by their redeployment yawned dangerously to the right of the 25th Ohio—and the Tigers, living up to their reputation, quickly found it. "On they came, with their wild, diabolical yells," one Buckeye shivered in recollection. Clambering over the stone fence in a furious "headlong charge," the Louisianans crashed through the gap just as water surges through a broken floodgate. "At this point, and soon all along my whole line," Colonel Harris remembered, "the fighting was obstinate and bloody." Men became fiends as they clubbed their muskets, stabbed with bayonets, swung their fists, and did anything that might stop the enemy. "Mr. Yank," one of the Tigers attested, "did not want to leave."[10]

But Harry Hays was not about to give the woefully outnumbered Buckeyes a choice. Though "driven up the hill," the 107th Ohio continued to resist; they "fell back fighting step by step." Under the cover of darkness (and despite "some disorder"), Adjutant Young rallied his out-of-breath remnants at the summit, around the guns of Captain Michael Nicholas Wiedrich's Battery I, 1st New York Light Artillery. Since their baptism of fire in the Shenandoah Valley the previous summer, Captain Wiedrich's gunners had managed to unlimber their six three-inch ordnance rifles "in the thickest" of every engagement. For the men from Buffalo, this bloody evening would prove no exception.[11]

After scaling the hill, the Louisianans yielded nothing of their momentum. They surged forth in a savage charge, "yelling like demons." Twenty-three-year-old Julius Geipel, a brown-haired, blue-eyed shoemaker from Elyria, defiantly mounted a stone fence and taunted the Tigers with the 107th Ohio's regimental colors. Standing five feet, eleven inches tall, the soldier made a conspicuous target. When a well-aimed rebel slug hit it, Young rushed forward to rescue the flag from the "rebel grasp." The Confederates, however, aiming for the tempting prize of Wiedrich's guns, began swarming the battery instead. The New Yorkers, armed with "hand-spikes, rammers, and staves," waged a savage, hand-to-hand fight, "defend[ing] themselves desperately." Not unreasonably, one Buckeye soldier supposed this struggle to be the "most sanguinary of the three days" at Gettysburg.[12]

Amid the "melee," Fritz Nussbaum alerted Adjutant Young to "the

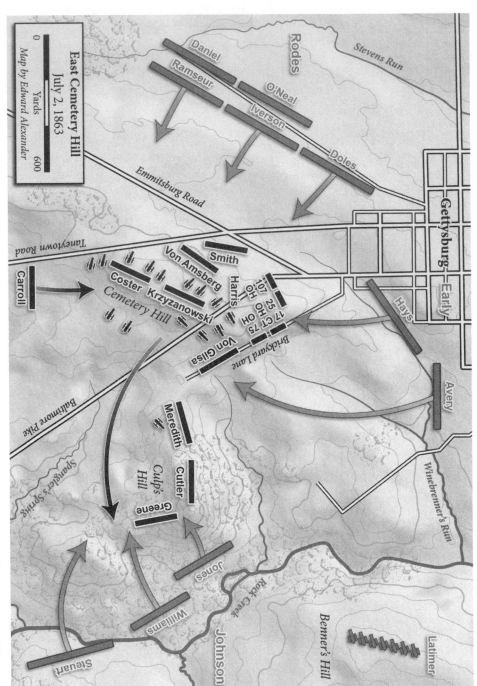

East Cemetery Hill
July 2, 1863

Map by Edward Alexander

Yards

0   600

Rodes

Stevens Run

Daniel

Ramseur

O'Neal

Iverson

Doles

Emmitsburg Road

Gettysburg

Early

Taneytown Road

Smith

Carroll

Von Amsberg

Coster

Krzyzanowski

Cemetery Hill

Harris

107 OH

25 OH

17 CT

75 OH

Von Gilsa

Brickyard Lane

Hays

Avery

Baltimore Pike

Spangler's Spring

Meredith

Cutler

Culp's Hill

Greene

Winebrenner's Run

Jones

Johnson

Rock Creek

Williams

Steuart

Benner's Hill

Latimer

color-bearer of the Eighth Louisiana Tigers," who was conspicuously "waving his flag near the Battery." Seizing the opportunity to avenge Geipel's wound, Young shoved ahead and emptied his revolver into the rebel's chest. A tiny knot of men—including George Billow, Philip Wang, Burkhart Gentner, Henry Brinker, and Fernando Suhrer—followed him into the fight. But just as soon as the color bearer fell (and before the Ohioans could seize the flag), Corporal Leon Gusman, a twenty-one-year-old ex-Centenary College student from Baton Rouge, "sprang forward" to rescue the colors. Young tried to "wrest" the flag from his "firm grip," but he "could not do it." Clutching the colors with his left hand, Corporal Gusman gripped a "large Navy revolver" with his right. He squeezed the trigger. Though badly wounded—shot through the shoulder—Young managed to fatally "plant his sabre in the color-bearer's breast." Then, after wrenching the "vile rag" of secession from his dead adversary's hands as a choice souvenir, the adjutant collapsed in Brinker's arms and was borne to the rear.[13]

At this point, the momentum that had carried the Louisianans up and over the hill seemed to falter. "For a time," one of the Ohioans recalled, "the opposing forces were much mixed up together." In the murk and smoke, it became "difficult to distinguish friend from foe." Still, the determined federals managed to maintain their fire. "Our boys stood like heroes," delighted George Billow. As it turned out, the flashes of their muskets served as a "guide" in the darkness for Colonel Samuel Sprigg Carroll, the impressively whiskered Marylander who delivered three regiments from his Second Corps brigade to the knob. Now realizing that the tide had turned against him, with none of his promised support in sight, Hays ordered his muddled squads "to retire to the stone wall at the foot of the hill"; he had lost more than two hundred men. As the rebels scrambled down the eminence, Captain Wiedrich offered them a parting salute. "I opened on them again with canister," he reported, and to "good effect."[14]

JUST BEFORE MIDNIGHT, the last wreath of battle smoke lifted into the air. The soft glow of a "brilliant" moon now illuminated evidence of a "heavy slaughter." "Another day has gone by, and with its passage scores and hundreds of our comrades have passed beyond the scenes of mortality," Jacob Smith confided to his diary. He marveled that men like Jacob Bise, a forty-six-year-old Prussian bookmaker from Tiffin, and Jacob McCormick, a twenty-one-year-old farmer from Tuscarawas County, now awaited their graves. So too did Private Daniel Palmer, whose remains would be identified days later by the pocket testament and a framed ambrotype discovered on his body. Smith could not be sure, however, what the losses of so many comrades ultimately meant. The repulse of the Louisiana Tigers might have secured the anchor of the Union army's position at Gettysburg, but the outcome of the battle—much less the war—remained anything but certain.

Indeed, Robert E. Lee believed that his army had come within a whisper of victory on July 2. The general was so encouraged by the reports trickling into his headquarters that he "determined to continue" the fight the next morning with synchronized strikes on the enemy's flanks. A "fresh" division under the command of Major General George Edward Pickett would brace Longstreet's attack; meanwhile, Ewell's capture of Culp's Hill would net the rebels a splendid artillery platform. "With proper concert of action," Lee wagered, "we should ultimately succeed."[15]

To Lee's great dismay, however, Longstreet did not "have Pickett on hand" for the planned dawn attack—and "before notice could be sent to General Ewell," eager federal artillerists renewed the contest for Culp's Hill. With his initial plan for coordinated flank attacks foiled, Lee proposed a daring frontal assault on the Union center instead. Seven minutes after one o'clock that afternoon, a signal gunner from New Orleans yanked his lanyard and commenced a massive bombardment of Cemetery Ridge. "The skies," one eyewitness gaped, "were converted into a pandemonium of howling, hissing, and exploding missiles." The cannonade emptied rebel ammunition chests, but did remarkably little to disable the federal batteries planted on the horizon. Finally, at three o'clock, Longstreet reluctantly nodded his men forward. Within the space of an hour, more than half of the nearly thirteen thousand rebels who made the assault would be added to the casualty registers. "The severe loss sustained by the army and the reduction of its ammunition," Lee concluded in a starchy official report that evaded any responsibility for the assault, "rendered another attempt to dislodge the enemy inadvisable."[16]

THE 107TH OHIO did not come under fire on July 3, but resting upon arms on a battlefield still crinkled their brows, tightened their throats, and tested their nerves. "Even the light-hearted soldiers, who would ordinarily never lose an opportunity for some outbreak of an hilarious mood," Carl Schurz made clear, "seemed to feel the oppression." Before eleven o'clock that morning, several "strange, unexpected hours of profound silence" replaced the distant sounds of battle atop Culp's Hill. Only the occasional crack of a sharpshooter's rifle disturbed the relative "tranquility." Nestled "in the houses and steeples," the rebel marksmen, still within easy range, "kept up a murderous fire from their safe retreats." For that reason alone, men "dared not raise [their] heads above the stone fence behind which [they] were sheltered."[17]

The Buckeyes crouched behind that fence throughout the frightful cannonade. "The earth," one soldier insisted, "seemed to rock from center to circumference." Hugging the ground, the men listened with "nervous anxiety" as the peals of cannon fire yielded to the distant rattle of musketry. Carl Schurz remembered that during Pickett's Charge, "some of the men occupied their minds by cleaning their gunlocks," burnishing their buttons, and "sewing up rents in their clothing." But such frenetic activity ultimately failed to distract them. From his perch atop Cemetery Hill, Charles Wainwright listened intently for the "sharp, quick reports of our guns" and the "alternate cheers and yells of the contestants." "The ring of [our] brass twelve-pounders," the artillerist boasted, "was easily distinguishable."[18]

By five o'clock it was apparent that Lee's gamble had failed spectacularly. But while some along the Union lines exulted in the verses of "John Brown's Body," the Ohioans were not quite ready to rejoice. After still another restless night ("we lay down upon our Arms among the dead bodies"), the men received orders to press down Baltimore Street and into the borough at dawn. "We could not understand what it meant," Fritz Nussbaum protested. "We were marched through the alleys expecting every step we made to be shot at by the enemy from the houses." Upon reaching the town square, however, they learned that Lee's baggage train—now heaped with injured soldiers—was trundling mournfully back into Virginia. His infantry columns would not be far behind.[19]

The news was no small relief. Still, as if to confirm the Duke of Wellington's insistence (the day after Waterloo) that "nothing except a battle lost can be half as melancholy as a battle won," there was hardly time for celebration. Gettysburg's panorama of death simply overwhelmed the senses. The bodies littering the field had "swollen to twice their original size"; a few even "burst asunder with the pressure of foul gases and vapors." "The odors were nauseating," one soldier gasped, "and so deadly that in a short time we all sickened and were lying with our mouths close to the ground, most of us vomiting profusely." Another soldier shuddered upon recollection of "two dead bodies blackened and bloated in the sun," wriggling "maggots filling their mouths and eyes." One could find corpses in almost any pose: curled on the ground, with arms in the air, slumped over a fence. Once again, battle did nothing so well as compile a catalogue of ghastly new ways to die. Charles Wainwright had "no fondness for looking at dead men," but, doubting that he would ever "get so good a chance again to see what slaughter is," the artillery chief indulged his morbid curiosity. He was more than repaid for his effort, for as one early battlefield visitor noted, "there was scarcely a rod that did not furnish evidence of the terrible scenes enacted."[20]

There was yet much work to do. While the men bagged prisoners in town (straggling rebels "who were tired of War and concluded not to go back to 'Dixie'"), Jacob Smith and his comrades on ambulance detail combed the battlefield and wound through makeshift hospitals in a search for the missing and maimed. On July 1, the retreat through

After three days of fighting, Gettysburg was a charnel house of human death and destruction. More than nine thousand bloated bodies littered the fields. *Library of Congress*

town had left scores of the regiment's injured men behind the enemy's lines and in urgent need of medical care. A thrashing rain made this unpleasant task even more "disagreeable," requiring the teams to ford swollen creeks, trudge through mud, and navigate "raging" floodwaters. Creaking wagons delivered loads of groaning and gangrenous men—among them a twenty-four-year-old shoemaker named Caspar Bohrer, whose gunshot wound below the right knee would require amputation, and Jacob Hof, a Clevelander who would not make it through the night—to the 156-acre farm of George and Elizabeth Spangler. Located on the Granite Schoolhouse Road, which stabs "between the Taneytown Road and the Baltimore Pike," their property now hosted the Eleventh Corps hospital.[21]

At the Spangler Farm, surgeons with "their sleeves rolled up to the elbows, their bare arms as well as their linen aprons smeared with blood," worked around the clock. An "unceasing procession of stretchers and ambulances" quickly overwhelmed the handsome house and barn, crowding the "hay mows, the feed room, the cow stable, the horse stable and loft." This obliged the newest arrivals to take whatever shelter they could find "under the eaves of the buildings." The piles of amputated limbs and pools of blood grew steadily larger, "but still the surgeons cut away." The side yard, meanwhile, became a makeshift graveyard, and Alfred Rider one of its undertakers. The regimental postmaster had been detailed to the hospital by the surgeon in charge, twenty-eight-year-old Dr. James Armstrong, an "able and efficient" graduate of the University of Pennsylvania Medical School. Rider worked without respite—burying the dead, recording their names, and collecting their effects for shipment back home.

It was physically and psychologically demanding labor. Rider actually wore through the soles of his brogans, tracking "back and forth" between the hospital and the regiment to deliver frequent updates to his impatient comrades. One of those updates concerned the regiment's young color bearer, who had been "shot in the wrist." After traveling up his arm, the spiteful slug lodged "near the elbow." The young soldier refused to let the surgeons operate. "I plead with him one evening when he was frying potatoes and onions to have the ball extracted," Rider recalled. It was with no small regret, then, that the next morning Rider recorded his comrade's name alongside the other interments.

EACH TIME HE recorded a name in that simple farm ledger, Rider must have felt the weight of history. He certainly did when he interred the hospital's most famous patient, Brigadier General Lewis A. Armistead, who had been mortally wounded after defiantly mounting the stone fence at the Angle on July 3. Rider placed the forty-six-year-old, North Carolina–born brigade commander's body in a "rough box," which he buried in the "Confederate part" of the Spangler cemetery. He would contemplate it all years later, for there was no time to pause now. The orchestra of human misery—"heart-rending groans" and "shrill cries of pain," the supple pleading of dying sons for their mothers—continued well into the night, the only serenade on this Fourth of July.[22]

BACK HOME, celebrations of the nation's eighty-seventh birthday began early. By nine o'clock in the morning, Wooster's public square was "already well filled with happy and patriotic people." Men, women, and children in Canton capped a festive, flag-festooned day ("a pageant the like of which was never before witnessed in this section," one observer commented) with a "filling, comfortable" ox roast. Notwithstanding some morning showers, "the masses poured along the streets" in Akron, eager to celebrate "a good old-fashioned Fourth of July" with a horse show and parade of fire companies. In downtown Cleveland, the evening sky was "illuminated with rockets, roman candles, and other pyrotechnical displays." The pop, pop, pop of fireworks "crackling" along Superior Street continued for hours.[23]

News of the victory at Gettysburg, of course, would not reach Ohio in time for the celebrations. But telegraphs clacked furiously throughout the weekend, conveying the latest news. From this fitful, sporadic, and imperfect traffic of real-time rumors and reports, editors slowly wrung a coherent chronicle of events. By July 6 that narrative had still not taken shape; instead, in a way that betrayed the agonizing confusion and uncertainty of the weeks after a battle, telegraphic dispatches from Washington, Philadelphia, Baltimore, and Harrisburg rushed frantically across the front page of the *Daily Cleveland Herald* without the slightest attempt at analysis. "It is really true," one war correspondent wrote, shrewdly anticipating that his report would be met with disbelief. "Lee has been totally routed, and is seeking to escape."[24]

As the public cheered the results of the battle, families and loved ones grew anxious and impatient for news from their soldiers. After major engagements, newspapers not infrequently published registers of the killed, wounded, and missing. But these hastily transcribed lists could be notoriously inaccurate; more than a few soldiers, for instance, had read their own obituaries over the course of the war. So it was that the citizens of Norwalk, Ohio, dispatched a delegation to Gettysburg "to look after the sick and wounded Ohio boys." After an exhausting, four-day journey by foot and freight car, the party reached the battlefield on the morning of July 9. Winding through overcrowded field hospitals, they visited with "many" wounded soldiers—including "several" men from the 107th Ohio—who appeared to be "well cared for" and "in excellent spirits." One of those men may well have been Augustus Vignos, who was recovering from the amputation of his right arm with the aid of twenty-five-year-old Rebecca Lane Price, a volunteer nurse who had earlier that week rushed to Gettysburg from her home near Philadelphia.[25]

Yet few communities had either the means or wherewithal to send out search parties; they instead waited on letters from their fathers, sons, and brothers to supply the latest and most up-to-date information. On the page, soldiers attempted to translate their raw memories into prose; not infrequently, however, their narrative momentum stalled, and crisp accounts of battle devolved into painstaking catalogues of human destruction. Take, for example, the letter that Barnet Steiner addressed to his brother, William, on July 8: "Our right was compelled for a short time to fall back," he began. "This was in the early part of the engagement. I was shot in the left shoulder blade, the ball lodging in my breast where it still is and will likely remain. H. Flora was shot through the left breast where the ball lodged. We are both in the hospital together. Among the others in the Company wounded are Hoagland, the little finger; Burnheimer, thigh, ball extracted; Tinkler, in head, pretty bad; L. McKinney, on cheek; Keiffer, same; Dine, forearm; Finkenbiner, shell struck on hip; Keedy and Exline, I think killed; also Palmer, and Lohm and Sinclare taken prisoners; several not heard from."[26]

Unable to furnish war correspondents, local and regional newspapers likewise relied on these communiqués to convey news from the front lines. On July 15, the *Stark County Democrat* could inform its readers that, "the 107th O.V.I. suffered severely in the late battles at Gettysburg." Still, two weeks after the fight for Blocher's Knoll, its editors had "heard but few particulars." The *Sandusky Register* was not able to communicate the details until the end of July, when Captain William Koch forwarded the lengthy list of Company F's "killed and wounded." Similarly, the *Summit County Beacon*'s reporting was indebted to a wrenching missive from George Billow, but it was not published until July 30. Wielding horrific losses—thirty men in his own Company I—as evidence of their courage, Billow concluded that, "the people of Summit County have every reason to be proud of the Germans in the 107th."[27]

For men and women like John and Catherine Heiss—eager for a report from their nineteen-year-old son William Henry, a private in Company B—it seemed as though the "particulars" would never arrive. Making their residence in a tiny dwelling on Cleveland's Parkman Street ("it was little better than a shanty"), the couple struggled to support their seven children. In fact, prior to his enlistment, William Henry worked in a spice mill to supplement his father's earnings as a planer at Sheppherd's Lumber. That autumn, the dreaded news arrived: the rebels shot their boy atop Blocher's Knoll, and he succumbed to typhoid fever in a hospital in York, Pennsylvania, some thirty miles east of Gettysburg. It was too much for John Heiss. He "[broke] down right after the boy died," one of his neighbors noted, "and was never afterward the man he had been." With her grief-stricken husband unable to work, Catherine was "compelled to take in washing" as she waited for the federal government to approve her son's pension money. But before that happened, and despite "a summer's worth of medicine," John Heiss "worried himself to death"—no less a casualty of the battle of Gettysburg than his beloved son.[28]

WHILE MEN at the front could supply details about their own participation in the fight and the fate of individual soldiers, they were often just as uninformed as folks back home when it came to matters of operational and strategic importance. On the morning of July 5 they swarmed a "newspaper boy" hawking the latest copy, eager to learn the "probable number of killed and wounded" and "the mortality of the enemy's forces." Losses of the kind they suffered over the last few days demanded context and meaning. The stilted after-action report filed by Captain Lutz ("exposed to a heavy fire of artillery and musketry," the regiment "suffered heavily in killed and wounded") provided neither.[29]

Just before dusk, the 107th Ohio "again started on the march." If loath to bid farewell to so many injured and dying comrades, the men were nonetheless impatient to leave behind Gettysburg's "destruction" and "desolation." Already, the heavy rains had opened many of the shallow graves strewn about the battlefield. "There was nothing to be found outside the dread results of war," Jacob Smith lamented, predicting accurately that it would require "months of labor" and "even years of time" to efface the physical scars the battle left on the landscape.[30]

The next three weeks pushed the bedraggled men to the brink of exhaustion. Hungry, aching, and itching, they trudged through thick mud, waded swollen streams, and twisted through tight mountain gaps. Narrow, uneven, and in places nearly vertical, the roads that reached over the hills and mountains were negotiated only with the "greatest difficulty." First, the men retraced their steps as far as Emmitsburg, Maryland, where they bivouacked in the vicinity of their old camp on the evening of July 6. Setting out before dawn the next morning, they tramped through Utica and Creagerstown, rounded High Knob (at more than fifteen hundred feet in elevation, the "loftiest peak" in the Catoctins afforded unrivaled views of the surrounding valley, including Harper's Ferry), and made one last push out to Middletown, a steepled village in the shadow of South Mountain. Though "half the men were bare footed," the troops logged a remarkable thirty-four miles that day.[31]

The next morning, a somewhat less strenuous march along the macadamized National Road—the first federal highway—delivered the men to Turner's Gap, a "narrow passage" through South Mountain that had seen pitched fighting during Lee's Maryland invasion the previous autumn. A most welcome respite on July 9 afforded the men an opportunity to wash their uniforms, now louse-infested and caked in a thick layer of dirt and grime. But before long it was off to Hagerstown, a "thriving" collection of "porches and verandas" located midway between South Mountain and the Potomac. Men and women choked the sidewalks to catch a glimpse of the massing troops.[32]

Perhaps unavoidably, these "long and tedious" marches invited questions about the army's intentions. Were they moving to intercept Lee's men, or "just marching leisurely along"? After such a costly, hard-earned victory, would Meade allow the enemy to escape unmolested back into Virginia? As they pondered the possibilities, their feet sore and blistered, an all too familiar dread began to gnaw at the rank and file.[33]

SINCE THAT unfortunate hour atop Blocher's Knoll, dread of a different sort had been gnawing at Seraphim Meyer. The colonel tendered his resignation on the Fourth of July, but rather than accept it, General Ames placed him under arrest. "Dragged along in the rear" of his regiment "like a culprit," the colonel now awaited the court-martial trial that would decide his fate. While courts-martial were not exactly rare occurrences during the Civil War—in a telling index of the earnestness with which the Union army enforced its code of conduct, well more than one hundred thousand Union soldiers responded to a court-martial inquiry between 1861 and 1865—they were much less common among officers. According to one estimate, two-thirds of all courts-martial involved privates; many of those cases, especially as the war entered its last two years, involved desertion. While several became high-profile because of the personalities involved, no more than ten percent of Civil War courts-martial cases implicated military commanders.[34]

During the Civil War, the military justice system distinguished between two sorts of court-martial inquiries. General courts-martial convened when the waywardness or misbehavior of a soldier or officer "threatened the security and success of the army," while regimental courts-martial were empaneled to mete out justice for "minor" misdeeds. Colonel Meyer would face a general court-martial because of the humorless charge—misbehavior in the face of the enemy—that Ames specified against him. The Articles of War, the regulations adopted by the War Department in 1806 to govern the conduct of soldiers and officers, prescribed a punishment up to and including death for "any officer or soldier who shall misbehave himself before the enemy, run away, or shamefully abandon any fort, post or guard which he or they may be commanded to defend." Though rules of procedure ensured equity and efficiency in general courts-martial inquiries—the accused was entitled to an advocate during the proceedings, had the right to object to members of the court of inquiry, and could not be tried by officers of a lesser rank, for example—a conviction required guilty votes from a simple majority of the panelists.[35]

On July 14, deeming it "a duty which I owe to myself as well as to my regiment," Meyer penned a forceful letter to Lieutenant Colonel Theodore Meysenburg, Howard's assistant adjutant general. Making a painstaking inventory of his sacrifices on behalf of the Union war effort, Meyer sought a "speedy" verdict. "As to my conduct on the field of battle," Meyer added, "I appeal to every soldier and officer of my regiment. Exposed to a most tremendous crossfire, which nearly destroyed my regiment, I kept on encouraging officers and men to stand fast, which they gallantly did, and carried out every order given to me." Still confident that the Army of the Potomac was moving to crush out Robert E. Lee, the colonel did not want to forgo the war's "final" showdown.

But on that last score, at least, Meyer needn't have worried. Earlier that morning, the rebels slipped back into Virginia, their supply trains and wagons trundling along the eight-hundred-foot long pontoon bridge that Lee's engineer corps extended across the swollen Potomac. When the men of the 107th Ohio reached Williamsport and realized that the "strong" enemy works ("built as if they meant to stand a month's siege," Charles Wainwright remarked) were empty, they erupted with "considerable profanity." Four-score miles away in Washington, D.C., President Lincoln, who had been tracking the army's progress, also found it difficult to contain his disappointment.

"Although he was not so profoundly distressed as he was when Hooker's army re-crossed the Rappahannock after the battle of Chancellorsville," the journalist and Lincoln intimate Noah Brooks observed, "his grief and anger were something sorrowful to behold." The president vented his frustration in a memorandum to Meade. "You had at least twenty thousand veteran troops directly with you," he scolded, "and as many more raw ones within supporting distance . . . I do not believe you appreciate the magnitude of the misfortune involved in Lee's escape."[36]

FOUR DAYS AFTER Lee slipped away, two narrow pontoon bridges carried a freshly provisioned Army of the Potomac across its namesake river. Once back in the Old Dominion, the men maintained a demanding itinerary—twenty-five miles to Aldie, a march at "sunrise" to New Baltimore ("we pushed on until dark and, after, still no orders were given to stop"), and a tramp out to Warrenton, the Fauquier County seat. Near that crossroads on the Manassas Gap Railroad, the men of the 107th Ohio, wearying under the remorseless July sun, staked their tents. Though a welcome reprieve from the grueling pace of the last few weeks, the new camp was located more than half a mile from the nearest source of fresh water—something that invited a squall of protest from the parched troops.[37]

Yet again, the soldiers exchanged the physical demands of life on campaign for the emotional demands of life in camp. Idle moments invited painful memories to prey upon the men. So too did Colonel Meyer's court-martial trial, which obliged men to relive that anguished hour north of the borough. Captain Edward Giddings convened the court just after ten o'clock on the morning of July 27. Once impatient for a thorough investigation of his conduct at Gettysburg, the colonel was now flooded with fear and misgiving. "What have I done to merit such treatment?" he demanded to know in yet another letter to Meysenburg, attempting unsuccessfully to head off his trial. "How ungrateful it seems to [me], after bringing all the sacrifices which I did."[38]

For the next week, tasked with deciding whether the colonel had behaved "in an improper and cowardly manner" atop Blocher's Knoll, a seven-member panel examined and cross-examined more than a dozen aides, staff officers, and enlisted men. The court heard from the prosecution's witnesses first. General Ames opened the testimony with a withering assessment of the colonel's performance, maintaining that Meyer's "excited" commands were "not such as should have been given according to the tactics adopted by the War Department." Captain John Marshall Brown assured the court that Meyer's "manner exhibited agitation," recalling how the colonel "crouch[ed] down on the neck of his horse at the sound of shells." The testimony of General Howard's aide-de-camp was equally devastating. With their intense scrutiny of Meyer's carriage and posture—even the modulation of his voice—the prosecution's witnesses revealed the unspoken rules that governed the expression of emotion on a Civil War battlefield.

Not surprisingly, witnesses for the defense roundly rejected the charge of cowardice, maintaining that Meyer made a "habit" of crouching upon his mount when delivering commands. "A spectator," as Lieutenant Philip Wang explained, "might be inclined to laugh at his manner." A captain, second lieutenant, and sergeant major from the 107th Ohio all agreed that there was nothing "unusual" about the way the colonel issued orders to the men that afternoon. The regimental surgeon even volunteered that Meyer's "weak" left lung, "still suffering" from the effects of exposure the previous winter, sometimes caused him to lean forward on the neck of his steed. Although one lieutenant admitted that the colonel "swore" when posting the regiment on Blocher's Knoll—something that was out of character—he insisted that Meyer remained with the regiment throughout the fight, and that he did not raise his voice "louder than was necessary."[39]

Judge Advocate Giddings was hardly persuaded. In his charge to the court, he urged careful consideration of "the circumstances under which the witnesses for the defence" supplied their statements. "A line officer testifying concerning the courage or the reverse of his Colonel is confessedly in a very embarrassing position," he reasoned. "I submit

that by the force of circumstances, their judgment would be as chari-
table [and] favorable as possible to the defendant." The judge advocate
then pointed to a more fundamental flaw in Meyer's trial strategy: the
colonel had hinged his case on the testimony of line officers. Yet it was
nearly impossible "for line officers to be cognizant of all the order[s]
received by a colonel." How could they affirm that Meyer executed
his orders when they were not privy to those orders in the first place?
"The preponderance of the evidence," Giddings concluded, sustained
the damning charges against Meyer.[40]

The court left no record of its deliberations, apart from reporting
that it "considered" the evidence "maturely." But with its members
hailing exclusively from Eleventh Corps regiments, Colonel Meyer's
acquittal was probably preordained. Still howling with indignation
over their treatment after Chancellorsville, the jurors were not about
to supply the press with extra copy. As such, the verdict was hardly vindication; all knew that another court would have reached a different
conclusion. Even as they exhaled, then, the colonel and his bone-tired
men shuddered at their brush with "lasting shame and infamy."[41]

On Thursday, August 6, at the invitation of the president, the
nation paused for a day of prayer and thanksgiving. The victories at
Gettysburg and Vicksburg, "so signal and so effective," required nothing less. From pulpits around the country, preachers exhaled that God
"was on the side of the pious" after all. The feast doubtless assumed
special meaning for the Ohioans, arriving as many men marked the
first anniversary of their enlistment—and just one day after the general court-martial returned its verdict in Colonel Meyer's case. The
next evening, "a sleepy, depressed column of troops" tramped out to
Catlett's Station, a march that brought them full circle to the site of
their first bivouac on the Gettysburg campaign.

But the men quickly abandoned any hope that providence might
finally shine upon them. At their now familiar depot on the Orange
& Alexandria, the soldiers learned that "as soon as transportation
could be obtained," they would be whisked to the war's margins—

transferred to the Department of the South in a humiliating move that would deny them the opportunity to demonstrate their mettle in another major eastern theater battle. On the orders of General Meade, the Eleventh Corps would no longer exist as a fighting unit in the Army of the Potomac.

Within twenty-four hours, the dazed troops obediently piled into forage and cattle cars. Their means of conveyance must have seemed all too appropriate. As the whistling locomotive lurched toward Alexandria, Virginia, the once bustling slave port where they would board "river boats" bound for Fortress Monroe, the men of the 107th Ohio could not help but wonder if misfortune was their fate as a regiment.[42]

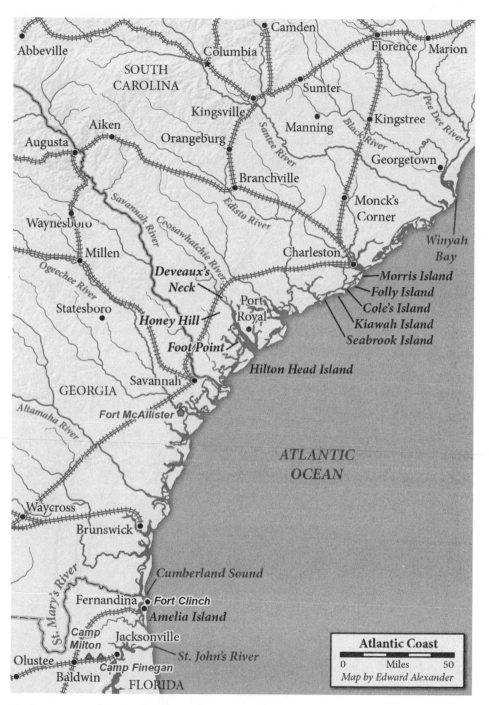

The Department of the South in the Civil War, 1863–1865

CHAPTER 7

"WE ARE NOT COWARDS"

August 1863 to February 1864

T HE QUARTERMASTER'S DEPARTMENT supplied the over-crowded boats that, one by one, thumped ashore on August 8, delivering the men of the 107th Ohio to Fortress Monroe. A squat pentagon of stone and masonry completed in 1834, the fort stood at the head of the historic Virginia peninsula that reaches into the Chesapeake Bay between the York and James Rivers. In May 1861, Fortress Monroe became famous as the place where three freedom-seeking slaves named Frank Baker, Shepherd Mallory, and James Townshend sought sanctuary behind Union lines, months before any federal policy on emancipation. Acting on his own clever accord, Union General Benjamin F. Butler declared them "contraband of war." Whatever Butler lacked in military acuity, he made up for with his wordsmithing; his ingenious turn of phrase, together with the determined strides of enslaved men, women, and children, placed the question of emancipation urgently and undeniably on the nation's agenda before the rebellion was even a month old.[1]

Rounding the peninsula, the troops entered the James River and sailed as far as Newport News, where they would wait for sturdier vessels to convey them to Charleston. Lone chimneys, shell-pocked walls, and heaps of rubble pointed their way. The "picturesque ruins" of Hampton, Virginia—torched by the rebels in 1861, lest it fall into the hands of the enemy—supplied an evocative tribute to the war's capacity for ruin and destruction. Later that evening, together with the seven other Eleventh Corps outfits shipped south, the 107th Ohio bivouacked along the river. That night and the ones that followed proved restive, for the ravenous mosquitoes were "so thick as to make sleep almost impossible."[2]

Three days later, a strapping fleet of side-wheeled ocean steamers—the S.R. *Spaulding, Empire City, New York, America, United States, Constitution,* and *Nelly Pentz*—collected the troops and set sail for South Carolina. The outline of Fortress Monroe "grew fainter and fainter" until it finally slid behind the horizon. Uncertainty about the future preyed upon the men as choppy waters tossed the vessels from side to side. Jacob Smith reported "the great majority of boys" experienced "nausea and sickness." Before long, however, the "tall masts" of the blockading squadron ringing Charleston harbor came into view. Bulging knapsacks and heavy muskets slung on their backs, the men wriggled down narrow rope ladders, leaping from the steamers into smaller boats able to pilot the warren of rivers and tiny inlets that shield the Low Country mainland from the sea.[3]

The line of boats navigated the shoals of Stono Inlet—a passage between two barrier islands "about two leagues from the south channel of Charleston"—and then steamed "up the Folly River." The men came ashore at Pawnee Landing on Folly Island, a narrow spit of sand choked by palmettos and shaded with live oaks and thick stands of pine. Six miles long but only half a mile wide, the island was, in John Brunny's initial survey, "loaded with sand hills and swamps." Because choleric passengers aboard Charleston-bound ships were routinely "quarantined" on its low-lying dunes, eighteenth-century maps sometimes labeled the island "Coffin Land." For many of the soldiers about to anchor their tents on Folly's windswept beaches, this seemed a fitting appellation indeed. The island was "one of the most dreary and worthless collection of sand hills we ever saw," one New Englander recollected. One enlisted man marveled that anyone "could live on such a baron place." Still another volunteer supposed that Folly Island assumed its name because "some fool landed here a long time ago."[4]

As the cradle of secession and the Confederacy's second largest city, Charleston, South Carolina, had been an object of federal military operations since the first rebel shells arched toward Fort Sumter during the wee morning hours of April 12, 1861. Still, apart from a few luckless attempts to seize the steepled peninsula by land and sea, Union forces did not mount a major campaign against Charleston until the summer of 1863. Choreographed by General Quincy Adams Gillmore, the Ohioan whose place at the head of his West Point class of 1849 earned him a commission in the Corps of Engineers, the joint army-navy effort twice stalled on the parapets of Battery Wagner in mid-July. The 54th Massachusetts Volunteers, an all-black regiment whose recruits were drawn from several northern states, famously spearheaded the second, failed attack on the fort's palmetto-log barricades.[5]

But Charleston was far "too important to be lost when so nearly won." Impatient for victory and persuaded that success would require at least eight thousand additional troops, on July 26 Secretary of the Navy Gideon Welles urged President Lincoln to forward "a few regiments to Charleston." The memorably whiskered Major General John Gray Foster lent two divisions of his North Carolina–based Eighteenth Corps to the cause, including the men of General Edward Wild's African Brigade. Then, on the morning of August 7, General in Chief Henry W. Halleck instructed eight regiments from the Eleventh Corps to set out for the Palmetto State—but not before upbraiding Gillmore, whose "urgent but unexpected application" for more men Halleck deemed "seriously embarrassing." This was the order that sent the 107th Ohio packing for the Department of the South.[6]

Despite the welcome arrival of these reinforcements, Quincy Adams Gillmore opted to dig in for a long siege. Notwithstanding the blistering summer heat, men heaped the loamy soil into miles of trenches and burrowed out ordnance magazines and bombproofs. Those who did not swing spades or fell trees laced "wire entanglements" along the zigzagging defenses, studded with mortars and masked batteries. On nearby Morris Island, federal troops constructed a platform

Occupying Union forces had turned palmetto-shaded Folly Island into a canvas city by the summer of 1863. *Library of Congress*

for an enormous Parrott gun they wryly dubbed the "Swamp Angel." Beginning in late August, dozens of shells from the "coal-black" rifle screamed across the harbor toward Fort Sumter.

Bit by bit, the men adjusted to the "strange and often harsh environment" of the Sea Islands. "We have made quite a change of front," George Billow explained to his friend Lane. John Brunny thought exotic and otherworldly the sprawling, moss-laureled branches of the live oaks, the "climbing plants," and the dense underbrush carpeting the island. The 107th Ohio pitched its new camp on the south end of Folly Island, now blanketed in white canvas that stretched as far as the eye could see. The sand, however, was "poor anchorage," and the "frail" shelter tents were especially unsuited for the fierce gales that howled across the island. "Our tents, which had proved fairly good shelter in Virginia," griped one enlisted man, "hardly met the requirements of our new location." One soldier swore that "if you fell asleep . . . on waking your face would be covered" in sand. Quarters were cramped, with three (and sometimes four) men packed into each A-framed tent. "Order is Heaven's first law," one officer remarked, "but not that of Folly Island—there was not room enough for order."[7]

On the island, it often seemed as though the men had exchanged their gray-clad enemies for a host of natural ones—fiddler crabs, sand fleas, wood ticks, gnats, scorpions, snakes, and giant "loud-mouthed locusts." After dark, the pests waged a relentless "campaign," gnawing, pinching, buzzing, and burrowing under the skin. "Wherever you went," Jacob Smith remarked, "the air was filled with mosquitoes, and no choir of singers or band of music ever rendered such an amount of melody as we had here." The muggy tropical climes also took some getting used to—especially for men accustomed to the crisp breezes of a northeastern Ohio autumn. "The weather is very warm [here]," one Stark County enlisted man exhaled. "One can go in his shirt sleeves any time." Though night afforded reprieve from the blistering sun, Jacob Lichty seemed to manage with just "one blanket." "We have fine weather," he commented.[8]

After the harried pace of the last few months, the most significant adjustment was to the languor of life on picket. Years later, when Colonel Joshua Lawrence Chamberlain tallied the most trying aspects of soldier life beyond combat, he gave pride of place to the picket line. In South Carolina, the war settled into dreary stretches of inactivity, interrupted only by the distant roar of siege guns or the occasional crack of a rebel picket's rifle. Men prowled through the palmettos, poised between duty and irrelevance. "Everything is very quiet here," Fritz Nussbaum explained. "Once a while some little firing can be heard in the front." One of his comrades confessed that, "we have not as much duty to perform here as we had." Even drill was "limited to squads." Nighttime not infrequently found the men of the regiment lost in reverie, visited by painful memories and lamenting departed comrades.

Indeed, the doleful drip of reports from the hospital wards and hometowns where men tended Gettysburg wounds persisted that fall—each one an unnecessary reminder that the pain of a battle never ended. Not long after their arrival on the island, the men of Company D learned that Captain Barnet Steiner, who had returned to Stark County in mid-July to nurse the ugly gunshot wound he received atop Blocher's Knoll, succumbed to his injury. The news came as a shock, for "until the last," the twenty-four-year-old anticipated a full recovery and "longed" to rejoin the regiment. "That for which he died," one of his men noted, "was the very same for which he most longed to live and labor and suffer." In camp that evening, Steiner's men penned "resolutions of respect" for their fallen commander. "While . . . now in humble submission to the will of Divine Providence," they resolved, "we deeply lament the death of our fellow soldier and deplore that in his death, our country has lost a patriotic, brave, and magnanimous defender, his comrades a warm and noble-hearted companion." Together with a preamble, the men forwarded their resolves ("but a faint expression of the feelings of the remaining fragment of heroes of the Captain's company") to the *Stark County Republican*. The captain, they wrote its editor, "cannot be erased from the tablet of our memories."[9]

Indeed, in the days that followed, Steiner's closest chum Jacob

Lichty labored under an enormous burden of grief and despair. One night, lost in one of memory's labyrinths, he stared vacantly across the moonlit ocean, "for some time listening" to the waves as they crashed, one after the other, against the sandbars. "How often I wish for some good old friend, with whom I could sit down on the top of some sand hill & look out upon the mighty waters & talk of many good things," he confided in a letter to his brother. "In that way Capt. Steiner & I passed many a pleasant hour, but now he is dead, & I cannot get over my loneliness." Doubting that he would ever find another friend so full of mirth and piety, so able to stimulate his mind, Lichty wondered how he would endure the war without him.[10]

It was a question to be repeated many times over. Now under the command of General Alexander Schimmelfennig, the brigade had been "reduced to a mere handful," with one Ohioan doubting that "the four regiments now composing it could muster one hundred and fifty men for duty a piece." To make matters worse, the sick rolls only continued to swell. Dysentery and diarrhea ravaged the ranks, the all too predictable consequences of the island's foul-smelling water. "The only drinking water," one enlisted man objected, "was obtained by digging about three feet in the sand, and this was so brackish that the thirsty were satisfied with a small quantity." Wincing with acute abdominal pain, twenty-seven of the fifty men in Company C were "sent sick" in August. Exhaustion finally caught up with others. Levied with "excessive and enormous duties" after Gettysburg, the sleep-deprived George Billow "was a mere wreck" by the time he arrived on Folly Island. When he fell "violently" ill, comrades carted his nearly "unconscious" body to the camp hospital, where he was diagnosed with a bout of typhoid fever "so malignant that his recovery was very doubtful." So it was that William Siffert, together with several of his comrades, was packed off to Ohio that autumn, assigned the daunting chore of recruiting new men.[11]

THE WEEKS OF numbing inactivity wore on, each one testing the regiment's resolve. Battle was no doubt taxing, but passivity made its own ironic demands. "Everything is so quiet here," one soldier explained, "that it is quite lonesome." Moored on an exotic barrier island far from home, subjected to mindless drill and monotonous fatigue duties, the men betrayed their feelings of dejection and gloom. "We looked every hour upon the same naked beaches of sand," another enlisted man explained, "the same drooping palmettos." Unable to escape the thought that they had been consigned to irrelevance, the troops no longer snapped to attention, shined their shoes, folded their gum blankets, or polished their muskets. Increasingly, they snubbed military conventions that now seemed but empty ceremony. In late September, an inspector from army headquarters groused that "little, if any attention is paid to the requirements of Army Regulations in regard to saluting." When General Gillmore asked the men to collect for a "grand review," Jacob Lichty supposed that the officer merely wished "to see if we noticed his new shoulder straps & the two stars."[12]

Indeed, throughout the regiment's time in South Carolina, officers struggled both to curb absenteeism and to maintain good order and discipline. "Too much which should be required by the officers is left to habit and violation of the men," one brigade inspector observed. Nineteen-year-old Private Joseph Hasenboeller abandoned the picket post he was ordered to guard for a lazy afternoon of fishing. When confronted by the corporal in charge of the post about his brazen neglect of duty, he replied that "he cared neither for the General or any one else" on the island. Days later, Hasenboeller's twin brother David, who had only recently returned to the regiment after recuperating from a minor injury at Gettysburg, displayed a similar contempt for authority. Ordered to help tidy camp, the self-assured private informed his first sergeant that, "he had nothing to command"—a retort that invited "much tumult" among the men. Directed to detail one man from his company for fatigue duty that same week, Sergeant Anthony Mainzer "cursed and swore and said he would be damned if he would do so."[13]

Of course, there was no greater or more ubiquitous threat to order and discipline than alcohol, many soldiers' preferred remedy for melancholy and listlessness. Enterprising sutlers kept soldiers plied with spirits until September, when a sharply worded circular from head-quarters forbade them from keeping "grog shops" on Folly Island. But the ingenuity of the enlisted men knew few limits when it came to procuring intoxicating liquors. The brigade surgeon's effort to fortify the troops against malaria—thrice weekly rations of whiskey "mixed with sulphate of quinoa"—hardly satisfied the thirsty soldiers. Private Joseph Greiner of Company A, for example, secured a gallon of whis-key by presenting a "forged" certificate to the post commissary. That night, he and his comrades on picket became so "drunk and intoxi-cated" that they were entirely "unable to discharge their duty."[14]

Such debauchery fairly scandalized teetotalers like Jacob Lichty. "I prefer spending my time & money in writing letters & receiving let-ters to buying whiskey," the soldier explained to his brother. The act of writing no doubt remedied long stretches of boredom and could help soldiers like Lichty maintain a sense of connection with loved ones, but the slothful pace of the mails merely reinforced their physical and emotional distance from home. "It takes letters so long to go & return that I get impatient sometimes," he confessed. "I must take it cool."[15]

MAKING A miraculous recovery after the amputation of his right arm—something he eagerly attributed to the tender care of nurse Rebecca Lane Price—Augustus Vignos rejoined the regiment in October. Upon his return, the major found his comrades especially anxious for the latest pickings from the political grapevine. In June, Ohio Republicans gathered in Columbus to nominate former state auditor John Brough for governor. Wreathed in a thick, white beard, the portly fifty-one-year-old railroad executive from Marietta looked every bit his part. Though a lifelong Democrat who had not supported President Lincoln in 1860, Brough quickly emerged as a vigorous sup-porter of the Union war effort. In the conflict's early months, he cho-reographed transportation to the front for thousands of soldiers on his Indianapolis, Pittsburgh and Cleveland Railroad. "Rigidly just and plain, even to bluntness," scandalized by the act of secession, Brough lent his stentorian voice to the cause of the republic. "How do you expect to get peace?" he asked an audience of fellow Democrats that summer. "Do you expect it by trammeling and binding the hands of the nation? Do you expect to get it by refusing men and money to carry on the war, or by putting in power an Administration opposed to the further prosecution of it?" He assured them that "sustaining the Government in the great work of suppressing this most wicked rebellion" was his only object.

Brough's broadmindedness and pledge to set aside partisanship appealed to leading Republicans throughout the state. So too did his embrace of emancipation. The peculiar institution, Brough believed, had afflicted the nation like a "leprous disease." "Either slavery must be torn out, root and branch," he told an enthusiastic crowd in Cleveland, "or our government will exist no longer." Testing the strategy that national party leaders would use in President Lincoln's reelection bid the following year, Ohio Republicans opted to nominate their slate of candidates on the "Union" ticket, discarding party labels in a nimble effort to persuade voters that "treason" and "loyalty" were the only true choices on the ballot. A "broad" party platform dodged old divisions and appealed to unity.[16]

Emboldened by their successes in the midterm elections, however, the Peace Democrats took precisely the opposite course—nominating Dayton's polarizing Clement Laird Vallandigham for the state's highest office. The most venomous of the Copperheads, Vallandigham had become a "martyr" in antiwar circles. That May, in one of his routine rehearsals of the war's affronts at a Democratic rally in Mount Vernon, Ohio, Vallandigham defied General Ambrose Burnside's recently issued General Order No. 38, which barred public expressions of "sympathy for the enemy" within his military department. Convicted by a military tribunal and then banished by President Lincoln to the enemy's lines, the sly former congressman fled to Bermuda on a blockade-running steamer before ultimately landing in Canada. There he resumed his bid for the Ohio governor's mansion from a hotel room in Windsor, turning what might have been a sleepy race into a marquee contest that commanded the nation's attention.[17]

Surrogates for the candidates barnstormed the state, drawing crowds that exceeded even the fabled turnouts for Old Tippecanoe in the celebrated "Log Cabin and Hard Cider" campaign of 1840. Secretary of the Treasury Salmon Chase, Hoosier congressman George Julian, Illinois governor Richard Yates, and General Franz Sigel took to the stump for Brough, while the Copperhead newspaper editor Samuel Medary of Columbus, former United States senator William Allen, and Ohio congressmen George Hunt Pendleton and Samuel Sullivan Cox crisscrossed the state to boost Vallandigham. "Political excitement," Governor Tod observed, "runs high in Ohio." On several occasions, "heated discussions" and torchlit rallies threatened to devolve into open violence; in August, a military company was required to restore order in Wooster after an exchange of sharp words between Copperheads and Union men resulted in "a serious riot."[18]

Nor was electioneering confined within the borders of the Buckeye State. In April, the Ohio state legislature passed a bill enfranchising soldiers in the field. For the first time, Ohioans away from home on active military duty could cast absentee ballots in local, state, and federal elections. Brough dispatched his old friend Edwin B. Olmstead to canvass the men of Ohio on Folly Island that autumn. The one-time Akron High School principal had served eighteen months as a captain in the Fourth Ohio before assuming a clerkship in the Treasury Department in Washington. In "short and meagre" remarks, he urged the men to remember "who it was that refused to vote them even food and clothing, while mocking their misfortunes and calamities." Vallandigham had "done everything within his power to arrest our progress and cripple the Administration and authorities." Only a few weeks before the election, "an Abolition agent" appeared on Folly Island and "labored faithfully for Brough," blanketing the camps with Union Party "tickets, circulars, and books." "Give him a gun," one Democratic soldier hissed, while another echoed, "Give him a cartridge box!"[19]

Officers also canvassed the regiment on behalf of the Republican cause. Captain Samuel Surburg ordered his company to cast their ballots for Brough, lest Ohio be plunged "into civil strife." In an emotional appeal, he warned that Vallandigham's election would "[turn] the tide in favor of Rebellion" and "crush" that "which has already cost the lives of many of our brethren of the regiment, whose bones are bleaching on the plains of Chancellorsville and Gettysburg." Surburg, of course, did not need to persuade obedient Republicans like George Billow. "Just give us soldiers of Ohio a chance to vote," the captain from Akron explained, "and we will show them in October next, who will carry the day—men that are really fighting for the freedom and liberty of their country, or those who are continually grumbling against their Government."

Still, more than a few soldiers either supported Vallandigham or at least seriously entertained his candidacy, supposing that his election might "offer relief for the suffering and inconveniences they faced at the front." Through "an incessant flood of newspapers," one captain lamented, the men "had been made to believe that with the election of [Vallandigham] would come speedily reconciliation, reunion, and peace, and that they would, without further struggles be restored to the bosoms of their families, &c." Beyond the usual electioneering, officers subjected these troops to threats, violence, and intimidation. Captain John Lutz promised to "punish" any man in his company who voted for Vallandigham, while his fellow officers "preached up the doctrine of rebellion" and "told us, that if we voted Vallandigham we would break our oaths." Other regimental leaders warned that "they would put [their men] in front of battle if [they] wouldn't vote for Brough." Men's faces puckered in anger at these taunts. "At Chancellorsville, we were in the front—at Gettysburg, we were in the front," one volunteer protested. "The next place you hear of us we will be in the front. That is where we always are and want to be," he continued. "We are no cowards."[20]

Leaving nothing to chance, General Schimmelfennig took matters into his own hands. A few days before election, he ordered "nearly the entire regiment" to Kiowa Island on another fatigue duty. "Soldiers," he smugly remarked, "had no business to vote." The move invited no small protest from the rank and file. "We were fairly cheated," one indignant Wayne County soldier objected in a tart letter that was widely reprinted in the press. "They kept us from voting because we would not vote the abolition ticket, as our officers wanted us to do." With no small irony, the Democratic press back home—including some of the same organs that decried Republican efforts to enfranchise soldiers in the field—wailed with outrage. "Here is a whole regiment, nearly cut off from the 'sacred rights' of voting, simply because they are Democrats!" frothed the *McArthur Democrat*.

The one hundred or so men left behind on Folly Island "insisted on exercising the elective franchise," but only those who had pledged support for Brough were permitted to cast ballots. Two dozen enlisted men voted for Brough. According to one account, a black quartermaster's cook likewise cast a ballot, bringing the final vote tally in the regiment twenty-five. "It is true," one soldier later reflected, "that by talking and voting we incurred the displeasure of our commanding officers; but our motto was and is, that nothing is worth fighting for that we would not vote for and advocate everywhere and at all times."

Enlisted men cast forty-four thousand ballots from the field that fall, and the Union Party nominee won ninety-four percent of them. Among the nearly two hundred Ohioans confined in Richmond's Libby Prison, Vallandigham earned not a single vote. Nor did the Dayton congressman find any supporters among the soldiers convalescing in Washington's Douglas Hospital. Ballot suppression was widespread, however, and we may never know how many soldiers were denied the franchise. Samuel Surburg supposed that "four-fifths of those [who] did not vote" in the 107th Ohio "were for Bough and the Union," but the taunts and threats suggest that the Democratic nominee may have easily triumphed on Folly Island. Surburg's need to reassure men and women back home of the unit's political convictions merely suggests the degree to which loyalty had become a question of partisan allegiance by the war's third autumn. Keenly aware that the regiment's political preferences would merely renew old questions about its mettle and conviction, Surburg simply declared that his comrades were loyal and true Republicans. In reality, their political allegiances proved malleable, responding to events at the front and functioning as a reliable index of morale.

As it turned out, Ohioans handed John Brough a margin of victory that exceeded a hundred thousand votes—an impressive showing considering the state's quarrelsome debates over the meaning of the war. President Lincoln wired the governor-elect once the last returns had been tabulated. "Glory to God in the highest," he exclaimed. "Ohio has saved the nation."[21]

ON NOVEMBER 28, a boat ferried the men of the 107th Ohio across the Folly River to Cole's Island, where the crumbling ruins of Fort Palmetto, an old War of 1812 garrison, still stood watch over Stono Inlet. No sooner had they established a camp than the skies released a thrashing rain. "The night was not a cold one," Jacob Smith remembered, "or we would certainly have suffered from the effects of our soaking." The men would pass the next six weeks on the island, keeping a watchful eye on the "very gay and happy" rebel pickets who were posted across the river in a belt of woods. "They are singing and dancing from morning till night," Fritz Nussbaum commented, "but I hope that their dancing and singing will soon be stopped."

The unit's new post afforded unobstructed views of Charleston and the fortifications that ringed its harbor. John Brunny was rather unimpressed at the sight of the garrison where the war began ("Sumter, to me, resembles a pile of stone and dirt," he informed a friend), but he was absolutely entranced by the shells that made it their target. "When one of Gilmore's 300-pound defensive artillery pieces hits it, a cloud of sand, rocks, and mortar will sometimes fly 40 feet in the air." At night, the men would survey the unremitting bombardment: "something that is dreadful to watch," Brunny confessed, "yet at the same time uncommonly beautiful." Cole's Island likewise remedied some of Folly's most notorious deficiencies. Here, the water was at least potable, and the sprawling oyster beds supplemented the soldiers' lifeless diets of salt pork and stale hardtack. Once the temperatures plummeted (December "came in quite rough and cold"), the pioneer corps could harvest the island's generous stands of pitch pine for fuel and firewood. In the evenings, huddled around the dancing sparks of "small fires," the men did their best to keep warm.

To be sure, life on Cole's Island was often numbing and disagreeable. Just days before Christmas, a private from Company G, pushed to the limits of endurance, fell asleep at his post on the picket line. "I had been on duty six days," he explained, "and been wet through twice . . . [I] felt almost too weak to stand my tour of duty." And yet even in the depths of despair, a faint hope flickered. Enemy deserters trickled into Union lines throughout the winter as Confederate morale flagged. "They say that many [more] would come over to us if they did not have families in Charleston," related Private John Geissler of Company I. "Even they believe that they will need to give up soon." Likewise, the shells that screamed across the harbor each night persuaded the men that Union victory was, if not inevitable, at least within reach. "We believe the war will come to an end this year, if it is God's will," Geissler told a friend shortly after New Year's Day.[22]

The new year also yielded up another reminder of the war's purpose. Notwithstanding the bitterly cold winds that whipped across nearby Morris Island, African-American soldiers solemnized the first anniversary of Lincoln's Emancipation Proclamation with a day of speeches and celebration—beginning a tradition that would continue well into the twentieth century. On the parade ground of the 54th Massachusetts, men fashioned a "speaker's stand" by draping a rubber blanket over an empty dry goods crate. When the makeshift rostrum collapsed midway through his "impassioned" oration, Sergeant Joseph Barquet quipped, "Gentlemen, I admire your principles, but damn your platform!"

While the day was freighted with special meaning on the windswept sea islands of South Carolina, whose rice marshes and cotton fields had been harvested by the toil of enslaved persons for generations, soldiers and civilians took note of the occasion far beyond

Charleston. Not far from "Freedom's Fortress," black soldiers in blue uniforms paraded through the streets of Norfolk. In Boston, veterans of the abolition movement gathered at Tremont Temple—the place where they had waited so anxiously for the news to arrive from Washington the year before—to observe "the new national anniversary."[23]

Weeks later, the 107th Ohio received orders to return to Folly Island. The seemingly interminable blizzard of circulars and general orders proscribing their movements made no more sense than they had in Virginia, and it was with no small frustration that the men acknowledged the latest dispatch. Supposing they would not tarry long, the men took little care in establishing a new camp, pitching tents over a hastily strewn carpet of grass, brush, and palmetto branches.[24]

Their intuition proved prescient. In December, with the war around Charleston fixed in a "holding pattern," General Gillmore began drawing up plans for a military expedition to Florida—an operation that would, at once, "recover all the most valuable portion of that State, cut off a rich source of the enemy's supplies, and increase the number of my colored troops." Gillmore knew that Florida's sizeable herds "kept a considerable number of Confederate soldiers fed." The rebels likewise harvested the state's bounteous stands of timber to corduroy roads, fortify battle lines, and feed campfires. Starved for new recruits and impatient for forward movement, the War Department quickly authorized the general's proposal. For his part, President Lincoln—his faith in southern Unionism abiding—hoped that Gillmore's expedition would midwife a loyal government in Florida, where there were whispers about "worthy gentlemen" desiring the state's return to the Union. In January, in a cocksure signal of his enthusiasm, the president dispatched his personal secretary John Hay, bearing a freshly inked major's commission, "to aid in the reconstruction."[25]

Led by thirty-nine-year-old, West Point–trained Brigadier General Truman Seymour, a detachment of some seven thousand federal troops—among them three African-American regiments—set sail for Jacksonville the first week of February, packed onto "twenty armed transports." Such a "large number of Union vessels headed out to sea from Port Royal," however, invited the curiosity of the Confederate sentinels perched at nearby Foot Point. Hoping to "distract the enemy's attention from the expedition to Jacksonville," Gillmore ordered Schimmelfennig's troops on Folly Island—among them the 107th Ohio—to stage a clever "demonstration."

On February 7, as General Seymour's contingent piloted its way up the St. John's River, "through the marshy lowlands" and beyond "the white bluffs and forests of pine and cedar," the Ohioans extinguished their campfires, stowed some stale bread and "cooked meat" in their knapsacks, and waited anxiously to move. "In the evening," one enlisted man later recalled, "we fell into line, and marched down the beach to the steamboat landing." At midnight, a boat collected the men and carried them across Stono Inlet to palmetto-choked Kiawah Island. The men tramped all night at a breakneck pace—all the more impressive when one contemplates their "difficult" route, which hooked through the stands of pine and tangled underbrush. At dawn they stopped to catch their breath in the shadow of the Vanderhorst Plantation, a dazzling three-story mansion whose stately, symmetrical façade and "broad, straight, amply shaded avenue" impressed even those who resented symbols of the slaveholder's abundance.[26]

That evening, the men forded the brackish, "waist deep" estuary that separated Kiawah and Seabrook Islands. Pausing a moment to wring the water from their "stockings and pantaloon legs," the column plodded on, marching until dawn. The soldiers struggled to see through the thick haze obscuring the island, but soon made out a large sugar plantation with its "negro quarters scattered around." The men had no more than identified those "foreign shapes" as a "cluster of buildings" when, all of the sudden, "a hundred or so" muskets released a "brisk" sheet of fire. Rebel skirmishers emerged from the woods and, after planting themselves behind a stout hedgerow, kept up their deadly work, squeezing their triggers just as quickly as they could reload. "The bullets," Mahlon Slutz remembered, "came thick and fast." Another of his regimental comrades marveled at the bullets "whizzing over our heads."

The blue-coated troops aimed their muzzles "in the direction from which the sounds of the firing came." Then they shook out into a line of battle with the men of the 107th Ohio anchoring the Union left. The blue-coated soldiers rushed forward at the double quick, undeterred by the "peculiar" trill of the rebel yell. "Our fellows gave a long and loud cheer," one Ohioan later reported, "and charged right over their rifle pits." After flushing the 150 South Carolinians and Virginians from their works and bagging a few prisoners, they chased the rebels more than two miles "through woods and swamps." Ultimately, however, the wheezing federals pulled back to trenches of their own, too depleted to keep up the pursuit in the face of swelling enemy numbers. In their freshly excavated rifle pits, they holed up for the better part of a day, awaiting an attack that never came. Finally, on the evening of February 12, with nearby federal gunboats supplying a lively covering fire, the soldiers evacuated their works and returned to their camp on Folly Island.

Though grueling, the expedition did not exact a great cost in human life or suffering. For men who still heard the moans of Chancellorsville's wounded and Gettysburg's dying, "it seemed miraculous that so much shooting should do so little execution." Slutz, in fact, was "the only one hit"; an enemy musket ball clipped and shattered his thumb. Augustus Vignos rushed to his side, inspected the injury, and then conveyed Slutz to a surgeon's tent, where he underwent a minor operation the next morning. He never forgot Vignos's act of kindness. More than a half century later, Slutz included the details in an elegant eulogy that he penned for the "capable" major.

But nor did the expedition produce much in the way of results. Jacob Smith pronounced the trek a flat "failure." Considering that the rebels quickly realized its true aim—as a "feint" for Seymour's excursion to Florida—his assessment came very near the mark.[27]

ONCE BACK IN their canvas city on Folly Island, the troops learned the fate of the Florida campaign. On February 8, after debarking in Jacksonville, Seymour's column trudged west, pressing deep into the

Florida interior. They aimed first for Baldwin, a modest map dot that possessed enormous strategic value as a vital rail junction. When the Union troops arrived, however, they found the town abandoned. Gleefully, they seized a stockpile of enemy supplies.

Despite an impressive haul, Seymour had second thoughts about advancing farther. "What has been said of the desire of Florida to come back [into the Union] now is a delusion," he informed Gillmore. To trudge farther into enemy territory would be to hazard "a sad termination to a project, brilliant thus far, but for which you could not answer, in case of mishap, to your military superiors." Gillmore agreed. It would be far better, he wagered, for Seymour's men to hold their "outposts" around Jacksonville than to move beyond their base of supply to Lake City, where Confederate general Joseph Finegan, the entrepreneurial Irishman who had served as delegate to Florida's secession convention, was busy huddling his command behind defensive works.

But then, abruptly and inexplicably, Seymour decided to reverse course. The general's contemporaries and historians alike have puzzled over this about-face, which ended in complete disaster. Driving west, Seymour collided with Finegan's command in an "open pine barren" at Olustee on February 20. "[We] had followed the rebels into the very jaws of death," one veteran shuddered. "The carnage became frightful." Indeed, the battle devolved into a racial massacre as rebel soldiers clubbed with muskets and furiously stabbed with bayonets. "Our men," one Georgia rebel acknowledged, "killed some of them after they had fell in our hands wounded." After a sharp fight, what remained of the federal column limped from the battlefield, "maimed, mangled and routed." To prevent the rebels from further exploiting Seymour's dazed troops, reinforcements—including the 107th Ohio—were summoned from Folly Island.[28]

Though uncertain about what Florida held in store for them, Jacob Smith and his comrades were eager to leave South Carolina. "A change of surroundings," he persuaded himself, "will be for the better." Other changes were afoot, too. Most momentously, Colonel Meyer would be returning home to Canton after tendering his resignation on February 13. In the letter he addressed to Assistant Adjutant General Edward Smith, the colonel cited his "rapidly declining" health. "I feel that I am unable to continue to fill my position," he explained. But while Meyer's health was "greatly impaired"—indeed, he had never really recovered from his spell in Libby Prison—the colonel had other reasons to take leave from the service. Just a few months before, he had appeared before a Union army examining board tasked with evaluating the "capacity, qualifications, propriety of conduct, and efficiency of commissioned officers." The officers found Meyer wanting in knowledge of tactics and administrative duties. He had been humiliated, but for the last time. "The good of the service and the welfare of his Regt.," a staff officer noted upon receiving Meyer's request, "demand the immediate acceptance of this resignation." Until a replacement could be appointed, Major Vignos would lead the regiment.[29]

As they bade farewell to that "island of desolation," then, the men felt the familiar push and pull of conflicting emotions. "It would be strange indeed had I felt any regrets at leaving," one veteran confessed decades later. "But I had passed seven long months with these surroundings, and somehow or other my own individuality took something from those familiar objects, despite the cares and vexations which had perplexed me." Months spent marking time in South Carolina had marked the regiment no less indelibly than its battles. Exiled to the war's margins, the men of the 107th Ohio once more had occasion to ponder the meaning of their sacrifices. But through their gloom and dejection, they resolved to stay the course. In early February, the Republican newspapers back home cheered the good news: all but a dozen of the regiment's enlisted men reenlisted in the service of the Union. "From the present outlook," Jacob Smith reasoned, "I felt confident that it would not add much to our time of service."[30]

CHAPTER 8

"SO MANY HARDSHIPS"

February 1864 to July 1865

ON FEBRUARY 24, the men of the 107th Ohio climbed aboard the iron steamship *Delaware* and bobbed down the Georgia coast to the St. John's River. Notwithstanding a thick curtain of fog and a "stiff cool breeze," the weather was cooperative. At noon the next day, after a voyage of 225 miles, they dropped anchor at Jacksonville— a neat grid of water-oak and magnolia-lined streets that sprawled along the coffee-colored river's west bank. Known to the French as Fort Caroline, to the Spanish as San Mateo, and later to the British as Cow Ford, the settlement in 1822 was named in honor of General Andrew Jackson, the hero of the First Seminole War. Four decades later, Jacksonville was the state's third largest city, boasting a population of more than two thousand. While it exported more than a few bales of "white gold," it was lumber—freshly hewn at one of six steam sawmills—that weighted down most of the port city's outbound schooners. The surrounding stands of yellow pine also supplied the timber for a two-story courthouse, a post office, Odd Fellows Hall, and Jacksonville's Episcopal, Presbyterian, Methodist, and Catholic churches.

By early 1864 the Civil War—and occupying Union soldiers—had visited Jacksonville on three occasions. Two years before, flames consumed several private dwellings, a hotel, and "at least a third of Jacksonville's main business area." Amid the "ruined gas-works, burned saw-mills and warehouses," the once "thriving, romantic town" now resembled "a devastated Northern city"; its streets were all but abandoned, save a stubborn collection of unapologetic rebels. "I believe myself that every citizen here," one soldier remarked, "would cut our throats in a minute if they dared to do it." One such holdout was attorney Rodney Dorman, who remonstrated against the federal war effort in general—and the sight of black men in blue uniforms in particular. "The use of [black troops] here," Dorman angrily told his diary, "is an insult & disgrace."

The newly arrived soldiers tramped through Jacksonville's deserted streets to "the edge of a pine forest." Amid the pines, about a mile beyond the city, they were instructed "to keep a sharp lookout for spies, guard runners, and rebel guerrillas." Though kept "under arms" in fresh rifle pits for three days, "all the noise I heard while on post," Jacob Smith regretted, was the "familiar" trill "of the southern mosquito."

To say the least, Florida did not make a good first impression. As they pressed into the southernmost state—the third to ratify a secession ordinance—soldiers encountered not a tropical paradise, but a land blighted with "poverty, ignorance, filth, fleas, alligators, and rebellion." One disenchanted volunteer, eager to find the healthful groves promoted prior to the war by Florida's energetic boosters, objected that he could "see nothing but pine woods, marsh, and every five or ten miles a cluster of dilapidated, deserted huts." A soldier from the 17th Connecticut offered a nearly identical assessment of the "very wild looking country of forest swamp and jungle." Unable to conceal his sense of taste and refinement, the soldier marveled at the "lonesome little shanties" inhabited by "half civilized creatures who probably lived by hunting and fishing."[1]

When it became evident that the enemy had no interest in launching an attack, however, at least a few soldiers set aside their bleak, initial perceptions of Florida. "We now enjoy a season of quiet," Isaac Loutzenheiser rejoiced, a "rest from previous hardships." Behind fresh fortifications and within easy range of friendly gunboats, the regiment established a new camp. "Every company has a good cook shanty with a large brick fireplace and bake oven," crowed one soldier. "The boys are faring sumptuously and growing fat." Enhancing their fare with local grapes, oranges, huckleberries, lemons, cherries, and watermelons—a raid of one orange grove yielded more than six hundred bushels of fruit—the regiment attempted to fortify itself against fever and disease. Florida's mild winter, which one soldier likened to "June in Ohio," was likewise a welcome departure from the gray cold of Brooke's Station. The camp's proximity to the St. John's River likewise promoted good hygiene, the crusade of the regiment's newly appointed surgeon, John Knaus. "For comfort and beauty," one Stark County volunteer concluded, "our camp cannot be excelled."[2]

But when the weeks wore on with little more to occupy their time than "tiresome" training exercises and interminable picket duties, the men grew restless. "Skirmish drill" invited particular ire from the ranks: "It is necessary that we understand the notes of the bugle in order to execute the proper movement required of us," Jacob Smith groaned. "We are kept running almost the entire time while engaged in it." The remonstrations from the ranks paled in comparison to the complaints many buglers registered about skirmish drill. "Since only two of us blow the lead part," the Zoar native John Brunny explained, "you can understand that it is not so very easy, with uniform on, parading around, until the lips are sore . . . the skin becomes thick as leather."[3]

To be sure, picket duty and drill demanded great strength, discipline, and forbearance. But what rendered them so objectionable was the intuition—increasingly difficult to deny—that this taxing work was contributing but little to the federal war effort. Elsewhere that spring, a war long punctuated by stalemates and set-piece battles at last yielded to the ambiguities and maneuvers of complex campaigns. Determined to wage a war of exhaustion that would prohibit the enemy from concentrating his strength or exploiting his interior lines, Ulysses S. Grant, the newly installed general-in-chief of all Union armies, choreographed five synchronous strikes into the Confederate heartland. After months of wrenching inactivity, telegraph operators finally—and feverishly—clicked out dispatches and reports from multiple fronts.

The news that spring was not entirely promising for those cheering the Union armies. In April, after driving up the Red River, Nathaniel Banks met with a humiliating defeat at Mansfield, in the pine barrens of northwestern Louisiana. Franz Sigel's efforts to lay waste to the Shenandoah Valley met with grief in the guise of Confederate general John Breckenridge's troops at New Market on May 15. The very next day, rebel soldiers stymied Major General Benjamin Butler, whose Army of the James crept along its namesake river, just south of Richmond at Drewry's Bluff. Coordinating the efforts of three federal armies—one hundred thousand men all told—William Tecumseh Sherman drove into Georgia, meeting Joe Johnston's Army of Tennessee in costly clashes at Rocky Face Ridge and Resaca, along the bed of the Western & Atlantic Railroad.

For its part, after splashing across the Rapidan at Ely's Ford, the Army of the Potomac once more pressed into the knotted scrub of the Wilderness, yet littered with the bleached bones of the Chancellorsville dead. For two days, Grant and Lee exchanged blows in that forlorn wood, their contest so close and savagely fought that the incessant blare of muskets ignited the underbrush. The battle exacted an enormous human toll, with each army losing a staggering seventeen percent of its men. But when Grant refused to retreat and attempted to swing around Lee's right flank instead, the northern press erupted in euphoric tones. "Bulletin after bulletin and extra after extra were eagerly read, and as every bit of news made the fact of Grant's victory clearer there were frequent cheers and more frequent congratulations," the *New York Herald* reported.[4]

The exultant headlines proved premature, however, as the Wilderness proved only the first bloody meeting in a long, grinding campaign—one in which soldiers exchanged the heroism of a peach orchard for the misery of a trench, the gleaming bayonet for the dirt-begrimed spade. The armies next battled at Spotsylvania Court House, a crossroads nine miles south of the Wilderness soon choked with miles of labyrinthine trenches. The slaughter at Spotsylvania slayed whatever sentimentalism remained, leaving it to putrefy alongside the bullet-riddled bodies lining the works. The northern public grew ever more impatient for victory ("our bleeding, bankrupt, almost dying country," Horace Greeley editorialized in the *New York Tribune*, "shudders at the prospect of fresh conscriptions, of further wholesale devastations, and of new rivers of human blood"). Still, many could sense that the war was marching to a promising new tempo. By June, with federal soldiers coiling breastworks around the rebels' crucial rail and supply hub of Petersburg, Virginia, even Grant's most exacting skeptics conceded that he had placed the armies on victory road.[5]

From a distance, the regiment looked on at these developments with an odd blend of satisfaction and regret. Earlier that spring, both armies began emptying their breastworks in Florida. Almost daily throughout April, transports packed with rebel soldiers embarked from Jacksonville, bound for Savannah and other points north. By early May, one federal commander estimated that more than nine thousand enemy soldiers had been withdrawn from the state. Federal army commanders responded in kind, extracting all but about three thousand men. The 107th Ohio would be among the few, unlucky outfits selected to stay. "Were it not for the consciousness that we are doing our duty at our assigned post," one of the volunteers confirmed, "we would certainly feel somewhat slighted for not having the privilege to share in the victories achieved by the larger armies."[6]

Yet clearly the men *did* feel slighted, and their sense of duty struggled to sustain them as the war in Florida faded into a "dismal series of forays," moonlit watches, and "false" alarms. "These boys are so fond of firing at *shadows*," one soldier explained, "that it keeps the officer of picket pretty nearly all the time running." Even so, it wasn't long before the men learned to ignore groaning limbs, creaking palms, and night winds howling through the reeds. In the barren swamps and stands of scrub pines, boredom became a rival as contemptible as any rebel—the source of renewed waywardness and misbehavior. Men began leaving their posts "without proper authority," prompting the provost marshal to impound all civilian boats. One summer evening, a superior officer asked Sergeant Henry Feldkamp for the time. "Any god dam dog can ask me that," he snapped in reply. "You are a humbugger, you have humbugged me long enough." A court-martial arraigned the riled soldier and reduced him to the rank of corporal.[7]

Detailed to the pioneer corps, Private John Foell registered his displeasure with "loud and boisterous" chatter in camp after quiet hours; the Cleveland cooper's "previous good conduct," however, resulted in a "lenient" fine. Notwithstanding a strident defense ("I *volunteered* to serve my Country in the times of her needs, and nothing has ever been more distant from my intentions than to neglect my duty"), the court was less forgiving in the case of Adam Regula, the Bavarian immigrant who returned from patrol one evening in a state of intoxication. "He talked very loud[ly] and made a great deal of disturbance," his sergeant recalled, "and after he was placed in the Guard House he vomited." The court not only reduced Regula to the ranks, but ordered him to forfeit eight dollars of his pay each month for the next four months.[8]

On at least one occasion, this mischief betrayed an ugly racism that thrived in the ranks—yet another reminder that even men who embraced emancipation as a war measure did so without abandoning old resentments. Private Michael Keichner was "making unnecessary noise" in camp one evening and defiantly refused repeated requests from the commander on guard—a white officer from the Third United States Colored Troops—that he return to his quarters. "You think more of a damned Nigger than you do of a white man," Keichner informed the dumbfounded first lieutenant, who "sent for the guard." Though the ensuing court-martial inquiry attributed the episode to drunkenness—comrades supplied ample testimony about the accused's good "character," even as they supposed that he "was under the influence of something stronger than water"—the utterance revealed the genuine resentment that some white soldiers felt for their new African-American comrades. While black men had labored as teamsters, cooks, and camp servants throughout the war, Florida would supply the Ohioans with an opportunity to fight alongside African-Americans for the first time.[9]

ON THE MORNING OF Wednesday, May 25, General Gordon roused the 107th Ohio with orders to reconnoiter the enemy's works. Spearheading a short column of white and black infantrymen led by Colonel James Shaw Jr., the thirty-three-year-old Rhode Islander who had recently assumed command of the Seventh United States Colored Troops, the men crossed Cedar Creek and felt their way through the thick timber toward Camp Finegan. Six guns trundled behind in support. At twilight, skirmishers exchanged "a brisk fire" with the enemy; unable to see, they aimed their muskets not at men, but at muzzle flashes. With the rebels ready to mount a counterattack, however, Shaw ordered his column to fall back to Jacksonville; he had "not men enough to spare any." As it was, the sortie through the swamps claimed the life of one Union soldier, blasted to death "by the premature explosion of a shell fired from one of our guns"; it was only some consolation that the affray was rumored to have been costlier for the rebels, whom one of the regiment's volunteers spied excavating fresh graves in the ensuing days.[10]

The "skirmish near Camp Finegan," as the events of the day came to be recorded in the war's official records, confirmed that the Confederates continued to export men and artillery from Florida. These tidings encouraged Gordon to attempt an ambush of the enemy's forces at Camp Milton, no more than a dozen miles west of Jacksonville, only six days later. Named for the archrebel who had occupied the governor's mansion in Tallahassee since October 1861, the bastion anchored a brawny system of log breastworks and revetments ("the labor of many thousands of men for many weeks") that twisted through the woods along the steep banks of McGirt's Creek.[11]

Gordon proposed a classic two-pronged assault. One column would press west and attack the Confederates head-on, while a second, slightly larger column would splash across McGirt's Creek, wing north, and gain the enemy's rear. The 107th Ohio was packed into the second column with remnants of the 157th New York and 17th Connecticut, two veteran Eleventh Corps outfits that had shared in the misfortunes of Chancellorsville and Gettysburg, and a pair of battle-tested African-American regiments, the 3rd and 35th United States Colored Troops, the latter led by the half-brother of Harriet Beecher Stowe. An arduous trudge through the "almost impassable swamps and sloughs" delivered the soldiers to a point behind the enemy's lines just after three o'clock on the morning of June 1. But the promise of a fight proved as empty as the enemy's works. By the time the blue-coated columns converged on Camp Milton, the rebels had slipped away, leaving plenty of "stores and forage" behind to evidence their sudden "flight."

Denied still another opportunity to prove their mettle in battle, the Ohioans obediently "fired and completely demolished" the rebel works before tromping back to their camp. In his after-action report, Gordon saluted their performance as "praiseworthy in the highest degree." Even so, decades later, regimental historian Jacob Smith was desperate to detect something of significance in this stretch of the unit's service. "Considering the number of men engaged in these movements," he concluded, "as much relatively was achieved by them as by the grander operations of large bodies of troops."[12]

TWO WEEKS LATER, orders arrived from headquarters that divided the companies of the 107th Ohio for the first time. Four companies would tarry in Jacksonville on provost guard and occupation duty—

mostly "town police work"—while four others, under the command of Major Vignos, would garrison Fort Clinch, the brick bastion on nearby Amelia Island whose seventy-seven batteries watched over Cumberland Sound. Until August, the remaining two companies would patrol the railroad bridge that spanned the Amelia River four miles south of the fort.[13]

At Fort Clinch, the men became prison guards and provost-marshals, commissaries and quartermasters. By the summer of 1864, the heavily armored fort had, like most other federal military installations in the Confederate South, become a destination for hundreds of freedom-seeking enslaved persons and starving refugees. The army acknowledged this steady movement of people across borders and boundaries—and their demands for shelter and subsistence—in the unusually exacting orders it prepared for Major Vignos upon the regiment's move to Fort Clinch. "You will see to it that refugees, contrabands, and all civilians whatsoever, asking subsistence from the Government, shall be forwarded to Jacksonville," Vignos was instructed. "You will furnish subsistence to them only for the time necessary to forward them to this point, except in cases of sickness or other cases of extreme necessity, of all which you will make immediate report to these headquarters."[14]

Throughout that long and drizzly summer, punctuated by company and heavy artillery drills, the demands of prison records and "tri-monthly" reports, the 107th Ohio ached for the latest news. Grumbling about the brutal delays between newspaper deliveries and mail calls, they subsisted mostly on rumor. "Rebel sourses" plied them with everything from premature accounts of Petersburg's fall to a spurious report that General Grant had been blown to bits by a torpedo. A deficit of reliable information was nothing new, of course, but in Florida it offered the men another, gnawing reminder of their remove from the war's primary front. The Fourth of July supplied still another, inviting the veterans of Gettysburg to measure how much had changed in the space of a year. As gunboats on the St. John's heralded the nation's eighty-eighth birthday with a cannon-fired salute, one soldier reflected that the year before, it was all that "we could do to keep from having our heads knocked off." Now, he marveled, "we have to be careful or we get our head eat[en] off by mosquitoes."[15]

Those ravenous pests carried the maladies that delivered scores of men to the United States General Hospital in St. Augustine, headquartered in an old ship captain's sprawling mansion at the edge of town. Late that summer, Jacob Smith was detailed to the hospital as a clerk, tasked with the huge chore of "keeping the books" and completing morning reports documenting the care and condition of soldiers taken with swamp fever, malaria, and exhaustion. Florida's oppressive climate thwarted speedy recoveries. "When a person gets down a little," one convalescing soldier explained, "it is almost impossible to get strength again."[16]

THAT FALL, with a token enemy doing but little to distract them, the men of the 107th Ohio turned their attention to Lincoln's bid for a second term. In August the Democrats gathered in Chicago to nominate General George B. McClellan for the presidency, selecting as his running mate George Hunt Pendleton, the Copperhead congressman from Cincinnati. The Democratic platform pledged "unswerving fidelity to the Union under the Constitution," reproving the Lincoln administration's "shameful" disregard of civil and military law. But it also pronounced the "experiment of war" a failure, and demanded that "immediate efforts be made for a cessation of hostilities." The platform recommended that a "convention of the states" might restore peace "on the basis of the Federal Union," but it was short on specifics—and evaded the question of emancipation. One final plank expressed the "sympathy of the Democratic party" for the "soldiery of our army and the sailors of our navy," promising them all the "care, protection, and regard" they had earned.[17]

Well into autumn, the race was tight—so tight, in fact, that nearby rebel pickets took to taunting the troops with "white rags" and cheers for McClellan, confident that recognition of Confederate independence was imminent. Back home, the antiwar factions once again stirred, reenergized by the lengthening casualty registers, dismal reports from the field, and the intuition that the war was eroding the national character. "We don't want a cold-blooded joker at Washington who, while the District of Columbia is infested with hospitals, and the atmosphere burdened by the groans and sighs of our mangled countrymen, when he can spare a minute from Joe Miller's Jest Book looks out upon the acres of hospitals and inquires 'What houses are those?'" snapped William Allen, who had represented Ohio in the United States Senate during the 1840s. Young men registered their opposition to the war by resisting Lincoln's July call for conscripts; a throng assembled in Canton for a "peace meeting" the next month. "As the ox knoweth his owner, and the ass his master's crib," one War Democrat scorned, "so do these mild and gentle souls yearn for their rightful proprietors, the rebels, to retake possession of, and to rule over them."[18]

The view from the ranks reflected the rancor back home. William Siffert delighted that Company A was "in for old Abraham to the hilt," adding that he and his comrades refused to offer the rebels "any other terms than" an unconditional surrender. Jacob Smith, too, hoped that Lincoln would "remain at the helm"; he believed that after steadying the ship of state through the perilous waters of war, the president deserved to pilot the nation into the peace. "There should be prompt and immediate action on the part of every true patriot at this stage of our national peril," one of the Stark County volunteers echoed in advocating the president's reelection. "*No Compromise. No measures of adjustment* with traitors in arms, but total submission to the Constitution and Laws of the United States." But these were hardly universal sentiments among the men, many of whom rejected national parties and politics—and the notion that the election was a contest between loyalty and lily-livered treason. By the fall, wearied of the war and its many slights, the men resolved to cast their votes "for the candidate they believed would end the war." Already derided as fainthearted and cowardly, after all, the men had no reason to fear that their votes for McClellan might out them as disloyal.[19]

On election eve, with his typical "earnest zeal and tenacity of purpose," Edward Meyer stumped for the president. Private Justus Silliman of the 17th Connecticut listened intently to Meyer's speech and
gave it good marks; still, he had little confidence it would persuade
the 107th Ohio's demoralized ranks. "It is strange," Silliman pondered, "that men who have endured so many hardships and periled
so much for their country should be so blind & ignorant as to try
to support that which is working to destroy all the good they have
ever accomplished." The regimental returns confirmed the Nutmeg-
ger's prediction. Of the three hundred men who voted, 188 marked
their ballots for McClellan. The results were unmistakable; more
than sixty percent of the regiment had rejected the war and President Lincoln.

Back home, the Copperheads made "considerable ado" about the
107th Ohio—the only Buckeye regiment to deliver a majority for the
Democrats and George B. McClellan. For the war's opponents, however, it proved little consolation. Buoyed by a string of Union victories
in the Shenandoah Valley and the fall of Atlanta, loyal northern voters
returned Lincoln to the Executive Mansion by a comfortable margin.
Despite many pockets of support in the Midwest, McClellan carried
just three states—his adopted home state of New Jersey and the slave-
holding border states of Delaware and Kentucky. In Ohio, the election
would not be close; Lincoln carried the Buckeye State by nearly thirteen percentage points, while Republican congressional candidates
notched victories in all but two of Ohio's nineteen districts. "It took
some nerve at that time to be a Democrat," one Union veteran concluded years later.[20]

Lincoln's triumph at the polls and the progress of the Union armies
and navies that fall invited despair in many quarters of the Confederacy. Before long, however, that resignation gave way to a newfound
resolve. In November, Jefferson Davis informed the rebel legislature in
Richmond that "no military success of the enemy" could destroy the
Confederacy. "There are no vital points on the preservation of which
the continued existence of the Confederacy depends," he daringly

asserted, pledging that the rebel armies would not capitulate even if Richmond, Wilmington, Savannah, Charleston, and Mobile—as seemed increasingly likely—fell into the enemy's hands. The "exhaustive drain of blood and treasure" would persist until southerners were secure in the recognition of their "indefeasible rights." Fittingly, the war's deadliest year drew to a close with the promise of even more killing.[21]

IT WAS William Tecumseh Sherman who first tested Davis's sincerity. Having captured Atlanta, Grant's red-haired, square-jawed lieutenant stepped off on his "March to the Sea" in mid-November, his armies spiritedly tramping to the evocative strains of "John Brown's Body." Sherman drove toward the Georgia coast virtually unopposed— pulling up bridges, twisting railroad tracks, torching foundries, and otherwise "living off the land" in country the war had scarcely visited. "Our men," one Illinois soldier marveled, "are foraging on the country with the greatest liberality."

Before setting out on the march, Sherman solicited a body of Union troops to slice the Charleston and Savannah Railroad. Severing those tracks would prevent the rebels from shuttling any reinforcements into the defensive works ringing Savannah. In late November, a fleet of steamers cut through "heavy fog" to transport five thousand blue-coated men from Hilton Head, Morris, and Folly Islands to Boyd's Neck, South Carolina. But once on land, the limited visibility prevented "Coastal Division" from exploiting their superior numbers; on the morning of November 30, the men blundered into a clumsy but fierce battle at Honey Hill, where the Confederates—mostly Georgia infantrymen—had filed hastily into a maze of old breastworks and wheeled several pieces of artillery into position. Fortified, the rebels staggered several determined enemy assaults. Union troops limped away from a battlefield littered with bodies, many "horribly mutilated by shells."[22]

Though the victorious rebels expected that the enemy would renew their efforts the next day, those attacks never came; instead, both armies simply spied on one another, swinging their spades and preparing new miles of works. In response to the steady buildup of enemy troops after Honey Hill—and with Sherman inching closer to Savannah—Army chief of staff Henry Halleck moved to reinforce the coastal division. On December 8, packed aboard the side-wheel steam gunboat USS *Sonoma*, the 107th Ohio finally bade farewell to Jacksonville. They would make this journey under the watchful eye of a new colonel. Nine long months after Colonel Meyer's departure, John Snider Cooper, a twenty-three-year-old native of Mount Gilead, Ohio, who had battled in the Shenandoah Valley, extended pontoon bridges across the Rappahannock before Fredericksburg, and more recently led a regiment of United States Colored Troops, assumed permanent leadership of the regiment. His reception was more than likely an icy one, given that none of the men made even the slightest mention of it.[23]

DROPPING ANCHOR at Gregorie's Point, the men ferried out to Deveaux's Neck, a slender, swampy, and thickly wooded peninsula that extends between the Tulifinny and Coosawatchie Rivers. The object of their expedition—the Charleston & Savannah Railroad—stretched nearby, still in possession of the rebels. For the next few weeks, the Ohioans laced Deveaux's Neck with earthworks, an errand made all the more disagreeable by the raw, bone-chilling winds that whipped across the island. Several companies mounded the loamy earth into a delicate perch for the guns of the Third New York Light Artillery.[24]

The weeks they passed in the knots of timber on Deveaux's Neck were among the most demanding the men would endure during the war and required renewed vigilance. "We expected an attack in force at any moment," one soldier recalled, "night or day." The rebels launched one of those attacks on the afternoon of December 26. "Our artillery had been firing up to the noon hour, but the enemy did not return the fire," Alfred Garner recalled. "Shortly after noon they let us have it." The "first shell" screamed into the regiment's camp with deadly accuracy, decapitating Joseph Stadelbauer. With his twin brother

Edward, the twenty-year-old Austrian-born immigrant had enlisted in Tiffin in the late summer of 1862. Stadelbauer's war had unfolded as a sequence of misfortunes. Not long after arriving in Washington, D.C., in November 1862, he took ill and was packed off to the U.S. Army General Hospital in Philadelphia. Making only a partial recovery, he returned to the front in time to freeze at Brooke's Station, fight at Chancellorsville, and brawl at Gettysburg, where he was bagged as a rebel prisoner on the battle's first day. Stadelbauer passed the next three months as a prisoner of war. Shortly after his exchange, his brother, who had likely contracted disease while detailed to the corps hospital in Gettysburg, was transferred to the Invalid Corps. Joseph passed the last, lonely year of his service as the company cook, addled with aches and tormented by painful memories of captivity. He was serving coffee to a comrade when the shell severed his head. Clots of brain matter and blood sprayed the men standing on either side of him.[25]

The rebels enjoyed an "enviable" range—within five hundred yards—and it was perhaps nothing short of miraculous that their steady torrent of shells produced just three casualties in the 107th Ohio that afternoon. The "sandy and soft" soil that had furnished such a poor platform for their own batteries, one veteran supposed, probably spared many men. While plenty of enemy missiles arced into and behind their lines, one soldier estimated that "not more than" half of them exploded upon striking the sand. The unremitting fire kept the Ohioans shivering in their rifle pits for several more weeks; still, with uncharacteristic confidence, they believed that it was only a matter of time before Sherman captured Savannah and Charleston. Deserters who surrendered to the enemy "almost every night," provided an index of enemy morale. "Both cities must fall ere long," Peter Young forecasted, "and this rebellion will soon be a thing of the past."[26]

The news about Savannah was not long in coming. The men awoke to the strident notes of a bugler one evening, after which they received orders to "fall in without arms" and snap to attention. Edward Meyer relieved their suspense by announcing that Fort McAllister had yielded to Sherman's men. With the fall of the stubborn Confederate garrison, the road to Savannah was open. Men in the ranks released lusty cheers, while the 127th New York took up the sprightly measures of "Yankee Doodle." Then, John Brunny and his fellow regimental band members joined in, finishing the cheering anthem their fifes had refused to whistle since that fateful afternoon along the Orange Turnpike at Chancellorsville. Within days, the rebels would abandon the Charleston & Savannah Railroad, leaving the Ohioans to inspect the damage they had wrought on the rails.[27]

In late December, Sherman and his men settled into Savannah—the general took as his headquarters a handsome, Gothic Revival mansion trimmed in black walnut—though they had no plans to linger. The troops struck north from Savannah in January, determined that the Palmetto State would at last know something of the war it began four years earlier. Brushing aside a token rebel force at the Salkehatchie River, Sherman's columns, marching at breakneck pace, converged on Columbia, the state's capital, in mid-February. On February 17, vengeful soldiers and stalwart winds fanned burning cotton bales into a hideous blaze that engulfed nearly a third of the city, adding Columbia to the lengthy inventory of destruction Sherman's armies visited on South Carolina. The next day, as embers crackled and columns of smoke choked Columbia, the city of Charleston finally surrendered—bringing the war's longest siege to an anticlimactic end.[28]

As it turned out, Charleston was the regiment's next destination. Wading "detestable swamps," flooded rice fields, and no fewer than nine rivers, the men struck for the coast, hastily hollowing out rifle pits as they felt their way toward the city. At Combahee Ferry they constructed a new bridge across the river, harvesting the lumber from abandoned slave dwellings nearby. Beyond the river, their route carried them over the old Monck's Corner battlefield, where Sir Henry Clinton's strapping British army scored a decisive victory over the besieged patriots in the spring of 1780.

Sherman's columns, meanwhile, drove toward Goldsboro and the North Carolina line. Though few enemy soldiers stood in the way—

after the loss of Columbia and Charleston, the rebels concentrated their strength in North Carolina—plenty of obstacles hindered their progress. Swollen streams, creeks, and rivers impeded the march, as did treacherous roads that required corduroying and bridges that demanded replanking. Even so, in a reprise of their performance in Georgia, Sherman's troops laid waste to "railroad tracks, stockpiles of ammunition, factories, mills, cotton" and to "an incalculable number of private homes, barns, and stores."[29]

To be sure, as Sherman's armies inched closer to their rendezvous with rebels in North Carolina, the general had little to chagrin him; his men had made short order of the enemy's supplies and knotted the rails between Columbia and Kingsville into "Sherman neckties." But there remained a "vast amount of rolling-stock" on the rails between Sumterville and Florence. In early March, two brigades of rebel cavalry and a small collection of infantry had turned back an understaffed federal expedition to Florence; the blue-coated column, dispatched by Oliver Otis Howard, "had not been sufficiently vigorous in its reconnaissance." On March 15, then, as his men continued their drive toward Goldsboro, Sherman scribbled a dispatch to General Gillmore. Deeming the destruction of those trains to be "all important," the general directed Gillmore to ready twenty-five hundred men from the forces garrisoning Savannah and Charleston for an expedition into the heart of South Carolina. "I want it done at once," he demanded, recommending that the men unsling their knapsacks and live off the land. "All real good soldiers must now be marching . . . keep them going all the time, even if for no other purpose than to exhaust the enemy's country."[30]

IT WAS forty-one-year-old Brigadier General Edward Elmer Potter who was selected to spearhead the expedition. Along with nearly three hundred thousand Americans, the New York City native and Columbia College graduate had rushed to California in 1849 to pan for riches in the South Fork American River. Although commissioned as a captain in the Union army early in the war, Potter's only real command experience had been threading a brigade into the battle at Honey Hill the previous November. His orderly charge that day, however, stood out among the other jumbled federal attacks; in March, he earned a brevet promotion that saluted his "bravery, discretion, and energy."

Potter did not tarry in assembling his force: two columns of infantry, a regiment of engineers, and the troopers of the 4th Massachusetts Cavalry. The six twelve-pounder Napoleons of Battery B, 3rd New York Artillery, would trundle behind. In late March, after steaming up the coast and navigating the shoals of the exquisite Winyah Bay— a journey of "ten or twelve hours"—ships conveyed the soldiers to Georgetown, one of South Carolina's oldest cities. Once the throne of the rice kingdom and a host to presidents, Georgetown's shabby streets and "decayed wharves" now told the story of the long-grained crop's collapse. Only the handsome headquarters of the Winyah Indigo Society, established in 1740 to debate "agricultural questions" and "discuss the latest news from London" each month, endured as a reminder of the social, cultural, and political capital once concentrated in cypress-shaded Georgetown.[31]

On April 2, General Gillmore reviewed the troops in "a large ploughed field." With the 25th Ohio and a pair of New York infantry regiments, the 107th Ohio packed into the first column, commanded by cerebral, forty-one-year-old Colonel Philip Perry Brown Jr. The second column, led by the handsomely mustached Colonel Edward Needles Hallowell, was composed exclusively of African-American soldiers: the 32nd United States Colored Troops, five companies of the 102nd United States Colored Troops, and Hallowell's own 54th Massachusetts Volunteers, the celebrated unit that had stormed Battery Wagner.[32]

Three mornings later the columns struck west, trudging through the marshy and meagre soil drained by the Black River. The march twisted through dense, "heavily timbered country," which Samuel Wildman of the 25th Ohio likened to the "chaparral of Mexico." Knots of vines laced through the "gloomy, frowning" pines as if to scorn and mock their efforts; still, Potter's men logged nineteen miles on the expedi-

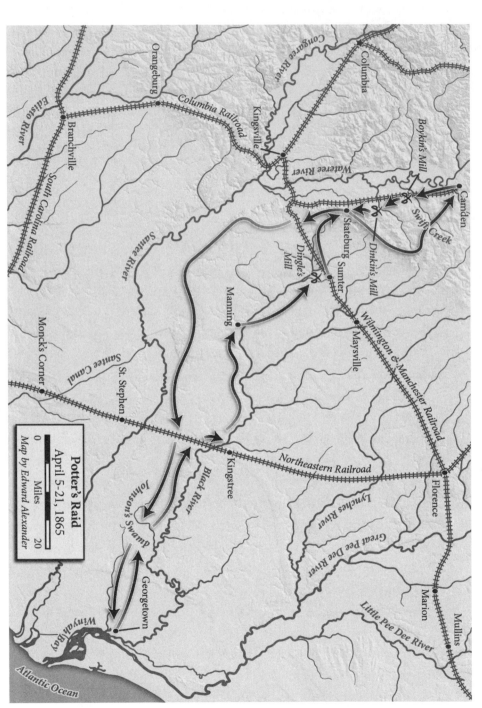

General Edward Potter's Raid, April 1865.

tion's first day, bivouacking for the night near Johnson's Swamp. Just after dawn, with Hallowell's column taking the lead, they resumed the march. It was a "close, warm day," and more than a few wearied men, their stomachs empty and feet blistered, fell out of the ranks. There was "little," one soldier carped, to "relieve the dull monotony of the march." All rejoiced, however, when foraging parties delivered their bounty of ham, bacon, and sweet potatoes to camp that evening. "The colored troops foraged nobly," one New York soldier applauded.[33]

AS THEY PRESSED into the interior of South Carolina, the men entered country that had scarcely been touched by the war. "Improvements could be observed," one soldier noted, "in private residences, outhouses and fences." The irony that the first state to pull itself out of the Union had known virtually nothing of the conflict was not lost on them, prompting many to indulge their darker side. The troops not only torched every gin mill and cotton bale in their path, but likewise resorted to pillage and "plunder" on a scale that Colonel Cooper deemed "absolutely sickening." With wry understatement, one soldier boasted the men were "living upon the fat of the land." Understandably, anxiety and dread consumed local civilians, who hastily stowed heirlooms and valuables in cellars and garrets. "We live in a whirl of excitement," acknowledged one young woman from nearby Camden, "and all things are unsettled and uncertain."[34]

Sated by their liberal foraging, the men broke camp at six thirty on the morning of April 8. A determined march of twenty miles delivered them to Manning, a handsome, well-manicured village of several hundred, by dusk. The route was onerous—requiring men to splash across muddy fords and wade through mucky, snake-choked swamps—but that hardly deterred the region's enslaved peoples from voting with their feet and joining the blue-coated columns. Hundreds of men and women and many young children, some cradled in their mothers' arms, seized this moment to flee their bondage. From the earliest days of the war, when enslaved persons wound their way to Benjamin Butler's lines at Fortress Monroe, geographic proximity to a Union army had opened windows of opportunity for freedom-seeking slaves. Now, after a long and impatient wait, the war had finally arrived in the South Carolina interior. "Such a sight for an artist it is to see these poor people just liberated," one enlisted man exclaimed, "going on happy, under such burdens as they bear, keeping up with veterans Soldiers in the long wearisome marching." Still, even as this soldier marveled at the social revolution unleashed by the war, he could not silence his doubts. "What is to become of this Race of uneducated, hopeful, anxious people?" he asked. His was a question that many more of his countrymen would pose in the months and years ahead.[35]

IF GENERAL POTTER's columns hoped for a warm welcome in Manning that evening, they were bound to be disappointed. As the men pressed into the city along a "fine, wide street," they learned that a stray round had picked off a soldier from the 4th Massachusetts Cavalry. "Deliberate murder," one soldier seethed. Until this point, the men had scarcely seen a rebel soldier. Hallowell's column easily punched through a thin Confederate cavalry screen on the way to Manning, but otherwise failed to encounter any serious opposition from the enemy.

That was about to change. A few miles up the road in Sumter, the Confederates were collecting frenziedly whatever men they could find to turn back the raiders. Among them was William Garland, a South Carolina infantryman who was recovering from the loss of his hand in a battle near Richmond the previous year. Rallying behind Lieutenant William Alexander McQueen, whose artillery pieces had rolled into action during Pickett's Charge, Garland and his fellow patients at the Confederate hospital in Sumter formed gun crews to man a pair of "brass howitzers." The convalescing soldiers joined a motley troop, which included Colonel George Washington Lee's 20th South Carolina Militia and the men of Colonel John W. Caldwell's 9th Kentucky Mounted Regiment. Mustered in at Bowling Green, Kentucky, that first autumn of the war, Caldwell's men had seen some hard service. They fought at Shiloh, defended Vicksburg, and were bloodied at Stone's River before mounting up to contest Sherman's March to the

Sea. In March 1865 they occupied Augusta, supposing—mistakenly, as it turned out—that its manufacturing houses and gunpowder works would make a tempting target for the Yankees. From Augusta, the Kentuckians set out for Sumter, ordered to defend the "rolling stock" the federals had set out to destroy.[36]

As the rebels prepared to make their stand before Sumter, Potter's men fanned through the streets of Manning. The 25th Ohio, along with a few mischievous boys from the 107th Ohio, seized the offices of W. J. N. Hammet's *Clarendon Banner*, the rebel rag which earlier in the week "recommended the assassination of General Potter." Perhaps moved by the sights of that day's march, they went to work on a "special edition" of the paper for the next morning, April 9, 1865. Throughout the night, they typeset original editorials in columns capped by a new masthead: *The Clarendon Banner—Of Freedom*. "We understand that our General does not intend to burn the town," the quick-witted soldiers wrote, "but if we have our way, this office shall no more poison the political atmosphere of the country with its foul odors."[37]

WHEN THE TROOPS broke camp and set out on the road to Sumter in the morning, a light drizzle dampening their march, they had no way to know that three hundred miles to the north, John Brown Gordon had just nodded forward the last charge of the Army of Northern Virginia. Just one week before, on April 2, Grant's troops broke through the threadbare Confederate works coiled around Petersburg, Virginia—prompting the rebels to evacuate both the supply hub and the city of Richmond. Hungry and bedraggled, Lee's men scurried west into the leafy tobacco fields drained by the Appomattox River, hoping to resupply before banking south to link hands with Joseph E. Johnston's Army of Tennessee in North Carolina. With Grant and Sheridan in pounding pursuit, one of the most intense weeks of the war in Virginia ensued. At Saylor's Creek, in a merciless rain on April 6, Lee lost a quarter of his army; defiant until the end, however, he rejected an initial invitation from Grant to discuss terms of surrender. Clinging to the faint hope that Gordon's men might punch through the federal cavalrymen straddling the Richmond-Lynchburg Stage Road just west of the village of Appomattox Court House, on this Palm Sunday morning, Lee held his breath.[38]

No more than three miles from Sumter, General Potter discovered that there were rebels ensconced in some fresh breastworks behind the cypress-shaded Turkey Creek. What was more, he learned that the enemy had pried up much of the wooden planking on the bridge that spanned the stream. Unable to dislodge some of the "stronger pieces" wedged in the banks, Sumter's defenders decided to set them ablaze. Still not satisfied, the rebels then torched the nearby millhouse, lest the federals seize it for a sharpshooter's nest. While these developments persuaded Potter that the enemy was in full retreat, his regimental commanders were more circumspect. As the 107th Ohio felt its way toward the creek, Colonel Cooper called for several soldiers to tear across the smoldering bridge and scout the enemy's position. Much to his surprise, Cooper found three eager volunteers in Henry Finkenbiner, Jacob Brobst, and Jacob James. None of these enlisted men had done very much to distinguish themselves as soldiers to this point in the war, though the thirty-two-year-old Finkenbiner, a blacksmith with a shock of reddish hair, had suffered a wound at Gettysburg.[39]

Without delay, as Sumter's church bells announced the three o'clock service, the trio crept across the burning bridge. When they reached the opposite bank, the rebels saluted them with a crackle of muskets. To make matters worse, the Ohioans were also "within the direct range and close fire" of the artillery pieces that Garland and his comrades had parked atop a "little knoll." Finkenbiner and his comrades managed to squeeze off a round of their own before another enemy volley erupted from the "dense thickets" choking the banks of the creek. The men dashed for the bridge, hoping to withdraw, but at least one Confederate round was accurate. Brobst crumpled to the ground, seriously wounded.

"Don't for God's sake let the rebels get me," he wailed. "Don't for God's sake let the rebels get me!"

Ducking and dodging shot and shell, Finkenbiner and James

turned back to retrieve their injured comrade. "We picked Brobst up and placed him on my rifle between us," the blacksmith recalled, "thus carrying him in safety over the burning bridge to an ambulance corps in the woods." At enormous personal risk to their own safety, Finkenbiner, Brobst, and James had established the enemy's position at Dingle's Mill. General Potter would have to give battle after all.[40]

THE FRUSTRATED GENERAL determined to flank the rebels. While the 107th Ohio shook out into a skirmish line and laid down a "covering fire" along the creek, Hallowell's column would coil down an old "plantation road" and gain the enemy's left. For their part, the

Henry Finkenbiner was awarded the Medal of Honor for his daring actions at Dingle's Mill on April 9, 1865. *Walter F. Beyer and Oscar F. Keydel,* Deeds of Valor: How America's Heroes Won the Medal of Honor *(Detroit: The Perrien Keydel Company, 1901), 495*

56th New York and 157th New York would loop to the left and trudge through a "waist deep" swamp, negotiating "broken timber, tangled vines, and drooping limbs" in an effort to turn the enemy's right.[41]

Hallowell's men set out on their march, but reversed course after their guide became disoriented in the impossible thickets. Piloted through the woods by a local African-American scout, however, the New Yorkers had better luck. Scaling a post-and-rail fence, they formed into a line of battle and prepared to make an attempt on the enemy's flank. From his commanding perch behind one of the Confederate howitzers, William Garland spied the New Yorkers readying their assault. "I happened to look down the swamp to our right and rear," he recalled, "and saw the Yankees jumping over the fence into the field a little over a quarter of a mile from us." By the time Garland and his frazzled gunners turned to meet the flanking column, it was already too late. The New Yorkers hoisted their muskets and squeezed out a devastating volley, killing one of the rebels' artillery commanders. For a time, the air "whistled" with "lively" shot and deadly canister. "Boys . . . take that battery!" the colonel of the 157th New York bellowed. Another federal shell severed the right shoulder of Lieutenant McQueen, killing the rebel officer instantly—no more than three miles from the place of his youth. "We were now flanked, vastly outnumbered, and both of our officers were killed," Garland sighed. "It was useless for us to attempt to continue the fight."

As the rebels scampered toward the rear "in great confusion," the New Yorkers seized one of their battle flags and hauled off both of their artillery pieces. At the cost of twenty-six men, the federals had brushed aside the first "opposition of consequence" on their raid into the South Carolina interior. "Had our Brigade been sent to the Rebel left earlier so as to have got on their flank," one soldier in the 54th Massachusetts contended, "we would have bagged them all." Confederate losses in the engagement were much larger, their killed and wounded left to litter the field where they fell. Before nightfall, they would be buried in hastily made graves. What was more, the 107th Ohio had turned in a most creditable performance, and at the cost of just one man—Brobst—wounded. But as luck would have it, their heroic deeds at Dingle's Mill would be immediately eclipsed by the news out of Virginia. John Brown Gordon's men had fought to a "frazzle," but could not cut through that Union cavalry screen at Appomattox. At the very moment the Ohioans laid down their covering fire, Robert E. Lee accepted his fate and waited for Ulysses S. Grant to meet him in Wilmer McLean's front parlor.[42]

AT DUSK, THE MEN strutted into Sumter, belting out the verses of "Rally 'Round the Flag" and "John Brown's Body." They would occupy the handsome town for the next two days, emptying its tobacco sheds and stores. Not to be outdone, the printers who issued the *Clarendon Banner—Of Freedom* gleefully went to work on a "loyal edition" of the *Sumter Watchman*. They had a ready-made headline when the news finally reached Sumter that Richmond and Petersburg had fallen into federal hands (the news about Lee's surrender would not arrive for a few more days). That evening, "wild with gladness," the men fired a thirteen-gun salute from one of the howitzers they had captured at Dingle's Mill.[43]

Notwithstanding the "hardships and sufferings" they had endured in the swamps of South Carolina, it was "the prospect of soon encountering the last of the armed foe," Jacob Smith later observed, that "cheered" the men in the spring of 1865. They sensed that the rebellion was at long last drawing to a close. Plantation slavery, for one, was unraveling before their eyes; with each mile, the number of refugees from slavery tramping behind them swelled. On April 16, one officer estimated that "as many as 3,000" men, women, and children of all "conditions" struggled to keep pace with Potter's winded columns. He gaped in awe at the "crippled men and women, little boys and girls just able to toddle, [and] women in the very agonies of child birth all moving along." The 107th Ohio could also measure progress in the miles of railroad track and trestle work they had twisted—and in the number of locomotive and train cars they had destroyed.[44]

Onward they marched into "one of the fairest portions of South Carolina," the roads now canopied by the interlocking limbs of sturdy live oaks. "There were Cotton Gins & Presses, horses, wagons & etc. at every house," one soldier marveled. "The women and children all sit on the Piazzas as we pass." Through this country, the columns encountered only a token opposition; as one lieutenant remarked, "not an able-bodied man was seen." Fixing their bayonets, the men rushed into line and charged some skirmishers entrenched near Statesburg on the evening of April 15. In a slashing rain after dark, the 107th Ohio drove in the enemy's right flank. Two days later, the men pressed into Camden, where Cornwallis notched an important victory during the Revolution. But the men would tarry just long enough to visit the marble obelisk marking the resting place of Baron de Kalb (Colonel Cooper recorded its elegant inscription in his diary). Learning that the rolling stock they had expected to find there had been whisked eight miles south to Boykin's Mill, they obediently reversed course and, before dawn, set out on the road to Statesburg.[45]

The enemy waited for them at Boykin's, ensconced in the rifle pits they planted along the commanding ridge overlooking Swift Creek. Their "strong force" was supported by two artillery pieces. Leaving nothing to chance, the rebels yanked up the bridge that spanned the creek and broke the mill dam, "flooding the road." As a result, Potter's men would be forced to wade through impossible ponds and breast-high swamps, practically moored in place under a spirited and well-trained fire.[46]

Linking hands with the 54th Massachusetts, the 107th Ohio attempted unsuccessfully to turn the enemy's right flank, but soon came to the support of the 25th Ohio which, in a stroke of remarkable fortune, discovered some "trestle work" that reached across the creek. After a fight that one veteran of the 54th Massachusetts deemed a "plucky affair," the outnumbered rebels yielded their position. Potter's men nipped at their heels, exchanging a few volleys with the enemy near Dinkin's Mill on April 19. Meanwhile, following the course of the railroad, the 107th Ohio wreaked havoc on every "bridge, culvert, box car, and steam locomotive" they could find. "Completely routed," the rebels sent up a flag of truce, conceding that further resistance was futile.

Early the next morning, Potter's men turned down the Santee River

Road and started on the march to Georgetown, their work finally finished. In the space of only seventeen days, they had razed one hundred
cotton gins, torched five thousand bales of cotton, collected more than
five thousand contrabands, wrecked thirty-two locomotives, captured
sixty-five prisoners, and destroyed nearly all of the railroad infrastruc-
ture between Sumter and Camden. For its part, the 107th Ohio had
met the enemy no fewer than four times and marched more than five
hundred miles. Unlike nearly every other episode of its service, the
regiment looked back on its participation in Potter's expedition self-
assuredly. If they felt any remorse for the ruin they exacted on South
Carolina, it was just as quickly quelled. "Circumstances uncontrolla-
ble," one of its enlisted men concluded years later, "had made it necessary to bring this last visitation on the state, guilty beyond all others,
of the sin of rebellion."[47]

ONLY A FEW HOURS into the march, halted on the grounds of a
stately old Greek Revival plantation, the troops learned that Generals Sherman and Johnston had agreed to a truce in North Carolina.
"Cheer on cheer went up from the troops," one soldier remembered.
"The joy that filled our hearts was supreme." Inspired by the report, a
sprightly gait delivered the men to Georgetown—one hundred miles
away—just four nights later.

For two weeks, the men caught their breath in Georgetown, inven-
torying their supplies, ordnance, and equipment amid the blizzard of
bulletins and dispatches attending the end of the war. But not all of
the news was heartening. At ten o'clock on the morning of May 4,
the regiment snapped to attention. Standing before them, clutching a
War Department circular trimmed with a thick, black border, Colonel Cooper started to read. "The distressing duty has devolved upon
the Secretary of War," he began, "to announce to the Armies of the
United States that at twenty-two minutes after seven o'clock, on the
morning of Saturday, the fifteenth day of April, 1865, Abraham Lincoln, President of the United States, died of a mortal wound inflicted
upon him by an assassin." The "soul that had taken all the people

into its care," Alfred Rider reflected, "had gone to its reward." The shocking news was sufficient to suspend all activities for the balance of the day. Even in a regiment that had voted for George McClellan, "strong men," as Jacob Smith recalled, "were bowed in grief." Some even thirsted for revenge; as was the case elsewhere throughout the South, Union officers moved to prevent enraged enlisted men from visiting violence on innocent rebel civilians. Their ardor cooled, however, the next afternoon, when a steamer from Charleston arrived with the report that John Wilkes Booth—one of the men pronounced the president's assassin a "deep dyed and consummate villain"—had been killed after a twelve-day manhunt.⁴⁸

The Holy City, as it turned out, would be the regiment's next destination. In early May, the men climbed aboard the steamer *Island City* for the short but turbulent voyage down the Carolina coast to the birthplace of secession. After the vessel dropped anchor, the 107th Ohio walked the streets of the "once proud" city, now reduced to ruins and heaps of rubble. "The splendid houses were all deserted, the glass in the windows broken, the walls dilapidated, the columns toppled over," one observer gaped. "Desolation and ruin sit monarchs of the place," he remarked. Men inventoried the "ploughed" pavements and "shivered" cornices, the "ghastly holes" in roofs and walls, the "fragments of brick and stone"—all damage visited upon Charleston by Gillmore's shells. The city's rough cobblestone streets, once alive with haughty secessionists, now teemed with newly freed slaves. The slave pens and markets were closed, no more to traffic in human flesh, but the Stars and Stripes once more fluttered over Fort Sumter. For his part, Jacob Smith took in the monument raised in honor of John C. Calhoun, the godfather of secession. "The marble bust of the senator upon the top of the shaft was without a head," he wrote with satisfaction, "that part of it having been shot off by the first shell fired into the city by our forces stationed upon Folly Island."⁴⁹

The troops filed into the entrenchments ringing Charleston, now under the command of Colonel Hallowell. The day must have seemed interminably long to the troops standing sentinel over the lifeless city. Nor did the blistering sun ("It is insupportably hot," one soldier groused) contribute much to their immediate comfort. Impatient for discharge papers, the troops grew anxious—especially once telegraphs began clicking feverishly with the news that Sherman's armies had started toward the nation's capital to strut down Pennsylvania Avenue behind the Army of the Potomac in a final, military review. Not unlike other "off duty officers," Surgeon Knaus remedied his boredom one evening by procuring a pass to enter the city. He rode directly to General Gillmore's headquarters for a night of heavy drinking.

One by one, Union regiments received orders to withdraw from the Charleston defenses. In late May, the 107th Ohio pitched a new camp in "a small rice swamp" near Magnolia Cemetery, the sprawling, oak-shaded maze of marble and granite on the banks of the Cooper River. But here they grew even more restive. "Local farmers" registered

Charleston, South Carolina, the cradle of secession, had been reduced to shell-pocked columns and heaps of rubble by the time the 107th Ohio strutted into the city in the spring of 1865. *Library of Congress*

"numerous complaints" about crops trampled and property damaged by wayward troops. In early June, twenty-one-year-old John Conrady confessed to desecrating a grave in Magnolia. He was ordered to march "along the line of the regiment at dress parade," displaying "a placard on his back naming his crime." Though the troops were "clean and well supplied," many refused to polish their muskets, maintain company records, or tend to the demands of drill. An inspector from army headquarters regarded discipline as "fair" or "middling" in eight of the regiment's ten companies.[50]

For weeks, locomotives and paddle-wheel steamers crowded with demobilized soldiers had been lurching north. From Washington, D.C., Quartermaster General Montgomery Meigs had expertly choreographed the disbanding of the armies—some eight hundred thousand men had returned to their homes by June—but from the perspective of men on the ground, demobilization made little sense. "We don't know anything of going home," an impatient Peter Zurbrugg grumbled in a letter to his father. Colonel Cooper implored headquarters to discharge his men, only to learn that they were being moored in place for want of blank muster rolls. "We are at a dead stand still in regard to them," he lamented in mid-June.

The maddening delay meant that the men would spend the Fourth of July in Charleston, parading through its streets as the harbor "resounded" with the tributes "fired from Sumter, Moultrie, Bee, Wagner, and Gregg." But these "national salutes," together with public readings of the Declaration of Independence and Emancipation Proclamation, contrasted sharply with the "perfectly outrageous" sentiments expressed by the locals. "Were I in command, I should put a bridle in the mouths of some of these men," the colonel confided to his diary, forecasting further turmoil once "the Yankees" abandoned the peninsula. Before long, Cooper's somber prophecy became a reality.[51]

Six days after celebrating the nation's birthday, the fatiguing work of making out its muster rolls completed, the men of the 107th Ohio finally received their coveted discharge papers. They had packed a lifetime into two years and ten months. Now they were going home.

CHAPTER 9

"THE FEELINGS OF A SOLDIER"

July 1865 and Beyond

THE MEN WERE RESTLESS as the passenger cars clacked along the Lake Shore, Cleveland & Erie Railroad that morning. It was July 18, and it had been nearly a week since the troops climbed aboard the *Salvor* in Charleston, the sturdy, square-rigged steamer whose enormous canvas masts "towered above its wooden decks." The four-day voyage to New York City—followed immediately by a two-day rail journey across the Empire State to the shores of Lake Erie—had afforded the men ample time to reflect on the war and their participation in it. Mourning the absence of slain comrades and carrying with them the enormous burden of the past, they tried to imagine the future. For nearly three years they had dreamt about this moment. But now that it had arrived, uncertainty and misgivings conspired to overwhelm them. Not surprisingly, as the cars slowed to a crawl, the city felt different. Cleveland's population had ballooned by an astounding fifty percent over the course of the war—demographic growth far exceeding that experienced by "any other northern city."

The locomotive sputtered into the old depot just after dawn, but Jack Leland's Band was there to greet it. The celebrated musicians—many of them veterans—escorted the men for the short march up Bank Street to Public Square, where Mayor Herman M. Chapin and a tiny knot of civilians had assembled to welcome them home. Anticipating its return, local newspapers heaped superlatives upon the regiment. Just a day after publishing a thumbnail sketch of the unit's service, the *Cleveland Daily Leader* declared that Ohio had recruited "no pluckier regiment," while the *Daily Cleveland Herald* noted that the outfit "was and is of the very best material." Another article applauded the men in turn as "healthy," "enterprising," and "brave"—descriptions that belied the physical condition of the 412 men who stepped off the train. Wracked by typhoid at Brooke's Station and afflicted with ague while in Florida—to say nothing of the spent rebel bullet that struck his right leg at Gettysburg—William Siffert was "so much depleted" upon his arrival in Cleveland that comrades Peter Gnau and Daniel Biddle carried him from the depot directly to a bed in the Marine Hospital.[1]

From the temporary rostrum erected in the square, the mayor introduced William Jarvis Boardman, who delivered prepared remarks. While the thirty-three-year-old Harvard-trained lawyer had not yet lived a decade in Cleveland, in that time he had emerged as an industrious civic leader, assuming the directorship of the city's Commercial National Bank, the presidency of the Cleveland Library Association, and a seat on the Adelbert College Board of Trustees. "The people of this county are able to say Old Cuyahoga has done her share, and nobly too, in the great work of crushing out this wicked rebellion," Boardman proclaimed. The soldiers had not only restored the Union; they had cleansed it of slavery, that "foul blot" upon the republic. The "pernicious doctrine of state's rights" had been laid bare. What was more, Billy Yank had reassured "the Union-loving masses of Europe" that democracy could be saved from itself. "You have shown to the world that our institutions make perfect soldiers of its civilians," he declared.[2]

The crowd looked to Colonel Cooper for a response. "No one who has not experienced the feelings of a soldier," he began, "can appreciate our feelings upon such an occasion as this." Cooper thanked the mayor for his "kind" reception, but he hastened to add that "it is not your provisions that we care about, nor the rest of the outward display." In polite yet measured remarks, he explained that only the loyalty of men and women back home could ever repay the regiment's great sacrifices. "There have been some who have not always sustained us," he alleged, "but you of the Western Reserve have always been true in our darkest days, and we have indeed had dark days."[3]

After a bounteous breakfast, the regiment paraded up Superior Avenue to the Weddell House, the regal, five-story brick-and-sandstone hotel whose two hundred guest rooms, appointed "with every attainable luxury," satisfied even the refined tastes of New Yorkers, among them the pinstriped politico Thurlow Weed. From its flag-festooned corner portico, General John Schofield reviewed the regiment, which had obediently filed onto Bank Street below. Not wishing to detain the troops very long, the general simply congratulated the men on "the termination of the war, and the inauguration of peace." Then they trudged out to Camp Cleveland, where they would be "paid off" and disbanded. As the veterans parted ways and the 107th Ohio passed into history, they expressed the "greatest good feeling for each other." Even if they could not yet articulate how, the men knew that the war had transformed their lives—and the life of their nation—forever. They would spend the next decades sorting out the meaning of the war and its unprecedented violence. "We are entering upon a new stage of being," one Cleveland newspaper nodded, "and will not be the same people hereafter, that we have been heretofore."[4]

"I WAS VERY ANXIOUS to get home," Jacob Smith remembered. From Cleveland, a train delivered him to Alliance, where he switched cars for the shorter trip into Canton. "One or two of the citizens of

Canton detained me for some time in relating parts of my experience in the service," he noted with regret, "so that it was past nine o'clock before I got out of town." Smith pressed on anyway, stopping several miles short of his home five hours later. Leaning against a "pile of wood alongside the road," the footsore veteran stole several hours of rest. Cresting the "large hill east of our house" early the next morning, he locked eyes with his parents, brothers, and sisters for the first time in three years. The reunion was a "very happy one," but Smith was most grateful for the chance to "rest and look back over the scenes passed through."⁵

The men were physically and emotionally exhausted. Like Smith, Colonel Cooper required a period of rest upon his return home. After a brief visit to Oberlin, a hotbed of abolitionism and his alma mater, he hastened to his family's home in rural Morrow County, eager to "enjoy a month's relaxation" after "years of life in the camp." For those flagging under the effects of painful infirmities and chronic diseases, rest was not a choice so much as it was a necessity. Christian Rieker returned to Zoar subject to severe bouts of diarrhea, which before long yielded to a constipation so extreme as to scorn every remedy. Wrenching cramps kept him prostrated in bed for days. Philip Seltzer "came home feeble and emaciated," laboring under a "hard," rasping cough that from time to time expelled blood. By the time George Billow reached his home in Akron, he had been "reduced to a physical wreck," the consequence of "protracted hardships and exposures."⁶

The condition of these young men, all of whom had marched off to war healthy and spry, doubtless startled friends and family members. Tom Hoagland returned from the war "a broken down man." His neighbors attested that "he suffered from general ill health and a broken constitution," describing his jaundiced complexion and recurring bouts of "constipation" and "indigestion." Casper Bohrer, Daniel Biddle, Frederick Tonsing, and Daniel Whitmer each lost a leg at Gettysburg; they returned home requiring the "constant aid and attendance of another person." Biddle journeyed more than two hundred miles to Cincinnati to be fitted with a wooden leg, but the prosthetic invited considerable frustration. "He would put it on," a friend recalled, "and after wearing it a short time the stump would get sore, and he would have to lay it aside." Moored in bed for at least two weeks on one of these occasions, he called upon his cousin to tend the "little grocery" he operated in Navarre. He soon resolved that he "would get around better on his crutches." Tonsing tried two prosthetics manufactured by Benjamin Franklin Palmer, the New Hampshire physician who held the patent for the artificial leg, before opting to lean into crutches for the rest of his life on Cleveland's West Side.[7]

No less distressing was the sight of so many young men mangled and disfigured. Joseph Kieffer, a musician in the regimental band, had suffered a gunshot wound atop Blocher's Knoll that destroyed the muscle tissue in his face; consequently, he could not open his left eye, which was "continuously inflamed" and constantly oozing. Ugly wounds prevented Frank Rothermel from opening his mouth more than a third of an inch, Theobald Hasman from raising his hands above his head, and Peter Schieb from extending his arm. A shell wound not only deafened Lanson McKinney but left his face badly disfigured. Together, these men bore witness to the war's violence; their furrowed brows and unsteady gaits supplied compelling testimony about all they had seen and experienced. The war was something indelibly inscribed on their bodies—something they were never again able to escape.[8]

Feeling the almost magnetic pull of the war, not every soldier was eager to return home. While awaiting their discharge papers at Camp Cleveland, more than a score of the regiment's veterans organized an "Emigration Society." Aiming to plant a soldier's colony in the "genial climate" of Florida, they deputized an "executive committee" to open negotiations with the government for "aid and assistance" acquiring land. The *Cleveland Daily Herald* cheered the proposal's promise of a "true" and thorough reconstruction of the South, but failed to consider how the project betrayed these veterans' not insignificant doubts about returning to civilian life.[9]

For their part, the Zoar volunteers wondered how—or even if— a community that had opposed the war would greet them. In 1875,

Constance Fenimore Woolson, the grandniece of James Fenimore Cooper, published "Wilhelmina," a short story that dramatized the return of the 107th Ohio to the separatist society on the "tranquil Tuscarawas." The eponymous character, a slender maiden who wears both a "stiff, short-waisted gown" and a "far-off dreamy expression," awaits Gustav, to whom she was betrothed before the war. Her "heavy lidded" eyes well with tears when she learns that the regiment will be paid off the following week—that the men "cannot be later than ten days from now." Wilhelmina claims to be elated, but she quietly dreads the reunion. Her father, the society's gardener, desires that his daughter marry Jacob, the thirty-year-old widower who, in refusing to go off to the war, remained true to the Separatists' principles.

An "unusual excitement" rouses Zoar as the veterans' arrival looms. When the men tramp "down the station road," still encumbered by their "knapsacks, guns, and military accoutrements," a large crowd is there to greet them, and their laughter and tears compete with the "drowsy, long-drawn chant" of a summer evening. Among Zoar's conscientious objectors, curiosity wins out over condemnation, and following "a half hour of general rejoicing," the townsfolk disperse. In the ensuing days, however, while some of the soldiers settle into "the old routine," Gustav, together with Karl, another of his comrades, opts to leave the "pleasant little village" of his youth behind. "I feel all cramped up here, with these rules and bells," he confesses. Wilhelmina, he adds, was "too quiet" for him. With no small "satisfaction," the Zoarites bid him farewell.

No more than a few miles beyond town, Wilhelmina catches up with Gustav, the color drained from her face. "Gustav, mein Gustav!" she shrieks, collapsing at his feet. A whisper of remorse compels the veteran to linger, but just a moment longer. "She looks bad," he says, "very bad." The veteran quickly quiets his conscience and kisses Wilhelmina goodbye, "impatient" to rejoin Karl on the road to Cleveland. Her worst fears confirmed, the young maiden wails with the grief that, despite her marriage to Jacob four weeks later, will place her in an early grave. Though fictional, Woolson's story nonetheless captured the knot of conflicting emotions that the regiment's veterans and their families worked to untangle that summer.[10]

THE VETERANS' first few weeks and months back home were nothing if not disorienting. In Akron, George Billow tried his hand as a grocer, but discovered a "once splendid" memory greatly diminished and his "mental faculties . . . alarmingly effected." The captain attributed both maladies to "leaving his accustomed routine of military service." After nearly three years of constant activity, he could not abide the thought of a stationary life. The "outlook," it seemed, was "dreary." Abandoning the grocery business, Billow next took up work as a traveling salesman, hawking Akron-manufactured stoneware throughout northeast Ohio. But his feeble frame could not endure the Western Reserve's numbing winters. In 1870, Billow decided to move to Huntsville, Alabama, hoping its "milder climate" might restore his delicate health.[11]

Some men seemed unfazed by their wounds. With a business partner, Peter F. Young, still nursing the gunshot wound he received in the left arm at Gettysburg, bought up the stock of a Painesville cashmere dealer. The duo advertised their custom, heavily discounted wares throughout the summer, with Young proudly billing himself as "formerly of the 107th Ohio Vol. Inf." But hardly all were so fortunate. Injuries and chronic ailments made it especially difficult for many of the regiment's veterans to find work. Philip May landed a job replacing track on the Pittsburgh, Cincinnati & St. Louis Railway the second summer after the war, but a rheumatic attack, which he attributed to the gunshot wound he received at Gettysburg, obliged him to quit. Not long after returning home, Arnold Streum began laboring at a "coal bank," but the musket ball lodged in his leg caused him such "great and continued pain" that he found it difficult to remain on his feet more than a few hours. "I work sometimes one day in a week, sometimes three and sometimes only half a day," he complained, "when I am forced to quit and go home." Adam Berghofer attempted to make ends meet as a "day laborer" on the abundant farms near his home in Sandusky, but crippling headaches and dizzy spells prevented him from working "more than one third of the time." Down in Zoar, Christian Rieker tried to pick up his blacksmithing hammer on several occasions, but his "greatly reduced" condition would not permit it. For Rieker, as for "many" of his comrades, "it seemed that ambitions cherished from boyhood would have to be given up."[12]

Men who were physically "broken down" depended on spouses, children, and even their former comrades for aid and assistance. Harrison Flora would lose the "entire use" of his right arm and hand "for days." The musket ball that struck his shoulder at Gettysburg remained burrowed beneath the skin for eighteen months—a painful souvenir of the battle. Confined to his home "three fourths of the time," he had "to be waited on as a child." Nicholas Lopendahl's wife and sister-in-law routinely washed, dressed, and fed him; the veteran's shattered right arm, first treated at a Gettysburg field hospital, rendered him "perfectly helpless." Alfred Rider's wife, Mary Ann, "use[d] to rub his knees every night before going to bed with 'nerve and bone liniment.'"

Perhaps the most dependent on assistance was Henry Feldkamp, who was no longer able to ply his trade as a carpenter. A matron made daily calls on the young sergeant, who rented a room in a boarding-house on Cleveland's Oregon Street. During the fight for Blocher's Knoll, a rebel slug lodged in the sergeant's left thigh, "just above the knee." The ball festered there for more than a decade, despite several heroic attempts at extraction. "Quite stiff," the irascible Feldkamp could not stand, could not sleep, and could "scarcely get about." His sore-pocked knee would swell to more than twice its natural circumference before discharging fluid and tiny fragments of bone.[13]

Survivors without a caretaker—or who lost one to death or divorce—sometimes sought sanctuary in a local, state, or federal soldiers' home. When John Hemmerling's wife passed away in 1885, the rheumatic veteran, still nursing the effects of a gunshot wound, moved from his home in Cleveland to the leafy Milwaukee campus of the National Home for Disabled Volunteer Soldiers. Yet suffering from an injury to his left shoulder, Frederick Jungling responded to his last roll call at the Ohio State Soldiers' and Sailors' Home, which domi-

ciled some one thousand veterans on a ninety-eight-acre site in Sandusky, near the shores of Lake Erie. Still others who sought admission
to these homes craved "the companionship of other soldiers." "Very
eas[ily] excited," Henry Klingaman supposed that "he would be better contented at the Soldiers' Home," where military discipline would
once more structure his days.[14]

Mental and emotional health issues delivered quite a few veterans
to these facilities, too. Emlen Landon, who suffered a severe gunshot wound to his head at Gettysburg, entered the Sandusky home
in March 1894, "subject to sudden attacks of violent pain" and "spells
of dizziness" during which he became "almost completely blind." The
twenty-year-old brickmaker from Stark County simply never got over
his injury. "His friends claim there has been an entire change in his dis-
position since receiving his wound," one pension examiner reported.
"[He] complains of being very nervous at times." After three years at
the Ohio Home, administrators discharged Landon for "violating the
rules"—more than likely the result of his whiskey habit. Somehow, he
found his way to the Danville, Illinois, branch of the National Home
in January 1899, but from it, too, he was "dishonorably discharged"
after five years. Fortunately for Landon, the administrators back in
Sandusky were willing to overlook his previous debauchery and read-
mitted him. But while absent without leave on the fourteenth anniversary of his first admission to a soldiers' home, Landon was found
dead, a victim of "acute alcoholism."[15]

Frederick Bross's injury "eventually [a]ffected his mind to such an
extent" that family members deposited him not at the soldiers' home
but at Columbus's Central Ohio Insane Asylum. The musket ball that
tore through his body had obliged the former blacksmith to "quit his
business." The loss of his trade, remorseless pain, and the "large" exit
wound that disfigured his body were simply too much. Charles Cordier continued to work in his butcher's shop after he returned home
from the war, but the shell that struck his head at Gettysburg likewise
continued to trouble him. The veteran suffered "fits every two or three
weeks," during which he would "lose control of his mind" and expe-

rience lapses in memory. Perhaps trusting that a warmer clime might improve his condition, Cordier moved to Jacksonville, not terribly far from where the regiment had twisted through the woods behind McGirt's Creek. Still, his health continued to wane. On the morning of August 10, 1889, his wife awoke to an empty house. Hours later, a police captain discovered her husband's body bobbing "in the St. John's River at the foot of Liberty Street." Considering that "for the past two weeks" he had "suffered much from an abscess on his cheek, and from wounds in the head received in the late war," the jury of inquest reckoned Cordier on "the verge of insanity" and deemed his death a suicide. For this veteran of the 107th Ohio, twenty-six years later and eight hundred miles away, the battle for Blocher's Knoll—and all of the pain it prompted—was finally over.[16]

GRIEVOUSLY WOUNDED veterans depended on federally funded pensions to make ends meet. So too did widowed mothers like Eliza Whisler, whose son, Laban, killed in the fight at Deveaux's Neck, had sustained her financially before the war. Yet the army of pension clerks in Washington was, within a year of Appomattox, "busy enough to be considered overworked and underpaid." The staggering volume of claims—more than 125,000 disabled veterans and widows appeared on the pension rolls by 1866—slowed processing times to a crawl. Just as the nation had been unprepared for the war, so too was it unprepared for the peace.[17]

For needy claimants, these delays could be devastating. Joseph Kieffer had been home no more than a week when he visited Dr. Lorenzo Whiting, the pension examining surgeon who maintained a medical practice in Canton. A native of Connecticut, Whiting earned his medical degree at Williams College in 1835 before relocating to Canton the following year. Though a staunch abolitionist, the genial scholar quickly earned the esteem of his neighbors. Whiting conducted a careful examination of the young musician's ghastly wound and then completed the required surgeon's certificate. Kieffer filed his claim three weeks later, but waited until January 1871 before he was added to the pension rolls. Amputees seemed to fare somewhat better, though they too met with maddening delays. David Sarbach, who could no longer elevate his left arm after a rebel musket ball ripped through his shoulder, waited just over a year for a pension certificate. Henry Feldkamp anticipated his first pension disbursement for seven agonizing months. Misfortune seemed to hound Theodore Blocher, the Stark County wagoner who was "slightly wounded" at Chancellorsville and then bagged as a prisoner at Gettysburg; he waited some nine years before the Pension Bureau took up his claim. Frustration with the application process (or perhaps an unjustly "low" rating) may have prompted Adam Berghofer to shred his pension certificate, the pieces of which were discovered littering a Dayton alley in 1885.[18]

Securing a pension claim obliged veterans to submit to a battery of invasive medical examinations. During annual or biennial visits, examining surgeons evaluated the "degree of disability" so as to determine the "appropriate" amount of compensation. Not surprisingly, veterans resented these exams. John Leffler, who endured recurring spells of numbness in his right leg, insisted frankly in the fall of 1883 that he was "entitled to a higher rate," his pension being "graded too low for degree of disability." Daniel Whitmer demanded an increase in the pension he received for the loss of his left leg, amputated in a Gettysburg field hospital after the fight for Blocher's Knoll. Disposed to falls and irritated by his government-issued artificial limb, which chafed his stump, the septuagenarian appealed for a higher rating in March 1905. This prompted the Pension Bureau to dispatch a medical investigator to his Canton home with precise instructions: measure and trace the stump, "determine definitely the point of amputation of claimant's left leg," and "describe the condition of the knee joint, stump, and cicatrix."[19]

Securing a pension also required veterans to navigate a thicket of rules, statutes, and federal legislation. Though veterans' newspapers dispensed routine advice about preparing pension applications, the process was so confounding that men frequently engaged pension claims attorneys to represent them. In Cleveland, many veterans and their families turned to Milo B. Stevens & Company, the Washington, D.C.–based firm that maintained a humming satellite office downtown on Superior Street—along with branches in Detroit and Chicago. The attorneys blanketed the city in handsomely printed circulars hawking their services. So too did William E. Preston, whose Cleveland-based "Soldiers' National War Claim Agency" pledged to *"exact justice"* for all pension-seekers. George Zuern, still suffering from the effects of captivity on Richmond's Belle Isle, retained George Lemon, a wounded New York veteran, to handle his claim, while Arnold Streum trusted George Hildt, who had commanded the 30th Ohio at Antietam, to prepare his application.[20]

Challenges unique to their wartime service rendered the veterans of the 107th Ohio especially labor-intensive clients. The Pension Bureau required applicants to establish the wartime origins of their disabilities by supplying notarized statements from both a regimental surgeon and a commissioned officer. But Surgeon Hartman was dead, and Surgeon Knaus relocated to New Alsace, Indiana, before reenlisting in the postwar army. For the next two decades, Knaus toiled as a hospital steward at far-flung military outposts in Nebraska, Minnesota, and the Dakota Territory. A yellowed envelope wedged in the surgeon's personal papers at the National Archives bulges with letters from anxious veterans desperate to find him. Some wrote to Knaus several times without so much as a reply. "I think it is impossible to get his affidavit," Albert Beck regretted, "for this is the second time I wrote to him and never received no answer." An impatient John Lutz scribbled out a plea directly to the Surgeon General. "As I require his certificate to complete certain pension papers," he explained, "I should be greatly obliged for an answer as soon as practicable." The regiment's notoriously poor record keeping also held up quite a few pensions. Henry Finkenbiner's claim stalled when the veteran could not produce a "hospital record" documenting his Gettysburg wound. His heroics at Dingle's Mill, which would earn for him the Medal of Honor, seem to have been insufficient evidence of his trustworthiness and character.[21]

Still, Finkenbiner was more fortunate than many of his comrades who suffered less conspicuous injuries. Those who froze at Brooke's Station or endured the tropical climes of Florida were often afflicted with rheumatism, chills, aches, ague, chronic diarrhea, and fever. But they struggled to establish the wartime origins of their swollen joints and halting limps with the exacting precision demanded by the Pension Bureau. Albert Beck had no doubt about the source of the rheumatic pains that besieged his limbs: "sleeping in the snow," he wrote, "with no protection but an oil cloth on the march Washington to Camp Fairfax." Several comrades even supplied testimony to that effect, noting how "very much exposed" the men were on this "very severe march." Still, pension examiners greeted his application with considered skepticism. "I think it is a sin and a shame to our government," Beck fumed.[22]

Betraying a keen understanding of the relationship between their bodies and unhygienic wartime environments, Alfred J. Rider marshaled evidence to support his claim that a winter of hard marching and exposure resulted in his "heart trouble," lameness, and vertigo, just as Philip Wang identified Deveaux's Neck as the location where he "ruined his health and contracted rheumatism and heart disease." But not until President Benjamin Harrison signed the Dependent and Disability Pension Act into law in June 1890—a sweeping measure that entitled all disabled, honorably discharged Union veterans to pension money—did the federal government finally acknowledge swollen limbs and nagging coughs as legacies of the war. By then, of course, it was much too late for many of the war's ailing and injured old soldiers. Still, that the government made these concessions at all was a tribute to the ordinary veterans who, in their urgent and unsteady appeals to the Pension Bureau, demanded a more sweeping definition of what constituted a wartime injury. For Union veterans, the struggle to secure pensions was merely a continuation of their struggle to wrest enduring recognition of their hardships and misfortunes.[23]

FOR THE 107TH OHIO, that struggle entered a new phase on September 15, 1869, when sixty of its survivors assembled at National Hall on Cleveland's Public Square—the very place where Colonel Meyer had appealed for recruits seven years before—to establish a permanent, regimental society. By adopting a constitution, electing officers—Captain Peter F. Young was appointed the first president—and pledging to meet once per year for the rest of their lives, the men validated the memories and shared suffering that united them. "Though our ranks were thinned by camp fever and the enemy's shot and shell," Young declared, "we will ever cherish the memory of our fallen comrades and brothers in arms."[24]

This they did. The men assembled faithfully each year, eager to rehearse the tale of their service and ready to revisit "the scenes through which the regiment passed." Reunions provided the veterans with a forum for piecing together a coherent narrative of the war. Akron hosted the regiment's second reunion on the Fourth of July, 1870. An early morning train delivered a contingent of the regiment's veterans from Cleveland. Led by a color bearer gripping their battle-worn standard and accompanied by Dustin Marble's renowned brass band, the men strutted down Market Street to Phoenix Hall, where they enjoyed a day of oratory and ovations. Following a "sumptuous banquet," they retired to the city rink for a "grand ball" in the regiment's honor.[25]

Though "but a remnant" of the Wooster company survived, the 107th Ohio resolved to meet in the elegant Wayne County seat in September 1872. Determined to "eclipse the hospitality and kindness" shown to the veterans in previous years, Woosterites spared no expense readying for the reunion. The meeting hall was handsomely appointed, garlanded with cords of fresh evergreen and festooned with German and American flags. Placards emblazoned with the names of the regiment's battles—Chancellorsville, Gettysburg, Deveaux's Neck, Pocotaligo Bridge, and Dingle's Mill—adorned the walls, while the regimental colors, "bullet riddled, bloody and battle-worn," were planted on stage. That evening, the seventy-five attendees enjoyed a "bountiful repast" prepared by the "ladies of Wooster." Few who attended that gathering ever forgot it.[26]

At their annual reunions, the regiment's survivors remembered a past that the nation preferred to forget. As it turned out, the hymns of victory that greeted Billy Yank upon his return home had but few verses. Within years of Appomattox, the desire to "clasp hands across the bloody chasm" threatened to efface not just the cause of the war, but also crucial details about how it was fought. As the nation ambled down the "road to reunion," many veterans deemed it all the more urgent to reflect on the war and its charge. Union veterans' periodicals brimmed with reports of the ugly white supremacist terrorism that gripped the South in the early days of Reconstruction. "That a system of wholesale murdering, whipping, and assaulting of the most brutal character has been inaugurated all over the south," one Ohio GAR newspaper shuddered, "cannot be longer questioned." In the face of presidential pardons for former rebels, repressive black codes, and rumors of another, even bloodier rebellion on the horizon, many indignant veterans refused to yield any authority over their past. "The same spirit of patriotism" that "actuated us in 1862," one veteran proclaimed, yet "pervades our hearts and thrills our souls." As one Cleveland newspaper predicted, "Men who fought to preserve the Union will vote to preserve the consequences of their victory."[27]

If the fate of Union victory remained unresolved, so too were many niggling details about their service. Most soldiers did not tramp home with a fixed, logical, or coherent narrative of events; they had experienced the conflict as a kaleidoscope of "countless minor scenes and interiors," each one demanding a larger context. Owing to the raw and inchoate nature of their memories, old soldiers sometimes found it difficult to partition time or propose turning points. Alfred Rider made this clear when he reflected on the regiment's participation in the battle of Gettysburg: "Just like every thing else concerning the fight," he bemoaned, "there is a great diversity of opinion . . . a grand admixture of conflicting testimony." The irksome questions only multiplied as the years accumulated into decades. What did that stand at the Talley place actually mean? What had those months in Florida contributed to the Union war effort? Was all the suffering and the loss worth it in the end?[28]

As self-appointed custodians of the war's history, veterans worked through these questions with zeal. In 1871, Seraphim Meyer attempted a short, narrative history of the regiment. That autumn, the colonel read his account to thunderous applause at the unit's third annual reunion, held at Schaefer's Opera House in Canton. Framing the war as a contest between treason and loyalty, his account emphasized the unit's selfless devotion amid trying circumstances. Lamenting the "very meagre" attention paid the regiment, he likewise hastened to point out that the 107th Ohio "lost more men in the Department of the South" than it had while serving in the Army of the Potomac—its bloody stands at Chancellorsville and Gettysburg notwithstanding.[29]

That the colonel struck a defensive chord was hardly a surprise, for the postwar years witnessed renewed attacks on the courage and battlefield performance of the Union army's ethnically German soldiers. Among ethnic soldiers, responding to these allegations became far more urgent than discussing slavery, debating the war's causes, or even spurning the Lost Cause—pursuits that preoccupied many other Union veterans. "We have had so much controversy over the misfortunes of the 11th corps," sighed a wearied old soldier, wracked with chronic diarrhea. "Bad conduct on the part of the Dutch has been so strongly impressed upon the native soldiers that fought the battles of the war of the rebellion, and upon the public outside of the army," another veteran supposed, "that I doubt if it [will] ever be eradicated and its character restored."[30]

The conflict's earliest chroniclers heaped more scorn and ridicule upon the men. "With wild yells the Confederates rushed on in overwhelming numbers, and the Germans, overborne, broke and fled in helpless confusion," the political economist Thomas Kettell wrote of the battle of Chancellorsville in his narrative history of the war, published just one year after Appomattox. "In vain officers stormed and entreated; the men sullenly made their way to the river." A decade later, the former army surgeon James Moore echoed Kettell's cruel assessment in his *Complete History of the Great Rebellion*. The "noblest effort of the brave Howard and his officers," he remarked, "could not arrest the panic, or stem the tide of fugitives rolling over the field." John Stevens Abbott likewise pitied his fellow Maine native Oliver Howard, "as heroic a commander and brave a man as ever stood upon a battlefield." The general's only misfortune, Abbott maintained, was his assignment to a corps "composed mainly of Germans," many of whom "could not speak English." Even more imaginative was the account of Chancellorsville produced by Benson J. Lossing, widely regarded for his illustrated history of the American Revolution. "In a few minutes," the historian sneered, "almost the entire Eleventh Corps was seen pouring out of the woods in the deepening twilight, and sweeping over the dusty clearing around Chancellorsville in the wildest confusion, in the direction of the Rappahannock, strewing and blockading the roads with the implements and accouterments of war."[31]

"Lies, lies, lies," one old soldier indignantly fumed. His sentiment was shared by a survivor of the 75th Ohio, who modestly declared, "We would all like to have the truth appear." "No occurrence of the war," still another veteran remonstrated, "has been more utterly and persistently misrepresented, to use a mild term, than has the behavior of the 11th Corps on the right" at Chancellorsville. Nearly three decades after the costly stand at the Talley Farm, this old soldier reckoned that "it is easier to fight battles than it is to dig out lies about them after they have become fairly embedded in history."[32]

After five years of hunching over maps and after-action reports— not to mention three extended visits to the battlefield—Augustus Choate Hamlin doubtless agreed. In the 1890s, the Harvard Medical School graduate who served as medical director of the Army of the Potomac resolved to conduct an "inquiry into the events of the battle of Chancellorsville," hoping to set the record straight about its many controversies. "The task has been entirely voluntary," he noted, "and of exceeding difficulty, mingled with much unpleasantness." Veterans of both armies plied him with a blizzard of personal reminiscences. "When the facts are told I do not think any man need ever apologize for the conduct of the rank and file of the command that wore the crescent," one veteran of the 55th Ohio affirmed.[33]

Hamlin's informants furnished meticulous accounts of what they had seen, felt, and experienced that fateful May afternoon. "My memory retains the events of that day very vividly," explained Charles T. Furlow, an old Georgia rebel who served on General George Doles's staff. "I think the men who were there," echoed one Union veteran who lost an arm in the fight, "can write the best kind of war history." For his part, Jacob Gano seized the opportunity to challenge the received wisdom about Jackson's flank attack. The former adjutant of the 75th Ohio felt that it was his duty to remedy the historical record. "It is stated by General Schimmelfennig in his official report that McLean's brigade stampeded without firing a shot," he began, "a statement so manifestly unjust that I feel impelled to deny it in the most emphatic manner." The hardware and cutlery wholesaler from Cincinnati dashed off several lengthy missives to Hamlin, describing the brigade's fraught stand at the Talley place. "You will pardon me for intruding upon your time," Gano implored, "but justice to McLean's Ohio Brigade demands the contradiction of such statements."[34]

Albert Peck was no less earnest in his letter to Hamlin. His forlorn company of the 17th Connecticut had suffered nearly seventy-five percent losses that afternoon—itself a powerful testament to the stand the Ohio brigade made before breaking for the rear. "There was no possible chance of holding our position, as we were surprised and most of our division were facing the wrong way," he held. "I have always thought, and still think that General Devens was more to blame for that disaster than any one else." While unable to agree on who was most responsible—Devens, McLean, or Howard—the veterans conceded almost in unison that they had fallen prey to inept leadership. "No men, caught in such a damnable trap, *could* stand," one New York veteran resolved. "For Howard (+ somewhat for Devens, who might have caught the infection from Howard) a thorough scathing must come out."[35]

Even so, not a few native-born veterans assigned blame to the ethnically German soldiers who had battled alongside them in the Eleventh Corps. In an 1892 letter to Hamlin, Colonel William H. Noble amplified a claim advanced by the captain who commanded the 17th Connecticut's picket line on May 2. "Wilson French saw apparently a full stack of arms back of rifle pits and no men behind them," he wrote. "They were those of the 107th Ohio . . . *That Regt.* had *no commander.*" Hamlin investigated the allegation at once. "I am quite sure it will prove to be a mistake," Captain Elias Riggs Monfort of the 75th Ohio assured him, pointing out that McLean's pickets "did not reach their regiments until dark after the fight." Monfort believed it impossible for French "to have reached the point where the 107 was located" without risking capture. "I am told the 107 were fully armed when rallied at night after the fight," he remarked, adding, "I have no interest in the 107th Ohio except to see them set right."[36]

OLD SOLDIERS like Henry Finkenbiner waited impatiently for Hamlin's history. A devoted reader of the largest newspaper for Union veterans, the hero of Dingle's Mill took seriously his role as a custodian of the war's history. When one New York captain maligned the record of the Eleventh Corps at Chancellorsville, Finkenbiner responded in kind with a letter to the editor of the *National Tribune*. "Allow me to say the comrade is a little off," he wrote. "I was a member of that Corps, and took part in the battle of May 2, 1863, when we were flanked and repulsed." After receiving an Eleventh Army Corps Association circular announcing the book's impending publication, one veteran of the 55th Ohio, domiciled at the National Home for the Disabled Volunteer Soldier in Dayton, begged for an advance copy. "I was on picket the afternoon when Jackson made his attack," he explained. "I am anxious to have the history."[37]

In the estimate of most veterans, the handsome tome was well worth the wait. "I have written to you twenty times in my imagination," the Brooklynite Horatio King explained to Hamlin. "I want to tell you how delighted I am with your book, and how completely you have answered the misinformed and clamorous critics of the Eleventh Corps." While Adelbert Ames worried that Hamlin had been "a little over indulgent with the Eleventh Corps," he nonetheless found the author's arguments reasoned and persuasive. "It is all very sad," the general mused, "and at the same time not a little ludicrous." Veterans devoured the text. "I took up the book the evening after it came and did not lay it down until I had again read every page and studied each map," one explained. Even former rebels extolled Hamlin's effort. "It is the only impartial history of the battle I have ever seen," affirmed one Georgian, "and as such I prize it very highly."[38]

SADLY, BY THE TIME Hamlin's book appeared in 1896, the last reveille had already sounded for many of the most grievously wounded and injured veterans. Time had not been kind to the regiment, nor would that change. New struggles loomed—fluttering of the heart and shortness of breath, rheumatic pain and paralysis, constipation and gout. Death claimed dozens of the regiment's veterans in the first decade of the new century—among them the Bavarian-born Andrew Backer, who succumbed to the effects of chronic dysentery at his home in Michigan, and Samuel Pfister, "a quiet, but very firm man," who lost his battle with consumption at his mother's home in Akron. By 1903, the pale horse visited the veterans with such frequency that the regimental association named a "condolences committee" at its annual reunion. This was hardly an encouraging development for John Geissler, who ached to attend the "Peace Jubilee" marking the fiftieth anniversary of the battle of Gettysburg. The Zoar veteran would not get his wish. Geissler passed away just days before he was to set out for Pennsylvania. Heartbreakingly, his transportation to the reunion—provided free of charge by the state of Ohio—had already arrived.[39]

One by one, the men of the regiment went to their graves—many still believing that their sacrifices and sufferings had not been adequately recognized by the nation at large. The forty-eight survivors who gathered for the regiment's nineteenth annual reunion, for example, applauded the melancholy stanzas of a popular poem, "The Weeds of the Army":

Some of the papers tell us that the boys of the G.A.R.
Never smelt smoke in battle, nor went to the front in war
They brazenly tell us our roster bears only the names of those
Who paused at the roar of conflict and northward pointed their toes
They say that the true, brave soldiers have never entered our ranks
That we never were known to muster but a lot of political cranks
As one of the papers put it, we are but the weeds of the crop
But loafers and shirks and cowards, who never heard muskets pop.

Who are these traitorous writers who are casting their venomous slime
O'er men who gave all to their country at that trying, terrible time?
They are the cringing cowards who never dared go to the front
And stand with our fearless soldiers and help bear the battle's brunt
They clung to the skirts of women, and soon as our backs were turned,
Our flag, our cause and our country the cowardly miscreants spurned.
Go seek them wherever they loiter, from the gulf to the northern lakes
And you'll find them but treacherous, venomous, hideous copper-
* head snakes.*

Let us pause on a shaded corner and see a procession pass
At a great Grand Army reunion, when the veterans form in mass
Just note the dismembered bodies, the crutches and canes and scars
That mutely tell us the story of the bloodiest of wars
Just gaze on the flags they are bearing, all riddled with shot and shell
The flags they carried undaunted right into the gateway of hell
See the bodies bent and disabled, made so in the battle's fierce blast;
Are these the weeds of the army at whom these insults are cast?[40]

By the summer of 1929, only twenty-six survivors of the 107th Ohio remained. That August, eight of them gathered in Navarre to reelect Augustus Vignos president of the regimental association. Five years later, with but a handful of survivors living, eighty-seven-year-old James M. Corl was the only veteran able to attend the regiment's annual reunion. On the appointed day, at the Navarre YMCA, Corl delivered a poignant address to a room lined with empty chairs, dutifully rehearsing the "many experiences of the regiment." Two summers later he was interred beneath a family headstone that was ordinary in every way, save the careful etching on its face: "Co. A, 107th Regt., OVI."[41]

TO THE VERY END, the men of the 107th Ohio believed that their many months of suffering—something symbolized by their tattered battle flags, pinned-up coat sleeves, and rotting wounds—had granted them a singular authority over the war and its legacies. During the conflict itself, they asserted that authority by resisting numbing fatigue duties and registering their distaste for discipline. As veterans, they drew on that authority to demand new and more capacious definitions of duty, sacrifice, and patriotism. More than extraordinary deeds, they seemed to insist, Union victory demanded everyday mettle—of the sort put on display in disease-choked camps and overcrowded hospital wards, on protracted marches and remote picket lines, as men impatiently marked time and suffered from self-doubt. Empty sleeves were "honorable scars," but so too, they maintained, were frostbitten toes and crooked fingers, raspy coughs and labored breaths.[42]

Neither convinced that they had climbed to the "snowy heights of honor" once described in elegy by Oliver Wendell Holmes Jr., nor entirely ready to concede that the war had been some irredeemable folly, the men of the regiment instead fused pain and pride into a single interpretation of the war. Loss and anguish were, even for the most sentimental among veterans, fundamental to the conflict's meaning. Celebrations of the war's results always implied a reckoning with its costs. As one scholar recently observed, veterans "revisited" the "terror of combat that had marked their service" after the war, "if only to take greater satisfaction in the comforts of a hard-won peace." Their sacrifices, they believed, bespoke their loyalty. While the legacy of emancipation divided the men in peace as it had divided them at war, no one could deny that they stood by the flag in the face of a treasonous rebellion.[43]

The nation, however, preferred to move on. So it was that in the twilight of the nineteenth century, Walt Whitman could declare that the "fervid atmosphere" and "typical events" of the war were "in danger of being totally forgotten." Not a few of the regiment's veterans sensed that their unique war had not gotten "in the books." In 1906, Martin Boyer appealed directly to the editor of the nation's leading periodical for Union veterans. "Please publish a short history of the 107th Ohio," he implored. "I am a reader of *The National Tribune*, but I have never seen anything in the paper concerning the 107th Ohio." The intuition that the regiment's experiences had not been adequately recorded similarly inspired Jacob Smith to put pen to paper on a unit history. The regiment's veterans were "fast growing feeble," after all, and "the gaps in the picket line" were "daily growing wider." Before long, the last of their number would be "mustered out of life's service." One cold winter's evening, Smith opened a tablet and began to write. Two years later, he had produced some five hundred manuscript pages, densely lined with his raw, unembellished prose.[44]

Work on *Camps and Campaigns* obliged Smith "to wander back through the mazes of memory," where the past presented itself again with "startling reality and vividness." He shouldn't have been surprised. Like so many of his comrades, he had never really been able to leave the war behind. Too many emotions and too many losses had crowded into those years. He belonged to a community of shared suffering—ordinary men welded together by their extraordinary circumstances. "I have never in thought or word regretted what little I had done for my country in the way of duty," Smith concluded at the end of his book, "but have always been proud that I had taken some humble part in the great strife." Confident but self-conscious, acknowledging the yawning void between the war he waged and the war the nation preferred to imagine, the old soldier had penned a fitting epitaph for his regiment.[45]

EPILOGUE

TWENTY-FOUR YEARS after they first rushed Blocher's Knoll, they did it again. This time, however, there was no unabated rush; they gripped walking sticks, not rifled muskets. No longer laureled with corps badges, the men donned bronze reunion medals and brightly colored ribbons. One pinned up an empty coat sleeve. The passage of nearly a quarter-century had furrowed and creased youthful faces; once vibrant beards and well-manicured chin fringe had faded into snow. Not all of the old boys made it, of course. Christian Ricker had been dead for a decade; he was just thirty-five years old when Zoar's elders laid him to rest, the young soldier having never recovered from the effects of exposure and rebel captivity. Still, some forty survivors of the 107th Ohio would assemble in Gettysburg on September 14, 1887—and those who made the journey wouldn't have missed it for the world. George Billow, Augustus Vignos, Alfred Rider, and William Siffert were all there, undeterred by the trials of the long railroad journey across Pennsylvania. Only John Brunny, who had moved to eastern Kansas very soon after the war, and Colonel Meyer, whose failing health prompted a physician-recommended move to Santa Cruz, where he passed away in April 1894, failed to make the trip.[1]

That morning, the men assembled at Christ Lutheran Church on Chambersburg Street. Shortly after noon they paraded through the flag-festooned borough to the slopes of Blocher's Knoll, where "a goodly number of Ohioans and citizens" awaited their arrival. Along their old lines, just beyond the lichened stones of the almshouse cemetery, they would dedicate their regimental monument. That once unremarkable rise was now laced with a tour road, conveying hacks and carriages over the wide, flat plain that in so many ways, they had never really left.[2]

BY THE TIME the veterans arrived, Gettysburg was already a maze of granite, marble, and bronze. In the 1870s and 1880s, in response to the relentless lobbying of Union veterans, northern state legislatures appropriated monies to adorn the field with tiny flank markers, tablets, and monuments. Ohio was no exception, approving funds to erect monuments saluting the two cavalry outfits, four artillery batteries, and thirteen infantry regiments from the Buckeye State that saw service at Gettysburg. In the summer of 1885, Vignos and Rider, together with Captain John Lutz, accompanied Ohio's adjutant general Ebenezer Finley to the battlefield to select a fitting and proper location for "Ohio's Token of Gratitude." The men were pleased that the Gettysburg Battlefield Memorial Association had not only connected important locations on the battlefield with a network of tour roads, but that care had been taken to "protect the natural and artificial defenses" used during the fight.[3]

Back in Columbus, the trio reviewed more than six hundred proposed designs for their regimental monument. After three days, they settled on Design No. 54 from the Smith Granite Works of Boston, one of two dozen contractors vying for the job. The handsome, somewhat understated block of Blue Westerly granite would be mounted atop Blocher's Knoll. Though planting a monument on East Ceme-

Forty survivors returned to Gettysburg in September 1887 to dedicate a regimental monument along the battle line on the slopes of Blocher's Knoll. *Camps and Campaigns of the 107th Ohio Volunteer Infantry, Huntington Library*

tery Hill would have recalled the fight with the Louisiana Tigers—the regiment's most distinguished service at Gettysburg—the men opted to commemorate a trying episode that entailed much suffering and sacrifice. "This Memorial," they proposed to etch, "is dedicated by the surviving members of the Regiment to their Fallen Comrades."[4]

Standing atop Blocher's Knoll, their minds flooded with painful memories, the men could not help but reflect back and take the measure of their lives. After returning home from the war, Augustus Vignos married his sweetheart, a twenty-seven-year-old Louisville girl named Phoebe DeVinney. For three years, they made a home in Marengo, Iowa, a steepled county seat located midway between Davenport and Des Moines, just south of the state's namesake river. What sent the young couple abruptly packing for the "sparsely settled" frontier is not entirely clear—perhaps the void at home created by the death of Augustus's father was too overwhelming—but before long, they were back in Canton. Even in familiar surroundings, however, Vignos struggled to find steady employment. He took on odd jobs to supplement his paltry earnings as a night watchman at a local lumber yard, a post the one-armed major left upon assuming new duties as janitor of the Stark County Court House.[5]

Vignos worked long hours to support his growing family—his son Henry Joseph was born in 1866, and seven more children followed over the next twelve years—but, as one descendant noted, "he never lost interest in his comrades of the war." Even in Iowa, he sought to "renew the acquaintance of those who had together shared the hardships of the camp, the march and the field," helping to stage a "sham battle" at a colossal reunion that invited the participation of some fifteen hundred veterans. Back in Canton, he became an outspoken Republican and, together with nearly three dozen former regimental comrades, an active member of Grand Army of the Republic Post No. 25, which met in a large hall stocked with complete sets of the *Official Records* and the *Medical and Surgical History of the War of the Rebellion*. These volumes were especially useful for Vignos, who was frequently called upon to support his comrades' pension claims.[6]

George Billow was one comrade who relied upon the major's aid. After five years of planting cotton in Alabama, Billow returned to Akron in 1875 with his wife, Anna, and their eight children—five sons and three daughters. Once back home, he converted his old wagons into horse-drawn hearses, establishing himself as an undertaker. By the time he traveled to Gettysburg, the captain was recognized as a leader in the budding funeral industry. (He would later serve as president of the Western Reserve Funeral Directors' Association and, in the early twentieth century, earned a seat on the state board tasked with examining embalmers.) Billow's success in family, business, and civic pursuits meant that friends and neighbors counted him among the war's self-assured heroes; in the public eye, he seemed the perfect picture of a veteran who had easily triumphed over the hardships of war. "There was no officer nor soldier in the whole command physically better constituted to endure the hardships & privations incident to a soldier's life than George Billow," one of his comrades asserted.

"He served his country faithfully from the beginning to the ending of the struggle," another echoed.[7]

But if the public image was useful—even something that Billow curated from time to time—it nonetheless consigned him to the legions of veterans who were left to suffer in silence. Many months of "camping under shelter tents in wet shoes and clothes, without fire" finally caught up with him. His feet, swollen and pocked with sores—stubborn reminders of those punishing winter marches in Virginia—continued to "break open" and ooze pus with painful regularity. Worse, he suffered from severe headaches, spells of dizziness, and "nervous prostration." Billow explained that very often he experienced the "sensation of flashes of heat" surging through his frame. Not surprisingly, in 1876, a pension examiner found him "irritable," wracked with "apprehension of coming misfortune."[8]

Hoping that he might "out grow" his ailments, and unable to

Though a successful entrepreneur and esteemed civic leader, George Billow quietly struggled with his Civil War past. *Cleveland: Plain Dealer Press, 1906, 260*

afford the services of a pension attorney, Billow waited a dozen years before filing a pension claim. Still more remarkably, after receiving an unjustly "low" rating, he held off any petition for an increase for two dozen years. Not only was the appeals process both daunting and "disheartening"—especially so for someone without a battle scar, but there was "considerable political feeling" gathering against pensions for Civil War veterans. Sensitive to his conspicuous place in local Republican politics and to his role in the Grand Army of the Republic, an order whose members were popularly derided as "pension beggars," Billow once more subordinated his needs to a greater cause—more concerned about needier comrades, whose own claims he frequently endorsed. Indeed, when Billow prepared his biography for inclusion in the enormous volume of "Personal War Sketches" maintained by the GAR's Colonel Lewis Buckley Post in Akron— a post Billow commanded for three years—it was characteristically modest. Beyond supplying his rank, company, and regiment, and the dates of his enlistment and discharge, the captain penned just a single sentence: "His Military Experience in the Civil War covered a period of 34 months."[9]

Perhaps more than most veterans, Billow cherished the opportunity to spend time with his old comrades. They affirmed his experiences and empathized with his anguish, all without demanding some sturdy, handsomely mustached hero. "I met him after the war at Akron," Vignos once recalled, but "he was not by any means a well man." In his work with the Buckley Post and with the regimental reunion association, he kept tabs on the old boys. Just down the road in Navarre, so too did Alfred Rider and William Siffert, both of whom attended, swapped stories, and munched hardtack at the Captain Samuel Miller Post of the GAR. Upon their return home, both veterans turned quickly to new business pursuits. Siffert tried his hand at the "milling business" with his old friend and regimental comrade James Corl, whose sister, Hettie, he married in 1867. Meanwhile, the "synonym for integrity" who always voted "the straight Republican ticket" prepared for the ministry; he earned his license to preach in the United Brethren Church in 1875 and was ordained a few years later. Rider went to work with his younger brother, Daniel, manufacturing harnesses and saddles in the "old stand" where their father had scraped out a living before the war. In 1872, the citizens of Navarre elected Rider as the village clerk; three years later he became the justice of the peace. His fidelity to the Republican Party would be further rewarded with his appointment as the "assistant superintendent" of the U.S. Post Office in Washington, D.C., where, appropriately enough, the old regimental postmaster served as the official government "inspector of mail bags."[10]

Like Billow, Rider suffered quietly after the war, depending on his wife, Mary Ann, for almost constant aid and assistance. He struggled with a lame foot, writhed with the chronic pain of rheumatism, and complained of frequent dizzy spells that prevented him from enjoying the evening newspaper. Attacks of vertigo could leave him prostrated for "days," and seized him abruptly. A neighbor with whom he shared a boardinghouse in Washington, for instance, sprang from bed one night after hearing a "heavy fall" in Rider's room. He found the veteran "very sick laying on the floor." Still another tenant observed that Rider's "nervous system" was "all torn to pieces."[11]

The war was something that Rider, stalked by these ailments, could never truly escape. Yet in a very real sense, like so many veterans, he did not want to. By remembering the war and acknowledging its pain and suffering, Rider resisted closure. He preserved his wartime letters (a "small hand truck full," as he explained to one comrade), both as a powerful material artifact of the war and as a rich archive to be mined. In October 1885, Rider agreed to assist the mutton-chopped John Badger Bachelder, recently appointed as the federal government's official historian of the battle of Gettysburg, in the daunting task of preparing a full and faithful chronicle of the war's bloodiest clash. Rider plied Bachelder with a few reminiscences, but pledged to rummage his letters that winter for still more details. "I may be able to find other interesting matter among those old letters," he assured, that might "enable me to do you some good." During these years, he became a real student of the battle, swapping stories with old comrades, exchanging copies of official reports, and even maintaining a small library of books and articles related to the fight—among them Pennsylvania College professor Michael Jacobs's *Notes on the Rebel Invasion of Maryland and Pennsylvania* (1864), the first contribution to the genre. Though he had wandered the fields "half a dozen times" after the battle, Rider confessed on the eve of the monument unveiling that he "had just begun to learn my ABCs of this fight."[12]

THE DEDICATION EXERCISES began "promptly at two o'clock," when the regiment posted its tattered colors, on loan from the Flag Room at the Ohio State House, atop Blocher's Knoll. Siffert invited his comrades to bow their heads in prayer before Vignos's young daughter, Blanche, led the audience in a stirring rendition of "America." After the handsome monument was unveiled, Captain Lutz introduced Rider, who had been tasked with delivering the keynote address.[13]

"Before we die," Rider declared, "we dedicate this monument to our fallen comrades, the cause of liberty and the Union, and charge the living to preserve that Constitution they died to defend." He trusted that the monument, recording the unit's grisly record of killed, wounded, missing, and captured, would prove an object of "unremitting study" among future generations. This "appropriate memento," he reflected, was not unlike the elegant obelisk marking the grave of Baron DeKalb, which the men had spied in Camden, South Carolina, at the climax of Potter's Raid. "The people of future days may read of the generous stranger, who came from a distant land, to fight their battles, and to water with his blood, the tree of their liberties."[14]

Standing in the National Cemetery where at least a dozen of the regiment's men had been interred earlier that morning, Ohio's walrus-mustached governor, Joseph Benson Foraker, delivered an address that alternated between appeals for sectional reconciliation and the best "bloody shirt" waving. "Gettysburg," he announced, "was more than a mere battle. It was more than the turning point of a great war. It was an epoch in the history of the world—a crowning triumph for the human race":

> Almost a quarter of a century has passed. The moving columns, glittering bayonets, flashing sabers and charging squadrons of that fearful time are gone forever. The rattling musketry and roaring cannon of the mighty struggle are hushed. Where was the carnage of war is now only peace.[15]

The governor's remarks were of a piece with the image of Civil War soldiering popular in the late nineteenth century. Granite soldiers gripping muskets began occupying northern town squares and village greens, standing quiet sentinel over the beguiling transformations of the Gilded Age. "Built around the idea of duty," one recent historian contends, these statues "created a new model of the citizen-soldier for the nation." Local and county histories, meanwhile, celebrated courage, patriotism, and bravery as the innate qualities of ordinary soldiers. In his history of Stark County, for instance, William Henry Perrin noted that the 107th Ohio's history was "written in the blood of the gallant men of whom it was composed." Meanwhile, the historian of neighboring Wayne County distinguished the 107th as a "fine regiment," acclaiming the "earnest patriotism and heroic valor" that its soldiers manifested on "many occasions."[16]

Over time, esteem of this sort served to obscure rather than preserve the memory of the regiment. In their conviction that the war's outcome was inevitable, popular narratives lost sight of the human and emotional realities of combat—the doubt, fear, grief, exhaustion, guilt, and sense of betrayal that animated the rank and file during and long after the Civil War. In a rush to deem every soldier a hero, many chroniclers wrung irony, ambiguity, and adversity from their narratives. Rather than engage with the lived immediacy of a struggle that did not always move in logical, rational, or easy-to-apprehend ways, Civil War histories brimmed with the quiet reassurance that the nation had been preserved. The struggle became an annealing fire that confirmed America's exceptionalism—a test of wills that celebrated the mettle of white, native-born men. Just as the war's history became segregated, so too did it become sanitized.

This emerging narrative vexed many veterans, but perhaps none more than William Siffert. Though the monument dedication exercises afforded him a welcome opportunity to once more grip the hands of old comrades, he returned from Gettysburg daunted by the thought that a "true" and complete history of the battle would never be recorded. The battle, he realized, was not a discrete event, but rather a dizzying mosaic of human experiences—each as unique as the regiments that endured them. That autumn, believing the artist's brush superior to the historian's pen, he outstretched large sheets of muslin and began to paint. By 1888, he had produced four oversized oil paintings illustrating the campaign and battle of Gettysburg. The largest painting crowded "the events of the three days of fighting" into a single panorama. All too predictably, Blocher's Knoll and the fields where the Eleventh Corps battled on July 1 commanded the canvas.[17]

In his Gettysburg series, Siffert did not reach for the realism or

William Siffert rode the war lecture circuit in the 1890s, regaling audiences throughout his native state with a stirring account of his participation in the war's bloodiest battle.

authenticity sought by artists like Paul Philippoteaux, whose cyclorama of Pickett's Charge—then on display in Boston—moved veterans to tears with its "life-like" fidelity to detail. Dominated instead
by distinct ensembles of men, Siffert rendered a vision of the battle
that foregrounded human will, agency, and individuality. The veteran
artist sought to critique—not to craft—a coherent narrative of the
battle. His paintings resisted grandeur and gore with the same, stead-
fast resolve; they exposed the eccentricities of war. The four paintings
would become Siffert's visual aids over the next decade as he crisscrossed Ohio, delivering the "war lecture" that he advertised on a stout,
handsomely printed business card: "My Experience as a Soldier."[18]

WILLIAM SIFFERT INSISTED that the human face of war could be
obscured, but never truly effaced. Today, one does not need to roam
in search of the regiment very long to grasp his point. Sturdy woods
once again populate the banks of Accokeek Creek. In the stands of
timber, subtle depressions pock the ground. These odd gouges in the
earth evocatively mark the locations where tiny log huts once sheltered
soldiers. Together with abandoned stretches of corduroy road and
the occasional pile of stone, they bear eloquent witness to the winter camps where men shivered, suffered, and resolved to preserve the
United States. South of the Rappahannock, vehicles navigate a curve
along congested Route 3, the name the Virginia State Highway Commission bestowed upon the old Orange Turnpike in the early twentieth century. The weather-boarded Talley farmhouse no longer stands
(after falling into disrepair, it was razed in 1926), but a local battlefield
preservation organization owns the surrounding acres—knotted with
thick brambles and briars—upon which the men of the 107th Ohio
made their fated stand on the second day at Chancellorsville.[19]

Up the road in Gettysburg, a rusty cyclone fence weaves along much
of the line the regiment held on the second day of July, among the least
visited sites on the nation's most visited battlefield. The few who take
the time or trouble to reach the site—a tiny patch of grass obscured by
an enormous green water tank—will find granite markers denoting

the flanks of the 107th Ohio, resolute reminders of the fight for East Cemetery Hill. The markers, just scores of feet apart, also testify eloquently to the devastating toll of the battle for Blocher's Knoll.[20]

Much farther south, Folly Island's city of canvas has been replaced by swarms of beach-goers, many of whom would be surprised to learn that their beloved spit of sand once played host to armies of occupying soldiers. Recent archeological work, however, has done much to unearth Folly's Civil War history. Down the coast in Jacksonville, prescient Florida officials spared a 124-acre tract of Camp Milton from its proposed fate as a sludge dump. A plank boardwalk lined with sun-bleached interpretive markers conveys park visitors to the remnants of the rebel works. A short drive away, the masonry walls of Fort Clinch still stand, the crown jewel of a state park where, as a glossy, color brochure boasts, "history, beauty, and nature meet in an experience like no other."[21]

In Sumter County, South Carolina, weather-beaten road signs point earnest Civil War buffs along the route of Potter's Raid, a campaign that scarcely scores a mention in most modern histories of the war. A cast-iron state historical marker informs the motorists who hurry along Route 521 that the clearing along Turkey Creek played host to "one of the last battles" of the war. With great fidelity to the Lost Cause, the sign relates that the fight was one against the overwhelming might of federal numbers. "A Confederate home guard of old men, boys, and convalescents here made a gallant stand in an effort to halt Potter's Raid," the sign boasts, claiming an historical authority it does not deserve. For the Medal of Honor won by Henry Finkenbiner, however, the marker has no words.[22]

IN NORTHEAST OHIO, a hunt for the 107th Ohio yields similar results. In Louisville, the Vignos tavern, recently fitted with a new copper roof, still stands—anchoring not a quiet village green, but the corner of a busy intersection. Cars hurry beyond the Town Tavern, almost certainly unaware of the Civil War history in their midst. Eight miles away, in a quaint Catholic cemetery at Canton's edge, Augustus rests in the grave where his four pallbearers—regimental comrades Alfred Garner, James Corl, Lanson McKinney, and Mahlon Slutz—lowered his casket in July 1926.[23]

Population booms and urban renewal projects have so reconfigured the streets of Akron that the regiment's veterans would scarcely know them. Only Glendale Cemetery, perched on the "high bluffs" immediately south of town, might be recognizable to the old boys. Established a generation before the war by city leaders seeking to fasten Akron to the rural cemetery movement, Glendale became a locus of Civil War commemorative activity in the late nineteenth century. In 1876, the Grand Army of the Republic dedicated a memorial chapel—a striking tribute in sandstone and slate, flanked by two brass cannon—at the cemetery gates. Its interior walls are ornamented with handsome plaques that are lined by the names of local veterans, including George Billow. The captain rests beneath a simple monolith at the top of the hill, the stone crooked and gnarled by a century's worth of Akron winters.[24]

In Cleveland, National Hall was razed long ago, and a wrecking ball demolished the Weddell House to create room for a seventeen-story office tower. But in the quiet Tremont neighborhood, at the intersection of West 7th Street and University Road, a bronze Ohio state historical marker recalls the heady days of Camp Cleveland. A year before that Buckeye laureled plaque went up, the state erected a similar sign at the corner of South Sandusky Street and Olentangy Avenue in Delaware—the site of Camp Delaware and the regiment's first fatalities.

The village of Zoar is now a National Historic Landmark. Five days per week between June and September, its well-manicured buildings and gardens—maintained by the private, not-for-profit Zoar Community Association—bustle with tourists eager to learn about the German separatist community from costumed interpreters. Only a few of those visitors will drive down Seventh Street to the Zoar Cemetery— the quiet oasis known to the settlers as "God's Acre." The decades have not been kind to the headstones, many leaning and lichened.

The ground has swallowed up some of the markers, while others will soon be ready for the piles of broken or toppled stones that line the cemetery's zagging rows. Christian Rieker's simple military headstone stands along the edge of a gravel road—still erect, but so weathered that its words are just ghostly impressions. But if one squints, the words, "107th Ohio Inf." can yet be made out. John Brunny's father, who died within a decade of the war, is buried here, too. His son, however, is interred nearly nine hundred miles away; the young bugler as far from Zoar in death as he was in life.[25]

Just up the road in Navarre, Union Lawn Cemetery consumes the better part of a city block. The graveyard contains the town's brawny Civil War monument, dedicated in the first decade of the twentieth century. Affixed to the striking granite boulder is a bronze tablet bearing the names of Navarre's Union soldiers—including fifty-two men from the 107th Ohio. Buried nearby are William O. Siffert and Alfred Rider, along with James M. Corl and other survivors of Company A. In cemeteries elsewhere throughout Cleveland, Akron, Canton, Massillon, New Philadelphia, and Elyria, the men of the 107th Ohio rest together in family plots, pauper's graves, and Grand Army of the Republic lots. Even in death, they never really demobilized.[26]

MORE THAN A century and a half later, genealogists are the most dutiful custodians of the regiment's history, sharing an urgent need to make sense of the great loss and tragedy that befell their forebears. Jim Finkenbiner conducted research on his grandfather, requesting copies of his pension records after touring the Chancellorsville battlefield in the late 1980s. Philip Scherag's great-grandson, a long-time high-school history teacher in Massillon, traveled to Germany in search of his ancestor. "The Germans were not real popular," he observed. "They were kind of like a sacrificial lamb." Chris Nelson, the great-great-grandson of John Flory, wrote an eight-page narrative history of the regiment—until this book, the only modern history of the 107th Ohio. "Not many regiments in the Union Army served all the way from Ohio to Florida and back," he concluded, "and not many fought in two of the most important battles of the war." While skeptics might be quick to dismiss Nelson's claim, it is no idle boast. Throughout its almost three years in the field, the men of the regiment whipsawed between the war's extremes. They trudged through snowbanks and sand bars, sampling victory and defeat. They learned about courage and cowardice, purpose and futility, resolve and despair. They took pride in their pain and solace from their suffering, keenly aware that emerging national narratives about the war captured nothing of their experiences.

More recently still, Andrew Suhrer, a direct descendant of Lieutenant Fernando Suhrer and a "lifelong history buff," self-published *The Flying Dutchmen*, a novel of "love, separation, friendship and tragedy" based on the unit's experiences. The book's imaginative scenes draw on years of original research, as well as the author's correspondence with descendants of Augustus Vignos and George Billow, who still live in northeastern Ohio. The bonds of regimental comradeship, it seems, are powerful enough to persist across several generations. "It is impossible to look back at our ancestors and not feel awe," Suhrer explained, "as well as thankfulness that we never had to endure such severe hardships and mortality."[27]

And so the men of the 107th Ohio endure still—urgent voices telling stories about who we are, how our country was saved, and what it means to go to war.

ACKNOWLEDGMENTS

NOT LONG AFTER RETURNING from a macabre expedition to inventory the graves of Union soldiers scattered throughout Kentucky, Georgia, and Tennessee, Colonel Edmund B. Whitman made a startling confession. "Called as I have been to spend three years and more among the *dead*," he explained, "it is not strange that I come to feel as though *their* dead were all *my* friends." After spending the last few years with the men of the 107th Ohio Volunteer Infantry, I empathize with Whitman's sentiment. As I chased the tracks they left in the archives, wandered around their camps and battlefields, and visited their graves, the soldiers of the 107th Ohio became my trusted companions. Though at times frustratingly elusive, I feel as though they have lived with me.

The journey of the last three years would not have been possible without the talented troop of librarians, archivists, and colleagues who helped me along the way. I salute here the fine folks at the Ohio History Connection in Columbus; the South Carolina Historical Society; the University of South Carolina; the Houghton Library at Harvard; the Huntington Library in San Marino, California; the Library of Virginia; the David M. Rubenstein Rare Book and Manuscript Library at Duke; Sterling Memorial Library at Yale; the Connecticut State Library; the Connecticut Historical Society; the Wayne

County Public Library; the Akron-Summit County Public Library Special Collections; the William McKinley Presidential Library; the Stark County Public Library; and last but certainly not least, the National Archives in Washington, D.C. I logged more hours at the National Archives than I did at any other repository. Will the thrill of cracking open dirt-begrimed volumes in the Central Reading Room ever get old?

More importantly, this book would not have come to fruition without the support, encouragement, and assistance of many dear friends and colleagues. Lesley J. Gordon's work has inspired me; I am grateful for her friendship. John J. Hennessy graciously provided reams of material on the Eleventh Corps from his personal research files and gave me unfettered access to the Fredericksburg & Spotsylvania National Military Park Library. Barbara Gannon, Jonathan W. White, and Adam H. Domby are talented historians but even better friends. Fellow Ohio native Daniel Welch shared valuable information about the care and treatment of the regiment's wounded at the George Spangler Farm, a site that he was instrumental in researching and interpreting for the public. Ronald Szudy of Parma, Ohio, sent me some valuable material on Peter F. Young. Lisa Tendrich Frank offered comments when I presented a portion of this book at the Society of Civil War Historians Biennial Meeting in Pittsburgh, and Mary Louise Roberts did the same when I presented at the American Historical Association Meeting in Chicago. Evan Rothera was, as always, a patient sounding board for ideas new and old. In record time, my friend and the talented historical cartographer Edward Alexander produced the splendid maps that illustrate this book.

My thanks to Terry Johnston of *The Civil War Monitor* for permission to reprint portions of an article that I published in his magazine about Seraphim Meyer's episode at Gettysburg. Andy Lang and Drew Bledsoe gave me the chance to try out some material on veteranhood in their fine anthology, *Upon the Fields of Battle*. My mentors Allen Guelzo, Gabor Boritt, Matthew Norman, Bruno Cabanes, Joanne

Freeman, and David Blight can no doubt detect their influence. It goes without saying that I have been unusually fortunate to work with such an august group of historians. I am a better historian—and a better person—for having worked with them.

It was a pleasure to once again publish with Liveright/W. W. Norton. Katie Adams, who edited my last book, believed in this project when it was still a shapeless proposal. Daniel Gerstle proved to be a smart and gifted editor. Dan's keen eye and discerning comments have made this a much better work of history than it might have been otherwise. Nancy Green was a careful copy editor, and Haley Bracken shepherded this book with great skill. I thank Bob Weil and the entire editorial, production, and marketing team at Liveright. They are truly the best in the business.

A few months before I began this project, Sam Houston State University became my academic home. Since then, it has become my family. Above all, I wish to thank Pinar Emiralioglu for her tireless support and friendship. Benjamin Park and I share many things—an editor, a publisher, and an office wall—but most important is our friendship, which sustained me in ways big and small through the writing of this book. Not many academicians can imagine spending eighteen days on the road in a rumbling bus with one of their departmental colleagues, but Willis Oyugi and I would do it again, so long as we had each other's company and conversation. Steve Rapp and his partner, Julie Nelson, have supplied many wonderful hours of food, conversation, and laughter. Jeremiah Dancy, now of the U.S. Naval War College, was a constant companion and loyal friend during the three years we spent together at Sam Houston State. CHSS Dean Abbey Zink deserves my thanks for her tireless support of my scholarly endeavors.

Carlotta Ford and Kellie Lawson have not only made my life easier, allowing me to spend precious hours at the keyboard, but have supplied plenty of good cheer over the years. Carlotta's friendship has seen me through difficult times. I likewise thank Haylee Furlow and

Ashley Nell, who provided able administrative support in the History Department office during the writing of this book.

I offer sincere thanks to my students, who challenge, teach, and inspire me every day. They've all known something of adversity, but never privilege. Their courage, work ethic, and genuine excitement for the study of history give me hope for the future. The world will be a better place when they are in charge of it. Here, I need to single out the two cohorts of undergraduates who have participated in Sam Houston State's Civil War Study Away program. I'll never forget those students contemplating the surreal savagery of the attack at Spotsylvania's Bloody Angle, or delivering my last lecture on the steps of the Lincoln Memorial. Thanks as well to my talented graduate students, past and present, and to the veterans of the "common soldier" seminar, in which parts of this book took shape.

More than anything else, tramping the battlefields of the American Civil War allowed me to write this book. I have been fortunate enough to walk the fields with some of the finest minds in the profession. Hours spent on the battlefield with John Hennessy, Frank O'Reilly, Greg Mertz, and Will Greene, in particular, have informed my thinking about the war and paid many dividends. John and I spent a wonderful afternoon poking around Stafford County in search of the 107th Ohio's winter campsites. Chapter 3 took shape in the car that afternoon. Thanks also to Roy Niedermayer, Johnson Fluker, and the participants in the six summer seminars I have led for Yale. I tested and refined many of the ideas in this book with them.

I've said it before, but I'll say it again—my parents, Ralph and Terri Jordan, are the best parents a son could ever ask for. Not only did they read most of this book in draft, but they carted me back and forth to the Ohio History Connection in Columbus, tolerated their fair share of 107th Ohio stories, and even cranked a few reels of microfilm at my request. They tramped cemeteries with me, tiptoed through the remnants of Fort Milton, and even made an ill-fated attempt to find the South Carolina plantation where the 107th Ohio learned of the

Lincoln assassination. At last, I can admit that I chose an Ohio topic so I could spend more time with them.

I can't spend any more time with Dick Klar, nor with Willard and Pat Jordan, but their memories burn on. So too does the memory of my friend Gary Dillon, who passed away as I labored over the first draft. Like the regiment at the heart of this book, you are not forgotten.

Brian Matthew Jordan
Willis, Texas
May 2020

BIBLIOGRAPHIC NOTE

PENNING THE HISTORY of a Civil War regiment is a difficult task, but the men of the 107th Ohio Volunteer Infantry posed unique challenges. While scholars of the nation's bloodiest conflict usually enjoy an embarrassing bounty of manuscript sources, only a few letters penned by the regiment's enlisted men survive in archival collections today. Three letters from Fritz Nussbaum found their way into the George Shane Phillips Papers at the Huntington Library in San Marino, California. Dispatches penned by John Brunny and Christian Rieker are preserved among the records of the Society of Separatists of Zoar at the Ohio History Connection in Columbus. Stray correspondence from Alvin Brown and Jacob Boroway is held by the Library of Virginia in Richmond and University of South Carolina. And thanks to the diligent spadework of Thomas J. Edwards, who toiled for many years on the 25th Ohio Volunteers, a folder's worth of material from the 107th made its way into the Center for Archival Collections at Ohio's Bowling Green State University. While all indispensable to this project, none of these sources provided a sustained look at life in the regiment, but captured snapshots of individual experiences at a particular moment in time.

Local newspapers provided richer fodder. Most historians have yet to mine these sources systematically for material from Civil War soldiers. Given the number of soldier letters that filled their columns—epistles from the front were more economical than dispatches from war correspondents—this is somewhat astonishing. Among other papers, the *Stark County Republican, Stark County Democrat, Summit County Beacon, Daily Cleveland Herald,* and *Elyria Independent Democrat,* all available on microfilm at the Ohio History Connection, were deep wells of source material. But here too, methodological problems abounded. Many Civil War soldiers penned letters keenly aware that they were writing for audiences beyond their addressees, but those who wrote to newspaper editors had no doubt. They attempted to shape the narrative of their service, turning back false-hearted allegations while seeking to present their sacrifices in the best possible light.

Though fully aware of the hazards of reminiscent testimony, I relied heavily on Jacob Smith's *Camps and Campaigns,* published in 1910. The regimental history was the first real "genre" of Civil War writing, and scholars have paid it too little notice. A surprising number of historians have regarded regimentals as unseemly exercises in self-promotion, serving "more a memorial purpose than a historical one." To be sure, unit histories served a commemorative function; they likewise brimmed with a level of detail that not infrequently arrested their narrative momentum. Disclaiming any "mercenary motives," their inexperienced writers cared little about achieving a readership or literary fame beyond the "small, closed world" of the regimental community. Yet regimental histories were also capable of advancing measured interpretations about the war's cause, conduct, and consequences. In many respects, they were ideal vessels for capturing the war in all of its complexities: it was incumbent upon them to explain how their experiences resounded beyond the regimental camp, but they could never lose sight of their own stubborn individuality. Unflinching and inclusive, they thrived somewhere between national histories and personal narratives.[1]

The records preserved in the National Archives afforded perhaps the most unvarnished look at the regiment. Regimental order books preserve muster rolls, general orders, records of disciplinary actions, and detailed information about the work of feeding, supplying, moving, and maneuvering Civil War regiments. I believe that no one can truly understand the huge logistical challenges posed by the war without reading these invaluable records. But here, too, the 107th Ohio posed challenges. Wartime inspectors noted the wretched state of the regiment's bookkeeping. Nor did the situation improve when some of the regiment's most fastidious clerks were detailed to brigade or division headquarters. Still, there is much to be gleaned about the regiment in these yellowed pages.

In an effort to capture something of the war as the 107th Ohio might have experienced it—to supply essential details about the weather, sensory experiences, the environment, and general sentiments in camp and on the march—it was necessary to rely on neighboring units. Each fighting regiment, of course, was a world of its own; nonetheless, units packed together in the same brigade or division made telling observations about one other—and very often supplied a more complete picture of events. Fortunately, the 17th Connecticut Volunteer Infantry, brigaded with the 107th Ohio throughout much of the war, left behind an enormous record of contemporaneous and reminiscent testimony. While less prolific, the soldiers of the 25th Ohio, 55th Ohio, and 75th Ohio were no less profound. When I did not have direct testimony from a soldier in the 107th Ohio, I relied on the words of men from neighboring units when their observations seemed plausible. Many of the volunteers quoted in the book did not fight in the 107th Ohio, but it is my belief that their expressions faithfully represent whatever slice of the war they shared with the regiment. Manuscript sources and published reminiscences supplied much fodder.

Ironically, owing to the rigorous evidentiary demands of the U.S. Pension Bureau, there is a much richer, more textured archival record of the 107th Ohio after the war. Pension files, which document in wrenching detail veterans' domestic situations, medical histories, daily struggles, and Civil War memories, were a logical place to begin. As Claire Prechtel Kluskens has pointed out, pension files are "underappreciated" sources that yield plenty of "untapped material for unit histories."[2] But my narrative benefited by reaching well beyond these records. Records of pension fraud investigations netted the stories of widows and veterans alike who became the prey of shark-like pension claim attorneys. By combing the seldom-used papers of Civil War volunteer surgeons at the National Archives, I uncovered many letters from veterans who, in their efforts to locate Surgeon Knaus, poignantly betrayed something of their desperation. Extant registers of the National Home for the Disabled Volunteer Soldier provided important information, as did the voluminous records of the Department of the Ohio, Grand Army of the Republic.

NOTES

PROLOGUE

1. On the battle of Chancellorsville, see Stephen W. Sears, *Chancellorsville* (New York: Houghton Mifflin, 1996).

2. *Daily National Intelligencer*, May 6, 1863; Union captain, as quoted in Wolfgang Helbich, "German-Born Union Soldiers: Motivation, Ethnicity, and 'Americanization'," in Wolfgang Helbich and Walter D. Kamphoefner, eds., *German-American Immigration and Ethnicity in Comparative Perspective* (Madison, WI: Max Kade Institute for German American Studies, 2004), 297. On tensions within the Union army, see Mark H. Dunkelman, "Hardtack and Sauerkraut Stew: Ethnic Tensions in the 154th New York Volunteers, Eleventh Corps, during the Civil War," *Yearbook of German-American Studies* 36 (2001): 69–90.

3. Henry Lee Scott, *Military Dictionary* (New York: D. Van Nostrand, 1863), 400; Wilhelm Stängel in the *Louisville Anzeiger*, January 9, 1862, as quoted in *A German Hurrah! Civil War Letters of Friedrich Bertsch and Wilhelm Stängel, 9th Ohio Infantry*, ed. Joseph R. Reinhart (Kent, OH: Kent State University Press, 2010), 202; Roberts Bartholow, *A Manual of Instructions of Enlisting and Discharging Soldiers* (Philadelphia: J. B. Lippincott & Co., 1864), 94; Mischa Honeck, "Men of Principle: Gender and the German-American War for the Union," *Journal of the Civil War Era* 5, no. 1 (March 2015): 38–67.

4. Whitelaw Reid, *Ohio in the War: Her Statesmen, Generals, and Soldiers* (Cincinnati: Robert Clarke Company, 1895), 2:135–36; Henry Howe, *Historical Collections of Ohio: An Encyclopedia of the State* (Cincinnati: C. J. Krehbiel & Co., Printers and Binders, 1902), 2:624; William Henry Perrin, ed., *History of*

Stark County, with an Outline Sketch of Ohio (Chicago: Baskin & Battey, 1881), 639–40; Charles Vignos, "Biography of Augustus Vignos," Ancestry.com, https://www.ancestry.com/mediaui-viewer/collection/1030/tree/31357887/ person/12448279419/media/04f4e235–7812–4270-b3f8-c44537516f86?_ phsrc=VlU146&usePUBJs=true [accessed March 15, 2020]; Cindy Vignos, "The Novelty Cutlery Company," *Oregon Knife Collectors Newsletter* (October 2002), posted to Ancestry.com, https://www.ancestry.com/mediaui-viewer/ collection/1030/tree/31357887/person/12448279419/media/6f9f6158-c8cf– 4be7-bfe8–5e5da261cc38?_phsrc=VlU146&usePUBJs=true [accessed March 15, 2020].

5. *OR*, vol. 10, pt. 1, pp. 310, 354–55, 357–58; Smith, *Shiloh: Conquer or Perish* (Lawrence: University Press of Kansas, 2014), 241, 336–38.

6. Helbich, "German-Born Union Soldiers: Motivation, Ethnicity, and 'Americanization'," in Wolfgang Helbich and Walter D. Kamphoefner, eds., *German-American Immigration and Ethnicity in Comparative Perspective*, 306; Cindy Vignos, "The Novelty Cutlery Company,": 1; Mahlon J. Slutz, *Tribute to Major Augustus Vignos* (Kent, OH: n.p., 1926), 1.

7. Samuel Alanson Lane, *Fifty Years of Summit County*; Mack Walker, *Germany and the Emigration, 1816–1885* (Cambridge, MA: Harvard University Press, 1964), 47, 69; Albert B. Faust, *The German Element in the United States.* 2 vols. (Boston and New York: Houghton Mifflin Company, 1909), 1:511–13; Christina Bearden-White, "Illinois Germans and the Coming of the Civil War: Reshaping Ethnic Identity," *Journal of the Illinois State Historical Society* 109, no. 3 (Fall 2016): 231–51; Walter D. Kamphoefner, Wolfgang Helbich, and Ulrike Sommer, eds., *News from the Land of Freedom: German Immigrants Write Home* (Ithaca: Cornell University Press, 1991). See also Gunter Moltmann, "The Pattern of German Emigration to the United States in the Nineteenth Century," in Frank Trommler and Joseph McVeigh, eds., *America and the Germans: An Assessment of a Three-Hundred-Year History* (Philadelphia: University of Pennsylvania Press, 1985), 1:14–24.

8. Stephen D. Engle, "Yankee Dutchmen: Germans, the Union, and the Construction of a Wartime Identity," in Susannah J. Ural, ed., *Civil War Citizens: Race, Ethnicity, and Identity in America's Bloodiest Conflict* (New York: New York University Press, 2010), 14–15; Dean B. Mahin, *The Blessed Place of Freedom: Europeans in Civil War America* (Washington, DC: Brassey's, 2002), 2; "When the Old School Wagon Maker was in Flower," *Carriage Monthly* 38, no. 1 (April 1902): 21–22. On the development of the carriage manufacturing industry in northeastern Ohio, see Thomas A. Kinney, "From Shop to Factory in the Industrial Heartland: The Industrialization of Horse-Drawn Vehicle Manufacture in the City of Cleveland" (PhD diss., Case Western Reserve University, 1998).

9. George Billow Pension File, RG 15, NA; *Summit County Beacon*, August 14, 1862.

10. Helbich, "German-Born Union Soldiers," 305; Walter Kamphoefner and Wolfgang Helbich, eds., *Germans in the Civil War: The Letters They Wrote Home* (Chapel Hill: University of North Carolina Press, 2006), 7–9, 20–34. On the Midwest, see Zachary Stuart Garrison, *German Americans on the Middle Border: From Antislavery to Reconciliation, 1830–1877* (Carbondale: Southern Illinois University Press, 2019).

11. William L. Burton, *Melting Pot Soldiers: The Union's Ethnic Regiments* (Ames: Iowa State University Press, 1988); Kamphoefner and Helbich, *Germans in the Civil War*, 20. On the population of ethnically German soldiers in the Union armies, see also Engle, "Yankee Dutchmen," 11–56, and Mahin, *Blessed Place of Freedom*, 15.

12. Kamphoefner and Helbich, eds., *Germans in the Civil War*, 20–21, 26; Don Doyle, *The Cause of All Nations: An International History of the American Civil War* (New York: Basic Books, 2014), 160; James M. Bergquist, "German Communities in American Cities: An Interpretation of the Nineteenth-Century Experience," *Journal of American Ethnic History* 4, no. 1 (Fall 1984): 9–30; Annette R. Hofmann, "One Hundred Fifty Years of Loyalty: The Turner Movement in the United States," *Yearbook of German-American Studies* 34 (1999): 63–82; Honeck, "Men of Principle." Recent scholars have done a much better job of recovering the hemispheric vision of Civil War Americans and understanding the "Civil War the world made." In addition to Doyle, see Evan C. Rothera, " 'The Men Are Understood to Have Been Generally Americans, in the Employ of the Liberal Government': Civil War Veterans and Mexico, 1865–1867," in Brian Matthew Jordan and Evan C. Rothera, eds., *The War Went On: Reconsidering the Lives of Civil War Veterans* (Baton Rouge: Louisiana State University Press, 2020), 37–60, and Gregory P. Downs, *The Second American Revolution: The Civil War–Era Struggle over Cuba and the Rebirth of the American Republic* (Chapel Hill: University of North Carolina Press, 2019). For a view of immigrant soldiers that aligns with the one posited by Kamphoefner and Helbich, see Burton, *Melting Pot Soldiers*, 58, 111, 227.

13. Perrin, *History of Stark County*, 555; Bryan S. Baker, "Biography of Alfred J. Rider," last updated January 2013 and posted by Robin Law, Ancestry.com, https://www.ancestry.com/mediaui-viewer/collection/1030/tree/11298984/person/-382004049/media/336e1424-281e-4d43-a8a2-fed9cc207dd5?_phsrc=VlU143&usePUBJs=true [accessed March 15, 2020]; Carol Sheriff, *The Artificial River: The Erie Canal and the Paradox of Progress* (New York: Hill and Wang, 1996); *Portrait and Biographical Record of Stark County, Ohio*, 443; Robert Swierenga, "The Settlement of the Old Northwest," *Journal of the Early Republic* 9, no. 1 (Spring 1989): 83; Faust, *The German Element in the United States*, 1:422.

14. Perrin, *History of Stark County*, 555; *Portrait and Biographical Record of Stark County, Ohio*, 443; Baker, "Biography of Alfred J. Rider."

15. Bruce Levine, *The Spirit of 148: German Immigrants, Labor Conflict, and the Coming of the Civil War* (Urbana and Chicago: University of Illinois Press, 1992), 250–52; Andre Fleche, *The Revolution of 1861* (Chapel Hill: University of North Carolina Press, 2010), 54; Kamphoefner and Helbich, eds., *Germans in the Civil War*, 3. See also John L. Brooke, *"There Is a North": Fugitive Slaves, Political Crisis, and Cultural Transformation in the Coming of the Civil War* (Amherst: University of Massachusetts Press, 2019); Don E. Fehrenbacher, *The Slaveholding Republic: An Account of the United States Government's Relations to Slavery* (New York: Oxford University Press, 2001).

16. *Portrait and Biographical Record of Stark County, Ohio*, 443–44.

17. According to historians Walter D. Kamphoefner and Wolfang Helbich, "Republican immigrants enlisted more eagerly in the Union army than did Democrats." Kamphoefner and Helbich, *Germans in the Civil War*, 7. Kathleen Fernandez, *Zoar: The Story of an Intentional Community* (Kent, Ohio: Kent State University Press, 2019), 1–29, 227, 233–34; Elizabeth Siber White, "The *Wiedergeburt* in the Religion of the Zoarites" (MA thesis, Western Michigan University, 1985), 1–9; and George Landis, "The Society of Separatists of Zoar, Ohio," *Annual Report of the American Historical Association* (1899): 169, 171. On Zoar, see also Philip E. Webber, *Zoar in the Civil War* (Kent, Ohio: Kent State University Press, 2007).

18. White, "The *Wiedergeburt* in the Religion of the Zoarites," 1–9.

19. Ibid.; Fernandez, *Zoar*, 1–29; Landis, "The Society of Separatists of Zoar," 172.

20. Fernandez, *Zoar*, 29, 68–69, 72, 233–34; see also R. Douglas Hurt, *The Ohio Frontier: Crucible of the Old Northwest, 1720–1830* (Bloomington: Indiana University Press, 1996), 305; Harry S. Stout, *Upon the Altar of the Nation: A Moral History of the Civil War* (New York: Viking, 2006); Fernandez, *Zoar*, 150–54.

21. Fernandez, *Zoar*, 29, 68–69, 72, 130–31, 150–54, 233–34; Landis, "The Society of Separatists of Zoar," 187.

22. Reid Mitchell, *The Vacant Chair: The Northern Soldier Leaves Home* (New York: Oxford University Press, 1993), 3–8.

23. Christian Rieker to dear sister, October 19, 1862, Society of Separatists of Zoar Records, Box 96, Folder 1, Ohio History Connection, Columbus; Christian Rieker to dear sister, November 13, 1862, Society of Separatists of Zoar Records, Box 96, Folder 1, Ohio History Connection; Declaration of Conscientious Objection, July 10, 1863, Society of Separatists of Zoar Records, Box 96, Folder 2, Ohio History Connection, Columbus. For a superb analysis of the links forged by homespun, see James J. Broomall, *Private Confederacies:*

The Emotional Worlds of Southern Men as Citizens and Soldiers (Chapel Hill: University of North Carolina Press, 2019), 36.

24. Brian Matthew Jordan, "The Unfortunate Colonel," *The Civil War Monitor* 6, no. 4 (Winter 2016): 62; George L. Kilmer, "First Actions of Wounded Soldiers," *Popular Science Monthly* (June 1892): 155–58.

25. Jordan, "The Unfortunate Colonel," 54–63, 74–76; Christian Rieker Pension File, National Archives Building.

26. David Van Tassel and John J. Grabowski, eds., *Encyclopedia of Cleveland History* (Bloomington and Indianapolis: Indiana University Press, 1996), c.v. 107th Ohio Volunteer Infantry Regiment.

27. On the experience of disability among Civil War soldiers, see Sarah Handley-Cousins, *Bodies in Blue: Disability in the Civil War North* (Athens: University of Georgia Press, 2019).

28. For accounts that emphasize the strength of ideological convictions, see James M. McPherson, *For Cause and Comrades: Why Men Fought in the Civil War* (New York: Oxford University Press, 1997); Michael Barton, *Goodmen: The Character of Civil War Soldiers* (University Park: Pennsylvania State University Press, 1981); Earl J. Hess, *The Union Soldier in Battle: Enduring the Ordeal of Combat* (Lawrence: University Press of Kansas, 1997); and Chandra M. Manning, *What This Cruel War Was Over: Soldiers, Slavery, and the Civil War* (New York: Alfred A. Knopf, 2007). For accounts that emphasize disillusionment, see Gerald F. Linderman, *Embattled Courage: The Experience of Combat in the American Civil War* (New York: Free Press, 1987), and Michael C. C. Adams, *Living Hell: The Dark Side of the Civil War* (Baltimore: Johns Hopkins University Press, 2014).

29. Beyond a renewed focus on the natural, physical, and material environments of war, recent scholars have applied the tools of sensory history and the history of emotions to the Civil War era. The result is a more textured understanding of the war as a lived human experience. In addition to James J. Broomall, *Private Confederacies*, see Amy Murrell Taylor, *Embattled Freedom: Journeys through the Civil War's Slave Refugee Camps* (Chapel Hill: University of North Carolina Press, 2018); Megan Kate Nelson, *Ruin Nation: Destruction and the American Civil War* (Athens: University of Georgia Press, 2012); Peter S. Carmichael, *The War for the Common Soldier: How Men Thought, Fought, and Survived in Civil War Armies* (Chapel Hill: University of North Carolina Press, 2018); Joan Cashin, *War Stuff: The Struggle for Human and Environmental Resources in the American Civil War* (Cambridge: Cambridge University Press, 2018); Evan A. Kutzler, *Living by Inches: The Smells, Sounds, Tastes, and Feelings of Captivity in Civil War Prisons* (Chapel Hill: University of North Carolina Press, 2019); Martha Hodes, *Mourning Lincoln* (New

Haven: Yale University Press, 2015); Judkin Browning and Timothy Silver, *An Environmental History of the Civil War* (Chapel Hill: University of North Carolina Press, 2020); and Mark M. Smith, *The Smell of Battle, The Taste of Siege: A Sensory History of the Civil War* (New York: Oxford University Press, 2015). Connecticut soldier, as quoted in *Danbury Times*, January 1, 1863.

30. Honeck, "Men of Principle": 39, 42–43.

31. Engle, "Yankee Dutchmen," 16, 32; Doyle, *Cause of All Nations*, 160; "Adopted Citizens and Slavery," *Douglass' Monthly* (August 1859); Kenneth Barkin, "Ordinary Germans, Slavery, and the U.S. Civil War," *Journal of African American History* 93, no. 1 (Winter 2008): 70–79; Andreas Dorpalen, "The German Element and the Issues of the Civil War," *Mississippi Valley Historical Review* 29, no. 1 (June 1942): 55–76; *Illinois Staats-Zeitung,* July 26, 1861, as quoted in Eric Benjaminson, "A Regiment of Immigrants: The 82nd Illinois Volunteer Infantry and the Letters of Captain Rudolph Mueller," *Journal of the Illinois State Historical Society* 94, no. 2 (Summer 2001): 142–43.

32. Perrin, *History of Stark County*, 264; Alfred J. Rider, "Memorial Address," *Gettysburg* [PA] *Star and Sentinel*, November 1, 1887; Leonard Weinstein, "The Relationship of Battle Damage to Unit Combat Performance," Institute for Defense Analysis Paper P–1903 (April 1986): 3–5.

33. Herrmann Nachtigall to Augustus Choate Hamlin, January 28, 1893, in Military Order of the Loyal Legion Papers, Ms 1084, Folder 1040, Houghton Library, Harvard University, Cambridge, MA. On veteranhood in the 107th Ohio, see Brian Matthew Jordan, "The Hour That Lasted Fifty Years: The 107th Ohio and the Human Longitude of Gettysburg," in Andrew F. Lang and Andrew S. Bledsoe, eds., *Upon the Fields of Battle: Essays on the Civil War's Military History* (Baton Rouge: Louisiana State University Press, 2018), 252–70. On the importance of regimental communities to "waging peace," see Susannah Ural, ed., *Hood's Texas Brigade: The Soldiers and Families of the Confederacy's Most Celebrated Unit* (Baton Rouge: Louisiana State University Press, 2017), and Barbara A. Gannon, "'She Is a Member of the 23rd': Lucy Nichols and the Community of the Civil War Regiment," in *This Distracted and Anarchical People: New Answers for Old Questions About the Civil War–Era North*, ed. Andrew L. Slap and Michael Thomas Smith (New York: Fordham University Press, 2013), 184–200. On the culture of veterans and sectional reunion, see Nina Silber, *The Romance of Reunion: Northerners and the South, 1865–1900* (Chapel Hill: University of North Carolina Press, 1993), and David W. Blight, *Race and Reunion: The Civil War in American Memory* (Cambridge, MA: Harvard University Press, 2001).

34. Arlette Farge, *The Allure of the Archives* (New Haven: Yale University Press, 2013), 6; Brigade Inspector's Report, December 24, 1863, in Company Order Books, 107th Ohio Volunteer Infantry, Companies A–E, vol. 5, RG 94, National Archives Building, Washington, DC.

35. Jacob Smith, *Camps and Campaigns of the 107th Ohio Volunteer Infantry, 1862–1865* (Reprint ed., Navarre, Ohio: Indian River Graphics, 2000), 3–8.

36. Ibid.

Chapter 1: "We Feel It Our Duty"

1. "War Meeting at National Hall," *Cleveland Morning Leader*, August 1, 1862; William Ganson Rose, *Cleveland: The Making of a City*, 315, 262; Sharon Gregor, *Rockefeller's Cleveland*, 22; John Malvin, "Incidents in the Racial History of Ohio, 1840–1860," in Robert Wheeler, ed., *Visions of the Western Reserve*, 359; *Daily Cleveland Herald*, July 31, 1862.

2. Eugene H. Roseboom, *The History of the State of Ohio* (Columbus: Ohio State Archaeological and Historical Society, 1944), 4:323–83; Jacob Dolson Cox, *Military Reminiscences of the Civil War* (New York: D. Appleton & Company, 1865), 1:20.

3. On Ohio politics in this period, see Stephen E. Maizlish, *The Triumph of Sectionalism: The Transformation of Ohio Politics, 1844–1856* (Kent, OH: Kent State University Press, 1983), and George Knepper, *Ohio and Its People* (Kent, OH: Kent State University Press, 1989).

4. Samuel S. Cox, *Eight Years in Congress* (New York: D. Appleton & Company, 1865), 235; Knepper, *Ohio and Its People*.

5. Jennifer L. Weber, *Copperheads: The Rise and Fall of Lincoln's Opponents in the North* (New York: Oxford University Press, 2006), passim; Cox, *Eight Years in Congress*, 246, Stephen D. Engle, *Gathering to Save a Nation. Lincoln and the Union's War Governors* (Chapel Hill: University of North Carolina Press, 2016), 207.

6. "War Meeting," *Daily Cleveland Herald*, July 24, 1862. Until Governor Tod scores a modern biographer, the best treatment of his political trajectory is Delmer John Trester, "The Political Career of David Tod" (PhD diss., Ohio State University, 1950). See also David Tod to Abraham Lincoln, July 28, 1862, Abraham Lincoln Papers, LC.

7. Gerald J. Prokopowicz, *All for the Regiment: The Army of the Ohio, 1861–1862* (Chapel Hill: University of North Carolina Press, 2001), 4–5, 27–3.

8. Constantine Grebner, *We Were the Ninth: A History of the Ninth Regiment, Ohio Volunteer Infantry: April 17, 1861 to June 7, 1864* (Reprint ed. Kent, OH: Kent State University Press, 1987), 5–8; William Burton, *Melting Pot Soldiers: The Union's Ethnic Regiments* (Ames, Iowa: Iowa State University Press, 1988).

9. Stephen D. Engle, *Yankee Dutchman: The Life of Franz Sigel* (Baton Rouge: Louisiana State University Press, 1993), xiv–xv.

10. "One Hundred and Seventh The German Regiment," *Daily Cleveland Herald*, July 25, 1862; "New German Regiment," *Daily Cleveland Herald*, July 14,

1862; *Cleveland Plain Dealer,* August 2, 1862; "New Appointments—S. Meyers, Esq.," *Cleveland Morning Leader,* August 1, 1862; *Stark County Republican* [Canton, Ohio], August 7, 1862; Smith, *Camps and Campaigns,* 9; "City Council Doings," *Ohio Repository* [Canton, Ohio], May 29, 1861; "A New Mayor," *Stark County Democrat,* August 27, 1862; *Stark County Republican,* October 16, 1862; Seraphim Meyer to Theodore A. Meysenburg, July 18, 1863, in Seraphim Meyer Court Martial Records, RG 153, National Archives, Washington, DC; Meyer to Meysenburg, July 14, 1863, in Seraphim Meyer Compiled Service Record, RG 94, National Archives; Richard F. Miller, ed., *States at War,* Vol. 5: *A Reference Guide for Ohio in the Civil War* (Hanover and London: University Press of New England, 2015), 167–68. On Hill, see Reid, *Ohio in the War,* 1:811–15. Burton, *Melting Pot Soldiers,* 95, 93; Engle, *Gathering to Save a Nation,* 150.

11. "War Meeting at National Hall," *Cleveland Morning Leader,* August 1, 1862; *Daily Cleveland Herald,* July 25, 1862; Rose, *Cleveland,* 203; James Harrison Kennedy and Wilson M. Day, *The Bench and Bar of Cleveland* (Cleveland: Cleveland Printing and Publishing Co., 1889), 66; *Annals of Cleveland,* 46:146; *The Biographical Cyclopedia and Portrait Gallery with an Historical Sketch of the State of Ohio* (Cincinnati: Western Biographical Publishing Company, 1887), 4:933–34; see also David D. Van Tassel and John J. Grabowski, eds., *The Encyclopedia of Cleveland History* (Bloomington and Indianapolis: Indiana University Press, 1996), 501–2.

12. Terry K. Woods, *Ohio's Grand Canal: A Brief History of the Ohio & Erie Canal* (Kent, OH: Kent State University Press, 2008), 17; Perrin, *History of Stark County,* 264, 320–21; William Neff, *Bench and Bar of Northern Ohio: History and Biography* (Cleveland: Historical Publishing Co., 1921), 121; *Tuscarawas Advocate* [New Philadelphia, Ohio], August 22, 1862.

13. "Hickory Club," *Weekly Ohio Statesman* [Columbus, Ohio], March 10, 1840; "Great German Mass Meeting," *Weekly Ohio Statesman,* August 7, 1844; "Gen. Taylor and Nativism," *Ohio Repository,* November 1, 1848; "General Taylor and Nativism," *Ohio Repository,* December 6, 1848; *Daily* [Columbus] *Ohio Statesman,* August 19, 1860; *Allen County Democrat* [Lima, Ohio], February 19, 1862; *Defiance Democrat,* August 9, 1862; *Revised Ordinances of the City of Canton,* 535; "Douglas & Johnson, Democratic Ticket," Alfred Whital Stern Collection of Lincolniana, Rare Book & Special Collections Division, LC.

14. *New York Herald,* April 17, 1861; "The Union Meeting," *Stark County Republican* [Canton, Ohio], May 16, 1861; *The Crisis* [Columbus, Ohio], April 18, 1861; William Kepler, *History of the Three Months' and Three Years' Service from April 16th, 1861 to June 22nd, 1864 of the Fourth Regiment Ohio Volunteer Infantry in the War for the Union* (Cleveland: Cleveland Leader Printing Company, 1886), 14.

15. Stephen Douglas, as quoted in Robert W. Johannsen, *Stephen A. Douglas*

(Urbana: University of Illinois Press, 1973), 867; "The Union Meeting," *Stark County Republican*, May 16, 1861; *Stark County Democrat*, October 2, 1861.

16. "The Union Meeting," *Stark County Republican*, May 16, 1861; *Stark County Democrat*, May 8, 1861, and May 15, 1861; "Army Correspondence," *Stark County Republican*, June 20, 1861; [Canton] *Ohio Repository*, August 28, 1861; Col. J. A. Chase, *History of the Fourteenth Ohio Regiment, O.V.V.I.* (Toledo: St. John Printing House, 1881), 8. On the war in western Virginia, see W. Hunter Lesser, *Rebels at the Gate: Lee and McClellan on the Front Line of a Nation Divided* (Naperville, IL: Sourcebooks, 2004). Edward S. Meyer, who later transferred to the 107th Ohio, served in the western theater with the 19th Ohio Volunteers. See William S. S. Erb, *Extract from "The Battles of the 19th Ohio"* (Washington, DC: Judd & Detweiler, Printers, 1893), 47.

17. *Stark County Republican*, July 18, 1861; *OR*, ser. 1, vol. 2, p. 215; Chase, *History of the Fourteenth Ohio*, 7–11; "Mr. Meyer's Speech," *Stark County Republican*, August 1, 1861. On the evolution of federal policy with respect to rebel civilians, property, and enslaved persons, see Mark Grimsley, *The Hard Hand of War: Union Military Policy Toward Southern Civilians, 1861–1865* (Cambridge: Cambridge University Press, 1995).

18. "Mr. Meyer's Speech," *Stark County Republican*, August 1, 1861; "Falsehood Exposed," *Stark County Republican*, August 22, 1861.

19. "Discouraging Enlistments," *Daily Cleveland Herald*, August 7, 1862; *Cleveland Plain Dealer*, August 2, 1862, *Stark County Republican*, August 7, 1862; *Stark County Democrat*, August 6, 1862, and July 23, 1862; Mahlon Slutz Reminiscences, Indiana State Library; Samuel Alanson Lane, *Fifty Years and Over of Akron and Summit County* (Akron, Ohio: Beacon Job Department, 1892), 387–88.

20. "An Appeal to the People of Northern Ohio," *Cleveland Plain Dealer*, August 2, 1862; "New German Regiment," *Daily Cleveland Herald*, July 14, 1862; *Stark County Republican*, August 14, 1862; George G. Lyon, "To the 107th Regiment," *Daily Cleveland Herald*, August 14, 1862; *Stark County Republican*, August 7, 1862; *Daily Cleveland Herald*, August 7, 1862; Smith, *Camps and Campaigns*, 9–10; *Tuscarawas Advocate*, August 22, 1862; "A Card of Thanks," *Cleveland Morning Leader*, September 10, 1862; *Annals of Cleveland*, 45:225; Jacob Lichty to Daniel Lichty, December 28, 1862, copy in Thomas J. Edwards Papers, Box 2, Folder 3, BGSU; *Biographical Record of Civil War Veterans Tuscarawas County, Ohio* (Reprint ed., New Philadelphia, Ohio: Tuscarawas County Genealogical Society, 1990), 581. Deeming it "wiser to depend upon loyalty and liberality of the people" than upon a bounty, Governor Tod "squelched" talk of a state-issued bounty in the summer of 1862. See Trester, "Political Career of David Tod," 134. *Summit County Beacon*, August 14, 1862; *Huron Reflector*, August 26, 1862.

21. Smith, *Camps and Campaigns*, 10; George Billow Pension File, RG 15, NA; *Annals of Cleveland*, 39:299, 43:317, 43:333; "Brief History of the 107th Reg't, O.V.I., Read By Colonel S. Meyer," *Canton Repository*, September 22, 1871; Charles A. Hartman to the Surgeon General, September 11, 1862, in RG 94, entry 561, box 250, NA. While the vast majority of its foreign-born soldiers hailed from Germany, the muster rolls of the 107th Ohio included men who hailed from Canada, Switzerland, and Ireland. See Regimental Descriptive Books, RG 94, NA.

22. Hartmann, as quoted in Jacob Mueller, *Memories of a Forty-Eighter: Sketches from the German-American Period of Storm and Stress in the 1850s* (Cleveland, OH: Western Reserve Historical Society, 1996), 218–21.

23. Mahlon Slutz Reminiscences, Indiana State Library; *Annals of Cleveland*, 45:226; *Daily Cleveland Herald*, August 20, 1862; *Cleveland Evening Leader*, August 21, 1862; "Special Order from Governor Tod, August 22, 1862," *Stark County Democrat*, August 27, 1862; "Our Soldiers Need Blankets," *Cleveland Morning Leader*, August 27, 1862; "The 107th Regiment," *Daily Cleveland Herald*, August 25, 1862; Rieker to his sister and brother-in-law, September 8, 1862 [typescript translation], in Society of Separatists of Zoar Records, Box 96, Folder 1, OHC; *The Civil War Diary of Private John Flory, Co. C, 107th Ohio, August 1862–July 1865*, 1–9, copy in Wayne County Public Library, Wooster, Ohio; Fritz Nussbaum to Friend Cary [Kauke], September 9, 1862, in George Shane Phillips Papers, Box 2, Huntington Library; Charles T. Clark to dear Tom, September 16, 1862, in Clark, *Opdycke Tigers, 125th O.V.I.: A History of the Regiment and of the Campaigns and Battles of the Army of the Cumberland*, 4; *Annals of Cleveland*, 45:225. For a compelling analysis of sleep (or the lack thereof) in the Civil War, see Jonathan W. White, *Midnight in America: Darkness, Sleep, and Dreams During the Civil War* (Chapel Hill: University of North Carolina Press, 2017), 1–26.

24. "First Ward Meeting," *Daily Cleveland Herald*, August 25, 1862; "Soldiers Need Blankets," *Cleveland Morning Leader*, August 27, 1862; Smith, *Camps and Campaigns*, 14; "To Our Branch Societies," *Daily Cleveland Herald*, September 8, 1862; *Daily Cleveland Herald*, September 1, 1862; *Cleveland Morning Leader*, September 10, 1862; Charles A. Hartman to the Surgeon General, September 11, 1862, in RG 94, entry 561, box 250, NA. On civilian presentations to the officers of the 107th, see also the *Norwalk* [Ohio] *Reflector*, September 23, 1862.

25. "Camp Cleveland," *Daily Cleveland Herald*, August 23, 1862; Smith, *Camps and Campaigns*, 5, 14; "Picnics at Camp Cleveland," *Daily Cleveland Herald*, August 29, 1862; "The Temperance Cause," *Daily Cleveland Herald*, September 3, 1862; G. W. Lewis, *The Campaigns of the 124th Regiment Ohio Volunteer Infantry* (Akron, OH: Werner Company, 1894), 14; "The 107th Capture

a Rebel Flag," *Cleveland Morning Leader,* September 9, 1862; Rose, *Cleveland,* 293; Kenneth E. Davison, *Cleveland during the Civil War* (Columbus: Ohio State University Press for The Ohio Historical Society, 1962), 18; "Cleveland's Interest in the State Fair," *Daily Cleveland Herald,* September 11, 1862; *Annals of Cleveland,* 45:340–42; *Seventeenth Annual Report of the Ohio State Board of Agriculture* (Columbus: Richard Nevins, State Printer, 1863), xliii and passim. Fair administrators were reportedly "disappointed" by a greatly diminished attendance, which one editor attributed to anxieties about the war. *Annals of Cleveland,* 45:341–42.

26. "No More Camp Picnics," *Daily Cleveland Herald,* August 30, 1862; *Annals of Cleveland,* 45:225.

27. Roger K. Spickelmier, "Training of the American Soldier During World War I and World War II" (Master's thesis, U.S. Army Command and General Staff College, 1987), passim; E. B. Sledge, *With the Old Breed: At Peleliu and Okinawa* (New York: Random House 1981); Kyle Longley, *Grunts: The American Combat Soldier in Vietnam* (New York: Routledge, 2015), 38–39, 64–66; Earl Hess, *Civil War Infantry Tactics: Training, Combat, and Small-Unit Effectiveness* (Baton Rouge: Louisiana State University, 2015), 61; Paddy Griffith, *Battle Tactics of the Civil War* (New Haven: Yale University Press, 1989), 105; *Cleveland Plain Dealer,* August 20, 1862; "107th Regiment," *Cleveland Morning Leader,* September 10, 1862; Smith, *Camps and Campaigns,* 14; *Annals of Cleveland* 45:235; Lewis, *The Campaigns of the 124th Regiment,* 14; Summary Statements of Quarterly Returns of Ordnance and Ordnance Stores on Hand in Regular and Volunteer Army Organizations, microfilm M1281, reel 4, NA. Soldiers from the 33rd Illinois reported that their Austrian longarms "would often fire when held at parade rest." See Victor Hicken, *Illinois in the Civil War,* 2nd ed. (Urbana and Chicago: University of Illinois Press, 1991), 14. The poor quality of the weapons must have especially enraged Valentine Kissel, the thirty-nine-year-old gunsmith who went to war with Company B.

28. Smith, *Camps and Campaigns,* 15; *Annals of Cleveland,* 45:236; Morning Reports, Company C, vol. 7, RG 94, National Archives; Matthew Elrod, "The Impact of the Civil War on Northern Kentucky and Cincinnati, 1861–1865" (Master's thesis, Northern Kentucky University, 2006), 4–5. The threat of Confederate invasion in the late summer and fall of 1862 ensured that a number of newly mustered volunteers would be hurried to the front, woefully unprepared for combat. See also Hess, *Civil War Infantry Tactics,* 63.

29. *Cincinnati Commercial,* as quoted in Trester, "Political Career of David Tod," 145; James M. McPherson, *Battle Cry of Freedom* (New York: Oxford University Press, 1988), 513–14, 517; *OR,* ser. I, vol. 16, pt. 1, pp. 931–33; Trester, "Political Career of David Tod," 143–44; Edison H. Thomas, *John Hunt Morgan and His Raiders* (Lexington: University Press of Kentucky, 1985), 34–45.

On Cincinnati as a supply depot, see Mark R. Wilson, *The Business of Civil War: Military Mobilization and the State 1861–1865* (Baltimore: Johns Hopkins University Press, 2006.

30. Trester, "Political Career of David Tod," 144–45; Nelson Edwards Jones, M.D., *The Squirrel Hunters, or Glimpses of Pioneer Life* (Cincinnati: Robert Clarke Co., 1898), 335–36, 339–41, 342; David Tod to George B. Wright, September 9, 1862, in David Tod Papers, Miscellaneous Manuscript Collection, LC; Smith, *Camps and Campaigns*, 15; "From the 107th," *Summit County Beacon*, October 23, 1862; John Heyard Pension File, RG 15, NA; "Brief History of the 107th Reg't," *Canton Repository*, September 22, 1871.

31. Richard Kesterman, "The Burnet House: A Grand Cincinnati Hotel," *Ohio Valley History* 12, no. 4 (Winter 2012): 60–68.

32. "Charges and Specifications Prepared Against Colonel Seraphim Meyer 107th Regiment Ohio Vols.," in Seraphim Meyer Compiled Service Record, RG 94, NA.

33. Smith, *Camps and Campaigns*, 15; General Orders No. 32, September 27, 1862, Regimental Order Book, vol. 4, RG 94, NA; Lewis, *Campaigns of the 124th Regiment*, 14; "The Bitter and the Sweet," *The Bivouac* 3, no. 9 (September 1885): 342.

34. John Brunny, entry in Descriptive Book for Company I, RG 94, National Archives; 1860 census; *Fort Scott* [Kansas] *Tribune*, June 12, 1909; *Stark County Republican*, October 16, 1862; *The Civil War Diary of Private John Flory, Co. C, 107th Ohio, August 1862—July 1865*, 10; William Huy Pension File, RG 15, NA.

35. John Brunny to esteemed friend, September 25, 1862 [typescript translation], in Society of Separatists of Zoar Records, Box 96, Folder 1, OHC; "From the 107th," *Summit County Beacon*, October 23, 1862. Robert E. Bonner emphasizes the candor of Civil War soldiers' letters—and a desire among the soldiers to accurately document their experiences in real time—in *The Soldiers' Pen: Firsthand Impressions of the Civil War* (New York: Hill & Wang, 2006).

36. John Brunny to esteemed friend, September 25, 1862; Smith, *Camps and Campaigns*, 17; "From the 107th," *Summit County Beacon*, October 23, 1862.

37. Smith, *Camps and Campaigns*, 19.

CHAPTER 2: "TO CRUSH OUT THE ... UNGODLY REBELLION"

1. "From the 107th," *Summit County Beacon*, October 23, 1862; "The 107th," *Summit County Beacon*, October 16, 1862.

2. "From the 107th" *Summit County Beacon*, October 23, 1862; "The 107th," *Summit County Beacon*, October 16, 1862; Smith, *Camps and Campaigns*, 20;

Stark County Republican, November 20, 1862; affidavit of William O. Siffert, October 6, 1893, in Alfred J. Rider Pension File, RG 15, NA; Christian Rieker to sister, October 19, 1862, in Society of Separatists of Zoar Records, Box 96, Folder 1, OHC. On pillage and plunder of foodstuff and crops, see Joan E. Cashin, *War Stuff: The Struggle for Human and Environmental Resources in the American Civil War* (Cambridge: Cambridge University Press, 2018).

3. Steps taken to maintain good physical health and hygiene both in camp and on the march have been termed soldier "self-care" by historian Kathryn Shively Meier. See *Nature's Civil War: Common Soldiers and the Environment in 1862 Virginia* (Chapel Hill: University of North Carolina Press, 2013).

4. Allen C. Guelzo, *Lincoln's Emancipation Proclamation: The End of Slavery in America* (New York: Simon & Schuster, 2004), 171; see also Glenn David Brasher, *The Peninsula Campaign & The Necessity of Emancipation* (Chapel Hill: University of North Carolina Press, 2012); James Oakes, *The Scorpion's Sting: Antislavery & the Coming of the Civil War* (New York: W. W. Norton, 2013); and Chandra Manning, *Troubled Refuge: Struggling For Freedom in the Civil War* (New York: Alfred A. Knopf, 2016).

5. Smith, *Camps and Campaigns*, 20; 107th Ohio Volunteers Regimental Descriptive Books, RG 94, NA; *Summit County Beacon*, December 18, 1862.

6. "From the 107th Regiment," *Stark County Republican*, November 20, 1862; *Daily Cleveland Herald*, November 6, 1862; Christian Rieker to his sister, October 22, 1862, in Society of Separatists of Zoar Records, Box 96, Folder 1, OHC; *Official Army Register of the Volunteer Force of the United States Army for The Years 1861–1865—Part V, Ohio and Michigan*, 204; Smith, *Camps and Campaigns*, 21; George Shambs Pension File, Civil War Widows' Pensions, WC14820, Fold3.com.

7. *Stark County Democrat*, October 8, 1862; "The 107th Reg't," *Summit County Beacon*, October 9, 1862; "From the 107th," *Summit County Beacon*, October 23, 1862.

8. "From the 107th," *Summit County Beacon*, October 23, 1862; Special Orders No. 1, October 17, 1862, in 107th Ohio Volunteers Regimental Descriptive Books, RG 94, NA; Smith, *Camps and Campaigns*, 23; *Stark County Republican*, October 16, 1862; Rieker to his sister, October 22, 1862, in Society of Separatists of Zoar Records, Box 96, Folder 1, OHC.

9. *Summit County Beacon*, November 27, 1862; Smith, *Camps and Campaigns*, 23; 107th Ohio Volunteers Regimental Descriptive Books, RG 94, NA; Joshua Budd Court Martial Records, RG 153, Case # OO–32, NA.

10. Joshua Budd Court Martial Records, RG 153, Case # OO–32, NA; "Letter from Virginia," *Stark County Republican*, December 18, 1862; Smith, *Camps and Campaigns*, 23; "From the 107th," *Summit County Beacon*, November 27, 1862.

11. "From the 107th," *Summit County Beacon*, November 27, 1862; on the controversy, see Jim Weeks, *Gettysburg: Memory, Market, and an American Shrine* (Princeton: Princeton University Press, 2003), 26.

12. Smith, *Camps and Campaigns*, 25, 29; *Canton Repository*, September 22, 1871; *Summit County Beacon*, November 27, 1862; "Letter from Virginia," *Stark County Republican*, December 18, 1862; Fritz Nussbaum to Friend Cary [Kauke], November 6, 1862, George Shane Phillips Papers, Box 2, Huntington Library. On deforestation, see Megan Kate Nelson, *Ruin Nation: Destruction and the American Civil War* (Athens: University of Georgia Press, 2012).

13. "The Elections," *The Liberator* [Boston, Mass.], October 24, 1862; "The Late Elections," *Newark Advocate*, October 24, 1862; "The Revolution in Ohio!" *Newark Advocate*, October 17, 1862; "The Popular Revolution at the Polls," *The Crisis* [Columbus, Ohio], October 29, 1862; "Celebrations," *The Crisis*, October 22, 1862; "The Hon. S.S. Cox on the Ohio Election," *Daily Cleveland Herald*, December 19, 1862; "An Unprecedented Vote," *Newark Advocate*, October 31, 1862; see also Frank L. Klement, *The Copperheads in the Middle West* (Chicago: University of Chicago Press, 1960), 37–38.

14. "Vote of the Volunteers," *Daily Cleveland Herald*, October 20, 1862; "A Raid in the Rear," *Morning Oregonian* [Portland, Oregon], October 25, 1862. On the soldier vote, see Jonathan W. White, *Emancipation, the Union Army, and the Reelection of Abraham Lincoln* (Baton Rouge: Louisiana State University Press, 2014), and Donald S. Inbody, *The Soldier Vote: War, Politics, and the Ballot in America* (New York: Palgrave Macmillan, 2016), 19; "What the Soldiers Think of the Butternut Jubilee," *Scioto Gazette* [Chillicothe, Ohio], December 2, 1862; "Soldiers of the Fifteenth Corps" to the Cincinnati *Commercial*, as quoted in *The Echo from the Army: What Our Soldiers Say About the Copperheads* (New York: William C. Bryant and Co., Printers, 1863), 4–5; "Another Soldier's Opinion of Copperheads," *Stark County Republican*, March 26, 1863. Mark E. Neely, Jr., suggests that the Republicans were not prepared for the fervor with which the Democrats opted to engage in partisan combat during the war. The midterm elections perhaps stung even more as a result.

15. "From the 107th," *Summit County Beacon*, December 18, 1862; "Letter from Virginia," *Stark County Republican*, December 18, 1862.

16. Meier, *Nature's Civil War*, 7; Smith, *Camps and Campaigns*, 29–30; *Canton Repository*, September 22, 1871; on corduroy roads, see Smith, *Camps and Campaigns*, 33, William Warren memoir, Bound Volume 391, FSNMP, and Leonard Mesnard [55th Ohio] Sketch, Civil War Collection, Box 20, Folder 3, Emory University Special Collections, Atlanta. Chandra Manning, *What This Cruel War Was Over: Soldiers, Slavery, and the Civil War* (New York: Alfred A. Knopf, 2007), contends that early in the war, Union soldiers "devel-

oped into emancipation advocates who expected their views to influence the prosecution of the war." Although she does not use the term "seasoning," Manning identified a transformation similar to the one described here.

17. *Annals of Cleveland*, 45:216; "From the 107th," *Summit County Beacon*, December 18, 1862; Julia S. Wheelock, *The Boys in White: The Experience of a Hospital Agent In and Around Washington*, 33; R. W. Rock, *History of the Eleventh Regiment, Rhode Island Volunteers in the War of the Rebellion* (Providence: Providence Press Company, Printers, 1881), 120; Christian Rieker to sister, November 13, 1862, in Society of Separatists of Zoar Records, Box 96, Folder 1, OHC; "Letter from Virginia," *Stark County Republican*, December 18, 1862. Scholars continue to debate how wide the chasm between the home front and the battlefield was, as well as the extent to which soldiers bridged it both during and after the war. Gerald F. Linderman, *Embattled Courage: The Experience of Combat in the American Civil War* (New York: Free Press, 1987), and Reid Mitchell, *The Vacant Chair: The Northern Soldier Leaves Home* (New York: Oxford University Press, 1993), remain the two poles of the debate, with Linderman portraying the wartime experience as disillusioning and Mitchell arguing that blue-coated soldiers remained tethered to their home communities and visions of domesticity. While the community no doubt wielded much influence over enlisted men throughout the war, and while volunteers yearned for home, I argue that a cognitive divide did increasingly separate soldiers and civilians.

18. *Canton Repository*, September 22, 1871; Smith, *Camps and Campaigns*, 30; *Stark County Republican*, January 1, 1863; Augustus Vignos, affidavit dated September 10, 1884, in Albert Beck Pension File, RG 15, NA; morning reports for Company C and Company D, 107th Ohio Regimental Descriptive Books, RG 94, NA; Charles Hartman to the 107th Ohio, November 18, 1862, in Regimental Order Book, vol. 4, RG 94, NA; Alfred J. Rider Pension File, RG 15, NA; Fritz Nussbaum to Friend Cary [Kauke], November 6, 1862, George Shane Phillips Papers, Box 2, Huntington Library; Fritz Nussbaum Carded Medical Records, RG 94, entry 534, Box 2844, NA; "A Man Killed in Euclid," *Daily Cleveland Herald*, July 22, 1858; "Dead Body Found," *Daily Cleveland Herald*, June 7, 1858, and "A Case of Infanticide," *Daily Cleveland Herald*, November 29, 1858; *Annals of Cleveland*, 43:192. Hartman's credentials are a reminder that Civil War regimental surgeons were often trained professionals, not "hacks" ignorant of surgical manuals and medical literature. For an important corrective to popular misperceptions about Civil War medicine and medical personnel, see Brian Craig Miller, *Empty Sleeves: Amputation in the Civil War South* (Athens: University of Georgia Press, 2015). See also Judkin Browning and Timothy Silver, *An Environmental History of the Civil War* (Chapel Hill: University of North Carolina Press, 2020), 16–21.

19. *Stark County Republican*, January 1, 1863; Smith, *Camps and Campaigns*, 30–31; Jonathan W. White, *Midnight in America*, 13; Christian Rieker to dear sister, November 13, 1862, in Society of Separatists of Zoar Records, Box 96, Folder 1, OHC.

20. Smith, *Camps and Campaigns*, 35; Seraphim Meyer Pension File, RG 15, NA. For a compelling argument about the significance of mud in soldiers' representations of their experiences at war, see Santanu Das, *Touch and Intimacy in First World War Literature* (Cambridge: Cambridge University Press, 2006); Smith, *Camps and Campaigns*, 34; *Stark County Republican*, January 1, 1863; George Billow and Daniel Umstaetler affidavits [circa 1890], in Seraphim Meyer Pension File, RG 15, NA; *The Civil War Diary of Private John Flory*, 11.

21. Engle, *Yankee Dutchman*, 152; *Stark County Republican*, January 1, 1863; *The Civil War Diary of Private John Flory*, 11; Jacob Lichty to Daniel Lichty, December 28, 1862, copy in Thomas J. Edwards Papers, Box 2, Folder 1, Center for Archival Collections, Jerome Library, BGSU.

22. George C. Rable, *Fredericksburg! Fredericksburg!* (Chapel Hill: University of North Carolina Press, 2002), 35; Daniel E. Sutherland, *Fredericksburg & Chancellorsville: The Dare Mark Campaign* (Lincoln: University of Nebraska Press, 1998); Thomas Francis Gawley, *The Valiant Hours: An Irishman in the Civil War* (Harrisburg, PA: Stackpole Company, 1961), 63; James I. Robertson, Jr., ed., *The Civil War Letters of General Robert McAllister* (Reprint ed., Baton Rouge: Louisiana State University Press, 1998), 244.

23. *Stark County Republican*, January 1, 1863; "From the 107th," *Summit County Beacon*, February 12, 1863; "Opening of the Great Battle at Fredericksburg," *Daily Cleveland Herald*, December 12, 1862; Thomas Evans Diary and Memoir, Miscellaneous Manuscript Collection, LC; "The Great Disaster," [San Francisco] *Daily Evening Bulletin*, December 19, 1862; Henry J. Blakeman to dear father, December 18, 1862, Bound Volume 105, FSNMP; William B. Southerton, "What We Did There, Or, Swamp Angel," typescript manuscript, VFM 3177, OHC; *New York Herald*, January 15, 1863; "How Long Must the War Last?" *Stark County Democrat*, December 24, 1862; "From the 75th Ohio Regiment," *Athens* [Ohio] *Messenger*, January 22, 1863; Lincoln, as quoted in Michael Burlingame, *The Inner World of Abraham Lincoln* (Chicago: University of Chicago Press, 1994), 105.

24. F. A. Wildman to dear wife, December 22, 1862, Wildman Family Papers, OHC; A. Wilson Greene, "Morale, Maneuver, and Mud: The Army of the Potomac, December 16, 1862—January 26, 1863," in Gary W. Gallagher, ed., *The Fredericksburg Campaign: Decision on the Rappahannock* (Chapel Hill: University of North Carolina Press, 1995), 179; Patrick R. Guiney to My Dear Jennie, December 15, 1862, in Christian G. Samito, ed., *Commanding Boston's*

Irish Ninth (New York: Fordham University Press, 2002), 155; Robertson, Jr., ed., *Civil War Letters of General Robert McAllister*, 247; Wildman to dear wife, December 22, 1862, Wildman Family Papers, OHC; Don Stewart to dear friend Lettie, January 18, 1863, Bonnifield Collection, Duke; *New York Times*, January 24, 1863. Ever self-aggrandizing, Joe Hooker did much to contribute to the narrative of a depleted and demoralized Army of the Potomac in a report he submitted to the Joint Committee on the Conduct of the War. See *Report of the Joint Committee on the Conduct of the War*, vol. 4 (Reprint ed., Wilmington, North Carolina: Broadfoot's Publishing Company, 1999), xli.

25. Smith, *Camps and Campaigns*, 40–41; Edward C. Culp, *The 25th Ohio Vet. Vol. Infantry in the War for the Union* (Topeka: Geo. W. Crane & Co., 1885), 58; Nathaniel Collins McLean to Louise McLean, May 15, 16, and 17, 1860, in Nathaniel McLean Correspondence, Miscellaneous Manuscript Collection, Manuscript Division, LC.

26. Reid, *Ohio in the War*, 1:921–922; John H. Matsui, *The First Republican Army: The Army of Virginia and the Radicalization of the Civil War* (Charlottesville: University Press of Virginia, 2016), 5; Scott C. Patchan, *Second Manassas: Longstreet's Attack and the Struggle for Chinn Ridge* (Washington, DC: Potomac Books, 2011), 12–13; "From the 107th Regiment," *Daily Cleveland Herald*, January 19, 1863; Augustus Choate Hamlin, *The Battle of Chancellorsville: The Attack of Stonewall Jackson and His Army Upon the Right Flank of the Army of the Potomac at Chancellorsville, Virginia, on Saturday Afternoon, May 2, 1863* (Published by the author, 1896), 44–45; "From the 107th," *Summit County Beacon*, February 12, 1863.

27. William H. Noble, *The Seventeenth Regiment Connecticut Volunteer Infantry in the War of the Rebellion, 1862–1865* (Hartford: Press of the Case, Lockwood & Brainard Company, 1889), 1; "William Noble's Regimental History," http://seventeenthcvi.org/blog/history-index/william-nobles -regimental-history (accessed July 8, 2017); Thomas Evans Diary, June 8, 1862, Miscellaneous Manuscript Collection, Manuscript Division, LC; Warren, "On To Washington," http://seventeenthcvi.org/blog/history -index/william-warren-history/articles–5–8/ [accessed July 15, 2017]; Southerton, "What We Did There," Ohio History Connection; Luther Mesnard Memoir, Bound Volume 45, FSNMP; Noah Stump to Dear Cousin, February 26, 1863, in Thomas J. Edwards Collection, Box 1, Folder 3, BGSU; William Noble to my darling wife, November 21, 1862, Lewis Leigh Collection, Box 24, Folder 1, United States Army Heritage & Education Center, Carlisle, Pennsylvania.

28. Smith, *Camps and Campaigns*, 46; "The Present Condition of the Army," *New York Herald*, January 11, 1863. For a narrative account of the Army of the Poto-

mac's winter encampment, see Albert Z. Conner, Jr., and Chris Mackowski, *Seizing Destiny: The Army of the Potomac's "Valley Forge" and the Civil War Winter that Saved the Union* (El Dorado Hills, CA: Savas Beatie, 2016).

29. Smith, *Camps and Campaigns*, 47, 53; F. A. Wildman to dear Sam, December 31, 1862, Wildman Family Papers, OHC; *Stark County Republican*, March 5, 1863.

30. Christian Rieker to sister and all, February 17, 1863, [typescript translation], Society of Separatists of Zoar Records, Box 96, Folder 1, OHC; Fritz Nussbaum to Friend Cary [Kauke], September 9, 1862, and November 14, 1863, George Shane Phillips Papers, Box 2, Huntington Library; "From the 107th," *Summit County Beacon*, October 23, 1862; "From the 107th," *Summit County Beacon*, February 12, 1863; Richard Magee Diary, May 6, 1863, RG 69:163, Connecticut State Library.

31. Mitchell, *Vacant Chair*, 33–34; Christian Rieker to dear sister, April 12, 1863, Society of Separatists of Zoar Records, Box 96, Folder 1, OHC; Alvin Brown to dear father, March 15, 1863, transcript at The Olive Tree Genealogy, http://www.pastvoices.com/usa/brownalvin1863.shtml [accessed November 25, 2017].

32. "From the 55th Ohio," *Tiffin Tribune*, May 1, 1863; Daniel Horn to Gelles Horn, October 2, 1863, Daniel Horn Papers, Box 2, Huntington Library.

33. Smith, *Camps and Campaigns*, 44; "From the 107th Regiment," *Stark County Republican*, February 26, 1863.

CHAPTER 3: "STOP ALL FIRING IN THE REAR OF US"

1. Phillip Oakleaf Carded Medical Records, RG 94, entry 534, Box 2844, NA; Smith, *Camps and Campaigns*, 46; William Williams, *History of The Fire Lands, Comprising Huron and Erie Counties, Ohio* (Cleveland: Press of Leader Printing Company, 1879), 95; Walt Whitman, December 26, 1862, as quoted in *Walt Whitman's Civil War*, ed. Walter Lowenfels (New York: Da Capo, 1961), 35, 36. Conversely, Nicholas Marshall, "The Great Exaggeration: Death and the Civil War," *Journal of the Civil War Era* 4, no. 1 (March 2014): 3–27, contends that scholars such as Drew Gilpin Faust have "exaggerated" the cultural impact of the war's human toll by discounting the grim "demographic realities" of nineteenth century America.

2. Christian Rieker to sister and all, February 17, 1863 [typescript translation], in Society of Separatists of Zoar Records, Box 96, Folder 1, OHC; Jacob Kummerle Carded Medical Records, RG 94, entry 534, Box 2843, NA; Thomas Evans Diary and Memoir, Miscellaneous Manuscript Collection, LC.

3. C. to Friend William, February 14, 1863, in *Stark County Democrat*, March 4, 1863; "From the Fifth," *Danbury* [Connecticut] *Times*, December 18, 1862.

4. *OR*, ser. 1, vol. 21, p. 127; William Marvel, *Burnside* (Chapel Hill: University of North Carolina Press, 1991; *OR*, ser. 1, vol. 21, p. 754; Sutherland, *Fredericksburg & Chancellorsville*, 89; *Daily Cleveland Herald*, January 23, 1863.

5. George C. Rable, *Fredericksburg! Fredericksburg!* (Chapel Hill: University of North Carolina Press, 2002), 412; "The Eleventh Army Corps," *New York Times*, January 25, 1863; *New York Times*, January 24, 1863; "From the 107th," *Summit County Beacon*, February 12, 1863; "The Army on the Rappahannock," [New Haven] *Daily Palladium*, January 24, 1863; *Stark County Republican*, February 26, 1863; "From Sigel's Column," *Cleveland Plain Dealer*, January 21, 1863.

6. Harold A. Winters, et al., *Battling the Elements: Weather and Terrain in the Conduct of War* (Baltimore: Johns Hopkins University Press, 1998), 38–39; James M. Greiner, Janet L. Coryell, and James R. Smither, eds., *A Surgeon's Civil War: The Letters and Diary of Daniel M. Holt, M.D.* (Kent, OH: Kent State University Press, 1994), 70; Daniel Umbstaetter, affidavit dated March 25, 1890, in Seraphim Meyer Pension File, RG 15, NA; *New York Herald*, January 26, 1863; "From the 107th," *Summit County Beacon*, February 12, 1863; "Latest From Burnside's Army," *Lowell Daily Citizen and News*, January 24, 1863; "Our Army on the Rappahannock," *New York Herald*, January 24, 1863; *New York Herald*, January 25, 1863; Smith, *Camps and Campaigns*, 48; Augustus Bronson to Dear Times, January 25, 1863, Bound Volume 391, FSNMP; Mark H. Dunkelman, *Gettysburg's Unknown Soldier: The Life, Death, and Celebrity of Amos Humiston* (Westport, CT: Praeger, 1999), 82; Thomas Evans Diary, Miscellaneous Manuscript Collection, Manuscript Division, LC, Harvey Henderson Civil War Diary, January 22, 1863, Huntington Library; William Swinton, as quoted in Hartwell Osborn, et al., *Trials and Triumphs: The Record of the Fifty-Fifth Ohio Volunteer Infantry* (Chicago: A. C. McClurg & Co., 1904), 58.

7. "The Army of the Potomac," *Daily National Intelligencer*, January 28, 1863; "Our Army on the Rappahannock," *New York Herald*, January 24, 1863; Ernst Damkoehler to Mathilde Damkoehler, February 2, 1863, Bound Volume 327, FSNMP; "The Obscurity of the Situation," *Philadelphia Inquirer*, January 26, 1863.

8. *Stark County Democrat*, February 4, 1863; A. Wilson Greene, "Morale, Maneuver, and Mud: The Army of the Potomac, December 16, 1862–January 26, 1863," in Gary W. Gallagher, ed., *The Fredericksburg Campaign: Decision on the Rappahannock*" (Chapel Hill: University of North Carolina Press, 1995), 205; Harvey Henderson Civil War Diary, January 23, 1863, Huntington Library; William H. Warren memoir, Bound Volume 391, FSNMP; "From

the Army of the Potomac," *Stark County* [Ohio] *Democrat*, February 11, 1863; *Bangor* [Maine] *Daily Whig & Courier*, January 23, 1863.

9. *Stark County Democrat*, February 4, 1863; *Lebanon* [Pennsylvania] *Courier*, February 5, 1863; *Stark County Republican*, February 26, 1863.

10. *The Liberator*, February 27, 1863; Henry Blakeman to dear friend, February 1, 1863, Bound Volume 105, FSNMP; Smith, *Camps and Campaigns*, 48; *Annals of Cleveland*, 46:112; Robert Hunt Rhodes, ed., *All for the Union: The Civil War Diary and Letters of Elisha Hunt Rhodes* (New York: Random House, 1992), 89–90; Charles H. Doerflinger, "Familiar History of The Twenty-Sixth [Wisconsin] Regiment," Bound Volume 75, FSNMP.

11. *Stark County Republican*, February 26, 1863.

12. "The Change of Commanders," *New York Times*, January 27, 1863; Carl Schurz, *The Reminiscences of Carl Schurz* (London: John Murray, 1909), 2:403; John Hennessy, "We Shall Make Richmond Howl: The Army of the Potomac on the Eve of Chancellorsville," in Gary W. Gallagher, *Chancellorsville: The Battle and Its Aftermath*, 7; Theodore Meysenburg, "Reminiscences of Chancellorsville," *B&L*, 1:301; Sears, *Chancellorsville* (New York: Houghton Mifflin, 1996), 54; *Hartford* [Connecticut] *Evening Press*, January 31, 1863; "A Soldier's Letter," *Stark County Democrat*, February 11, 1863.

13. *New York Times*, January 28, 1863; *OR*, ser. 1, vol. 25, pt. 2, p. 5; Lincoln to Hooker, January 26, 1863, in Roy P. Basler, ed., *The Collected Works of Abraham Lincoln* (New Brunswick, NJ: Rutgers University Press, 1953), 6:78–79; *OR*, ser. I, vol. 25, pt. 2, pp. 11, 38–39, 50–51, 54–59, 152, 161–63, 582; Brig. Gen. Williams, letter to XI Corps, March 22, 1863, RG 393, entry 5315, NA; Wilson French to dear wife, April 19, 1863, Bound Volume 391, FSNMP.

14. "Circulation of Disloyal Papers Stopped," *Stark County Republican*, March 5, 1863; *The Liberator*, February 27, 1863; *Hartford Daily Courant*, February 21, 1863.

15. Smith, *Camps and Campaigns*, 51–52; Southerton, "What We Did There," Ohio History Connection; D. G. Brinton Thompson, ed., "From Chancellorsville to Gettysburg: A Doctor's Diary," *Pennsylvania Magazine of History and Biography* 89, no. 3 (July 1965): 297n15; "Stafford County Civil War Sites Database: Army of the Potomac Camps, 2nd Brigade, 1st Division, 11th Army Corps," from the research files of John J. Hennessy [copy in author's possession]. More than fifty miles to the south in Richmond, one Confederate War Department underling held "that the thermometer on the night of [February] 3rd had dropped to 8 degrees below zero." Robert K. Krick, *Civil War Weather in Virginia* (Tuscaloosa: University of Alabama Press, 2007), 86, 88. Seraphim Meyer Pension File, RG 15, NA. Not surprisingly, George Billow reported that several officers resigned their commissions "on account of ill health." "From

the 107th," *Summit County Beacon*, February 12, 1863. See also Henry J. Blakeman to dear mother, February 4, 1863, Bound Volume 105, FSNMP.

16. Smith, *Camps and Campaigns*, 51–52; Culp, *The 25th Ohio Vet. Vol. Infantry*, 57; F. A. Wildman to my dear wife, January 22, 1863, Wildman Family Papers, OHC; William H. Warren memoir, Bound Volume 391, FSNMP; *Danbury Times*, January 29, 1863; "A Soldier's Letter," *Stark County Democrat*, March 4, 1863; Alvin Brown to his father, February 15, 1863, in Personal Papers Collection, Library of Virginia, Richmond.

17. Smith, *Camps and Campaigns*, 54; Nelson, *Ruin Nation*, 137; Charles Carleton Coffin, *Marching to Victory: The Second Period of the War of the Rebellion, Including the Year*, 99; *OR*, ser. 1, vol. 25, pt. 1, p. 196; John A. Black to dear father, March 19, 1863, Bound Volume 197, FSNMP; William H. Warren memoir, Bound Volume 391, FSNMP; Anton Lang Pension File, RG 15, NA; "Life in the Seventeenth," *Danbury* [Connecticut] *Times*, February 26, 1863. On fatalities beyond combat, see Brian Steel Wills, *Inglorious Passages: Noncombat Deaths in the American Civil War* (Lawrence: University Press of Kansas, 2017). On the relationship between deforestation and mud, see Cashin, *War Stuff*, 104.

18. "From the 107th," *Summit County Beacon*, March 19, 1863; "An Army Letter," *Tiffin Tribune*, February 27, 1863; "A Soldier's Letter," *Stark County Democrat*, March 4, 1863; Smith, *Camps and Campaigns*, 53; Thomas Evans Diary, Miscellaneous Manuscript Collection, LC; Reid, *Ohio in the War*, 2:177; Henry J. Blakeman to dear brother, February 15, 1863, and to dear mother, March 15, 1863, Bound Volume 105, FSNMP; Erastus Fouch diary, March 12, 1863, Bound Volume 229, FSNMP; "Life in the Seventeenth," *Danbury Times*, February 26, 1863; Charles Mueller, order dated February 25, 1863, 107th Ohio Regimental Order Books, vol. 5, RG 94, NA; Smith, *Camps and Campaigns*, 53; "From the Army of the Rappahannock," *Stark County Democrat*, February 11, 1863.

19. Invoking the memory of Valley Forge and the rugged Revolutionary encampment of 1777–1778, authors Albert Z. Conner, Jr., and Chris Mackowski contend that for the men of the Army of the Potomac, the winter of 1862–1863 constituted "a strategic pause." According to these authors, a "strategic pause" is "a protracted halt to fighting in a theater of operations" that enables men to "rest, restore, resupply, and regroup forces." Further, it "provides opportunities to develop plans; revise tactics, procedures, and techniques; and make necessary personnel and organizational changes." This framework is very useful; however, I argue that the "strategic pause" was equally significant in that it provided enlisted men with ample time to ruminate about their participation in the war, the sniping of Copperhead Democrats back home, and the potential consequences of defeat. As they reflected on the growing anti-

war movement arresting the North, men encamped along the Rappahannock increasingly defined themselves in opposition to "disloyal" civilians. An army that was divided on emancipation (to say nothing about its fierce disagreements over what constituted appropriate military tactics and policies toward southern civilians) would come to find common ground—and perhaps a previously unknown level of internal cohesion—by condemning the so-called "fire in the rear." Conner Jr. and Mackowski, *Seizing Destiny,* xii. See also James S. Pula, *Under the Crescent Moon with the XI Corps in the Civil War,* Vol. 1: *From the Defenses of Washington to Chancellorsville, 1862–1863* (El Dorado Hills, CA: Savas Beatie, 2017), 77–78; Henry J. Blakeman to dear friend, February 1, 1863, Bound Volume 105, FSNMP. *Annals of Cleveland,* 46:45. Almost a decade before the war, the publication of the *Cleveland Leader* began with the merger of "a Free Soil organ, the *True Democrat,* and an antislavery Whig paper, the *Forest City.*" Davison, *Cleveland during the Civil War,* 15. Jennifer L. Weber has pointed out that, "The strength of the Peace Democrats generally ran in inverse relation to the successes (or failures) of the armies." Weber, *Copperheads: The Rise and Fall of Lincoln's Opponents in the North* (New York: Oxford University Press, 2006), 8–10. I rely on the periodization of Copperheadism proposed by Weber, who contends that, "Copperheadism developed in three distinct phases." In her view, the movement's "second phase" commenced "with the preliminary Emancipation Proclamation in September 1862 and extended into the following spring, when the Union adopted a draft." In a sharp departure from the seminal work of historian Frank L. Klement, perhaps the Copperheads' most important chronicler, Weber contends that, "the peace movement was broad, and so influential by August 1864 that it very nearly took over the Democratic Party." Her thesis has invited much debate, but I find it persuasive. See also George Knepper, *Ohio and Its People* (Kent, OH: Kent State University Press, 1989), 237–38.

20. Roseboom, *The History of the State of Ohio,* 4:404; Clement Laird Vallandigham, "Speech On The Great Civil War in America," January 14, 1863, in *Speeches, Arguments, Addresses, and Letters of Clement L. Vallandigham* (New York: J. Walter & Co., 1864), 436, 438, 440, 429, 430; James L. Vallandigham, *A Life of Clement L. Vallandigham* (Baltimore: Turnbull Brothers, 1872), 53; Stephen Middleton, *The Black Laws: Race and the Legal Process in Early Ohio* (Athens: Ohio University Press, 2005), 212.

21. "The Northern Peace Party," *Fayetteville* [North Carolina] *Observer,* January 26, 1863; *Semi-Weekly Raleigh Register,* January 24, 1863; Frank L. Klement, *The Limits of Dissent: Clement L. Vallandigham & The Civil War* (Lexington: University Press of Kentucky, 1970), 124–25, 127–28; "Great Speech of Hon. C. L. Vallandigham on the War," *Newark* [Ohio] *Advocate,* January 23, 1863; *Newark Advocate,* January 30, 1863; "Reaction Against Vallandigham's

Speech," *Daily Cleveland Herald*, January 19, 1863; *Lowell Daily Citizen and News*, January 20, 1863; Thomas Beer, as quoted in Klement, *Limits of Dissent*, 136.

22. "Treason," *Ripley* [Ohio] *Bee*, February 19, 1863; "Echoes from the Army," *Hartford* [Connecticut] *Evening Press*, February 28, 1863. On the "groundswell for peace and compromise that swept over the land" in early 1863, see Klement, *Limits of Dissent*, 128; *Ripley Bee*, January 22, 1863; *Annals of Cleveland*, 46:45; George Templeton Strong, diary entry, January 24, 1863, in Allan Nevins, ed., *Diary of the Civil War, 1860–1865 by George Templeton Strong*, (New York: Macmillan Company, 1962), 289–90; "Jeff. Davis and His Dog," *Scioto Gazette*, February 17, 1863; "Peace Movements," *Lowell* [Massachusetts] *Daily Citizen and News*, February 17, 1863. Echoing George Templeton Strong, one modern scholar concludes that, "no single man outside the Confederate armies represented a greater threat to the Union than Clement L. Vallandigham," Giovanna Dell'Orto, "The Arrest and Trial of Clement L. Vallandigham in 1863," in *Words at War: The Civil War and American Journalism*, ed. David B. Sachsman, S. Kittrell Rushing, and Roy Morris, Jr. (West Lafayette, IN: Purdue University Press, 2008), 189.

23. "Another Soldier's Opinion of Copperheads," *Stark County Republican*, March 26, 1863; John J. Hennessy, "'We Shall Make Richmond Howl: The Army of the Potomac on the Eve of Chancellorsville," in Gary W. Gallagher, ed., *Chancellorsville: The Battle and Its Aftermath* (Chapel Hill: University of North Carolina Press, 1996), 5; John J. Hennessy, "Evangelizing for Union, 1863: The Army of the Potomac, Its Enemies at Home, and a New Solidarity," *Journal of the Civil War Era* 4, no. 4 (December 2014): 533–58. For further analysis of how Buckeye soldiers responded to the Copperhead movement, see Keith Fellows Altavilla, "Can We Call It Anything but Treason? Loyalty and Citizenship in Ohio Valley Soldiers" (PhD diss., Texas Christian University, 2013); "A Soldier's Response," *Stark County Republican*, March 19, 1863; *Annals of Cleveland*, 45:47.

24. "The Voice of the Ohio Soldiers," resolutions of the 4th and 8th Ohio Volunteer Infantry, *Stark County Republican*, March 6, 1863. At least one Ohio soldier was less modest—or perhaps more candid. "With regard to the probable reception of the miserable Vallandigham," he wrote, "my opinion is that were he to come to our brigade lines and make himself known or intrude upon the soldiers, he would not get out alive," *Annals of Cleveland*, 45:47.

25. Hennessy, "Evangelizing for Union, 1863"; "What Another Soldier Says," *Tuscarawas Advocate*, March 20, 1863, and *Stark County Republican*, March 26, 1863; *Wooster Republican*, May 7, 1863. See also *Summit County Beacon*, March 19, 1863, *Norwalk Reflector*, April 21, 1863, *Ohio Repository*, March 18, 1863, and *Stark Country Republican*, March 6, 1863. N. A. Patterson, a soldier from the

90th Ohio, flatly rejected one report that "four-fifths of the army" opposed the Emancipation Proclamation. "I will venture the assertion that one-tenth is the more truthful amount," he wrote. *Annals of Cleveland*, 45:47. On von Gunden, see Mike Fitzpatrick et al., "Immigrants in the Ranks: A Collection of Vignettes of Foreigners in the Union Army," *Military Images* 19, no. 3 (November/December 1997): 21–22.

26. *Stark County Republican*, March 26, 1863. See also "From the 55th Ohio," *Tiffin* [Ohio] *Tribune*, May 1, 1863; "What Another Soldier Says," *Tuscarawas Advocate*, March 20, 1863; *Wooster Republican*, May 7, 1863; *Stark County Republican*, March 26, 1863; "Another Soldier's Opinion of Copperheads," *Stark County Republican*, March 26, 1863; see also *The Bivouac* 3, no. 9 (September 1885): 343.

27. Perrin, *History of Stark County*, 205–6; Marc R. Warner, "History of the Stark County Courthouse," http://www.starkcountyohio.gov/StarkCounty/media/Common-Pleas/History-of-the-Courthouse.pdf [accessed December 13, 2017]; David Tod to William H. Seward, July 29, 1862, in "Appendix," *Journal of the House of Representatives of the State of Ohio for the Second Session of the Fifty-Fifth General Assembly*, 7; Bryon C. Andreasen, "Lincoln's Religious Critics: Copperhead Christian Reactions to the President and the War," in Daniel M. McDonough and Kenneth W. Noe, eds., *Politics and Culture of the Civil War Era: Essays in Honor of Robert W. Johannsen* (Selinsgrove, PA: Susquehanna University Press, 2006), 200; Edson Baldwin Olds, *Arbitrary Arrests: Speech of Hon. Edson B. Olds, For Which He Was Arrested, And His Reception Speeches on his Return from The Bastille* (Circleville, OH: n.p., 1862).

28. "The Copper-Head Meeting—Speech of Dr. Olds," *Stark County Republican*, March 6, 1863.

29. "The Copperhead Meeting Winds Up in a Fight," *Stark County Republican*, March 6, 1863.

30. Roseboom, *The History of the State of Ohio*, 4:409–10; Thomas H. Smith, "Crawford County 'Ez Trooly Dimecratic': A Study of Midwestern Copperheadism," *Ohio History* 76, nos. 1–2 (Winter/Spring 1967): 45; Wayne Jordan, "The Hoskinsville Rebellion," *Ohio State Archaeological and Historical Quarterly* 47, no. 1 (January 1938): 320, 330, 332; Klement, *The Limits of Dissent*, 143; Joseph Allan Frank, *With Ballot and Bayonet: The Political Socialization of American Civil War Soldiers*, 180; *Stark County Republican*, February 26, 1863; "Stark County Sound As a Butternut," *Stark County Democrat*, April 15, 1863.

31. Klement, *The Copperheads in the Middle West*, 118; Andrew Harris to Friend Lough, March 25, 1863, Andrew Harris Papers, Box 1, Folder 1, OHC; *Stark County Republican*, February 26, 1863; Hennessy, "Evangelizing for Union, 1863."

32. Smith, *Camps and Campaigns*, 56; "Army Correspondence," *Norwalk Reflec-*

tor, April 21, 1863; Darius N. Couch, "The Chancellorsville Campaign," in *Battles and Leaders of the Civil War* (Reprint ed., New York & London: Thomas Yoseloff, 1956), 3:155; Smith, *Camps and Campaigns*, 63; Erastus Fouch diary, April 20, 1863, Bound Volume 229, FSNMP; "List of the 11th Army Corps, April 10, 1863," in RG 393, entry 5319, Letters Received 1863–1864, NA; Special Requisition of Peter F. Young in Warren Russell Papers, Box 3, Folder 2, BGSU.

33. Smith, *Camps and Campaigns*, 61, 63; Christian Rieker to dear sister, April 12, 1863, Society of Separatists of Zoar Records, Box 96, Folder 1, OHC; *Tiffin* [Ohio] *Tribune*, May 1, 1863; John Bigelow, Jr., *The Campaign of Chancellorsville: A Strategic and Tactical Study* (New Haven: Yale University Press, 1910), 35; "From the 17th Regiment," *Danbury Times*, March 12, 1863; *OR*, ser. I, vol. 25, pt. 2, p. 239; Augustus Bronson to Dear Times, March 5, 1863, Bound Volume 391, FSNMP; Hennessy, "We Shall Make Richmond Howl," 10; William H. Warren memoir, Bound Volume 391, FSNMP; Stephen Crofutt to "Excellent Mother," February 27, 1863, Bound Volume 521, FSNMP; Smith, *Camps and Campaigns*, 63.

34. *Norwalk Reflector*, April 21, 1863; *Wooster Republican*, May 7, 1863; Greiner, Coryell, and Smither, *A Surgeon's Civil War*, 90–91; *Ohio Repository*, June 24, 1863; William A. Aiken, quoted in *Seventeenth Regiment C.V.I. Reunion at Fairfield, Ct., 1862–1883, August 28, 1883* (Bridgeport, CT: The Standard Association, Printers, 1884), 34; Christian Rieker to dear sister, April 12, 1863, Society of Separatists of Zoar Records, Box 96, Folder 1, OHC.

CHAPTER 4: "COMPLETELY AND SCIENTIFICALLY FLANKED"

1. Orin Buttles to dear Fred, April 6, 1863, Bound Volume 327, FSNMP; Seth Williams to Oliver Otis Howard, April 26, 1863, in Register of Letters Received, January 1863–April 1864, RG 393, entry 5315, NA; Samuel Surburg diary, as quoted in *Ohio Repository*, June 24, 1863; E. C. Culp to dear Ma, May 7, 1863, copy in Thomas J. Edwards Papers, Box 1, Folder 2, BGSU.

2. *Ohio Repository*, June 24, 1863.

3. Smith, *Camps and Campaigns*, 64–67; "From the 107th Regiment," *Stark County Republican*, May 21, 1863; *The Civil War Diary of Private John Flory*, 13; Eric J. Wittenberg, *The Union Cavalry Comes of Age: Hartwood Church to Brandy Station, 1863* (Washington, DC: Brassey's, 2003, 40–42; Conner and Mackowski, *Seizing Destiny*, 259; Edward J. Stackpole, *Chancellorsville: Lee's Greatest Battle*, 2nd ed. (Harrisburg, PA: Stackpole Books, 1988), 42–47; Alexander W. Black to dear father, May 13, 1863, and John A. Black to dear father, May 31, 1863, Bound Volume 197, FSNMP; *OR*, ser. 1, vol. 25, pt.

1, pp. 640, 642; Osborn, et al., *Trials and Triumphs*, 274; "Life in the Seventeenth No. 10—Under Fire," *Danbury Times*, May 14, 1863; Robert Hubbard to darling Nellie, May 8, 1863, Bound Volume 353, FSNMP; Erastus Fouch diary, April 28, 1863, Bound Volume 229, FSNMP; William H. Warren memoir, Bound Volume 391, FSNMP; Luther B. Mesnard Memoir, Bound Volume 45, FSNMP; Daniel Biddle, affidavit dated April 6, 1896, Alfred Rider Pension File, RG 15, NA; Thompson, "From Chancellorsville to Gettysburg: A Doctor's Diary," 298; *Stark County Republican*, May 21, 1863; Theodore Meysenberg, "Reminiscences of Chancellorsville," in *War Papers and Personal Reminiscences, 1861–1865, Read Before the Commandery of the State of Missouri, Military Order of the Loyal Legion of the United States* (St. Louis: Becktold & Co., 1892), 1:298; Joseph R. Reinhart, ed., *Yankee Dutchmen under Fire: Civil War Letters from the 82nd Illinois Infantry* (Kent, OH: Kent State University Press, 2013), 71; Noble, *The Seventeenth Regiment Connecticut Volunteer Infantry*, 2; *Tiffin Weekly Tribune*, May 29, 1863, and June 5, 1863; Richard Magee Diary, May 6, 1863, RG 69:163, Connecticut State Library; E. C. Culp to dear Ma, May 7, 1863, copy in Thomas J. Edwards Papers, Box 1, Folder 2, Center for Archival Collections, Jerome Library, BGSU.

4. Oliver Otis Howard, "The Eleventh Corps at Chancellorsville," in *Battles and Leaders of the Civil War*, 3:192, 190; Earl J. Hess, *Trench Warfare Under Lee and Grant: Field Fortifications in the Overland Campaign*, 20; Osborn, et al., *Trials and Triumphs*, 62; G.K. Warren, report of May 12, 1863, in *Report of the Joint Committee on the Conduct of the War*, 4:54.

5. Howard, "The Eleventh Corps at Chancellorsville," 3:191; William S. McFeely, *Yankee Stepfather: General O. O. Howard and the Freedmen* (New York: W. W. Norton, 1968), 31, 33; "Fighting Them Over," *National Tribune*, December 25, 1884.

6. Orin Buttles to dear Fred, April 6, 1863, Bound Volume 327, FSNMP; Oliver Otis Howard, *Autobiography of Oliver Otis Howard* (New York: Baker & Taylor Company, 1907), 1:348–349; Engle, *Yankee Dutchman*, 156–59; Smith, *Camps and Campaigns*, 64; [Harrisburg] *Weekly Patriot and Union*, March 5, 1863; Culp, *The 25th Ohio Vet. Vol. Infantry*, 59; "The Eleventh Corps," *National Tribune*, December 11, 1884.

7. G. K. Warren, report of May 12, 1863, in *Report of the Joint Committee on the Conduct of the War*, 4:54; *OR*, ser. 1, vol. 25, pt. 1, p. 197; *OR*, ser. 1, vol. 25, pt. 2, p. 151; A. Wilson Greene, "Stoneman's Raid," in Gallagher, *Chancellorsville*, 65–106; Stackpole, *Chancellorsville*, 108–9; Daniel E. Sutherland, *Fredericksburg & Chancellorsville: The Dare Mark Campaign* (Lincoln: University of Nebraska Press, 1998), 130; testimony of G. K. Warren, March 11, 1865, in *Report of the Joint Committee on the Conduct of the War*, 4:116; Ernest B. Furgur-

son, *Chancellorsville 1863: The Souls of the Brave* (New York: Alfred A. Knopf, 1992), 65, 67; Edward G. Longacre, *The Commanders of Chancellorsville—The Gentleman versus the Rogue: The Opposing Strategies and Personalities of Lee and Hooker* (Nashville: Rutledge Hill Press, 2005), 117; Joseph Hooker to Abraham Lincoln, April 27, 1863, Abraham Lincoln Papers, LC.

8. Smith, *Camps and Campaigns*, 68–70; *OR*, ser. 1, vol. 25, pt. 1, p. 628; testimony of Daniel Sickles, February 25, 1864, in *Report of the Joint Committee on the Conduct of the War*, 4:4; *OR*, ser. 1, vol. 25, pt. 1, pp. 171, 633; Justus M. Silliman memoir, Bound Volume 353, FSNMP; Jesse M. Spooner to cousin William, May 14, 1863, Bound Volume 281, FSNMP; *Tiffin Tribune*, May 29, 1863; William H. Warren memoir, Bound Volume 391, FSNMP.

9. *OR*, ser. 1, vol. 25, pt. 1, pp. 796–97, 849–50; "Special Orders No. 121," *OR*, ser. 1, vol. 25, pt. 2, p. 762; James Power Smith, "Stonewall Jackson's Last Battle," in *Battles and Leaders of the Civil War*, 3:203; Joseph T. Glatthaar, *General Lee's Army: From Victory to Collapse* (New York: Free Press, 2008), 245; Sutherland, *Fredericksburg & Chancellorsville*, 142.

10. *Battles and Leaders of the Civil War*, 3:204; *OR*, ser. 1, vol. 25, pt. 1, p. 797; *Ohio Repository*, June 24, 1863; Meysenberg, "Reminiscences of Chancellorsville," 1:299–300.

11. *B&L*, 3:161.

12. *B&L*, 3:205; *OR*, ser. 1, vol. 25, pt. 1, p. 651; *OR*, ser. 1, vol. 25, pt. 1, p. 797; Sutherland, *Fredericksburg & Chancellorsville*, 148.

13. Justus M. Silliman memoir, Bound Volume 353, FSNMP; Erastus Fouch diary, May 1, 1863, Bound Volume 229, FSNMP; Smith, *Camps and Campaigns*, 69; *OR*, ser. 1, vol. 25, pt. 1, pp. 167, 633, 642, 644; Fred W. Cross to "The Ladies Who Reside at the Talley Homestead on the Chancellorsville Battlefield," May 2, 1926, Talley Farm Vertical File, FSNMP; pencil drawing, "Hatch House Div. & Brigade Headquarters, 1st Div. 2nd Brigade 11th Corps," accession number 1999.161.432, Virginia Historical Society, Richmond; "Family accounts of death of Stonewall," *Washington Times*, May 3, 2003, copy in Talley Farm Vertical File, FSNMP; Charles Doerflinger map, Bound Volume 483, FSNMP; William H. Warren memoir, Bound Volume 391, FSNMP; Howard, "The Eleventh Corps at Chancellorsville," *B&L*, 3:191; *Norwalk Reflector*, May 19, 1863; *New Philadelphia Democrat*, May 22, 1863; *Tiffin Tribune*, May 29, 1863; "Statement of Capt. S. Surburg," *Ohio Repository*, June 24, 1863; "Army Correspondence," *Tuscarawas Advocate*, May 22, 1863; Meysenberg, "Reminiscences of Chancellorsville," 1:299–300; *Norwalk Reflector*, May 19, 1863; Alexander W. Black to dear father, May 13, 1863, Bound Volume 197, FSNMP; E. R. Monfort, "The First Division, Eleventh Corps, at Chancellorsville," in Monfort, H. B. Furness, and Fred H. Alms, eds., *G.A.R.*

War Papers: Papers Read Before Fred C. Jones Post, No. 401, Department of Ohio, G.A.R. (Cincinnati: Fred C. Jones Post, 1891), 1:60–61; "Chancellorsville," *National Tribune*, October 22, 1891.

14. *Norwalk Reflector,* May 19, 1863; Erastus Fouch Diary, May 2, 1863, Bound Volume 229, FSNMP; "A Private's Account of the Late Battle," *Tiffin Tribune,* May 29, 1863; *OR,* ser. 1, vol. 25, pt. 1, p. 650; *OR,* ser. 1, vol. 25, pt. 1, p. 637; William H. Warren memoir, Bound Volume 391, FSNMP; Culp, *The 25th Ohio Vet. Vol. Infantry,* 60–62; William O. Dauchy letter, May 31, 1863, Bound Volume 479, FSNMP; Justus M. Silliman Memoir, Bound Volume 353, FSNMP; J. C. Hall to Augutus Choate Hamlin, November 12, 1891, Augustus Choate Hamlin Papers, Houghton Library; E. C. Culp to dear Ma, May 7, 1863, Thomas J. Edwards Papers, Box 1, Folder 2, BGSU.

15. Culp, *The 25th Ohio Vet. Vol. Infantry,* 61–62, 64; John W. Black to dear father, May 31, 1863, Bound Volume 197, FSNMP; William O. Dauchy letter, May 31, 1863, Bound Volume 479, FSNMP; J. C. Hall to Augustus Choate Hamlin, November 12, 1891, Augustus Choate Hamlin Papers, Houghton Library; Smith, *Camps and Campaigns,* 72–73; *Tiffin Tribune,* May 29, 1863; "Somebody's Blunder," *National Tribune,* March 19, 1885.

16. *OR,* ser. 1, vol. 25, pt. 1, p. 652; Hans L. Trefousse, *Carl Schurz: A Biography* (Knoxville: University of Tennessee Press, 1982), 133; Carl Schurz, *The Reminiscences of Carl Schurz,* 2:418; Thompson, "From Chancellorsville to Gettysburg: A Doctor's Diary," 299; "Chancellorsville," *National Tribune,* October 22, 1891; "Letter from the 107th Regiment," *Defiance Democrat,* May 23, 1863; Lucius B. Swift, "An Enlisted Man in the Chancellorsville Campaign," John Bigelow Papers, Box 54, Manuscript Division, LC; Sears, *Chancellorsville,* 264–65; "Chancellorsville," *National Tribune,* June 11, 1891.

17. Culp, *The 25th Ohio Vet. Vol. Infantry,* 64; William H. Warren memoir, Bound Volume 391, FSNMP; Luther Mesnard Memoir, Bound Volume 45, FSNMP; *Norwalk Reflector,* May 19, 1863.

18. *Daily Cleveland Herald,* May 25, 1863; *Stark County Republican,* May 21, 1863; "On Picket at Chancellorsville: Captain A. B. Searles Tells How the Eleventh Corps Was Flanked," *Boston Journal,* February 24, 1893; Thomas Evans Diary, Manuscript Division, LC; Reinhart, *Yankee Dutchmen Under Fire,* 72; Smith, *Camps and Campaigns,* 73; *OR,* ser. 1, vol. 25, pt. 1, pp. 639, 642; *Tiffin Weekly Tribune,* May 29, 1863; "Letter from the Rappahannock," *Portage County Democrat,* May 27, 1863.

19. *OR,* ser. 1, vol. 25, pt. 1, pp. 644, 641; "Army Correspondence," *Daily Cleveland Herald,* May 14, 1863; "Lieut. Col. Mueller," *New Philadelphia Democrat,* May 22, 1863; "Chancellorsville," *National Tribune,* October 22, 1891; *Tuscarawas Advocate,* May 22, 1863; *Elyria Independent Democrat,* May 27, 1863.

20. "Life in the Seventeenth Under Fire," *Danbury Times,* May 14, 1863; *OR,* ser.

1, vol. 25, pt. 1, pp. 636–37, 644; Augustus Choate Hamlin, "Chancellorsville," *National Tribune*, August 3, 1893.

21. *Wooster Republican*, May 21, 1863; Christian Rieker to dear sister, May 11, 1863, Society of Separatists of Zoar Records, Box 96, Folder 1, OHC; *Daily Cleveland Herald*, May 25, 1863; *OR*, ser. 1, vol. 25, pt. 1, p. 638; Osborn, et al., *Trials and Triumphs*, 71; *OR*, ser. 1, vol. 25, pt. 1, p. 644; Monfort, "The First Division, Eleventh Corps, at Chancellorsville," 66–67; *National Tribune*, October 22, 1891; "The Eleventh Corps," *National Tribune*, December 11, 1884; Smith, *Camps and Campaigns*, 74; Thomas Evans Diary, Manuscript Division, LC; Robert Hubbard to dear Nellie, May 9, 1863, Bound Volume 353, FSNMP; Justin Keeler letter, Bound Volume 353, FSNMP; James Middlebrook to his wife, May 10, 1863, Middlebrook Family Papers, MSS 73139, Connecticut Historical Society; "Life in the Seventeenth Under Fire," *Danbury Times*, May 14, 1863.

22. "107th Ohio Regiment," *Stark County Republican*, June 11, 1863; "Wounded Ohio Soldiers in Washington Hospital," *Cleveland Morning Leader*, May 15, 1863; "The Killed and Wounded," *Stark County Democrat*, May 13, 1863; *Norwalk Reflector*, May 19, 1863; "The 107th Ohio at Fredericksburg," *Cleveland Plain Dealer*, May 8, 1863; "From the 107th Ohio Regiment," *Tuscarawas Advocate*, May 22, 1863; Conrad Messig Pension File, RG 15, NA; "From the 107th Regiment," *Stark County Republican*, July 2, 1863; M. N. French to my dear husband, May 7, 1863 and May 10, 1863, Bound Volume 391, FSNMP. My ideas in this paragraph are deeply influenced by Hodes, *Mourning Lincoln*.

23. "Capt. A. J. Dewaldt," *Sandusky Register*, June 12, 1863; *Norwalk Reflector*, June 23, 1863; C. H. Gallup, et al., *The Firelands Pioneer* (Norwalk, OH: American Publishers Company, 1915), 2100; Morning Reports for Company C, 107th Ohio Regimental Order Books, vol. 7, RG 94, NA; Ernst Damkoehler to dear Mathilde, May 13, 1863, Bound Volume 327, FSNMP; Robert Hubbard to dear Nellie, May 9, 1863, Bound Volume 353, FSNMP; Christian Rieker to his sister, May 11, 1863, Society of Separatists of Zoar Records, Box 96, Folder 1, OHC; "Touching Letter," *Salem Observer*, July 14, 1863; Robert Hubbard to darling Nellie, May 8, 1863, Bound Volume 353, FSNMP; Smith, *Camps and Campaigns*, 75.

24. "List of Union Officers Taken By the Rebels," *New York Tribune*, May 12, 1863; Christian Rieker to his sister, May 11, 1863, and May 30, 1863, both in Society of Separatists of Zoar Records, Box 96, Folder 1, OHC; George Billow affidavit, March 5, 1890, and Edward S. Meyer affidavit, December 4, 1889, Seraphim Meyer Pension File, RG 15, NA; *Defiance* [Ohio] *Democrat*, May 16, 1863; Edward S. Meyer to Captain McBailey, June 22, 1864, Edward S. Meyer Compiled Service Record, RG 94, NA; *Defiance Democrat*, May 16, 1863. In waiting a week for medical attention, Captain Meyer, it seems, was hardly alone. Stephen Crofutt, a soldier in the 17th Connecticut, explained that some

"poor fellows lay on the field" for "nearly a whole week" before they received care. Crofutt to dear parents, May 16, 1863, Bound Volume 521, FSNMP.

25. Edward S. Meyer affidavit, December 4, 1889, Seraphim Meyer Pension File, RG 15, NA.

26. Stephen Crofutt to dear parents, May 16, 1863, Bound Volume 521, FSNMP; Justus M. Silliman memoir, Bound Volume 353, FSNMP; Christian Rieker to dear sister, May 11, 1863, Society of Separatists of Zoar Records, Box 96, Folder 1, OHC; Robert Hubbard to dear Nellie, May 9, 1863, Bound Volume 353, FSNMP; Thomas Evans Diary, Manuscript Division, LC; Jesse M. Spooner to cousin William, May 14, 1863, Bound Volume 281, FSNMP; William Southerton Memoir, VFM 3177, OHC. On noise, smell, and sight as portals to the lived experience of war, see Mark M. Smith, *The Smell of Battle, The Taste of Siege*.

27. Reid, *Ohio in the War*, 2:577; Ben Douglass, *History of Wayne County, Ohio*, 757; *Canton Repository*, September 22, 1871; Christian Rieker to his sister, May 11, 1863, and May 30, 1863, Society of Separatists of Zoar Records, Box 96, Folder 1, OHC; Special Order No. 22, June 11, 1863, in 107th Ohio Regimental Order Books, vol. 4, RG 94, NA; "107th Ohio Regiment," *Stark County Republican*, June 11, 1863; "From the 107th Ohio," *Daily Cleveland Herald*, May 25, 1863; *Stark County Republican*, June 4, 1863; on Franklin Bow, see 107th Ohio Regimental Order Books, vol. 1, RG 94, NA; *Defiance Democrat*, May 23, 1863; *Daily Cleveland Herald*, May 14, 1863.

28. Robert K. Krick, *The Smoothbore Volley That Doomed the Confederacy: The Death of Stonewall Jackson and Other Chapters on the Army of Northern Virginia*, 1–2; Stackpole, *Chancellorsville*, 259–260, 269, 280, 283, 285–286, 262; Sutherland, *Fredericksburg & Chancellorsville*, 161; Carol Reardon, "The Valiant Rearguard: Hancock's Division at Chancellorsville," in Gallagher, *Chancellorsville*, 143–75.

29. Stackpole, *Chancellorsville*, 288; Sutherland, *Fredericksburg & Chancellorsville*, 163; Sears, *Chancellorsville*, 312–13, 365; John W. Black to dear father, May 31, 1863, Bound Volume 197, FSNMP; Erastus Fouch diary, May 3, 1863, Bound Volume 229, FSNMP; Noah Brooks, *Washington in Lincoln's Time*, 57–58.

30. Thomas Evans Diary, Manuscript Division, LC; Clay MacCauley, "From Chancellorsville to Libby Prison," in *Glimpses of the Nation's Struggle: A Series of Papers Read Before the Minnesota Commandery of the Military Order of the Loyal Legion of the United States* (St. Paul: St. Paul Book and Stationery Company, 1887), 193–94, 200; Christian Rieker to Mary Rouf, May 30, 1863, Society of Separatists of Zoar Records, Box 96, Folder 1, OHC; William B. McCreery, *"My Experiences as a Prisoner of War, and Escape from Libby Prison"* (Detroit: Winn & Hammond, 1893), 11.

31. Seraphim Meyer Pension File, RG 15, NA; Seraphim Meyer Compiled Service

Record, RG 94, NA; Federico Fernandez Cavada, *Libby Life: Experiences of a Prisoner of War in Richmond, Virginia, 1863–64* (Philadelphia: King & Baird, 1864), 23. On Libby's odors, see Evan A. Kutzler, *Living by Inches: The Smells, Sounds, Tastes, and Feeling of Captivity in Civil War Prisons* (Chapel Hill: University of North Carolina Press, 2019), 37.

32. Richard Magee Diary, May 6, 1863, in RG 69:163, Connecticut State Library; Mahlon Slutz Reminiscences, Indiana State Library; Smith, *Camps and Campaigns*, 77.

33. Special Field Orders No. 52, May 8, 1863, in RG 393, pt. 2, entry 2282, NA; Washington A. Roebling to John Bigelow, December 9, 1910, John Bigelow Papers, Box 54, Manuscript Division, LC; Richard Magee Diary, May 6, 1863, RG 69:163, Connecticut State Library; Christian Rieker to his sister, May 11, 1863, in Society of Separatists of Zoar Records, Box 96, Folder 1, OHC; *OR*, ser. 1, vol. 25, pt. 1, p. 644; *Sandusky Register*, June 12, 1863; *Norwalk Reflector*, June 23, 1863.

34. Francis Foote, as quoted in Bound Volume 76, FSNMP; Jesse M. Spooner to cousin William, May 14, 1863, Bound Volume 281, FSNMP; Robert Hubbard to darling Nellie, May 8, 1863, Bound Volume 353, FSNMP; William Noble, "History of the Seventeenth Connecticut," Bound Volume 353, FSNMP; *Hartford Evening Press*, May 7, 1863; E. C. Culp to dear ma, May 7, 1863, Thomas J. Edwards Collection, Box 1, Folder 2, BGSU; "History of the Seventeenth Connecticut by Colonel William H. Noble," Bound Volume 391, FSNMP.

35. *The Battle of Chancellorsville and the Eleventh Army Corps*, 3; [Washington, D.C.] *Daily National Intelligencer*, May 6, 1863; *New Hampshire Sentinel*, May 7, 1863. See also Christian Keller, *Chancellorsville and the Germans: Nativism, Ethnicity, and Civil War Memory* (New York: Fordham University Press, 2007).

36. "From the 107th Ohio," *Wooster Republican*, May 28, 1863; George Templeton Strong diary, May 5, 1863.

37. *Stark County Republican*, May 28, 1863.

38. John W. Black to dear father, May 31, 1863, Bound Volume 197, FSNMP; William O. Dauchy letter, May 31, 1863, Bound Volume 479, FSNMP; "From the 107th Regt.," *Sandusky Register*, May 11, 1863.

CHAPTER 5: "HEAPING UPON US . . . IGNOMINY AND SHAME"

1. *The Battle of Chancellorsville and the Eleventh Army Corps* (New York: G. B. Teubner, Printer, 1863), 9; Robert E. Wright and George David Smith, *Mutually Beneficial: The Guardian and Life Insurance in America* (New York and London: New York University Press, 2004), 27.

2. *The Battle of Chancellorsville and the Eleventh Army Corps,* 9; "The German Soldiers at the Battle of Chancellorsville," *New York Herald,* June 3, 1863; Harold Holzer, *Lincoln at Cooper Union: The Speech That Made Abraham Lincoln President* (New York: Simon and Schuster, 2004).

3. *The Battle of Chancellorsville and the Eleventh Army Corps,* 7; *New York Herald,* June 3, 1863; "The German Troops in the 11th Corps," *Sandusky Register,* June 6, 1863; on Kapp, see Daniel Moran and Arthur Waldron, eds., *The People in Arms: Military Myth and National Mobilization since the French Revolution* (Cambridge: Cambridge University Press, 2003), 91.

4. Friedrich Kapp and Charles Goepp, as quoted in *The Battle of Chancellorsville and the Eleventh Army Corps,* 25–26, 19–20; on Goepp, see Julius Goebel, *Deutsch-amerikanische Geschichtsblätter* (Chicago: German-American Historical Society of Illinois, 1913), 12:479–480.

5. William H. Warren Memoir, in MS 619: Civil War Manuscripts Collection, Series I, Box 24, Sterling Memorial Library, Yale; Erastus Fouch Diary, May 16, 1863, Bound Volume 229, FSNMP; 107th Ohio Descriptive Books, vol. 1, RG 94, NA; Smith, *Camps and Campaigns,* 77; *Sandusky Register,* May 23, 1863; *Stark County Republican,* June 4, 1863; *Stark County Republican,* June 18, 1863; "Wounded Ohio Soldiers in Washington Hospital," *Cleveland Morning Leader,* May 15, 1863.

6. See the various Special Orders in RG 313, pt. 2, entry 5367, General and Special Orders, May 1863–February 1864, NA.

7. Smith, *Camps and Campaigns,* 77; Henry Blakeman, letter, May 22, 1863, Bound Volume 105, FSNMP; Schurz, *The Reminiscences of Carl Schurz,* 7–8. Seraphim Meyer reported that upon his return to the regiment, he found "great discontent and complaints in the regiment" with respect to the allegedly "harsh and severe treatment" doled out by these new officers. See Seraphim Meyer to Theodore Meysenburg, July 14, 1863, Seraphim Meyer Compiled Service Record, RG 94, NA.

8. Carl Schurz to Oliver O. Howard, June 17, 1863, in RG 393, entry 5315: Register of Letters Received, January 1863–April 1864, NA; Smith, *Camps and Campaigns,* 79–80; Compiled Records Showing Service of Military Units in Volunteer Union Organizations, microfilm M594, reel 158, NA; Howard, *Autobiography,* 1:390–91; Richard Magee Diary, June 12–June 30, 1863, RG 69:163, Connecticut State Library; Silas Shuler to Asa Shuler, July 16, 1863, in *Pennsylvania Folklife* 29, no. 3 (Spring 1980), 107th Ohio Volunteer Infantry Vertical File, Gettysburg National Military Park Library.

9. *OR.* On the Confederate invasion of Pennsylvania, see Allen C. Guelzo, *Gettysburg: The Last Invasion* (New York: Alfred A. Knopf, 2013), and Jason Frawley, "Marching Through Pennsylvania: The Story of Soldiers and Civilians in the Gettysburg Campaign" (PhD diss., Texas Christian University, 2008).

10. On the fight at Winchester, see Eric J. Wittenberg and Scott L. Mingus, Sr., *The Second Battle of Winchester: The Confederate Victory That Opened the Door to Gettysburg* (El Dorado Hills, CA: Savas Beatie, 2016); Guelzo, *Gettysburg*, 71; David Schley Schaff, *The Life of Philip Schaff: In Part Autobiographical* (New York: Charles Scribner's Sons, 1897), 214.

11. Smith, *Camps and Campaigns*, 84.

12. Smith, *Camps and Campaigns*, 85–86; Alfred E. Lee, "Reminiscences of the Gettysburg Battle," *Lippincott's Magazine* 6 (July 1883): 54; Oliver Howard, "Campaign and Battle of Gettysburg, June and July, 1863," *Atlantic Monthly* 38 (July 1876): 52; Thompson, "From Chancellorsville to Gettysburg: A Doctor's Diary," 311; James Montgomery Bailey, "Under Guard or Sunny Slices in the South," *Danbury Times*, September 17, 1863; Richard Magee Diary, June 29–June 30, 1863, RG 69:163, Connecticut State Library, Hartford; J. Henry Blakeman to his dear mother, June 27, 1863, in Lewis Leigh Collection, Box 21, Folder 33, United States Army Heritage and Education Center, Carlisle, Pennsylvania. See also Eric Burke, "Facing the Enemy: The Crucible of Combat Forged Unique Unit Cultures Within Civil War Regiments," *Civil War Times Illustrated* (June 2019): 30–38.

13. Vanderslice, *Gettysburg, Then and Now,* 43.

14. Hess, *Lee's Tar-Heels*, 115–17.

15. Howard, "Campaign and Battle of Gettysburg," 52–53; Harry W. Pfanz, *Gettysburg—The First Day* (Chapel Hill: University of North Carolina Press, 2001), 48–49; Guelzo, *Gettysburg*, 162; William Henry Warren, "The Battle of Gettysburg, As Seen By the Writer, Wednesday, July 1st, 1863," 17th Connecticut Volunteer Infantry Vertical File, Gettysburg National Military Park Library.

16. Smith, *Camps and Campaigns*, 86; Coddington, *The Gettysburg Campaign*, 278; RG 313, pt. 2, entry 5367, NA; William H. Warren Diary, July 1, 1863, Civil War Manuscripts Collection, Group 619, Series I, Box 24, Manuscripts and Archives, Sterling Memorial Library, Yale; Lee, "Reminiscences of the Gettysburg Battle," 55.

17. Smith, *Camps and Campaigns*, 86; Howard, "Campaign and Battle of Gettysburg," 54; Pfanz, *Gettysburg—The First Day*, 137.

18. Howard, "Campaign and Battle of Gettysburg," 54; *OR*, vol. 27, no. 1, p. 701.

19. A. Wilson Greene, "From Chancellorsville to Cemetery Hill: O. O. Howard and Eleventh Corps Leadership," in Gallagher, *The First Day at Gettysburg*, 70; *OR*, vol. 27, no. 1, p. 727; Edward N. Whittier, in *Civil War Papers Read Before the Commandery of the State of Massachusetts, Military Order of the Loyal Legion of the United States* (Reprint ed., Wilmington, NC: Broadfoot Publishing Company, 1993), 1:75; Hartwig, "The Unlucky 11th," 33; Culp, *The 25th Ohio Vet. Vol. Infantry*, 76–77; Schurz, *The Reminiscences of Carl Schurz*, 5.

20. Lee, "Reminiscences of the Gettysburg Battle," 55; Warren, "The Battle of Gettysburg, As Seen By the Writer," 17th Connecticut Volunteer Infantry Vertical File, Gettysburg National Military Park; Guelzo, *Gettysburg*, 1801–181; Hartwig, "The Unlucky 11th," 37; *OR*, vol. 27, no. 1, p. 229; Busey and Martin, *Regimental Strengths and Losses*, 209; Greene, "From Chancellorsville to Cemetery Hill," 74; Kiefer, *History of the One Hundred and Fifty-Third Regiment*, 68; see also William B. Southerton Memoir, MS 3177, OHC.

21. *OR*, vol. 27, no. 1, p. 727; "Historical Significance of Adams County Poor Farm Lands, Tracts 02–138 and 02–139," and Edward Roach, "Maintaining the Poor: An Introduction to the Almshouse and Public Relief in Adams County, Pennsylvania, 1817–1968," Adams County Almshouse Vertical File, 9–20a, Gettysburg National Military Park; "Adams County Almshouse," http://www.asylumprojects.org/index.php/Adams_County_Almshouse.

22. William Henry Warren, "The Great Rebellion: A History of the 17th Conn. Vol. Infantry," vol. 2, in Civil War Manuscripts Collection, MS 619: Civil War Manuscripts Collection, Series I, Manuscripts and Archives, Yale; Hartwig, "The Unlucky 11th," 40; William H. Warren Scrapbook, in Civil War Manuscripts Collection, Series I, Box 26, Yale; Carol Reardon and Tom Vossler, *A Field Guide to Gettysburg: Experiencing the Battlefield Through Its History, Places, and* People (Chapel Hill: University of North Carolina Press, 2013), 104; *OR*, vol. 27, no. 1, p. 727; New York Monuments Commission, *Final Report of the Battlefield of Gettysburg* (Albany: J. B. Lyon Company, Printers, 1902), 1:19–20; *National Tribune*, March 19, 1885.

23. Schurz, *The Reminiscences of Carl Schurz*, 8–9; Hartwig, "The Unlucky 11th," 40; *OR*, vol. 27, pt. 1, pp. 727–29; Pfanz, *Gettysburg—The First Day*, 232; Culp, *The 25th Ohio Vet. Vol. Infantry*, 78; *OR*, vol. 27, pt. 1, p. 719; Howard, "Campaign and Battle of Gettysburg," 56. The 41st New York was likewise attached to von Gilsa's brigade, though on July 1 it remained behind in Emmitsburg, Maryland, on a guard duty.

24. Campbell Brown, as quoted in Jones, *Campbell Brown's Civil War*, 208–9; Joseph T. Butts, ed., *A Gallant Captain of the Civil War: Being the Record of the Extraordinary Adventures of Frederick Otto Baron Von Fritsch* (New York and London: F. Tennyson Neely, 1902), 75–76; Bradley M. Gottfried, *The Artillery of Gettysburg* (Nashville: Cumberland House, 2008), 66.

25. Ibid.; Fritz Nussbaum, as quoted in Smith, *Camps and Campaigns*, 225; Ralph Lowell Eckert, *John Brown Gordon: Soldier, Southerner, American* (Baton Rouge: Louisiana State University Press, 1989), 2, 35–36; Robert Stiles, *Four Years Under Marse Robert* (New York and Washington: Neale Publishing, 1910), 210–11; *OR*, vol. 27, pt. 2, p. 492; Busey and Martin, *Regimental Strengths and Losses*, 285.

26. Kiefer, *History of the One Hundred and Fifty-Third Regiment*, 78; J. Clyde Miller to John B. Bachelder, March 2, 1884, in David L. Ladd and Audrey J. Ladd, eds., *The Bachelder Papers: Gettysburg in Their Own Words*. 3 vols. (Dayton, Ohio: Morningside Books, 1994), 2: 1025–26; Butts, *A Gallant Captain*, 75; William Henry Mayo Diary, July 1, 1863, in Mayo Family Papers, Box 1, Huntington Library.

27. Henry W. Thomas, *History of the Doles-Cook Brigade, Army of Northern Virginia* (Atlanta: Franklin Printing & Publishing Company, 1903), 8–9; Guelzo, *Gettysburg*, 184–85; Bradley M. Gottfried, *The Maps of Gettysburg: An Atlas of the Gettysburg Campaign, June 3–July 13, 1863* (El Dorado Hills, CA: Savas Beatie, 2007), 124–25; Noble, *The Seventeenth Regiment Connecticut Volunteer Infantry in the War of the Rebellion*, 2.

28. *OR*, vol. 27, pt. 1, pp. 712–13; Andrew L. Harris to John B. Bachelder, March 14, 1881, in Ladd and Ladd, *The Bachelder Papers*, 2:742–44; J. Henry Blakeman to his dear Mother, July 21, 1863, in Lewis Leigh Collection, Box 21, Folder 33, United States Army Heritage & Education Center; Butts, ed., *A Gallant Captain*, 75; Kiefer, *History of the One Hundred and Fifty-Third Regiment*, 213–14; Jones, *Campbell Brown's Civil War*, 209; Guelzo, *Gettysburg*, 183; Ames, as quoted in Seraphim Meyer Court Martial Records, RG 153, NA; G. W. Nichols [61st Georgia], as quoted in Hartwig, "The Unlucky 11th," 44; Sears, 213–14. See also lecture, n.d., by Augustus Choate Hamlin, in Military Order of the Loyal Legion Collection, MS 1084 (1053), Houghton Library

29. Seraphim Meyer Court Martial Records, RG 153, NA; William H. Warren Memoir, 17th Connecticut Volunteer Infantry Vertical File, GNMP.

30. Seraphim Meyer Court Martial Records, RG 153, NA; William H. Warren Memoir, 17th Connecticut Volunteer Infantry Vertical File, GNMP; Henry Chase, ed., *Representative Men of Maine* (Portland: Lakeside Press, 1893), 231; Andrew Harris to John B. Bachelder, March 14, 1881, *Bachelder Papers*, 2:742–44; Mahlon Slutz Reminiscences, Indiana State Library.

31. William B. Southerton Memoir, William B. Southerton Papers, MS 3177, OHC; Andrew Harris to John B. Bachelder, March 14, 1881, *Bachelder Papers*, 2:742–44; "Gettysburg, July 1–3, 1863," 17th Connecticut Volunteer Infantry Vertical File, GNMP; John Henry Ahrens Diary, in 75th Ohio Volunteer Infantry Vertical File, GNMP.

32. James Montgomery Bailey, "Slice Second," 17th Connecticut Volunteer Infantry Vertical File, GNMP; J. Henry Blakeman to dear mother, July 21, 1863, Lewis Leigh Collection, Box 21, Folder 33, United States Army Heritage & Education Center; *OR*, vol. 27, pt. 2, p. 492; Culp, *The 25th Ohio Vet. Vol. Infantry*, 78; Jere Williams to John Bachelder, June 18, 1880, Licensed Battlefield Guide Files, 25th Ohio Volunteer Infantry, GNMP; Andrew Harris

speech, Andrew Linton Harris Papers, Box 1, Folder 3, OHC; Jacob Boroway to his brother, July 10, 1863, in Raynors' Historical Collectible Auction Catalog, HCA 2014-08, lot no. 362, http://www.hcaauctions.com/lot–36565.aspx.

33. "Gettysburg, July 1–3, 1863," in 17th Connecticut Volunteer Infantry Vertical File, GNMP; see also Hartwig, "The Unlucky 11th," 49.

34. Seraphim Meyer Court Martial Records, RG 153, NA; *National Tribune*, April 23, 1885; Smith, *Camps and Campaigns*, 88; Augustus Vignos to J. B. Bachelder, April 17, 1864, *Bachelder Papers*, 1:155.

35. Southerton, "What We Did There, Or, Swamp Angel," OHC; Howard, "Campaign and Battle of Gettysburg," 58; Howard, *Autobiography*, 1:418; Smith, *Camps and Campaigns*, 88.

36. Smith, *Camps and Campaigns*, 88–89.

37. Ibid.

38. Ibid.; Howard, *Autobiography*, 1:419; Fritz Nussbaum, as quoted in Smith, *Camps and Campaigns*, 225.

39. Smith, *Camps and Campaigns*, 88, 226; Seraphim Meyer Court Martial Records, RG 153, NA; Howard, *Autobiography*, 1:419; "From the 25th Ohio," *National Tribune*, June 4, 1885.

40. Smith, *Camps and Campaigns*, 90; George Billow Pension File, RG 15, NA; Andrew L. Harris to John Bachelder, March 14, 1881, *Bachelder Papers*, 2:748; Peter F. Young to John Bachelder, August 12, 1867, *Bachelder Papers*, 1:311; Mahlon Slutz Reminiscences, Indiana State Library; Kiefer, *History of the One Hundred and Fifty Third Regiment*, 85; E. C. Culp to my dear Lucy, July 5, 1863, Thomas J. Edwards Collection, Box 1, Folder 2, BGSU; 107th Ohio Regimental Order Books, RG 94, NA. Fritz Nussbaum supposed that there were "only about one hundred men" drawn up behind the fence on East Cemetery Hill, but the numbers he provides elsewhere are unreliable. Nussbaum, as quoted in Smith, *Camps and Campaigns*, 225–26. On injuries among the rank and file, see also Busey and Martin, *The Last Full Measure*, 104–5.

CHAPTER 6: "ALL THAT MORTAL[S] COULD DO"

1. Gallagher, *The Second Day at Gettysburg*, 189n47; Smith, *Camps and Campaigns*, 93; William Seymour, as quoted in Jones, *Cemetery Hill*, 53; Stephen A. Wallace Diary, July 2, 1863, Licensed Battlefield Guide Files, 153rd Pennsylvania Volunteer Infantry, GNMP; Butts, *A Gallant Captain of the Civil War*, 83.

2. Smith, *Camps and Campaigns*, 98; *OR*, vol. 27, no. 2, p. 446; Howard, "Campaign and Battle of Gettysburg," 63; Archer, *East Cemetery Hill at Gettysburg*, 15; Butts, *A Gallant Captain of the Civil War*, 83. For a provocative analysis of temporality in Civil War America, see Cheryl Wells, *Civil War Time: Tem-*

porality and Identity in America, 1861–1865 (Athens: University of Georgia Press, 2005).

3. *OR*, vol. 27, no. 2, pp. 543–44; Cyrus Kingsbury Remington, *A Record of Battery I, First N.Y. Light Artillery Vols., Otherwise Known As Wiedrich's Battery during the War of the Rebellion, 1861–'65* (Buffalo: Press of the Courier Company, 1891), 19; William Seymour, typescript manuscript, Licensed Battlefield Guide File for "Hays' Brigade, Early's Division, Second Corps," GNMP; Howard, "Campaign and Battle of Gettysburg," 63; Smith, *Camps and Campaigns*, 98; Butts, *A Gallant Captain*, 84; Allan Nevins, ed., *A Diary of Battle: The Personal Journals of Colonel Charles S. Wainwright, 1861–1865* (Reprint ed., Gettysburg: Stan Clark Military Books, 1962), 242–43; Jones, *Campbell Brown's Civil War*, 216–17; William Henry Mayo Diary, July 2, 1863, Mayo Family Papers, Box 1, Huntington Library; Silas Schuler to Asa Schuler, July 16, 1863, in William T. Parsons and Mary Shuler Heimburger, ed., "Shuler Family Correspondence," *Pennsylvania Folklife* 29, no. 3 (Spring 1980): 112; Albert Peck [17th Connecticut], as quoted in Archer, *East Cemetery Hill at Gettysburg*, 26–27, 29–30; Theodore Ayrault Dodge, as quoted in Thomas L. Elmore, "The Whistle and Hiss of The Iron: The Effects of Artillery Fire on Infantry at Gettysburg," *Gettysburg Magazine* 5 (July 1991): 121; Schurz, *The Reminiscences of Carl Schurz*, 3:28.

4. Archer, *East Cemetery Hill at Gettysburg*, 26, 30; *OR*, vol. 27, no. 2, pp. 446–47, 544; Guelzo, *Gettysburg*, 338; Nevins, ed., *A Diary of Battle*, 243; Whittier, "The Left Attack (Ewell's) at Gettysburg," 1:79.

5. *OR*, vol. 27, no. 2, pp. 447, 480, 504; William Henry Mayo Diary, July 2, 1863, Mayo Family Papers, Box 1, Huntington Library; Terry L. Jones, *Lee's Tigers Revisited: The Louisiana Infantry in the Army of Northern Virginia* (Baton Rouge: Louisiana State University Press, 2017), 272–77, 378; J. W. Jackson as quoted in Gottfried, *The Maps of Gettysburg*, 218; Arthur W. Bergeron, Jr., *Guide to Louisiana Confederate Military Units, 1861–1865* (Baton Rouge: Louisiana State University Press, 1989), 90–91; Busey and Martin, *Regimental Strengths and Losses*, 286; Guelzo, *Gettysburg*, 339; Whittier, "The Left Attack (Ewell's) at Gettysburg," 1:77; Kiefer, *History of the One Hundred Fifty Third Regiment*, 219–20.

6. Kiefer, *History of the One Hundred Fifty Third Regiment*, 219–20; Parsons and Heimburger, "Shuler Family Correspondence," 112; Butts, *A Gallant Captain*, 84; Nevins, *A Diary of Battle*, 245; J. W. Jackson as quoted in Merle Reed, ed., "The Gettysburg Campaign—A Louisiana Lieutenant's Eye-Witness Account," *Pennsylvania History* 30 (April 1963): 189.

7. Andrew L. Harris to John Bachelder, March 14, 1881, *Bachelder Papers*, 2:744–745; *OR*, vol. 27, pt. 1, p. 706.

8. *Bachelder Papers*, 2:746; Whittier, "The Left Attack (Ewell's) at Gettysburg,"

1:90; *OR*, vol. 27, pt. 1, pp. 715, 718; Charles P. Hamblen and Walter Powell, eds., *Connecticut Yankees at Gettysburg* (Kent, OH: Kent State University Press, 1993), 55; *OR*, vol. 27, pt. 1, p. 480; Harris to John Bachelder, April 7, 1864, *Bachelder Papers*, 1:138–139.

9. Smith, *Camps and Campaigns*, 101; Nevins, *A Diary of Battle*, 245; Thomas E. Causby, "Storming the Stone Fence at Gettysburg: A Morganton Confederate Veteran Tells of the Charge," *Southern Historical Society Papers* 29 (1901): 339–41; Nussbaum, as quoted in *Camps and Campaigns*, 225–26; Parsons and Heimburger, ed., "Shuler Family Correspondence," 112; Culp, *The 25th Ohio Vet. Vol. Infantry*, 79; E. C. Culp to my dear Lucy, July 5, 1863, Thomas J. Edwards Collection, Box 1, Folder 2, BGSU; Southerton, "What We Did There, Or, Swamp Angel," typescript manuscript, VFM 3177, OHC.

10. *OR*, vol. 27, pt. 1, pp. 718, 720, 731; Whittier, "The Left (Ewell's) Attack at Gettysburg," 90; Ohioan, as quoted in Jones, *Lee's Tigers Revisited*, 280; Andrew Harris to John B. Bachelder, March 14, 1881, *Bachelder Papers*, 2:745–46; Kiefer, *History of the One Hundred and Fifty Third Regiment*, 87; Smith, *Camps and Campaigns*, 101; Parsons and Heimburger, ed., "Shuler Family Correspondence," 112; J. W. Jackson, as quoted in Reed, ed., "The Gettysburg Campaign," 189; "From the 11th Army Corps," *Norwalk Reflector*, July 21, 1863.

11. Jones, *Lee's Tigers Revisited*, 281–82; George B. Fox to A. L. Harris, November 14, 1885, *Bachelder Papers*, 2:1144–45; Michael Wiedrich to John B. Bachelder, January 20, 1886, *Bachelder Papers*, 2:1181–82; J. Clyde Miller to John B. Bachelder, March 2, 1886, *Bachelder Papers*, 2:1210–13; Alfred J. Rider to J. B. Bachelder, August 20, 1885, *Bachelder Papers*, 2:1118–19; Peter F. Young to J. B. Bachelder, August 12, 1867, *Bachelder Papers*, 1:310–11; *OR*, vol. 27, pt. 1, p. 752; Fritz Nussbaum, as quoted in Smith, *Camps and Campaigns*, 226; Henry Perry Smith, ed., *History of the City of Buffalo and Erie County* (Syracuse: D. Mason & Co., 1884), 1:294; J. W. Jackson, as quoted in Reed, "The Gettysburg Campaign—A Louisiana Lieutenant's Eye-Witness Account," 189; Fred Smith, "Historical Sketch," in New York Monuments Commission for the Battlefields of Gettysburg and Chattanooga, *Final Report of the Battlefield of Gettysburg*, 3:1247.

12. Peter F. Young to J. B. Bachelder, August 12, 1867, *Bachelder Papers*, 1:310–11; Alfred J. Rider to John B. Bachelder, October 3, 1885, *Bachelder Papers*, 2:1129; 107th Ohio Descriptive Books, RG 94, NA; Culp, *The 25th Ohio Vet. Vol. Infantry*, 79; M. Browne to J. B. Bachelder, April 8, 1864, *Bachelder Papers*, 1:148–49; Schurz, *The Reminiscences of Carl Schurz*, 3:25; "From the 11th Army Corps," *Norwalk Reflector*, July 21, 1863.

13. Schurz, *The Reminiscences of Carl Schurz*, 3:25; Nussbaum, as quoted in Smith, *Camps and Campaigns*, 226; *National Tribune*, July 15, 1909; Young to Bachelder, August 12, 1867, *Bachelder Papers*, 1:310–12; Peter F. Young Carded Med-

ical File, RG 94, entry 534, Box 2845, NA; George Billow Pension File, RG 15, NA; *Semi-Centennial Register of the Members of the Phi Kappa Sigma Fraternity, 1850–1900*, 171; Andrew B. Booth, comp., *Records of Louisiana Confederate Soldiers and Louisiana Confederate Commands*, 139; Jones, *Lee's Tigers Revisited*, 285; *Tuscarawas Advocate*, August 7, 1863; Richard Rollins, *"The Damned Red Flags of the Rebellion": The Confederate Battle Flag at Gettysburg* (Redondo Beach, CA: Rank and File Publications, 1997), 131; *OR*, vol. 27, pt. 1, p. 713; "A Tiger at Gettysburg," *The Opelousas Courier* [Opelousas, Louisiana], August 7, 1909.

14. Smith, *Camps and Campaigns*, 101; J. W. Jackson as quoted in Reed, "The Gettysburg Campaign," 189; Whittier, "The Left (Ewell's) Attack at Gettysburg," 90–93; Guelzo, *Gettysburg*, 342–43; George Billow, "Casualties of the 107th in the Gettysburg Battle," *Summit County Beacon*, July 30, 1863; *OR*, vol. 27, pt. 1, pp. 372, 456–57, 752; *OR*, vol. 27, pt. 2, p. 475, 480–81; William Henry Mayo Diary, July 2, 1863, Mayo Family Papers, Box 1, Huntington Library.

15. Culp, *The 25th Ohio Vet. Vol. Infantry*, 79; Richard Magee Diary, Connecticut State Library; Smith, *Camps and Campaigns*, 104; *OR*, vol. 27, no. 2, p. 320; 107th Ohio Regimental Descriptive Books, RG 94, NA; Busey and Martin, *Regimental Losses*, 107.

16. William Garrett Piston, "Cross Purposes: Longstreet, Lee, and Confederate Attack Plans for July 3 at Gettysburg," in Gary W. Gallagher, ed., *The Third Day at Gettysburg & Beyond* (Chapel Hill: University of North Carolina Press, 1994), 45; *OR*, vol. 27, pt. 2, pp. 320–22, 360–61; Alfred Lee, "Reminiscences of the Gettysburg Battle," *Lippincott's Magazine* 6 (July 1883), 59; James Longstreet, "Lee's Right Wing at Gettysburg," *B&L*, 3:339–354.

17. Schurz, *The Reminiscences of Carl Schurz*, 3:27; Fritz Nussbaum, as quoted in Smith, *Camps and Campaigns*, 227; Smith, *Camps and Campaigns*, 105.

18. Smith, *Camps and Campaigns*, 109; Nevins, *A Diary of Battle*, 249; Schurz, *The Reminiscences of Carl Schurz*, 3:29, 31–33.

19. Andrew Harris to Friend Lough, July 11, 1863, Andrew L. Harris Papers, Box 1, Folder 1, OHC; Harris to Bachelder, *Bachelder Papers*, 2:747; Nussbaum, as quoted in Smith, *Camps and Campaigns*, 227; *The Civil War Diary of Private John Flory, Co. C, 107th Ohio*, 19.

20. Gregory A. Coco, *A Strange and Blighted Land: Gettysburg: The Aftermath of a Battle* (El Dorado Hills, CA: Savas Beatie, 2017), 6; Stiles, *Four Years Under Marse Robert*, 220; F. A. Wildman to dear wife, July 12, 1863, Wildman Family Papers, OHC; Smith, *Camps and Campaigns*, 120; Nevins, ed., *A Diary of Battle*, 251–52; Schurz, *The Reminiscences of Carl Schurz*, 3:37; "Editorial Correspondence," *Norwalk Reflector*, July 21, 1863; Busey and Martin, eds., *Regimental Strengths and Losses*, 104–5.

21. Harris to Bachelder, March 14, 1881, *Bachelder Papers*, 2:747; Smith, *Camps*

and Campaigns, 123–24; Gregory A. Coco, *A Vast Sea of Misery: A History and Guide to the Union and Confederate Field Hospitals at Gettysburg, July 1– November 20, 1863* (Reprint ed., El Dorado Hills, CA: Savas Beatie, 2017), 105; Daniel Welch to the author, email correspondence, August 8, 2017; Caspar Bohrer Pension File, RG 15, NA; *Medical and Surgical History of the Civil War* (Reprint ed. Wilmingrton, NC: Broadfoot Publishing Co., 1991), 12:489, NA; 107th Ohio Regimental Descriptive Books, RG 94, NA.

22. Schurz, *The Reminiscences of Carl Schurz*, 3:39–40; Thompson, "From Chancellorsville to Gettysburg: A Doctor's Diary," 313; "300 Arms and Legs," *Ohio Democrat*, July 17, 1863; Andrew Harris to Friend Lough, July 11, 1863, Andrew L. Harris Papers, Box 1, Folder 1, OHC; Butts, ed., *A Gallant Captain*, 88; Ronald D. Kirkwood, *"Too Much for Human Endurance": The George Spangler Farm Hospitals and the Battle of Gettysburg* (El Dorado Hills, CA: Savas Beatie, 2019), 313; Alfred J. Rider to John B. Bachelder, October 3, 1885, *Bachelder Papers*, 2:1128–30.

23. "The Firemen's Celebration," *Wooster Republican*, July 16, 1863; "The Fourth in Canton," *Stark County Republican*, July 9, 1863; "The 4th in Akron," *Sandusky Register*, July 8, 1863; "The Fourth in The City," *Daily Cleveland Herald*, July 6, 1863.

24. "Telegraphic," *Daily Cleveland Herald*, July 6, 1863.

25. "Editorial Correspondence," *Norwalk Reflector*, July 21, 1863; *Elyria Independent Democrat*, July 22, 1863; Lee, "Reminiscences of the Gettysburg Battle," 60; Kirkwood, *"Too Much for Human Endurance,"* 210–11, 221–22.

26. Barnet T. Steiner to William Steiner, July 8, 1863, in Smith, *Camps and Campaigns*, 235–36.

27. "The 107th," *Stark County Democrat*, July 15, 1863; "The 107th at Gettysburg," *Sandusky Register*, July 28, 1863; "Casualties of the 107th in the Gettysburg Battle," *Summit County Beacon*, July 30, 1863.

28. William H. Heiss Pension File, RG 15, NA; 107th Ohio Regimental Descriptive Books, RG 94, NA.

29. Smith, *Camps and Campaigns*, 124; *OR*, vol. 27, pt. 1, p. 720.

30. Ibid., 120, 126.

31. Ibid., 120, 126, 135; *OR*, vol. 27, no. 1, pp. 146–47, 708–9; John Thomas Scharf, *History of Western Maryland* (Philadelphia: Louis H. Evarts, 1882), 1:570; Thomas Chalmers Harbaugh, *Middletown Valley in Song and Story* (N.p.: T. C. Harbaugh, 1910), 155; Leander Schooley, as quoted in Eric J. Wittenberg, J. David Petruzzi, and Michael F. Nugent, *One Continuous Fight: The Retreat from Gettysburg and the Pursuit of Lee's Army of Northern Virginia, July 4–14, 1863* (El Dorado Hills, CA: Savas Beatie, 2008), 152, 196; 107th Ohio Regimental Descriptive Books, RG 94, NA.

32. Smith, *Camps and Campaigns*, 135; *OR*, vol., 27, pt. 1, pp. 708–9; *Summit*

County Beacon, July 30, 1863; 107th Ohio Regimental Descriptive Books, RG 94, NA; Wittenberg, Petruzzi, and Nugent, *One Continuous Fight*, 254; Richard Slotkin, *The Long Road to Antietam* (New York: Liveright, 2012), 196; Thomas Brownfield Searight, *The Old Pike: A History of the National Road* (Uniontown, PA: Published by the Author, 1894).

33. 107th Ohio Regimental Descriptive Books, RG 94, NA; Smith, *Camps and Campaigns*, 135–50, quote at 137; *OR*, vol. 27, pt. 1, pp. 709–10. Meade's retreat from Gettysburg has invited no shortage of debate and controversy. For a perceptive analysis, see A. Wilson Greene, "From Gettysburg to Falling Waters: Meade's Pursuit of Lee," in Gallagher, *The Third Day at Gettysburg & Beyond*, 161–201.

34. Steven J. Ramold, *Baring the Iron Hand: Discipline in the Union Army* (DeKalb: Northern Illinois University Press, 2009), 316–43.

35. Ramold, *Baring the Iron Hand*, 316–43; *Revised United States Army Regulations of 1861* (Washington: Government Printing Office, 1863), 493.

36. Seraphim Meyer to Theodore Meysenburg, July 4, 1863, and Meysenburg to Meyer, July 5, 1863, Seraphim Meyer Court Martial Records, RG 153, NA; Meyer to Meysenburg, July 14, 1863, Seraphim Meyer Compiled Service Record, RG 94, NA; *OR*, vol. 27, pt. 2, pp. 322–23; Wittenberg, Petruzzi, and Nugent, *One Continuous Fight*, 299; Kent Masterson Brown, *Retreat from Gettysburg: Lee, Logistics, and the Pennsylvania Campaign* (Chapel Hill: University of North Carolina Press, 2005), 322; Nevins, *A Diary of Battle*, 261; Smith, *Camps and Campaigns*, 139; Brooks, *Washington in Lincoln's Time* (New York: Century Co., 1896), 96; John G. Selby, *Meade: The Price of Command, 1863–1865* (Kent: Kent State University Press, 2018), offers a vigorous defense of Meade in the weeks after Gettysburg.

37. Smith, *Camps and Campaigns*, 140–42, 150; *OR*, vol. 27, no. 1, pp. 149–50.

38. Seraphim Meyer Court Martial Records, RG 153, NA; Seraphim Meyer to Theodore A. Meysenburg, July 18, 1863, Seraphim Meyer Court Martial Records, RG 153, NA; Thomas P. Lowry, *Curmudgeons, Drunkards, & Outright Fools: Courts-Martial of Civil War Union Colonels* (Lincoln: University of Nebraska Press, 2003); Brian Matthew Jordan, "The Unfortunate Colonel," *The Civil War Monitor* 6, no. 4 (Winter 2016): 54–63, 74–76.

39. Seraphim Meyer Court Martial Records, RG 153, NA; Brian Matthew Jordan, "Forming Up, Falling Back, Digging In: The Politics of Movement in a Civil War Regiment," paper delivered at Society of Civil War Historians Biennial Meeting, Pittsburgh, Pennsylvania, June 1, 2016.

40. Seraphim Meyer Court Martial Records, RG 153, NA.

41. Ibid.

42. "Our Recent Victories," *Milwaukee Daily Sentinel*, August 3, 1863; "National Thanksgiving," *New York Herald*, August 4, 1863; George Henry Gordon,

A War Diary of Events in the War of the Great Rebellion, 1863–1865 (Boston: James R. Osgood and Company, 1882), 168–69; Smith, *Camps and Campaigns*, 146–47; Noble, *The Seventeenth Regiment Connecticut Volunteer Infantry*, 2; Harry S. Stout, *Upon the Altar of the Nation*, 248–49.

CHAPTER 7: "WE ARE NOT COWARDS"

1. Franklin McGrath, comp., *The History of the 127th New York: "Monitors" in the War for the Preservation of the Union—September 8th, 1862, June 30th 1865* (N.p.: n.d.), 68; Gordon, *A War Diary of Events in the War of the Great Rebellion*, 169–70.

2. McGrath, *History of the 127th New York*, 68; Gordon, *A War Diary of Events in the War of the Great Rebellion*, 169–70. On ruins and lone chimneys, see Nelson, *Ruin Nation*.

3. Gordon, *A War Diary of Events in the War of the Great Rebellion*, 173–74; Smith, *Camps and Campaigns*, 152; McGrath, *History of the 127th New York Volunteers*, 69; Albert Rowe Barlow, *Company G: A Record of the Services of One Company of the 157th New York Volunteers in the War of the Rebellion* (Syracuse: A. W. Hall, 1899), 147.

4. John Purdy, *The Colombian Navigator, or Sailing Directory for the American Coasts* (London: R. H. Laurie, 1839), 128; McGrath, *History of the 127th New York*, 70–73; Stratton Lawrence, *Folly Beach* (Charleston, SC: Arcadia, 2013), 12; Barlow, *Company G*, 148; Henry F. W. Little, *The Seventh Regiment New Hampshire Volunteers in the War of the Rebellion* (Concord: Ira C. Evans, Printer, 1896), 102; "At the Siege of Charleston," *Independent Statesman* [Concord, New Hampshire], December 2, 1875; Smith, *Camps and Campaigns*, 152–54; John Brunny to esteemed friend, December 29, 1863, in Society of Separatists of Zoar Records, Box 96, Folder 1, OHC; enlisted man, as quoted in Stephen R. Wise, *Gate of Hell: Campaign for Charleston Harbor, 1863* (Columbia: University of South Carolina Press, 1994), 38; "From the 107th O.V.I.," *Stark County Republican*, November 19, 1863; James B. Legg and Steven D. Smith, *"The Best Ever Occupied . . ." Archaeological Investigations of a Civil War Encampment on Folly Island, South Carolina* (Columbia: South Carolina Institute of Archaeology and Anthropology, 1989), 18; Gordon, *A War Diary of Events*, 224.

5. Robert N. Rosen, "Charleston, Siege of (1863–1865)," in Walter B. Edgar, ed., *South Carolina Encyclopedia* (Columbia: University of South Carolina Press, 2006); Wise, *Gate of Hell*. On the Fifty-fourth, see Egerton, *Thunder at the Gates: The Black Civil War Regiments That Redeemed America* (New York: Basic Books, 2016).

6. *OR*, vol. 28, pt. 2, pp. 29–30, 39; Gideon Welles, diary, July 26, 1863, in William E. Gienapp and Erica L. Gienapp, eds., *The Civil War Diary of Gideon Welles, Lincoln's Secretary of the Navy: The Original Manuscript Edition* (Urbana, Chicago, and Springfield: University of Illinois Press, 2014), 258–59; George H. Gordon to E. W. Smith, September 11, 1863, RG 393, pt. 2, entry 2282: Letters Sent January 1863–March 1864, NA; Wise, *Gate of Hell*, 137–38.

7. "From the 107th," *Summit County Beacon*, September 24, 1863; John Brunny to esteemed friend, December 29, 1863, in Society of Separatists of Zoar Records, Box 96, Folder 1, OHC; McGrath, *History of the 127th New York*, 73; Smith, *Camps and Campaigns*, 153; Gordon, *A War Diary of Events*, 224–25; Wise, *Gate of Hell*, 119–20; Legg and Smith, *"The Best Ever Occupied...",* 13, 18, 21; Moore, *Complete History of the Great Rebellion* (Philadelphia: W. S. Burlock and Company, 1881), 388; E. Milby Burton, *The Siege of Charleston, 1861–1865* (Columbia: University of South Carolina Press, 1970); W. Scott Poole, *South Carolina's Civil War: A Narrative History* (Macon, GA: Mercer University Press, 2005), 92.

8. Smith, *Camps and Campaigns*, 160–61; Gordon, *A War Diary of Events*, 224; Jacob Lichty to dear brother, September 27, 1863, Thomas J. Edwards Papers, Box 2, Folder 1, BGSU; Kelby Ouchley, *Flora and Fauna of the Civil War: An Environmental Reference Guide* (Baton Rouge: Louisiana State University Press, 2010).

9. Fritz Nussbaum to Friend Cary, November 14, 1863, in George S. Phillips Papers, Box 2, Folder 1, Huntington Library; Mahlon Slutz Reminiscences, Indiana State Library; McGrath, *History of the 127th New York*, 73–74; *Stark County Republican*, November 19, 1863; Jacob Lichty to dear brother, September 27, 1863, Thomas J. Edwards Papers, Box 2, Folder 1, BGSU; "Death of Capt. Steiner," *Stark County Republican*, August 20, 1863; "From Company D, 107th Regiment," *Stark County Republican*, October 8, 1863.

10. Jacob Lichty to dear brother, September 27, 1863, Thomas J. Edwards Papers, Box 2, Folder 1, Jerome Library, BGSU.

11. Andrew Harris to dear Sir, August 6, 1863, Andrew L. Harris Papers, MSS 322, Box 1, Folder 1, OHC; Oscar D. Ladley to Mother, July 16, 1863, Oscar D. Ladley Papers, Wright State University; Smith, *Camps and Campaigns*, 153–54; George Billow Pension File, RG 15, NA; 107th Ohio Regimental Descriptive Books, RG 94, NA; Jacob Lichty to dear brother, September 26, 1863, Thomas J. Edwards Papers, Box 2, Folder 1, Jerome Library, BGSU; William Siffert Compiled Service Record, RG 94, NA.

12. General Orders No. 34, September 24, 1863, RG 393: Records of United States Continental Army Commands, 1821–1920, pt. 2, entry 5367: General and Special Orders May 1863–February 1864, NA; Report of Division Inspector, December 22, 1863, 107th Ohio Regimental Books, RG 94, NA; Jacob Lichty to dear brother, September 26, 1863, Thomas J. Edwards Papers, Box

2, Folder 1, BGSU; enlisted man, as quoted in Legg and Smith, *"The Best Ever Occupied,"* 23; Brigade Inspector's Report, December 24, 1863, 107th Ohio Regimental Books, vol. 5, RG 94, NA; John E. Florance, Jr., "Morris Island: Victory or Blunder?" *The South Carolina Historical Magazine* 55, no. 3 (July 1954): 143–52.

13. General Orders No. 27, December 18, 1863, in 107th Ohio Regimental Books, RG 94, NA; 107th Ohio Regimental Books, vol. 4, RG 94, NA; Ramold, *Baring the Iron Hand.*

14. 107th Ohio Regimental Books, RG 94, NA; General Orders No. 36, September 30, 1863, RG 313, pt. 2, entry 5367: General and Special Orders May 1863–February 1864, NA; Mark Will-Weber, *Muskets and Applejack: Spirits, Soldiers, and the Civil War* (Washington, DC: Regnery History, 2017); Arnold James Cooley, *Cooley's Cyclopaedia of Practical Receipts,* 6th ed. (New York: D. Appleton and Company, 1897), 2:1418–19; McGrath, *History of the 127th New York,* 87–88.

15. Jacob Lichty to dear brother, September 26, 1863, Thomas J. Edwards Papers, Box 2, Folder 1, BGSU; Christopher Hager, *I Remain Yours: Common Lives in Civil War Letters* (Cambridge, MA: Harvard University Press, 2018).

16. Daniel Joseph Ryan, *A History of Ohio, with Biographical Sketches of Her Governors and the Ordinance of 1787* (Columbus: A. H. Smythe, 1888), 186–87; Frank Conover, ed., *Centennial Portrait and Biographical Record of the City of Dayton and of Montgomery County, Ohio* (Chicago: A. W. Bowen & Co., 1897), 151; Reid, *Ohio in the War,* 1:1025; James W. Low, *Low's Railroad Directory for 1862* (New York: Wynkoop, Hallenbeck & Thomas, Printers, 1862), 97; Wood Gray, *The Hidden Civil War: The Story of the Copperheads* (New York: Viking Press, 1964), 150–51; John Brough, as quoted in Richard F. Miller, ed., *States at War,* Vol. 5: *A Reference Guide for Ohio in the Civil War* (Hanover and London: University Press of New England, 2015), 230; Arnold Shankman, "Soldier Votes and Clement L. Vallandigham in the 1863 Ohio Gubernatorial Election," *Ohio History* 82, nos.1–2 (Winter-Spring 1973): 90; Richard H. Abbott, *Ohio's Civil War Governors* (Columbus: Ohio State University Press, 1962), 36–38; *Speech of John Brough at the Union Mass Meeting, at Marietta, Ohio, June 10, 1863* (Springfield, OH: Springfield Republic, 1863); Jonathan W. White, *Emancipation, The Union Army, and the Reelection of Abraham Lincoln* (Baton Rouge: Louisiana State University Press, 2014), 25; "Brough's Platform," *Newark* [Ohio] *Advocate,* August 21, 1863; "The Meeting on the Square Last Night," *Daily Cleveland Herald,* June 16, 1863; "The State Union Convention—The Ticket," *Daily Cleveland Herald,* June 18, 1863.

17. Shankman, "Soldier Votes and Clement L. Vallandigham," 88; White, *Emancipation, the Union Army, and the Reelection,* 25; Vallandigham, *A Life of Clement L. Vallandigham,* 314.

18. Arnold Michael Shankman, "Candidate in Exile: Clement Vallandigham and the 1863 Ohio Gubernatorial Election" (PhD diss., Emory University, 1969), 146, 182; "Birthplace of John Brough," *Ohio Archaeological and Historical Quarterly* 28 (1919): 373; David Tod, as quoted in Miller, ed., *States at War,* Vol. 5: *A Reference Guide for Ohio in the Civil War*, 237–38; "Riot at Wooster," *Tiffin Tribune*, August 14, 1863.

19. Shankman, "Soldier Votes and Clement L. Vallandigham," 90; "From the 107th Ohio," *Wooster Republican*, January 21, 1864; Kepler, *History of the Three Months and Three Years Service of the Fourth Regiment Ohio Volunteer Infantry*, 275; White, *Emancipation, the Union Army, and the Reelection*, 20; "Appeal to the Soldiers," *Daily Cleveland Herald*, October 9, 1863.

20. "From the 107th Ohio," *Wooster Republican*, January 21, 1864; Shankman, "Soldier Votes and Clement L. Vallandigham," 90; "From the 107th," *Summit County Beacon*, September 24, 1863; "From the 107th Regiment," *Newark* [Ohio] *Advocate*, November 27, 1863; White, *Emancipation, the Union Army, and the Reelection*, 110; *Wooster Republican*, January 4, 1864.

21. *The Tribune Almanac and Political Register for 1864* (New York: Tribune Association, 1864), 69; "How the Soldiers Voted," *Lowell Daily Citizen and News*, October 15, 1863; "Telegraphic," *Daily Cleveland Herald*, October 22, 1863; "From the 107th Regiment—The Democratic Soldiers not Permitted to Vote," *Stark County Democrat*, December 2, 1863; "The Election in Ohio," *Ohio Repository*, October 21, 1863; Smith, *Camps and Campaigns*, 155; Lincoln to Brough, as quoted in Christopher Dell, *Lincoln and the War Democrats: The Grand Erosion of Conservative Tradition* (Cranbury, NJ: Associated University Presses, 1975), 245; *McArthur Democrat* [Vinton County, Ohio], January 7, 1864; *Holmes County* [Ohio] *Farmer*, November 5, 1863.

22. Smith, *Camps and Campaigns*, 156 60; John Brunny to friend, December 29, 1863, Society of Separatists of Zoar Records, Box 96, Folder 1, OHC; John Geissler to esteemed friend, January 8, 1864, Society of Separatists of Zoar Records, Box 96, Folder 1, OHC; Fritz Nussbaum to Friend Cary, November 14, 1863, George Shane Phillips Papers, Box 2, Huntington Library; Mahlon Slutz Reminiscences, Indiana State Library; Order of December 29, 1863, 107th Ohio Regimental Books, RG 94, NA; Fritz Nussbaum to Friend Cary, November 14, 1863, George S. Phillips Papers, Box 2, Huntington Library; Court Martial Case File LL–1584, RG 153, NA; McGrath, *History of the 127th New York*, 77–78; Wise, *Gate of Hell*, 9–10, 147–48; "The 107th Re-Enlisted," *Wooster Republican*, February 4, 1864.

23. *The Liberator*, January 8 and January 15, 1864; Smith, *Camps and Campaigns*, 159; Luis Fenollosa Emilio, *The History of the Fifty-fourth Regiment of Massachusetts Volunteer Infantry, 1863–1865* (Boston: Boston Book Company, 1894), 144.

24. Dispatch to Seraphim Meyer, February 6, 1864, RG 393, pt. 2, entry 5364: Letters Sent May 1863–May 1864.

25. *OR*, vol. 28, pt. 2, pp. 129–30, 134–35; *OR*, vol. 35, pt. 1, p. 279; Robert A. Taylor, *Rebel Storehouse: Florida's Contribution to the Confederacy* (Tuscaloosa: University of Alabama Press, 2003), 111, and chaps. 5 and 6, passim; William H. Nulty, *Confederate Florida: The Road to Olustee* (Tuscaloosa: University of Alabama Press, 1990), 53–55, 72–73; John G. Nicolay and John Hay, *Abraham Lincoln: A History* (New York: Century Company, 1909), 8:281–82; Emilio, *History of the Fifty-fourth Regiment*, 148.

26. H. David Stone, Jr., *Vital Rails: The Charleston & Savannah Railroad and the Civil War in Coastal South* (Columbia: University of South Carolina Press, 2008), 177–78; Daniel L. Schafer, *Thunder on the River: The Civil War in Northeast Florida* (Gainesville: University Press of Florida, 2010), 178; George F. Baltzell, "The Battle of Olustee (Ocean Pond), Florida," *Florida Historical Quarterly* 9, no. 4 (April 1931): 202–3; Emilio, *History of the Fifty-fourth Regiment*, 151; Oscar D. Ladley to Mother and Sisters, February 1864, Oscar D. Ladley Papers, Wright State; Smith, *Camps and Campaigns*, 161; *OR*, vol. 35, pt. 1, p. 31; William Warren Memoir, https://seventeenthcvi.org/blog/history-index/william-warren-history/the-warren-articles–18–22/; *OR*, vol. 35, pt. 1, pp. 31, 106–7; "Letter from the 107th," *Stark County Republican*, March 10, 1864.

27. Oscar D. Ladley to Mother and Sisters, February 1864, Oscar D. Ladley Papers, Wright State; William Warren Memoir, https://seventeenthcvi.org/blog/history-index/william-warren-history/the-warren-articles–18–22/; *OR*, vol. 35, pt. 1, pp. 31, 106–7, 144–45; Smith, *Camps and Campaigns*, 162; Stone, Jr., *Vital Rails*, 179–80; *Stark County Republican*, March 10, 1864; Mahlon Slutz, *Tribute to Major Augustus Vignos*, 2–3.

28. My narrative of the Florida expedition draws heavily on *OR*, vol. 35, pt. 1, pp. 281–86; Schafer, *Thunder on the River,* chap. 9; David James Coles, "Far From Fields of Glory: Military Operations in Florida during the Civil War, 1864–1865" (PhD diss., Florida State University, 1996), 40–65; and Nulty, *Confederate Florida*. Ezra J. Warner, *Generals in Gray: Lives of Confederate Commanders* (Baton Rouge: Louisiana State University Press, 2006), 142; Emilio, *History of the Fifty-fourth*, 173; Georgia soldier, as quoted in David J. Coles, "'Shooting Niggers Sir': Confederate Mistreatment of Black Soldiers at the Battle of Olustee," in Gregory J. W. Urwin, ed., *Black Flag Over Dixie: Racial Atrocities and Reprisals in the Civil War* (Carbondale: Southern Illinois University Press, 2004), 74.

29. Meyer to Edward W. Smith, February 13, 1864, Seraphim Meyer Compiled Service Record, RG 94, NA.

30. Smith, *Camps and Campaigns*, 163; Gordon, *A War Diary of Events*, 289; "The 107th Re-Enlisted," *Wooster Republican,* February 4, 1864.

CHAPTER 8: "SO MANY HARDSHIPS"

1. Justus M. Silliman to My Dear Mother, February 24, 1864, February 28, 1864, and March 11, 1864, in Edward Marcus, ed., *A New Canaan Private in the Civil War: Letters of Justus M. Silliman, 17th Connecticut Volunteers* (New Canaan. CT: New Canaan Historical Society, 1984), 62–63, 65; Smith, *Camps and Campaigns*, 163–64; "From the 107th Regiment," *Stark County Republican*, April 7, 1864; John Adams, *Warrior at Heart: Governor John Milton, King Cotton, and Rebel Florida, 1860–1865* (Victoria, BC, Canada: Friesen Press, 2015), 3, 31; Otis L. Keene, "Jacksonville, Fifty-Three Years Ago: Recollections of a Veteran," *Florida Historical Quarterly* 1 (January 1909): 9–12; Thomas Addison Richards, ed., *Appleton's Companion Hand-Book of Travel* (New York: D. Appleton & Company, 1864), 181; "From the 107th O.V.I.," *Stark County Republican*, November 24, 1864; journalist, as quoted in Egerton, *Thunder at the Gates*, 214; George E. Stephens, as quoted in Ouchley, *Flora and Fauna of the Civil War*, 87; P. J. Staudenraus, ed., "A War Correspondent's View of St. Augustine and Fernandina: 1863," *Florida Historical Quarterly* 41, no. 1 (July 1962): 60–61; *The Traveller's Tour Through the United States: An Instructive Pastime, Performed on a Map* (New York: Roe Lockwood, 1842), 32; Paul Ortiz, *Emancipation Betrayed: The Hidden History of Black Organizing and White Violence in Florida from Reconstruction to the Bloody Election of 1920* (Los Angeles: University of California Press, 2005), 15; Charlie Duren to Dear Mother, February 15, 1864, in "The Occupation of Jacksonville, February 1864 and the Battle of Olustee: Letters of Lt. C. M. Duren, 54th Massachusetts Regiment, U.S.A.," *Florida Historical Quarterly* 32, no. 4 (April 1954): 264; Emilio, *History of the Fifty-fourth Regiment*, 151; Gordon, *A War Diary of Events*, 297, 301; Ira Bisbee to his brother, June 28, 1862, Spared & Shared blog [accessed January 9, 2019]; Hodes, *Mourning Lincoln*, 17–18, 211–12; Samuel Proctor, "Jacksonville During the Civil War," *Florida Historical Quarterly* 41, no. 4 (April 1963): 353; "From the 107th Regiment," *Stark County Republican*, April 7, 1864; Coles, "Far From the Fields of Glory" (PhD diss., Florida State University, 1996), 47–48; Frederic Denison, *Shot and Shell: The Third Rhode Island Heavy Artillery Regiment in the Rebellion 1861–1865* (Providence: J. A. & R. A. Reid, 1879), 242.

2. "From the 107th O.V.I.," *Stark County Republican*, April 28, 1864; James Harvey McKee, *Back "In War Times": History of the 144th Regiment, New York Volunteers* (Unadilla, NY: Horace E. Bailey, 1903), 154; Smith, *Camps and Campaigns*, 175, 178; "From the 107th Regiment," *Stark County Republican*, April 7, 1864; O. D. Ladley to Dear Mother and Sisters, June 5, 1864, in Carl M. Becker and Ritchie Thomas, eds., *Hearth and Knapsack: The Lad-*

ley Letters, 1857–1880 (Athens: Ohio University Press, 1988), 172; "Biography of John Knaus, M.D., A Candidate for Asst Surg U.S.A.," Records of the Adjutant General's Office, Entry 561, Box 321, RG 94, NA. On soldier "self-care," see Kathryn Shively Meier, *Nature's Civil War: Common Soldiers and the Environment in 1862 Virginia* (Chapel Hill: University of North Carolina Press, 2013).

3. Smith, *Camps and Campaigns*, 166; John Brunny to a friend, December 29, 1863, in Society of Separatists of Zoar Records, Box 96, Folder 1, OHC.

4. Brooks D. Simpson, "Great Expectations: Ulysses S. Grant, the Northern Press, and the Opening of the Wilderness Campaign," in Gary W. Gallagher, ed., *The Wilderness Campaign* (Chapel Hill: University of North Carolina Press, 1997), 19–21. The literature on these campaigns is voluminous; for the best, one volume treatment, see Mark Grimsley, *And Keep Moving On: The Virginia Campaign, May –June 1864* (Lincoln: University of Nebraska Press, 2002).

5. Simpson, "Great Expectations"; Gordon C. Rhea, *The Battles for Spotsylvania Court House and the Road to Yellow Tavern, May 7–12, 1864* (Baton Rouge: Louisiana State University Press, 1997); Horace Greeley, as quoted in Noah Brooks, *Abraham Lincoln* (New York and London: G. P. Putnam's Sons, 1888), 397; Steven R. Sodergren, *The Army of the Potomac in the Overland and Petersburg Campaigns* (Baton Rouge: Louisiana State University Press, 2017).

6. "From the 107th Regiment," *Stark County Republican*, June 16, 1864; Taylor, *Rebel Storehouse*, 152, 154; William Watson Davis, *The Civil War and Reconstruction in Florida* (New York: Columbia University Press, 1913), 297; *OR*, vol. 35, pt. 1, pp. 371–72; Smith, *Camps and Campaigns*, 170–71; Gordon, *A War Diary*, 294; *Canton* [Ohio] *Repository*, September 22, 1871.

7. Davis, *The Civil War and Reconstruction in Florida*, 297–98; Smith, *Camps and Campaigns*, 167, 170; Oscar Ladley to Dear Mother and Sister, May 10, 1864, Oscar D. Ladley Papers, Wright State; John E. Johns, *Florida During the Civil War* (Gainesville: University of Florida Press, 1963), 203; C. M. Duren to Dear Father, March 15, 1864, in "The Occupation of Jacksonville, February 1864 and the Battle of Olustee," *Florida Historical Quarterly* 32, no. 4 (April 1954): 278.

8. Proceedings of Garrison Court Martial, August 19, 1864, and Order of the Provost Marshal, July 16, 1864, 107th Ohio Regimental Books, vol. 5, RG 94, NA; Court Martial Case File 00–566, RG 153, NA; 107th Ohio Regimental Descriptive Books; Court Martial Case File MM1863, RG 153, NA. See also *Stark County Democrat*, May 11, 1864, and *Biographical Record of Civil War Veterans Tuscarawas County, Ohio*, 625–26.

9. Court Martial Case File NN2836, RG 153, NA; "Report of Persons and Articles Employed and Hired in the Field in Va. During the Month of April 1863,"

Warren Russell Papers, Box 1, Folder 2, BGSU. Company D's "colored servant" was known by the name of "Yelper." See Smith, *Camps and Campaigns*, 165. For a fresh analysis of camp servants and race in Union armies, see Kristopher Teters, *Practical Liberators: Union Officers in the Western Theater during the Civil War* (Chapel Hill: University of North Carolina Press, 2018).

10. *OR*, vol. 35, pt. 1, p. 399; Smith, *Camps and Campaigns*, 168–69; Richard F. Miller, ed., *States at War*, Vol. 4: *A Reference Guide for Delaware, Maryland, and New Jersey in the Civil War* (Hanover and London: University Press of New England, 2015), 537; William M. Jones, "A Report on the Site of Camp Finegan," *Florida Historical Quarterly* 39, no. 4 (April 1961): 366–73; Davis, *Civil War and Reconstruction in Florida*, 303.

11. *OR*, vol. 35, pt. 1, p. 399; *OR*, vol. 35, pt. 1, pp. 401–2; Daisy Parker, "John Milton, Governor of Florida: A Loyal Confederate," *Florida Historical Quarterly* 20 (April 1942): 346–61; Davis, *Civil War and Reconstruction in Florida*, 296. On Milton, see also Adams, *Warrior at Heart*.

12. *OR*, vol. 35, pt. 1, pp. 401–2, 403; Davis, *Civil War and Reconstruction in Florida*, 296; Smith, *Camps and Campaigns*, 172; Gordon, *A War Diary of Events*, 303–4.

13. Smith, *Camps and Campaigns*, 172; Frank A. Ofeldt, III, *Fort Clinch* (Charleston, NC: Arcadia, 2017), 7; *OR*, ser. 1., vol. 35, pt. 2, pp. 128–29.

14. *OR*, ser. 1., vol. 35, pt. 2, pp. 128–29; William J. Gladwin, Jr., "Men, Salt, Cattle, and Battle: The Civil War in Florida, November 1860–July 1865" (Research paper, U.S. Naval War College, 1992).

15. Oscar Ladley to Dear Mother & Sisters, August 8, 1864, in Becker and Thomas, *Hearth and Knapsack*, 175–76, Smith, *Camps and Campaigns*, 170.

16. Oscar Ladley to Dear Mother & Sisters, July 31, 1864, and August 8, 1864, in Becker and Thomas, *Hearth and Knapsack*, 174–76; Smith, *Camps and Campaigns*, 176–77.

17. 1864 Democratic Party Platform, as quoted in David E. Long, *The Jewel of Liberty: Abraham Lincoln's Re-election and the End of Slavery* (Mechanicsburg, PA: Stackpole Books, 1994), 283–84.

18. William Allen, as quoted in Roseboom, *The History of the State of Ohio*. Vol. 4, 434; "A Few Paragraphs on 'Peace,'" *Stark County Republican*, August 11, 1864; "Lieut. Harrison," *Stark County Republican*, October 27, 1864; *Annals of Cleveland* 47 (1864): 289; Weber, *Copperheads*, 154; James W. Geary, *We Need Men: The Union Draft in the Civil War* (DeKalb: Northern Illinois University Press, 1991), 151.

19. "Company A, 107th O.V.I.," *Stark County Republican*, October 27, 1864; "From the 107th O.V.I.," *Stark County Republican*, November 24, 1864; Smith, *Camps and Campaigns*, 179; White, *Emancipation, the Union Army, and the Re-Election of Abraham Lincoln*, 98–128. On the election of 1864, see

Long, *Jewel of Liberty*, and John C. Waugh, *Re-Electing Lincoln: The Battle for the 1864 Presidency* (New York: Da Capo, 2001). Jonathan W. White has persuasively argued that soldiers in the 1864 election "voted for the candidate they believed would end the war quickly and honorably." White likewise documents widespread voter intimidation within the ranks. See White, *Emancipation, the Union Army, and the Re-Election of Abraham Lincoln*, 103–4.

20. Justus Silliman to My Dear Mother, November 9, 1864, in Marcus, ed., *A New Canaan Private*, 83; "From the 107th O.V.I.," *Stark County Republican*, November 24, 1864; "Vote of the 107 Ohio Regiment for President," *Stark County Democrat*, December 7, 1864; *Stark County Republican*, December 15, 1864; Knepper, *Ohio and Its People*, 250. Democratic soldier, as quoted in White, *Emancipation, the Union Army, and the Re-Election of Abraham Lincoln*, 125. Meyer's speech no doubt enthused the Stark County contingent, which cast fifty-eight votes for Lincoln and just four for McClellan.

21. Jefferson Davis, as quoted in Jesse Ames Spencer, *History of the United States: From the Earliest Period to the Administration of Andrew Johnson* (New York: Johnson, Fry and Company, 1866), 504.

22. Smith, *Camps and Campaigns*, 180; *OR*, vol. 39, pt. 3, p. 740; Paul M. Angle, ed., *Three Years in the Army of the Cumberland: The Letters and Diary of Major James A. Connolly* (Bloomington: Indiana University Press, 1987), 311; Frank J. Welcher, *The Union Army, 1861–1865: Organization and Operations* (Bloomington: Indiana University Press, 1989), 1:120; Mahlon Slutz Reminiscences, Indiana State Library; Leonne M. Hudson, "A Confederate Victory at Grahamville: Fighting at Honey Hill," *South Carolina Historical Magazine* 94, no. 1 (January 1993): 19–33, quote from *Savannah Republican*, December 3, 1864, at 30; C. C. Jones, Jr., "The Battle of Honey Hill," *Southern Historical Society Papers* 13 (1885): 362; Stone, Jr., *Vital Rails*, 210–25, 232; Justus Silliman to Dear Mother, December 12, 1864, in Marcus, ed., *A New Canaan*, 86–87; OR, vol. 44, pp. 535, 636. On Sherman's March to the Sea, see also Mark Grimsley, *The Hard Hand of War*, and Joseph T. Glatthaar, *The March to the Sea and Beyond: Sherman's Troops in the Savannah and Carolinas Campaign* (Baton Rouge: Louisiana State University Press, 1985).

23. Stone, Jr., *Vital Rails*, 228–29; Smith, *Camps and Campaigns*, 180.

24. Smith, *Camps and Campaigns*, 181–82; McKee, *Back "In War Times,"* 200.

25. Joel C. Fisk and William H. D. Blake, *A Condensed History of the 56th Regiment, New York Veteran Volunteer Infantry* (Newburgh, NY: Newburgh Journal Printing House and Book Bindery, 1906), 64; Smith, *Camps and Campaigns*, 182–83; *OR*, vol. 44, p. 824; Company K roster in 107th Ohio Regimental Books, RG 94, NA. On the harrowing experience of rebel captivity and the struggles of survivors to wrestle with those experiences, see Brian

Matthew Jordan, *Marching Home: Union Veterans and Their Unending Civil War* (New York: Liveright, 2014), chap.5.

26. *OR*, vol. 44, pp. 824–25; Fisk and Blake, *A Condensed History of the 56th Regiment*, 65–66; McGrath, *History of the 127th New York*, 142; *Annals of Cleveland* 47 (1864): 326; Smith, *Camps and Campaigns*, 185.

27. Smith, *Camps and Campaigns*, 184; McGrath, *History of the 127th New York*, 143.

28. Glatthaar, *March to the Sea,* 143–46. The burning of Columbia has invited no shortage of controversy; see Marion Brunson Lucas, *Sherman and the Burning of Columbia* (College Station: Texas A&M University Press, 1988).

29. Denison, *Shot and Shell*, 287–88; Howard, *Autobiography*, 2:131–132; Glatthaar, *March to the Sea,* 12; Smith, *Camps and Campaigns*, 185 87; *OR*, vol. 47, pt. 1, p. 202; Fisk and Blake, *A Condensed History of the 56th Regiment*, 74.

30. *OR*, vol. 47, pt. 1, pp. 254–55; *OR*, vol. 47, pt. 2, p. 856; Howard, *Autobiography*, 2:135; Emilio, *History of the Fifty-fourth Regiment*, 289; Culp, *The 25th Ohio Vet. Vol. Infantry*, 121.

31. *OR*, vol. 47, pt. 1, pp. 1025, 1027, 1033; *OR*, vol. 47, pt. 2, pp. 856–57; Noah Andre Trudeau, *Out of the Storm: The End of the Civil War, April-June 1865* (Boston: Little, Brown and Company, 1994), 245; Charles Joyner, *Down by the Riverside: A South Carolina Slave Community* (Urbana and Chicago: University of Illinois Press, 2009), 5, 9–11; Ramona LaRoche, *Georgetown County, South Carolina* (Charleston, SC: Arcadia, 2000), 7; Mary H. Leonard, "An Old Industry," *Popular Science Monthly* 46 (1895): 649, 657–58; Smith, *Camps and Campaigns*, 187. For a compendium of documents on Potter's Raid, see Allan D. Thigpen, ed., *The Illustrated Recollections of Potter's Raid, April 5–21, 1865* (Sumter, SC: Gamecock City Printing, 1998).

32. Ezra J. Warner, *Generals in Blue: Lives of the Union Commanders* (Baton Rouge: Louisiana State University Press, 2006), 380–81; *OR*, vol. 47, pt. 1, p. 1028; Emilio, *History of the Fifty-fourth*; *OR*, vol. 47, pt. 3, p. 98; John Hammond Moore, ed., "The Last Officer: April 1865," *South Carolina Historical Magazine* 67, no. 1 (January 1966): 3; John Snider Cooper Diary, April 2, 1865, David M. Rubenstein Rare Book and Manuscript Library, Duke. After a hard march that required its men to wade through waist-deep water, the 25th Ohio would not arrive until late on the evening of April 2. It did not participate in Gillmore's review. See A. P. Zurbrugg to Dear Brother Frederick, March 15, 1865, in Thomas Edwards Collection, Box 2, Folder 1, BGSU.

33. *OR*, vol. 47, pt. 1, pp. 1028, 1033; Emilio, *History of the Fifty-fourth*, 291–92; Samuel Wildman, as quoted in Tom J. Edwards, ed., *Raising the Banner of Freedom: The 25th Ohio Volunteer Infantry in the War for the Union by Bvt. Col. Edward C. Culp* (Bloomington, IN: iUniverse, 2003), 128; John Snider

Cooper Diary, April 6, 1865, Rubenstein Library, Duke; Barlow, *Company G*, 218; Culp, *The 25th Ohio Vet. Vol. Infantry*, 121–22.

34. Emma Holmes, diary, April 7, 1865, as quoted in *The Diary of Miss Emma Holmes*, ed. John F. Marszalek (Baton Rouge: Louisiana State University Press, 1994), 432–33; Mary Boykin Chesnut, *A Diary from Dixie*, ed. Isabella D. Martin and Myrta Lockett Avary (New York: D. Appleton and Company, 1906), 387; *Watchman and Southron*, November 16, 1886.

35. Culp, *The 25th Ohio Vet. Vol. Infantry,* 122; John Snider Cooper Diary, April 7–8, 1865, Rubenstein Library, Duke; Emilio, *History of the Fifty-fourth*, 292; Barlow, *Company G*, 218–19; Moore, "The Last Officer," 4–6. Employing new, digital tools, scholars have demonstrated that the proximity of Union armies was the single most reliable predictor of "emancipation events." See "Visualizing Emancipation," dsl.richmond.edu/emancipation.

36. Moore, "The Last Officer," 6; Cooper Diary, April 8, 1865, Rubenstein Library, Duke; W. H. Garland, "The Battle of Dingles's Mill, Fla.," *Confederate Veteran* 24, no. 12 (December 1916): 549; *Watchman and Southron* [Sumter, South Carolina], May 15, 1901. Garland was a native of Fernandina, Florida; the *Confederate Veteran* editorial team—in a testament to the battle's obscurity among contemporaries—mistakenly identified the South Carolina clash's location. William C. Davis, *The Orphan Brigade: The Kentucky Confederates Who Couldn't Go Home* (New York: Doubleday, 1980); Edwin Porter Thompson, *History of the Orphan Brigade* (Louisville, KY: Lewis N. Thompson, 1868), 436–37; "Dingle's Mill Battle Site Is Marked," *Watchman and Southron*, April 12, 1913.

37. Edwards, *Raising the Banner of Freedom*, 151; Cooper Diary, April 8, 1865, Rubenstein Library, Duke; Robert W. Andrews, *The Life and Adventures of Robert W. Andrews, of Sumter, South Carolina* (Boston: Printed for the Author by E. P. Whitcomb, 1887), 54; https://repository.duke.edu/dc/broadsides/ bdssco22682. On the *Clarendon Banner*, see https://chroniclingamerica.loc .gov/lccn/sn85042899/. On the role of southern newspapers in the coming of the war, see Donald E. Reynolds, *Editors Make War: Southern Newspapers in the Secession Crisis* (Carbondale: Southern Illinois University Press, 2006).

38. The literature is vast, but see Elizabeth R. Varon, *Appomattox: Victory, Defeat, and Freedom at the End of the Civil War* (New York: Oxford University Press, 2013), and William Marvel, *Lee's Last Retreat: The Flight to Appomattox* (Chapel Hill: University of North Carolina Press, 2002).

39. John S. Cooper to H. B. Shively, November 16, 1897, Henry S. Finkenbiner Medal of Honor File, RG 94, File 501,443, Box No. 747, NA; "Don't Let Them Get Me," in W. F. Beyer and O. F. Keydel, eds., *Deeds of Valor: How America's Civil War Heroes Won the Congressional Medal of Honor* (Reprint ed., Stamford, CT: Longmeadow Press, 1994), 494–96; Henry S. Finkenbiner Pension File, RG 94, NA; Smith, *Camps and Campaigns*, 188–89; Thompson, *Orphan*

Brigade, 438; "The Battle of Dingle's Mill," *New Orleans Daily Democrat*, July 21, 1878.

40. Beyer and Keydel, *Deeds of Valor*, 496; P. Brown to 107th Ohio, April 12, 1865, in Henry S. Finkenbiner Medal of Honor File, RG 94, NA; "A Daring Passage," *National Tribune*, April 28, 1898.

41. Moore, "The Last Officer," 6; Cooper Diary, April 9, 1865, Rubenstein Library, Duke; Garland, "The Battle of Dingles's Mill, Fla.," 549; Smith, *Camps and Campaigns*, 188; Emilio, *History of the Fifty-fourth*, 293–94; John S. Cooper to H. B. Shively, November 16, 1897, Henry S. Finkenbiner Medal of Honor File, RG 94, NA; *OR*, vol. 47, pt. 1, pp. 1028, 1033, 1036–37; Barlow, *Company G*, 220; *Columbia* [South Carolina] *Phoenix*, April 12, 1865.

42. Garland, "The Battle of Dingle's Mill, Fla.," 549; Barlow, *Company G*, 221; *OR*, vol. 47, pt. 1, pp. 1026, 1028–29, 1033–34; "The Affair at Dingles's Mill," *National Tribune*, July 7, 1910; Moore, "The Last Officer," 7–8.

43. Culp, *The 25th Ohio Vet. Vol. Infantry*, 125; Garland, "The Battle of Dingle's Mill, Fla.," 549; Smith, *Camps and Campaigns*, 190; Emilio, *History of the Fifty-fourth*, 295; Moore, "The Last Officer," 7; Alfred J. Rider, "Memorial Address," *Gettysburg Star and Sentinel*, November 1, 1887.

44. Smith, *Camps and Campaigns*, 195; Cooper Diary, April 11 and 16, 1865, Rubenstein Library, Duke; Culp, *The 25th Ohio Vet. Vol. Infantry*, 126; *OR*, vol. 47, pt. 1, pp. 1033–34.

45. Culp, *The 25th Ohio Vet. Vol. Infantry*, 126–29; Moore, "The Last Officer," 6; *OR*, vol. 47, pt. 1, pp. 1034–35; Emilio, *History of the Fifty-fourth*, 299–300; Cooper Diary, April 15–18, 1865, and endpapers, Rubenstein Library, Duke.

46. Cooper Diary, April 18, 1865, Rubenstein Library, Duke; *OR*, vol. 47, pt. 1, pp. 1029–30, 1034–35; "Boykin's Mill," in *The Union Army: Cyclopedia of Battles* (Wisconsin: Federal Publishing Co., 1908), 5:155.

47. Cooper Diary, April 18, 1865, Rubenstein Library, Duke; *OR*, vol. 47, pt. 1, pp. 1029–10, 1034–35; "Boykin's Mill," in *The Union Army: Cyclopedia of Battles* (Wisconsin: Federal Publishing Co., 1908), 5:155; *OR*, vol. 47, pt. 1, pp. 1036–37; Barlow, *Company G*, 229; "The Fight at Boykin's & DeSaussure's," *Journal and Confederate* [Camden, South Carolina], April 24, 1865, as quoted in Thigpen, *Illustrated Recollections of Potter's Raid*, 549–55; Smith, *Camps and Campaigns*, 195; *OR*, vol. 47, pt. 1, p. 1031; Emilio, *History of the Fifty-fourth*, 304.

48. *OR*, vol. 47, pt. 1, p. 1031; Smith, *Camps and Campaigns*, 195–96, 205–6; Emilio, *History of the Fifty-fourth*, 305–8; Barlow, *Company G*, 232; Cooper Diary, May 4, 5, and 8, 1865, Rubenstein Library, Duke; General Orders No. 66, April 16, 1865, Alfred Whital Stern Collection of Lincolniana, LC; Culp, *The 25th Ohio Vet. Vol. Infantry*, 133; Orders of May 3, 1865, 107th Ohio Regimental Books, vol. 5, RG 94, NA; Alfred J. Rider, "Memorial Address," *Gettysburg Star and Sentinel*, November 1, 1887; Hodes, *Mourning Lincoln*, 122.

49. Cooper Diary, May 9, 1865, Rubenstein Library, Duke; Edward Cary, *The Trip of the Steamer Oceanus to Fort Sumter and Charleston, S.C., April 14, 1865* (New York: "The Union" Steam Printing House, 1865), 21, 34, 38, 94–95; John Worrell Northrop, *Chronicles from the Diary of a War Prisoner in Andersonville and Other Military Prisons in 1864* (Wichita: Published by the Author, 1904), 187; Peter Zurbrugg to dear Father, May 19, 1865, www.excelsiorbrigade .com/products/details/LTR–5220; John Townsend Trowbridge, *The South: A Tour of Its Battlefields and Ruined Cities*, 514; Emilio, *History of the Fifty-fourth*, 310–12; Smith, *Camps and Campaigns*, 211; Nelson, *Ruin Nation*.

50. Orders of June 6, 1865, 107th Ohio Regimental Books, vol. 5, RG 94, NA; Emilio, *History of the Fifty-fourth*, 310–11; Cooper Diary, May 10, 1865, and June 2, 1865, Rubenstein Library, Duke; Smith, *Camps and Campaigns*, 210; General Orders No. 34, June 22, 1865, 107th Ohio Regimental Books, vol. 5, RG 94, NA. On Magnolia Cemetery, see Thomas J. Brown, *Civil War Canon: Sites of Confederate Memory in South Carolina* (Chapel Hill: University of North Carolina Press, 2005).

51. Jordan, *Marching Home*; Cooper Diary, June 15–20, 1865, Rubenstein Library, Duke; Emilio, *History of the Fifty-fourth*, 314; Peter Zurbrugg to his father, May 19, 1865.

CHAPTER 9: "THE FEELINGS OF A SOLDIER"

1. Portions of this chapter were previously published as "The 107th Ohio and the Human Longitude of Gettysburg," in Lang and Bledsoe, *Upon the Fields of Battle*, 252–70. Kenneth E. Davison, *Cleveland during the Civil War*, 24; *New York Herald*, July 17, 1865; "Arrival of Ohio Troops," *Cleveland Daily Leader*, July 19, 1865; "Arrival of Battery 'B' and the 107th Ohio Regiment," *Daily Cleveland Herald*, July 18, 1865; "Roster of Company A, 107th O.V.I.," *Stark County Republican*, August 3, 1865; Samuel Peter Orth, *A History of Cleveland, Ohio* (Chicago: S. J. Clarke, 1910), 1:455; *Boston Daily Advertiser*, July 17, 1865; *North American and United States Gazette* [Philadelphia], July 17, 1865; "Marine Intelligence," *North American and United States Gazette,* July 18, 1865; *Daily Cleveland Herald*, July 29, 1865; *Canton Repository*, September 22, 1871; William O. Siffert Pension File, RG 15, NA; William O. Siffert Carded Medical File, RG 94, entry 534, Box 2845. Bank Street was the regiment's likeliest route from the Union train depot down to Public Square. See the 1869 Cleveland Directory Map, http://usgenwebsites.org/OHCuyahoga/ Maps/1869%20Map.jpg.

2. "Arrival of Ohio Troops," *Cleveland Daily Leader*, July 19, 1865; Van Tassel

and Grabowski, *Encyclopedia of Cleveland History*, c.v. William Jarvis Boardman, https://case.edu/ech/articles/b/boardman-william-jarvis.

3. *Cleveland Leader*, July 19, 1865; *Daily Cleveland Herald*, July 18, 1865.

4. *Cleveland Leader*, July 19, 1865; *Daily Cleveland Herald*, July 18, 1865; Orth,
A History of Cleveland, 1:431; *Cleveland Daily Leader*, July 25, 1865; Cooper
Diary, July 1865, Rubenstein Library, Duke; "Local Matters," *Daily Cleveland
Herald*, July 25, 1865; "Local Notices," *Daily Cleveland Herald*, July 29, 1865;
Encyclopedia of Cleveland History, c.v. Weddell House, https://case.edu/ech/
articles/w/weddell-house; *Annals of Cleveland* 47 (1864): 289.

5. Smith, *Camps and Campaigns*, 215.

6. Ibid.; Cooper Diary, July 1865, Rubenstein Library, Duke; John Cooper Pension File, RG 15, NA; Christian Rieker Pension File, RG 15, NA; Jacob Thumm
Pension File, RG 15, NA; Philip Seltzer Pension File, RG 15, NA; George Billow Pension File, RG 15, NA.

7. Tom Hoagland Pension File, RG 15, NA; Daniel Biddle Pension File, RG 15,
NA; Frederick Tonsing Pension File, RG 15, NA. On amputation in the Civil
War, see Nelson, *Ruin Nation*; Brian Craig Miller, *Empty Sleeves: Amputa-
tion in the Civil War South* (Athens: University of Georgia Press, 2015); and
Handley-Cousins, *Bodies in Blue*.

8. Joseph Kieffer Pension File, RG 15, NA; Casper Bohrer Pension File, RG 15,
NA; Daniel Biddle Pension File, RG 15, NA; Daniel Whitmer Pension File,
RG 15, NA; Frederick Tonsing Pension File, RG 15, NA; Theobald Hasman
Pension File, RG 15, NA; Peter Schieb Pension File, RG 15, NA; Frank Rothermel Pension File, RG 15, NA; Tom Hoagland Pension File, RG 15, NA. Other
scholars have explored the notion that traumatic memories can be inscribed
on the body. For one example, see Edward Linenthal, *The Unfinished Bombing: Oklahoma City in American Memory* (Oxford: Oxford University Press,
2001), 69.

9. "A Landable Enterprise," *Daily Cleveland Herald*, July 25, 1865. While Union
veterans established a number of "colonies" after the war, this is the earliest
such project I have been able to document. On Civil War veterans' colonies,
see Kurt Hackemer, "Civil War Veteran Colonies in the Western Frontier," in
Jordan and Rothera, eds., *The War Went On*.

10. No more than a week after the battle of Gettysburg, two dozen Zoar men registered their conscientious objection to the war. See Society of Separatists of
Zoar Records, Box 96, Folder 2, Ohio History Connection. Constance Fenimore Woolson, "Wilhelmina," in *Castle Nowhere: Lake-Country Sketches*
(Boston: James R. Osgood and Company, 1875), 270–303. The story was also
published in the *Atlantic Monthly* and the *Tuscarawas Advocate* [New Philadelphia, Ohio]. "Wilhelmina" errs in identifying the 107th Ohio as a western-

theater unit, referencing its service at Lookout Mountain. On Woolson, see Anne Boyd Rioux, *Constance Fenimore Woolson: Portrait of A Lady Novelist* (New York: W. W. Norton, 2016); Kathleen Diffley, *To Live and Die: Collected Stories of the Civil War, 1861–1876* (Durham: Duke University Press, 2002), and Kathleen M. Fernandez, "The Happy Valley: Constance F. Woolson's View of Zoar" [unpublished paper in author's possession].

11. George Billow Pension File, RG 15, NA; *Akron Daily Beacon*, July 5, 1870.

12. Norine S. Hendricks, "An Illustrated Lecture: The Civil War Paintings of William Siffert," *Timeline* 16, no. 3 (May-June 1999): 46; *Jeffersonian Democrat* [Chardon, Ohio], September 8, 1865; Philip May Pension File, RG 15, NA; Arnold Streum Pension File, RG 15, NA; Adam Berghofer Pension File, RG, NA; *Akron Daily Beacon*, July 5, 1870.

13. Harrison Flora Pension File, RG 15, NA; Nicholas Lopendahl Pension File, RG 15, NA; Henry Feldkamp Pension File, RG 15, NA; Alfred J. Rider Pension File, RG 15, NA.

14. John Hemmerling Pension File, RG 15, NA; *The Ohio Guide* (New York: Oxford University Press, 1946), 477. For recent scholarship on life in local, state, and federal soldiers' homes, see Patrick J. Kelly, *Creating a National Home: Building the Veterans' Welfare State, 1860–1900* (Cambridge, MA: Harvard University Press, 1997); James A. Marten, *Sing Not War: The Lives of Union and Confederate Veterans in Gilded Age America* (Chapel Hill: University of North Carolina Press, 2011); Jordan, *Marching Home*.

15. Emlen Morgan Landon Pension File, RG 15, NA; Admissions Records for Emlen Landon, Ohio State Soldiers' and Sailors' Home, Microfilm 3399, Ohio History Connection; Historical Register of National Homes for Disabled Volunteer Soldiers, 1866–1938, Microfilm M1749, 282 rolls, RG 15, NA.

16. Frederick Bross Pension File, RG 15, NA; Charles Cordier Pension File, RG 15, NA.

17. Claire Prechtel Kluskens, " 'A Reasonable Degree of Promptitude': Civil War Pension Claim Application Processing, 1861–1865," *Prologue* 42, no. 1 (2010): 1–26; Eliza Whisler Widow's Pension File, RG 15, NA.

18. Linda Leigh Geary, *Balanced in the Wind: A Biography of Betsey Mix Cowles* (Lewisburg, PA: Bucknell University Press, 1989), 67–68; Perrin, *History of Stark County*, 275; Joseph Kieffer Pension File, RG 15, NA; David Sarbach Pension File, RG 15, NA; Henry Feldkamp Pension File, RG 15, NA; *Biographical Record of Civil War Veterans Tuscarawas County, Ohio*, 571; *Dayton Herald*, March 30, 1885.

19. John Leffler Pension File, RG 15, NA; Daniel Whitmer Pension File, RG 15, NA.

20. Jordan, "The Hour That Lasted Fifty Years," in Lang and Bledsoe, *Upon the Fields of Battle*, 258–59; William Heiss Pension File, RG 15, NA; *Cleveland*

Directory for the Year Ending July, 1897, 995; Arnold Streum Pension File, RG 15, NA; George Zuern Pension File, RG 15, NA; *Army Herald* [Cleveland, Ohio], May 1865. George Lemon became the editor of the *National Tribune*, the largest Union veterans' newspaper, which became an important hub of information about the pension application process. See Steven R. Sodergren, "'Exposing False History': The Voice of the Union Veteran in the Pages of *The National Tribune*," in Jordan and Rothera, *The War Went On*. On Milo B. Stevens & Company and its circulars, see Marten, *Sing Not War*, 210.

21. John Lutz to the Surgeon General, U.S. Army, March 12, 1879, Records of the Adjutant General's Office, RG 94, Entry 561, Records Relating to Medical Officers and Physicians, Box 321, NA; Albert Beck Pension File, RG 15, NA; Gotlieb Buettinger to Surgeon General, U.S. Army, March 23, 1883; H. Hines to Surgeon General, U.S. Army, December 3, 1883; and G. Schrieber to Surgeon General, n.d., RG 94, Entry 561, Box 321, NA; John S. Cooper to H.B. Shively, November 16, 1897, Henry S. Finkenbiner Medal of Honor File, Records of the Adjutant General's Office, RG 94, Box No. 747, File No. 501,443, NA; *Biographical Record of Civil War Veterans Tuscarawas County, Ohio*, 571.

22. Albert Beck Pension File, RG 15, NA.

23. Alfred Rider Pension File, RG 15, NA; Philip Wang Pension File, RG 15, NA.

24. *Daily Cleveland Herald*, September 16, 1869; David Dirck Van Tassel and John Vacha, *"Behind Bayonets": The Civil War in Northern Ohio* (Kent, OH: Kent State University Press, 2006), 61; *Cleveland Plain Dealer*, September 16, 1869; "The 107th O.V.I.," *Cleveland Plain Dealer*, September 16, 1869; *Wooster Republican*, September 26, 1872; *The Republic* [Cincinnati, Ohio], October 1, 1868.

25. "Re-Union of the 107th," *Wooster Republican*, September 28, 1871; "Third Annual Re-Union of the 107th Regiment, Ohio Vol. Inf.," *Canton Repository*, September 15, 1871; Lane, *Fifty Years and Over of Akron and Summit County*, 445; *Akron Daily Beacon*, July 5, 1870; *Democratic Press* [Ravenna, Ohio], July 7, 1870; *Daily Cleveland Herald*, June 13, 1870, and July 6, 1870; *Annals of Cleveland*, 53:802.

26. "Re-Union of the 107th," *Wooster Republican*, September 28, 1871; "The 107th Regiment," *Wooster Republican*, September 26, 1872; "The 107th Regiment," *Canton Repository*, October 4, 1872; *Canton Repository*, September 20, 1872.

27. Brian Matthew Jordan, "'Our Work Is Not Yet Finished': Union Veterans and Their Unending Civil War, 1865–1872," *Journal of the Civil War Era* 5, no. 4 (December 2015): 484–503; Silber, *The Romance of Reunion*; Blight, *Race and Reunion*; *Wooster Republican*, September 26, 1872; *The Republic* [Cincinnati, Ohio], October 1, 1868; *Annals of Cleveland*, 52:594; "Resolutions of Sympathy," *Stark County Democrat*, September 22, 1881; *Annals of Cleveland*, 50:751.

28. Walt Whitman, "The Real War Will Never Get in the Books," in *Complete*

Prose Works (New York: G. P. Putnam's Sons, 1902), 74; Jordan and Rothera, "The Hour That Lasted Fifty Years," in Lang and Bledsoe, *Upon the Fields of Battle*, 265. My thinking here has benefited from many stimulating conversations with John J. Hennessy.

29. *Canton Repository*, September 22, 1871; Alfred J. Rider to John B. Bachelder, October 3, 1885, *Bachelder Papers*, 2:1129.

30. *Canton Repository*, September 22, 1871; J. S. Robinson to Augustus Choate Hamlin, November 12, 1890, Military Order of the Loyal Legion Collection, MS 1084, folder 1046, Houghton Library; James Wood to Augustus Choate Hamlin, June 11, 1891, Military Order of the Loyal Legion Collection, MS 1084, folder 1050, Houghton Library; I. S. Bangs to Augustus Choate Hamlin, December 29, 1896, Military Order of the Loyal Legion Collection, MS 1084, folder 1010, Houghton Library.

31. Thomas Prentice Kettell, *History of the Great Rebellion* (Hartford: L. Stebbins, 1865), 1:446; Moore, *Complete History of the Great Rebellion*, 348; John S. C. Abbott, *The History of the Civil War in America* (New York: Henry Bill, 1866), 2:384; Benson J. Lossing, *Pictoral History of the Civil War in the United States of America* (Hartford: Thomas Belknap, 1877), 3:30; Keller, *Chancellorsville and the Germans*.

32. Dana King to Augustus Choate Hamlin, January 15, 1897, Military Order of the Loyal Legion Collection, MS 1084, folder 1033, Houghton Library; J. C. Hall to Augustus Choate Hamlin, November 5, 1891, Military Order of the Loyal Legion Collection, MS 1084, folder 1028, Houghton Library; I. F. Huntington to Francis Irsch [1891], Military Order of the Loyal Legion Collection, MS 1084, folder 1032, Houghton Library.

33. Augustus Choate Hamlin, *The Battle of Chancellorsville*, preface (Bangor, ME: Published by the Author, 1896); "Reviews and Exchanges," newspaper clipping in Augustus Choate Hamlin Papers, Military Order of the Loyal Legion Collection, MS 1084, folder 1011, Houghton Library; H. M. Kellogg to Augustus Choate Hamlin, December 9, 1891, Military Order of the Loyal Legion Collection, MS 1084, folder 1034, Houghton Library.

34. Charles T. Furlow to Augustus Choate Hamlin, May 11, 1892, Military Order of the Loyal Legion Collection, MS 1084, folder 1016, Houghton Library; J. M Davis to Augustus Choate Hamlin, February 18, 1893, Military Order of the Loyal Legion Collection, MS 1084, folder 1023, Houghton Library; Jacob Gano to Augustus Choate Hamlin, Military Order of the Loyal Legion Papers, MS 1084, Houghton Library.

35. A. W. Peck to Augustus Choate Hamlin, June 1, 1891, Military Order of the Loyal Legion Papers, MS 1084, folder 1037, Houghton Library; John Calvin Owen to Augustus Choate Hamlin, October 14, 1893, Military Order of the

Loyal Legion Papers, MS 1084, folder 1045, Houghton Library; see also Alfred S. Roe to Augustus Choate Hamlin, December 29, 1900, Military Order of the Loyal Legion Papers, MS 1084, folder 1044, Houghton Library.

36. William H. Noble to Augustus Choate Hamlin, January 8, 1892, Military Order of the Loyal Legion Papers, MS 1084, Houghton Library; Elias Riggs Monfort to Augustus Choate Hamlin, February 17, 1892, Military Order of the Loyal Legion Papers, MS 1084, Houghton Library.

37. "The Eleventh Corps at Chancellorsville," *National Tribune*, October 22, 1885; Augustus Wormley to John Lockman, March 31, 1896, Military Order of the Loyal Legion Papers, MS 1084, folder 1036, Houghton Library.

38. J. H. Peabody to Augustus Choate Hamlin, November 16, 1892, Military Order of the Loyal Legion Papers, MS 1084, folder 1043, Houghton Library; E. C. Culp to Augustus Choate Hamlin, Military Order of the Loyal Legion Papers, MS 1084, folder 1023, Houghton Library; Adelbert Ames to Augustus Choate Hamlin, December 21, 1896, Military Order of the Loyal Legion Papers, MS 1084, folder 1020, Houghton Library; William Freeman Fox to Augustus Choate Hamlin, December 8, 1896, Military Order of the Loyal Legion Papers, MS 1084, folder 1028, Houghton Library; Charles T. Furlow to Augustus Choate Hamlin, February 4, 1897, Military Order of the Loyal Legion Papers, MS 1084, folder 1016, Houghton Library; A. J. Cavanaugh to Augustus Choate Hamlin, Military Order of the Loyal Legion Papers, MS 1084, folder 1018, Houghton Library.

39. *Marysville* [Ohio] *Journal-Tribune*, June 23, 1913; *St. Joseph* [Michigan] *Saturday Herald*, June 6, 1908; *Akron Beacon Journal*, December 23, 1903; *Stark County* [Ohio] *Democrat*, July 10, 1903. For a superb treatment of the 1913 reunion, see Thomas R. Flagel, *War, Memory, and the 1913 Gettysburg Reunion* (Kent, OH: Kent State University Press, 2019).

40. "Weeds of the Army," in H. E. Gerry, *Camp Fire Entertainment and True History of Robert Henry Hendershot, The Drummer Boy of the Rappahannock* (Chicago: Hack and Anderson, 1900), 94.

41. *Marysville* [Ohio] *Journal-Tribune*, August 23, 1929; *Evening Independent* [Massillon, Ohio], September 20, 1934, and September 22, 1960.

42. My ideas here have been shaped by Thaddeus M. Romansky, "'Deeds of Our Own': Loyalty, Soldier Rights, and Protest in Northern Regiments of the United States Colored Troops," in Robert M. Sandow, ed., *Contested Loyalty: Debates Over Patriotism in the Civil War North* (New York: Fordham University Press, 2018), 288–89.

43. Robert E. Bonner, *The Soldier's Pen: Firsthand Impressions of the Civil War* (New York: Hill & Wang, 2006), 112. Recent arguments that the "dark turn" in Civil War history imperils our understanding of the conflict neglect this

crucial reality. On the advent of neorevisionism, see Yael A. Sternhell, "Revisionism Reinvented? The Antiwar Turn in Civil War Scholarship," *Journal of the Civil War Era* 3, no. 2 (June 2013): 239–56.

44. Walt Whitman, "The Real War Will Never Get in The Books," in *Complete Prose Works of Walt Whitman*, 1:140; Rider to John Bachelder, August 20, 1885, *Bachelder Papers*, 2: 1118–19; *National Tribune*, February 15, 1906; Smith, *Camps and Campaigns*, 5–7. At that fourth reunion, Young implored his comrades to come "to each other's aid in time of need," and trusted that they would neither neglect "the wants of the widows, and the care and education of the orphans." *Wooster Republican*, September 26, 1872. See also Steven R. Sodergren, " 'Exposing False History': The Voice of the Union Veteran in the Pages of *The National Tribune*," in Jordan and Rothera, eds., *The War Went On*; "The Joys of Reminiscence," *Toledo* [Ohio] *Blade*, September 3, 1908; "The Bitter and The Sweet," *The Bivouac* 3, no. 9 (September 1885): 342.

45. Smith, *Camps and Campaigns*, 216.

EPILOGUE

1. Christian Rieker, Ancestry.com, https://www.ancestry.com/family-tree/person/tree/16693970/person/140145640190/gallery [accessed March 15, 2020]; John Brunny, Ancestry.com, https://www.ancestry.com/family-tree/person/tree/62136961/person/32343703534/story [accessed March 15, 2020].

2. "Ohio at Gettysburg," *Cincinnati Commercial Tribune*, August 17, 1885; Franklin Sawyer, *The Eighth Ohio at Gettysburg* (Washington, DC: E. J. Gray, Printer, 1889), 1; "The 107th Dedication at Gettysburg," *Canton Weekly Repository*, September 29, 1887; "Ohio at Gettysburg," *Cleveland Plain Dealer*, September 14, 1887; "Memorial Address," *Gettysburg Star and Sentinel*, November 1, 1887; Smith, *Camps and Campaigns*, 126–27, 133.

3. Minutes of the Ohio Gettysburg Memorial Commission, BV 1837: Series 2381, OHC; "Ohio at Gettysburg," *Cincinnati Commercial Tribune*, August 17, 1885; Franklin Sawyer, *The Eighth Ohio at Gettysburg* (Washington DC: E. J. Gray, Printer, 1889), 1; "The 107th Dedication at Gettysburg," *Canton Weekly Repository*, September 29, 1887; "Ohio at Gettysburg," *Cleveland Plain Dealer*, September 14, 1887; "Memorial Address," *Gettysburg Star and Sentinel*, November 1, 1887; Smith, *Camps and Campaigns*, 126–27, 133.

4. Minutes of the Ohio Gettysburg Memorial Commission, BV 1837: Series 2381, OHC; "Ohio at Gettysburg," *Cincinnati Commercial Tribune*, August 17, 1885.

5. Perrin, *History of Stark County*, 639–40; Charles Vignos, "Biography of Augustus Vignos," posted to Ancestry.com, https://www.ancestry.com/mediaui-viewer/collection/1030/tree/31357887/person/12448279419/media/04f4e235–7812–4270

-b3f8-c44537516f86?_phsrc=VlU146&usePUBJs=true [accessed March 15, 2020]; Cindy Vignos, "The Novelty Cutlery Company," *Oregon Knife Collectors Newsletter* (October 2002), posted to Ancestry.com, https://www.ancestry.com/mediaui-viewer/collection/1030/tree/31357887/person/12448279419/media/6f9f6158-c8cf-4be7-bfe8-5e5da261cc38?_phsrc=VlU146&usePUBJs=true [accessed March 15, 2020].

6. Ibid.; Jordan, *Marching Home*, 67–68.

7. *Cincinnati Enquirer*, July 14, 1910; George Billow Pension File, RG 15, NA; Sarah Handley-Cousins, 83, 86–94.

8. Handley-Cousins, *Bodies in Blue* 86–94; George Billow Pension File, RG 15, NA.

9. George Billow Pension File, RG 15, NA; Personal War Sketches, Lewis Buckley Post, GAR, OHC.

10. George Billow Pension File, RG 15, NA; William Otterbein Siffert, Ancestry.com; Alfred Rider Pension File, RG 15, NA; Bryan S. Baker, "Biography of Alfred J. Rider," last updated January 2013 and posted by Robin Law, Ancestry.com [accessed March 15, 2020].

11. Alfred J. Rider Pension File, RG 15, NA; Perrin, *History of Stark County*, 993–95; Bryan S. Baker, "Biography of Alfred J. Rider," last updated January 2013 and posted by Robin Law, Ancestry.com, https://www.ancestry.com/mediaui-viewer/collection/1030/tree/11298984/person/-382004049/media/336e1424-281e-4d43-a8a2-fed9cc207dd5?_phsrc=VlU143&usePUBJs=true [accessed March 15, 2020].

12. Alfred J. Rider to John Badger Bachelder, October 20, 1885, *Bachelder Papers*, 2:1129–30; Michael Jacobs, *Notes on the Rebel Invasion of Maryland and Pennsylvania* (Philadelphia: J. B. Lippincott & Co., 1864).

13. "The 107th Dedication at Gettysburg," *Canton Repository*, September 29, 1887; State Archives Series 4060, Box 50,765A: Applications to Borrow Regimental Colors, 1865–1906.

14. "The 107th Dedication at Gettysburg," *Canton Repository*, September 29, 1887.

15. Ibid.

16. Kirk Savage, *Standing Soldiers, Kneeling Slaves: Race, War, and Monument in Nineteenth Century America* (Princeton: Princeton University Press, 1999), 163–64; Alice Fahs, *Imagined Civil War: Popular Literature of the North and South: 1861–1865* (Chapel Hill: University of North Carolina Press, 2001); Blight, *Race and Reunion*; Robert E. Bonner, *The Soldier's Pen: Firsthand Impressions of the Civil War* (New York: Hill & Wang, 2006); Thomas J. Brown, *Civil War Monuments and the Militarization of America* (Chapel Hill: University of North Carolina Press, 2019); Perrin, *History of Stark County*, 264; Douglass, *History of Wayne County, Ohio*, 758.

17. Hendricks, "An Illustrated Lecture: The Civil War Paintings of William Siffert," 44–53.

18. Ibid.; *Cyclorama of the Battle of Gettysburg by Paul Philippoteaux Permanently Located in Boston, Mass.* (1868), n.p.

19. Site visit to Brooke's Station, Virginia, January 10, 2018; Talley Farm Vertical File, FSNMP.

20. Max Reihmann, "A Gettysburg Story of Interest," *Case Shot & Canister: A Publication of the Delaware Valley Civil War Round Table* 27, no. 8 (August 2017): 18–19.

21. Ron Ward, "Jacksonville's Camp Milton a little-known Civil War jewel," *Orlando Sentinel*, August 17, 2009; Florida State Parks Website, https://www.floridastateparks.org/fortclinch.

22. Tom Elmore, *Potter's Raid Through South Carolina: The Final Days of the Confederacy* (Charleston, SC: History Press, 2015), 94; site visit to Dingle's Mill, South Carolina, March 5, 2017.

23. Slutz, *Tribute to Major Augustus Vignos*.

24. Lane, *Fifty Years and Over of Akron and Summit County*, 238–54.

25. Site visit to Zoar, Ohio, April 23, 2017.

26. This point is amplified by a census of Union veterans undertaken by the state of Ohio in 1866. Perhaps the first such exercise conducted anywhere in the country, the census revealed the significant number of old regimental comrades who lived together in the same communities. See "Numerical Returns of Civil War Veterans by County and Township, 1866," State Archives Series 2986, Box 50, 640B, OHC.

27. Jim Finkenbiner to Robert K. Krick [n.d.], Bound Volume 183, FSNMP; Doug Staley, "Civil War soldier's story takes shape," *Massillon Independent*, May 31, 2010; Chris Nelson, typescript history of the 107th Ohio Volunteers, Thomas J. Edwards Collection, BGSU; Chris Nelson, "An Unlucky XI Corps Regiment: The 107th Ohio Volunteer Infantry," *Military Images* 22, no. 6 (May/June 2001): 16–20; Andrew B. Suhrer, *The Flying Dutchmen* (Bloomington, IN: AuthorHouse, 2008).

BIBLIOGRAPHIC NOTE

1. Aaron Sheehan-Dean, "The Blue and Gray in Black and White: Assessing the Scholarship on Civil War Soldiers," in Aaron Sheehan-Dean, ed., *The View from the Ground: Experiences of Civil War Soldiers* (Lexington: University Press of Kentucky, 2007), 10; Stephen Z. Starr, "The Grand Old Regiment," *Wisconsin Magazine of History* 48, no. 1 (Autumn 1964): 21–31; Crompton B. Burton, "'The Dear Old Regiment': Maine's Regimental Associations and the Memory of the American Civil War," *New England Quarterly* 84, no. 1 (March 2011): 104–22; Smith, *Camps and Campaigns*, 3–8. For useful med-

itations on the regimental history, see also Peter C. Luebke, introduction, in Albion Winegar Tourgee, *The Story of a Thousand: A History of the 105th Ohio Volunteer Infantry*, ed. Peter C. Luebke (Kent, OH: Kent State University Press, 2011); M. Keith Harris, "Slavery, Emancipation, and Veterans of the Union Cause: Commemorating Freedom in the Age of Reconciliation, 1885–1915," *Civil War History* 53, no. 3 (September 2007): 264–90; Jordan, *Marching Home*; and Lesley J. Gordon, *A Broken Regiment: The 16th Connecticut's Civil War* (Baton Rouge: Louisiana State University Press, 2014).

2. Claire Prechtel Kluskens, "Anatomy of a Union Civil War Pension File," *NGS Newsmagazine* 34, no. 3 (July–September 2008): 42–45.

BIBLIOGRAPHY

ARCHIVAL MATERIAL

Center for Archival Collections, Bowling Green State University, Bowling Green, OH
　　Thomas J. Edwards Papers
　　Warren Russell Papers
Connecticut Historical Society, Hartford, CT
　　Middlebrook Family Papers
Connecticut State Library, Hartford, CT
　　Richard Magee Diary
Emory University Special Collections Library, Atlanta, GA
　　Civil War Collection
　　Luther B. Mesnard Sketch
Fredericksburg and Spotsylvania National Military Park Library, Fredericksburg, VA
　　Henry J. Blakeman Letters
　　John and Alexander Black Letters
　　Augustus Bronson Letter
　　Stephen Crofutt Letters
　　Ernst Damkoehler Letters
　　William Dauchy Letter
　　Charles H. Doerflinger Memoir
　　Francis Foote Letters
　　Erastus Fouch Diaries
　　Wilson French Letters
　　Robert Hubbard Letters

Justin Keeler Letter

Luther Mesnard Memoir

Franklin Sauter Diary

Justus Silliman Memoir and Correspondence

Jesse M. Spooner Letter

Talley Farm Vertical File

Douglas Tedrow Letter

William Warren Memoir

Gettysburg National Military Park Library, Gettysburg, PA

Park Vertical Files

17th Connecticut Volunteer Infantry

25th Ohio Volunteer Infantry

75th Ohio Volunteer Infantry

John Henry Ahrens Diary

107th Ohio Volunteer Infantry

153rd Pennsylvania Volunteer Infantry

Stephen A. Wallace Diary

Adams County Almshouse Vertical File

Hays' Brigade, Early's Division, Second Corps

Henry E. Huntington Library, San Marino, CA

Harvey Henderson Civil War Diary

Daniel Horn Papers

Mayo Family Papers

John Page Nicholson Collection

George Shane Phillips Papers

Houghton Library, Harvard University, Cambridge, MA

Military Order of the Loyal Legion Collection

Augustus Choate Hamlin Papers

Indiana State Library, Indianapolis, IN

Mahlon Slutz Reminiscences

Library of Virginia, Richmond, VA

Alvin Brown Letter

Manuscripts and Archives, Sterling Memorial Library, Yale University, New Haven, CT

Civil War Manuscript Collection

Robert Hubbard Papers

William Henry Warren Papers

Manuscript Division, Library of Congress, Washington, DC

John Bigelow Papers

Abraham Lincoln Papers

Miscellaneous Manuscripts Collection

Thomas Evans Diary and Memoir

Nathaniel McLean Correspondence

David Tod Correspondence

National Archives Building, Washington, DC

RG 15: Records of the Department of the Interior

Civil War Pension Files

Historical Register, National Homes for Disabled Volunteer Soldiers, 1866–1938

RG 94: Records of the Adjutant General's Office

Carded Medical Files

Compiled Service Records

Henry S. Finkenbiner Medal of Honor File

Records Relating to Medical Officers and Physicians

Charles A. Hartman Papers

John Knauss Papers

Regimental Orders Books, 107th Ohio Volunteer Infantry

RG 153: Records of the Office of the Judge Advocate General

Civil War Court Martial Cases

RG 393: Records of United States Continental Army Commands, 1821–1920

Ohio History Connection, Columbus, OH

Andrew Harris Papers

Grand Army of the Republic Collection

Ohio Gettysburg Memorial Commission Records

Ohio State Soldiers' and Sailors' Home Admission Records

Society of Separatists of Zoar Records

William B. Southerton Memoir

Wildman Family Papers

Rubenstein Library, Duke University, Durham, NC

John Snider Cooper Diary

United States Army Heritage and Education Center Library and Archives, Carlisle, PA

Lewis Leigh Collection

University of South Carolina Library, Columbia, SC

Jacob Boroway Letter

Wayne County Public Library, Wooster, OH

John Flory Diary

William McKinley Presidential Library and Museum, Canton, OH

William McKinley Post No. 25, Grand Army of the Republic Records

Wright State University, Dayton, OH

Oscar D. Ladley Papers

Government Documents and Official Records

Busey, John W., and David G. Martin. *Regimental Strengths and Losses at Gettysburg*, 4th ed. Hightstown, NJ: Longstreet House, 2005.

————. *The Last Full Measure: Burial in the Soldiers' National Cemetery at Gettysburg*. Hightstown, NJ: Longstreet House, 1988.

Journal of the House of Representatives of the State of Ohio for the Second Session of the Fifty-Fifth General Assembly. Columbus: Richard Nevins, State Printer, 1863.

Medical and Surgical History of the Civil War. Reprint ed. Wilmington, North Carolina: Broadfoot Publishing Company, 1991.

Report of the Joint Committee on the Conduct of the War. Reprint ed. Wilmington, NC: Broadfoot's Publishing Company, 1999.

Revised Ordinances of the City of Canton. Canton, OH: Roller Press, 1916.

Revised United States Army Regulations of 1861. Washington, DC: Government Printing Office, 1863.

Seventeenth Annual Report of the Ohio State Board of Agriculture. Columbus: Richard Nevins, State Printer, 1863.

Summary Statements of Quarterly Returns of Ordnance and Ordnance Stores on Hand in Regular and Volunteer Army Organizations, microfilm M1281, reel 4, NA.

United States War Department. *The War of the Rebellion: A Compilation of the Official Records of the Union and Confederate Armies*. Washington, DC: Government Printing Office, 1880–1901.

Newspapers and Periodicals

Akron Daily Beacon	*Cleveland Daily Herald*
Allen County Democrat	*Cleveland Daily Leader*
Annals of Cleveland	*Cleveland Morning Leader*
The Army Herald	*Cleveland Plain Dealer*
Athens Messenger	*Columbia Phoenix*
Atlantic Monthly	*Concord Independent Statesman*
Bangor Daily Whig & Courier	*Confederate Veteran*
The Bivouac	*The Crisis*
Boston Daily Advertiser	*Daily Cleveland Herald*
Boston Journal	*Daily National Intelligencer*
Canton Repository	*Daily Ohio Statesman*
The Carriage Monthly	*Danbury Times*
Cincinnati Commercial	*Dayton Herald*
Clarendon Banner	*Defiance Democrat*

Elyria Independent Democrat
Fayetteville Observer
Gettysburg Star and Sentinel
Harper's Weekly
Harrisburg Weekly Patriot and Union
Hartford Daily Courant
Hartford Evening Press
Holmes County Farmer
Jeffersonian Democrat
Lebanon Courier
The Liberator
Lippincott's Magazine
Lowell Daily Citizen and News
Marysville Journal-Tribune
Massillon Independent
McArthur Democrat
Milwaukee Daily Sentinel
Morning Oregonian
National Tribune
New Hampshire Sentinel
New Haven Daily Palladium
New Orleans Daily Democrat
New Philadelphia Democrat
New York Herald
New York Times
New York Tribune
Newark Advocate
North American and United States Gazette

Norwalk Experiment
Norwalk Reflector
Ohio Democrat
Ohio Repository
The Opelousas Courier
Orlando Sentinel
Philadelphia Inquirer
Popular Science Monthly
Portage County Democrat
The Republic
Ripley Bee
Sacramento Daily Union
Salem Observer
San Francisco Daily Evening Bulletin
Sandusky Register
The Semi-Weekly Raleigh Register
Scioto Gazette
Southern Historical Society Papers
Stark County Democrat
Stark County Republican
Summit County Beacon
Sumter Watchman
Tiffin Tribune
Toledo Blade
Tuscarawas Advocate
Washington Chronicle
The Watchman and Southron
Weekly Ohio Statesman
Wooster Republican

Printed Primary Sources

Abbott, John S. C. *The History of the Civil War in America*. New York: Henry Bill, 1866.

Andrews, Robert W. *The Life and Adventures of Robert W. Andrews, of Sumter, South Carolina*. Boston: Printed for the Author by E. P. Whitcomb, 1887.

Angle, Paul M., ed. *Three Years in the Army of the Cumberland: The Letters and Diary of Major James A. Connolly*. Bloomington: Indiana University Press, 1987.

Barlow, Albert Rowe. *Company G: A Record of the Services of One Company of the 157th New York Volunteers in the War of the Rebellion*. Syracuse, NY: A. W. Hall, 1899.

Bartholow, Roberts. *A Manual of Instructions of Enlisting and Discharging Soldiers*. Philadelphia: J. B. Lippincott & Co., 1864.

Basler, Roy P., ed. *The Collected Works of Abraham Lincoln*. New Brunswick, NJ: Rutgers University Press, 1953.

The Battle of Chancellorsville and the Eleventh Army Corps. New York: G. B. Teubner, Printer, 1863.

Battles and Leaders of the Civil War. Reprint ed. New York and London: Thomas Yoseloff, 1956.

Becker, Carl M., and Ritchie Thomas, eds. *Hearth and Knapsack: The Ladley Letters, 1857–1880*. Athens: Ohio University Press, 1988.

Beyer, W. F., and O. F. Keydel, eds. *Deeds of Valor: How America's Civil War Heroes Won the Congressional Medal of Honor*. Reprint ed. Stamford, Connecticut: Longmeadow Press, 1994.

The Biographical Cyclopedia and Portrait Gallery with an Historical Sketch of the State of Ohio. Cincinnati: Western Biographical Publishing Company, 1887.

Biographical Record of Civil War Veterans Tuscarawas County, Ohio. Reprint ed. New Philadelphia, OH: Tuscarawas County Genealogical Society, 1990.

Booth, Andrew B. *Records of Louisiana Confederate Soldiers and Louisiana Confederate Commands*. New Orleans: n.p., 1920.

Brooks, Noah. *Abraham Lincoln*. New York and London: G. P. Putnam's Sons, 1888.

———. *Washington in Lincoln's Time*. New York: Century Co., 1896.

Butts, Joseph T., ed. *A Gallant Captain of the Civil War: Being the Record of the Extraordinary Adventures of Frederick Otto Baron von Fritsch*. New York and London: F. Tennyson Neely, 1902.

Cary, Edward. *The Trip of the Steamer Oceanus to Fort Sumter and Charleston, S.C., April 14, 1865*. New York: "The Union" Steam Printing House, 1865.

Cavada, Federico Fernandez. *Libby Life: Experiences of a Prisoner of War in Richmond, Virginia, 1863–64*. Philadelphia: King & Baird, 1864.

Chase, Henry, ed., *Representative Men of Maine*. Portland: Lakeside Press, 1893.

Chase, J. A. *History of the Fourteenth Ohio Regiment, O.V.V.I.* Toledo: St. John Printing House, 1881.

Chesnut, Mary. *A Diary from Dixie*, ed. Isabella D. Martin and Myrta Lockett Avary. New York: D. Appleton and Company, 1906.

Clark, Charles T. *Opdycke Tigers, 125th O.V.I.: A History of the Regiment and of the Campaigns and Battles of the Army of the Cumberland*. Columbus: Spahr & Glenn, 1895.

Cleveland Directory for the Year Ending July, 1897. Cleveland: Cleveland Directory Publishing Co., 1896.

Coffin, Charles Carleton. *Marching to Victory: The Second Period of the War of the Rebellion, Including the Year 1863*. New York: Harper & Brothers, 1888.

Conover, Frank, ed. *Centennial Portrait and Biographical Record of the City of Dayton and of Montgomery County, Ohio*. Chicago: A. W. Bowen & Co., 1897.

Cooley, Arnold James. *Cooley's Cyclopaedia of Practical Receipts*. 6th ed. New York: D. Appleton and Company, 1897.

Cox, Jacob Dolson. *Military Reminiscences of the Civil War*. New York: D. Appleton & Company, 1865.

Cox, Samuel S. *Eight Years in Congress*. New York: D. Appleton & Company, 1865.

Culp, Edward C. *The 25th Ohio Vet. Vol. Infantry in the War for the Union*. Topeka: Geo. W. Crane & Co., 1885.

Denison, Frederic. *Shot and Shell: The Third Rhode Island Heavy Artillery Regiment in the Rebellion, 1861–1865*. Providence: J. A. & R. A. Reid, 1879.

Douglass, Ben. *History of Wayne County, Ohio*. Indianapolis: Robert Douglass, Publisher, 1878.

Duren, Charlie. "The Occupation of Jacksonville, February 1864 and the Battle of Olustee: Letters of Lt. C. M. Duren, 54th Massachusetts Regiment, U.S.A." *Florida Historical Quarterly* 32, no. 4 (April 1954): 264.

The Echo from the Army: What Our Soldiers Say About the Copperheads. New York: William C. Bryant and Co., Printers, 1863.

Emilio, Luis Fenollosa. *The History of the Fifty-fourth Regiment of Massachusetts Volunteer Infantry, 1863–1865*. Boston: Boston Book Company, 1894.

Erb, William S. S. *Extract from "The Battles of the 19th Ohio."* Washington, DC: Judd & Detweiler, Printers, 1893.

Faust, Albert B. *The German Element in the United States*. 2 vols. Boston and New York: Houghton Mifflin Company, 1909.

Fisk, Joel C., and William H. D. Blake. *A Condensed History of the 56th Regiment, New York Veteran Volunteer Infantry*. Newburgh: Newburgh Journal Printing House and Book Bindery, 1906.

Gallup, C. H., et al. *The Firelands Pioneer*. Norwalk, OH: American Publishers Company, 1915.

Garland, W.H. "The Battle of Dingles's Mill, Fla.," *Confederate Veteran* 24, no. 12 (December 1916): 549.

Gawley, Thomas Francis. *The Valiant Hours: An Irishman in the Civil War*. Harrisburg, PA: Stackpole Company, 1961.

Gerry, H. E. *Camp Fire Entertainment and True History of Robert Henry Hendershot, The Drummer Boy of the Rappahannock*. Chicago: Hack and Anderson, 1900.

Gienapp, William E. and Erica L., eds. *The Civil War Diary of Gideon Welles, Lincoln's Secretary of the Navy: The Original Manuscript Edition*. Urbana, Chicago, and Springfield: University of Illinois Press, 2014.

Goebel, Julius. *Deutsch-amerikanische Geschichtsblätter*. Chicago: German-American Historical Society of Illinois, 1913.

Gordon, George Henry. *A War Diary of Events in the War of the Great Rebellion, 1863–1865*. Boston: James R. Osgood and Company, 1882.

Grebner, Constantin. *We Were the Ninth: A History of the Ninth Regiment, Ohio Volunteer*

Infantry, April 17, 1861, to June 7, 1864. Reprint ed. Kent, OH: Kent State University Press, 1987.

Greiner, James M., Janet L. Coryell, and James R. Smither, eds. *A Surgeon's Civil War: The Letters and Diary of Daniel M. Holt, M.D.* Kent, OH: Kent State University Press, 1994.

Hamlin, Augustus Choate. *The Battle of Chancellorsville: The Attack of Stonewall Jackson and His Army Upon the Right Flank of the Army of the Potomac at Chancellorsville, Virginia, on Saturday Afternoon, May 2, 1863.* Bangor, ME: Published by the Author, 1896.

Harbaugh, Thomas Chalmers. *Middletown Valley in Song and Story.* N.p.: T. C. Harbaugh, 1910.

Howard, Oliver Otis. *Autobiography of Oliver Otis Howard.* New York: Baker & Taylor Company, 1907.

———. "Campaign and Battle of Gettysburg, June and July, 1863," *Atlantic Monthly* 38 (July 1876): 48–70.

———. "The Eleventh Corps at Chancellorsville," in *Battles and Leaders of the Civil War.* Reprint ed. New York and London: Thomas Yoseloff, 1956.

Jacobs, Michael. *Notes on the Rebel Invasion of Maryland and Pennsylvania.* Philadelphia: J. B. Lippincott & Co., 1864.

Jones, C.C., Jr. "The Battle of Honey Hill," *Southern Historical Society Papers* 13 (1885): 362.

Jones, Nelson Edwards, M.D. *The Squirrel Hunters, or Glimpses of Pioneer Life.* Cincinnati: Robert Clarke Co., 1898.

Jones, Terry L., ed. *Campbell Brown's Civil War: With Ewell in the Army of Northern Virginia.* Baton Rouge: Louisiana State University Press, 2001.

Keene, Otis L. "Jacksonville, Fifty-Three Years Ago: Recollections of a Veteran," *Florida Historical Quarterly* 1 (January 1909): 9–12.

Kennedy, James Harrison, and Wilson M. Day. *The Bench and Bar of Cleveland.* Cleveland: Cleveland Printing and Publishing Co., 1889.

Kepler, William. *History of the Three Months' and Three Years' Service from April 16th, 1861 to June 22nd, 1864 of the Fourth Regiment Ohio Volunteer Infantry in the War for the Union.* Cleveland: Leader Printing Company, 1886.

Kettell, Thomas Prentice. *History of the Great Rebellion, From Its Commencement to Its Close.* Hartford: L. Stebbins, 1865.

Kiefer, William R. *History of the One Hundred and Fifty-Third Regiment, Pennsylvania Volunteers.* Easton, PA: Chemical Pub. Co., 1909.

Kilmer, George L. "First Actions of Wounded Soldiers," *Popular Science Monthly* (June 1892): 155–58.

Ladd, David L., and Audrey J. Ladd, eds. *The Bachelder Papers: Gettysburg in Their Own Words.* 3 vols. Dayton, OH: Morningside Books, 1994.

Lee, Alfred E. "Reminiscences of the Gettysburg Battle," *Lippincott's Magazine of Popular Literature and Science* 6 (July 1883): 54–60.

Leonard, Mary H. "An Old Industry," *Popular Science Monthly* 46 (March 1895): 649–58.

Lewis, G. W. *The Campaigns of the 124th Regiment Ohio Volunteer Infantry*. Akron: Werner Company, 1894.

Little, Henry F. W. *The Seventh Regiment New Hampshire Volunteers in the War of the Rebellion*. Concord: Ira C. Evans, Printer, 1896.

Lossing, Benson J. *Pictoral History of the Civil War in the United States of America*. Hartford: Thomas Belknap, 1877.

Low, James W. *Low's Railroad Directory for 1862*. New York: Wynkoop, Hallenbeck & Thomas, Printers, 1862.

Lowenfels, Walter, ed. *Walt Whitman's Civil War*. New York: Da Capo, 1961.

MacCauley, Clay. "From Chancellorsville to Libby Prison," in *Glimpses of the Nation's Struggle: A Series of Papers Read Before the Minnesota Commandery of the Military Order of the Loyal Legion of the United States*. St. Paul. St. Paul Book and Stationery Company, 1887.

Marcus, Edward, ed. *A New Canaan Private in the Civil War: Letters of Justus M. Silliman, 17th Connecticut Volunteers*. New Canaan, CT: New Canaan Historical Society, 1984.

Marszalek, John, ed. *The Diary of Miss Emma Holmes*. Baton Rouge: Louisiana State University Press, 1994.

McCreery, William B. *"My Experiences as a Prisoner of War, and Escape from Libby Prison."* Detroit: Winn & Hammond, 1893.

McGrath, Franklin, comp. *The History of the 127th New York Volunteers: "Monitors" in the War for the Preservation of the Union—September 8th, 1862, June 30th 1865*. N.p.: n.d.

McKee, James Harvey. *Back "In War Times": History of the 144th Regiment, New York Volunteers*. Unadilla, NY: Horace E. Bailey, 1903.

Meysenberg, Theodore. "Reminiscences of Chancellorsville," in *War Papers and Personal Reminiscences, 1861 1865, Read Before the Commandery of the State of Missouri, Military Order of the Loyal Legion of the United States*. St. Louis: Becktold & Co., 1892.

Monfort, E. R. "The First Division, Eleventh Corps, at Chancellorsville," in H. B. Furness Monfort and Fred H. Alms, eds. *G.A.R. War Papers: Papers Read Before Fred C. Jones Post, No. 401, Department of Ohio, G.A.R.*, vol. 1. Cincinnati: Fred C. Jones Post, 1891.

Moore, James. *A Complete History of the Great Rebellion*. Philadelphia: W. S. Burlock and Company, 1881.

Moore, John Hammond, ed. "The Last Officer: April 1865." *South Carolina Historical Magazine* 67, no. 1 (January 1966): 3.

Mueller, Jacob. *Memories of a Forty-Eighter: Sketches from the German-American Period of Storm and Stress in the 1850s*. Cleveland, OH: Western Reserve Historical Society, 1996.

Neff, William. *Bench and Bar of Northern Ohio: History and Biography*. Cleveland: Historical Publishing Co., 1921.

Nevins, Allan, ed. *A Diary of Battle: The Personal Journals of Colonel Charles S. Wainwright, 1861–1865*. Reprint ed. Gettysburg: Stan Clark Military Books, 1962.

———. *Diary of the Civil War, 1860–1865 by George Templeton Strong*. New York: Macmillan Company, 1962.

New York Monuments Commission. *Final Report of the Battlefield of Gettysburg.* Albany: J. B. Lyon Company, Printers, 1902.

Nicolay, John G., and John Hay. *Abraham Lincoln: A History.* New York: Century Company, 1909).

Noble, William H. *The Seventeenth Regiment Connecticut Volunteer Infantry in the War of the Rebellion, 1862–1865.* Hartford: The Press of the Case, Lockwood & Brainard Company, 1889.

Northrop, John Worrell. *Chronicles from the Diary of a War Prisoner in Andersonville and Other Military Prisons in 1864.* Wichita: Published by the Author, 1904.

Official Army Register of the Volunteer Force of the United States Army for The Years 1861–1865—Part 5: *Ohio and Michigan.* Washington, DC: Published by Order of the Secretary of War, 1865.

The Ohio Guide. New York: Oxford University Press, 1946.

Olds, Edson Baldwin. *Arbitrary Arrests: Speech of Hon. Edson B. Olds, For Which He Was Arrested, And His Reception Speeches on his Return from The Bastille.* Circleville, OH: n.p., 1862.

Orth, Samuel Peter. *A History of Cleveland, Ohio.* Chicago: S. J. Clarke, 1910.

Osborn, Hartwell, et al. *Trials and Triumphs: The Record of the Fifty-Fifth Ohio Volunteer Infantry.* Chicago: A. C. McClurg & Co., 1904.

Perrin, William Henry, ed. *History of Stark County, with an Outline Sketch of Ohio.* Chicago: Baskin & Battey, 1881.

Portrait and Biographical Record of Stark County, Ohio. Chicago: Chapman Brothers, 1892.

Public Documents, Concerning the Ohio Canals, Which Are to Connect Lake Erie with the Ohio River, Comprising a Complete Official History of These Great Works of Internal Improvement. Columbus: Olmsted, Bailhache & Camron, Printers, 1828.

Purdy, John. *The Colombian Navigator, or Sailing Directory for the American Coasts.* London: R. H. Laurie, 1839.

Reed, Merle, ed. "The Gettysburg Campaign—A Louisiana Lieutenant's Eye-Witness Account." *Pennsylvania History* 30 (April 1963): 189.

Reid, Whitelaw. *Ohio in the War: Her Statesmen, Generals, and Soldiers.* Cincinnati: Robert Clarke Company, 1895.

Reinhart, Joseph R., ed. *A German Hurrah! Civil War Letters of Friedrich Bertsch and Wilhelm Stängel, 9th Ohio Infantry.* Kent, OH: Kent State University Press, 2010.

———. *Yankee Dutchmen under Fire: Civil War Letters from the 82nd Illinois Infantry.* Kent, OH: Kent State University Press, 2013.

Remington, Cyrus Kingsbury. *A Record of Battery I, First N.Y. Light Artillery Vols., Otherwise Known As Wiedrich's Battery during the War of the Rebellion, 1861–'65.* Buffalo: Press of the Courier Company, 1891.

Rhodes, Robert Hunt. *All for the Union: The Civil War Diary and Letters of Elisha Hunt Rhodes.* New York: Random House, 1992.

Richards, Thomas Addison, ed. *Appleton's Companion Hand-Book of Travel*. New York: D. Appleton & Company, 1864.

Robertson, Jr., James I., ed. *The Civil War Letters of General Robert McAllister*. Reprint ed. Baton Rouge: Louisiana State University Press, 1998.

Rock, R. W. *History of the Eleventh Regiment, Rhode Island Volunteers in the War of the Rebellion*. Providence: Providence Press Company, Printers, 1881.

Ryan, Daniel Joseph. *A History of Ohio, with Biographical Sketches of Her Governors and the Ordinance of 1787*. Columbus: A. H. Smythe, 1888.

Samito, Christian, ed. *Commanding Boston's Irish Ninth: The Civil War Letters of Colonel Patrick R. Guiney, Ninth Massachusetts Volunteer Infantry*. New York: Fordham University Press, 1998.

Schaff, David Schley. *The Life of Philip Schaff: In Part Autobiographical*. New York: Charles Scribner's Sons, 1897.

Scharf, John Thomas. *History of Western Maryland*. Philadelphia: Louis H. Everts, 1882.

Schurz, Carl. *The Reminiscences of Carl Schurz*. London: John Murray, 1909.

Scott, Henry Lee. *Military Dictionary*. New York: D. Van Nostrand, 1863.

Searight, Thomas B. *The Old Pike: A History of the National Road*. Uniontown, PA: Published by the Author, 1894.

Semi-Centennial Register of the Members of the Phi Kappa Sigma Fraternity, 1850–1900. Philadelphia: Avil Printing Co., 1900.

Seventeenth Regiment C.V.I. Reunion at Fairfield, Ct., 1862–1883, August 28, 1883. Bridgeport, CT: The Standard Association, Printers, 1884.

Sledge, E. B. *With the Old Breed: At Peleliu and Okinawa*. New York: Random House, 1981.

Slutz, Mahlon. *Tribute to Major Augustus Vignos*. Kent, OH: n.p., 1926.

Smith, Henry Perry, ed. *History of the City of Buffalo and Erie County*. Syracuse: D. Mason & Co., 1884.

Speech of John Brough at the Union Mass Meeting, at Marietta, Ohio, June 10, 1863. Springfield, OH: Springfield Republic, 1863.

Speeches, Arguments, Addresses, and Letters of Clement L. Vallandigham. New York: J. Walter & Co., 1864.

Spencer, Jesse Ames. *History of the United States: From the Earliest Period to the Administration of Andrew Johnson*. New York: Johnson, Fry and Company, 1866.

Staudenraus, P. J., ed. "A War Correspondent's View of St. Augustine and Fernandina: 1863." *Florida Historical Quarterly* 41, no. 1 (July 1962).

Stiles, Robert. *Four Years Under Marse Robert*. New York and Washington: Neale Publishing Company, 1910.

Thigpen, Allan D., ed. *The Illustrated Recollections of Potter's Raid, April 5–21, 1865*. Sumter, SC: Gamecock City Printing, 1998.

Thomas, Henry W. *History of the Doles-Cook Brigade, Army of Northern Virginia*. Atlanta: Franklin Printing & Publishing Company, 1903.

Thompson, D. G. Brinton, ed. "From Chancellorsville to Gettysburg: A Doctor's Diary." *Pennsylvania Magazine of History and Biography* 89, no. 3 (July 1965).

Thompson, Edwin Porter. *History of the Orphan Brigade*. Louisville, KY: Lewis N. Thompson, 1868.

The Traveller's Tour Through the United States: An Instructive Pastime, Performed on a Map. New York: Roe Lockwood, 1842.

The Tribune Almanac and Political Register for 1864. New York: Tribune Association, 1864.

Trowbridge, John T. *The South: A Tour of Its Battlefields and Ruined Cities*. Hartford: L. Stebbins, 1866.

The Union Army: Cyclopedia of Battles. Madison, WI: Federal Publishing Co., 1908.

Vallandigham, James L. *A Life of Clement L. Vallandigham*. Baltimore: Turnbull Brothers, 1872.

Vanderslice, John Mitchell. *Gettysburg, Then and Now: The Field of American Valor*. New York: G. W. Dillingham Co., 1897.

Wheeler, Robert A., ed. *Visions of the Western Reserve: Public and Private Documents of Northeastern Ohio, 1750–1860*. Columbus: Ohio State University Press, 2000.

Wheelock, Julia S. *The Boys in White: The Experience of a Hospital Agent In and Around Washington*. New York: Lange & Hillman, 1870.

Whitman, Walt. *The Complete Prose Works of Walt Whitman*. New York: G. P. Putnam's Sons, 1902.

Whittier, Edward N. "The Left Attack (Ewell's) at Gettysburg," in *Civil War Papers Read Before the Commandery of the State of Massachusetts, Military Order of the Loyal Legion of the United States*. Reprint ed. Wilmington, NC: Broadfoot Publishing Company, 1993.

Williams, William. *History of the Fire Lands, Comprising Huron and Erie Counties, Ohio*. Cleveland: Press of Leader Printing Company, 1879.

Woolson, Constance Fenimore. *Castle Nowhere: Lake-Country Sketches*. Boston: James R. Osgood and Company, 1875.

Secondary Sources

Abbott, Richard H. *Ohio's Civil War Governors*. Columbus: Ohio State University Press, 1962.

Adams, John. *Warrior at Heart: Governor John Milton, King Cotton, and Rebel Florida, 1860–1865*. Victoria, BC, Canada: Friesen Press, 2015.

Adams, Michael C. C. *Living Hell: The Dark Side of the Civil War*. Baltimore: Johns Hopkins University Press, 2014.

Andreasen, Bryon C. "Lincoln's Religious Critics: Copperhead Christian Reactions to the President and the War," in Daniel M. McDonough and Kenneth W. Noe, eds., *Politics and Culture of the Civil War Era: Essays in Honor of Robert W. Johannsen*. Selinsgrove, PA: Susquehanna University Press, 2006.

Archer, John M. *East Cemetery Hill at Gettysburg: "The Hour Was One of Horror."* Gettysburg: Thomas Publications, 1997.

Baltzell, George F. "The Battle of Olustee (Ocean Pond), Florida." *Florida Historical Quarterly* 9, no. 4 (April 1931).

Barton, Michael. *Goodmen: The Character of Civil War Soldiers.* University Park: Pennsylvania State University Press, 1981.

Bearden-White, Christina. "Illinois Germans and the Coming of the Civil War: Reshaping Ethnic Identity." *Journal of the Illinois State Historical Society* 109, no. 3 (Fall 2016).

Bergeron, Jr., Arthur W. *Guide to Louisiana Confederate Military Units, 1861–1865.* Baton Rouge: Louisiana State University Press, 1989.

Bergquist, James M. "German Communities in American Cities: An Interpretation of the Nineteenth-Century Experience." *Journal of American Ethnic History* 4, no. 1 (Fall 1984).

Bigelow, Jr., John. *The Campaign of Chancellorsville: A Strategic and Tactical Study.* New Haven: Yale University Press, 1910.

Blight, David W. *Race and Reunion: The Civil War in American Memory.* Cambridge, MA: Harvard University Press, 2001.

Bonner, Robert E. *The Soldier's Pen: Firsthand Impressions of the Civil War.* New York: Hill & Wang, 2006.

Brasher, Glenn David. *The Peninsula Campaign & The Necessity of Emancipation.* Chapel Hill: University of North Carolina Press, 2012.

Brooke, John. *"There Is a North": Fugitive Slaves, Political Crisis, and Cultural Transformation in the Coming of the Civil War.* Amherst: University of Massachusetts Press, 2019.

Broomall, James J. *Private Confederacies: The Emotional Worlds of Southern Men as Citizens and Soldiers.* Chapel Hill: University of North Carolina Press, 2019.

Brown, Kent Masterson. *Retreat from Gettysburg: Lee, Logistics, and the Pennsylvania Campaign.* Chapel Hill: University of North Carolina Press, 2005.

Brown, Thomas J. *Civil War Canon: Sites of Confederate Memory in South Carolina.* Chapel Hill: University of North Carolina Press, 2015.

———. *Civil War Monuments and the Militarization of America.* Chapel Hill: University of North Carolina Press, 2019.

Browning, Judkin, and Timothy Silver. *An Environmental History of the Civil War.* Chapel Hill: University of North Carolina Press, 2020.

Burke, Eric. "Facing the Enemy: The Crucible of Combat Forged Unique Unit Cultures Within Civil War Regiments." *Civil War Times Illustrated* (June 2019).

Burlingame, Michael. *The Inner World of Abraham Lincoln.* Urbana and Chicago: University of Illinois Press, 1994.

Burton, Crompton B. "'The Dear Old Regiment': Maine's Regimental Associations and the Memory of the American Civil War." *New England Quarterly* 84, no. 1 (March 2011).

Burton, E. Milby. *The Siege of Charleston, 1861–1865.* Columbia: University of South Carolina Press, 1970.

Burton, William L. *Melting Pot Soldiers: The Union's Ethnic Regiments.* Ames: Iowa State University Press, 1988.

Carmichael, Peter S. *The War for the Common Soldier: How Men Thought, Fought, and Survived in Civil War Armies.* Chapel Hill: University of North Carolina Press, 2018.

Cashin, Joan. *War Stuff: The Struggle for Human and Environmental Resources in the American Civil War.* Cambridge: Cambridge University Press, 2018.

Coco, Gregory A. *A Strange and Blighted Land: Gettysburg: The Aftermath of a Battle.* Reprint ed. El Dorado Hills, CA: Savas Beatie, 2017.

———. *A Vast Sea of Misery: A History and Guide to the Union and Confederate Field Hospitals at Gettysburg, July 1–November 20, 1863.* Reprint ed. El Dorado Hills, CA: Savas Beatie, 2017.

Coddington, Edwin B. *The Gettysburg Campaign: A Study in Command.* New York: Touchstone Books, 1997.

Coles, David J. "'Shooting Niggers Sir': Confederate Mistreatment of Black Soldiers at the Battle of Olustee," in Gregory J. W. Urwin, ed., *Black Flag Over Dixie: Racial Atrocities and Reprisals in the Civil War.* Carbondale: Southern Illinois University Press, 2004.

Conner, Jr., Albert, and Chris Mackowski. *Seizing Destiny: The Army of the Potomac's "Valley Forge" and the Civil War Winter that Saved the Union.* El Dorado Hills, CA: Savas Beatie, 2016.

Cronon, William. "Storytelling," *The American Historical Review* 118, no. 1 (February 2013).

Das, Santanu. *Touch and Intimacy in First World War Literature.* Cambridge: Cambridge University Press, 2006.

Davis, William C. *The Orphan Brigade: The Kentucky Confederates Who Couldn't Go Home.* New York: Doubleday, 1980.

Davis, William Watson. *The Civil War and Reconstruction in Florida.* New York: Columbia University Press, 1913.

Davison, Kenneth E. *Cleveland during the Civil War.* Columbus: Ohio State University Press for The Ohio Historical Society, 1962.

Dell, Christopher. *Lincoln and the War Democrats: The Grand Erosion of Conservative Tradition.* Cranbury, NJ: Associated University Presses, 1975.

Dell'Orto, Giovanna. "The Arrest and Trial of Clement L. Vallandigham in 1863," in *Words at War: The Civil War and American Journalism,* ed. David B. Sachsman, S. Kittrell Rushing, and Roy Morris, Jr. West Lafayette, IN: Purdue University Press, 2008.

Diffley, Kathleen, ed. *To Live and Die: Collected Stories of the Civil War, 1861–1876.* Durham: Duke University Press, 2002.

Downs, Gregory P. *The Second American Revolution: The Civil War–Era Struggle over Cuba and the Rebirth of the American Republic.* Chapel Hill: University of North Carolina Press, 2019.

Doyle, Don. *The Cause of All Nations: An International History of the American Civil War.* New York: Basic Books, 2014.

Dunkelman, Mark H. *Gettysburg's Unknown Soldier: The Life, Death, and Celebrity of Amos Humiston*. Westport, CT: Praeger, 1999.

———. "Hardtack and Sauerkraut Stew: Ethnic Tensions in the 154th New York Volunteers, Eleventh Corps, during the Civil War." *Yearbook of German-American Studies* 36 (2001).

Eckert, Ralph Lowell. *John Brown Gordon: Soldier, Southerner, American*. Baton Rouge: Louisiana State University Press, 1989.

Edwards, Tom J., ed. *Raising the Banner of Freedom: The 25th Ohio Volunteer Infantry in the War for the Union by Bvt. Col. Edward C. Culp*. Bloomington, IN: iUniverse, 2003.

Egerton, Douglas R. *Thunder at the Gates: The Black Civil War Regiments that Redeemed America*. New York: Basic Books, 2016.

Elmore, Thomas. "The Whistle and Hiss of The Iron; The Effects of Artillery Fire on Infantry at Gettysburg." *Gettysburg Magazine* 5 (July 1991).

Elmore, Tom. *Potter's Raid through South Carolina: The Final Days of the Confederacy*. Charleston, SC: History Press, 2015.

Engle, Stephen D. *Gathering to Save a Nation: Lincoln and the Union's War Governors*. Chapel Hill: University of North Carolina Press, 2016.

———. *Yankee Dutchman: The Life of Franz Sigel*. Baton Rouge: Louisiana State University Press, 1993.

Fahs, Alice. *The Imagined Civil War: Popular Literature of the North and South, 1861–1865*. Chapel Hill: University of North Carolina Press, 2001.

Farge, Arlette. *The Allure of the Archives*. New Haven: Yale University Press, 2013.

Fehrenbacher, Don E. *The Slaveholding Republic: An Account of the United States Government's Relations to Slavery*. New York: Oxford University Press, 2001.

Fernandez, Kathleen. "The Happy Valley; Constance F. Woolson's View of Zoar." [Unpublished paper in author's possession].

———. *Zoar: The Story of an Intentional Community*. Kent, OH: Kent State University Press, 2019.

Fitzpatrick, Mike, et al. "Immigrants in the Ranks: A Collection of Vignettes of Foreigners in the Union Army." *Military Images* 19, no. 3 (November/December 1997).

Flagel, Thomas R. *War, Memory, and the 1913 Gettysburg Reunion*. Kent, OH: Kent State University Press, 2019.

Fleche, Andre. *The Revolution of 1861*. Chapel Hill: University of North Carolina Press, 2010.

Florance, Jr., John E. "Morris Island: Victory or Blunder?" *South Carolina Historical Magazine* 55, no. 3 (July 1954).

Frank, Joseph Allan. *With Ballot and Bayonet: The Political Socialization of American Civil War Soldiers*. Athens: University of Georgia Press, 1998.

Furgurson, Ernest B. *Chancellorsville 1863: The Souls of the Brave*. New York: Alfred A. Knopf, 1992.

Gallagher, Gary W., ed. *Chancellorsville: The Battle and its Aftermath*. Chapel Hill: University of North Carolina Press, 1996.

———. *The First Day at Gettysburg: Essays on Union and Confederate Leadership*. Kent, OH: Kent State University Press, 1992.

———. *The Fredericksburg Campaign: Decision on the Rappahannock*. Chapel Hill: University of North Carolina Press, 1995.

———. *The Second Day at Gettysburg: Essays on Union and Confederate Leadership*. Kent, OH: Kent State University Press, 1993.

Gannon, Barbara A. " 'She Is a Member of the 23rd': Lucy Nichols and the Community of the Civil War Regiment," in *This Distracted and Anarchical People: New Answers for Old Questions About the Civil War–Era North*, ed. Andrew L. Slap and Michael Thomas Smith. New York: Fordham University Press, 2013.

Garrison, Zachary Stuart. *German Americans on the Middle Border: From Antislavery to Reconciliation, 1830–1877*. Carbondale: Southern Illinois University Press, 2019.

Geary, James W. *We Need Men: The Union Draft in the Civil War*. DeKalb: Northern Illinois University Press, 1991.

Geary, Linda Leigh. *Balanced in the Wind: A Biography of Betsey Mix Cowles*. Lewisburg, PA: Bucknell University Press, 1989.

Glatthaar, Joseph T. *General Lee's Army: From Victory to Collapse*. New York: Free Press, 2008.

———. *The March to the Sea and Beyond: Sherman's Troops in the Savannah and Carolinas Campaign*. Baton Rouge: Louisiana State University Press, 1985.

Gordon, Lesley J. *A Broken Regiment: The 16th Connecticut's Civil War*. Baton Rouge: Louisiana State University Press, 2014.

Gottfried, Bradley M. *The Artillery of Gettysburg*. Nashville: Cumberland House, 2008.

———. *The Maps of Gettysburg: An Atlas of the Gettysburg Campaign, June 3–July 13, 1863*. El Dorado Hills, CA: Savas Beatie, 2007.

Gray, Wood. *The Hidden Civil War: The Story of the Copperheads*. New York: Viking Press, 1964.

Greene, A. Wilson. "From Chancellorsville to Cemetery Hill: O. O. Howard and Eleventh Corps Leadership," in Gary W. Gallagher, ed., *The First Day at Gettysburg*. Kent, OH: Kent State University Press, 1992.

———. "From Gettysburg to Falling Waters: Meade's Pursuit of Lee," in Gary W. Gallagher, ed., *The Third Day at Gettysburg & Beyond*. Chapel Hill: University of North Carolina Press, 1994.

———. "Morale, Maneuver, and Mud: The Army of the Potomac, December 16, 1862—January 26, 1863," in Gary W. Gallagher, ed., *The Fredericksburg Campaign: Decision on the Rappahannock*. Chapel Hill: University of North Carolina Press, 1995.

Gregor, Sharon. *Rockefeller's Cleveland*. Charleston, SC: Arcadia, 2010.

Griffith, Paddy. *Battle Tactics of the Civil War*. New Haven: Yale University Press, 1989.

Grimsley, Mark. *And Keep Moving On: The Virginia Campaign, May–June 1864*. Lincoln: University of Nebraska Press, 2002.

———. *The Hard Hand of War: Union Military Policy Toward Southern Civilians, 1861–1865*. Cambridge: Cambridge University Press, 1995.

Guelzo, Allen C. *Gettysburg: The Last Invasion*. New York: Alfred A. Knopf, 2013.

———. *Lincoln's Emancipation Proclamation: The End of Slavery in America*. New York: Simon & Schuster, 2004.

Hager, Christopher. *I Remain Yours: Common Lives in Civil War Letters*. Cambridge, MA: Harvard University Press, 2018.

Hamblen, Charles P., and Walter Powell, eds. *Connecticut Yankees at Gettysburg*. Kent, OH: Kent State University Press, 1993.

Handley-Cousins, Sarah. *Bodies in Blue: Disability in the Civil War North*. Athens: University of Georgia Press, 2019.

Harris, M. Keith. "Slavery, Emancipation, and Veterans of the Union Cause: Commemorating Freedom in the Age of Reconciliation, 1885–1915." *Civil War History* 53, no. 3 (September 2007).

Hartwig, D. Scott. "The Unlucky 11th: The 11th Army Corps on July 1, 1863." *Gettysburg Magazine* 2 (January 1990).

Hebert, Walter H. *Fighting Joe Hooker*. Indianapolis: Bobbs-Merrill Company, 1944.

Helbich, Wolfgang, and Walter D. Kamphoefner, eds. *German-American Immigration and Ethnicity in Comparative Perspective*. Madison, WI: Max Kade Institute for German-American Studies, 2004.

Hendricks, Norine S. "An Illustrated Lecture: The Civil War Paintings of William Siffert," *Timeline* 16, no. 3 (May-June 1999).

Hennessy, John J. "Evangelizing for Union, 1863: The Army of the Potomac, Its Enemies at Home, and a New Solidarity," *The Journal of the Civil War Era* 4, no. 4 (December 2014).

———. "We Shall Make Richmond Howl: The Army of the Potomac on the Eve of Chancellorsville," in Gary W. Gallagher, ed., *Chancellorsville: The Battle and Its Aftermath*. Chapel Hill: University of North Carolina Press, 1996.

Hess, Earl J. *Civil War Infantry Tactics: Training, Combat, and Small-Unit Effectiveness*. Baton Rouge: Louisiana State University Press, 2015.

———. *Lee's Tar-Heels: The Pettigrew-Kirkland MacRae Brigade*. Chapel Hill: University of North Carolina Press, 2002.

———. *Trench Warfare Under Lee and Grant: Field Fortifications in the Overland Campaign*. Chapel Hill: University of North Carolina Press, 2007.

———. *The Union Soldier in Battle: Enduring the Ordeal of Combat*. Lawrence: University Press of Kansas, 1997.

Hicken, Victor. *Illinois in the Civil War*. 2nd ed. Urbana and Chicago: University of Illinois Press, 1991.

Hodes, Martha. *Mourning Lincoln*. New Haven: Yale University Press, 2015.

Hofmann, Annette. "One Hundred Fifty Years of Loyalty: The Turner Movement in the United States." *Yearbook of German-American Studies* 34 (1999).

Holzer, Harold. *Lincoln at Cooper Union: The Speech That Made Abraham Lincoln President*. New York: Simon and Schuster, 2004.

Honeck, Mischa. "Men of Principle: Gender and the German American War for the Union," *Journal of the Civil War Era* 5, no. 1 (March 2015).

Howe, Henry. *Historical Collections of Ohio: An Encyclopedia of the State.* Cincinnati: C. J. Krehbiel & Co., 1902.

Hudson, Leonne M. "A Confederate Victory at Grahamville: Fighting at Honey Hill." *South Carolina Historical Magazine* 94, no. 1 (January 1993).

Hurt, R. Douglas. *The Ohio Frontier: Crucible of the Old Northwest, 1720–1830.* Bloomington: Indiana University Press, 1996.

Inbody, Donald S. *The Soldier Vote: War, Politics, and the Ballot in America.* New York: Palgrave Macmillan, 2016.

Johannsen, Robert W. *Stephen A. Douglas.* Urbana: University of Illinois Press, 1973.

Johns, John E. *Florida During the Civil War.* Gainesville: University of Florida Press, 1963.

Jones, Terry L. *Cemetery Hill: The Struggle for the High Ground, July 1–3, 1863.* New York: Da Capo Press, 2003.

———. *Lee's Tigers Revisited: The Louisiana Infantry in the Army of Northern Virginia.* Baton Rouge: Louisiana State University Press, 2017.

Jones, William M. "A Report on the Site of Camp Finegan." *Florida Historical Quarterly* 39, no. 4 (April 1961).

Jordan, Brian Matthew. "The Hour That Lasted Fifty Years: The 107th Ohio and the Human Longitude of Gettysburg," in Andrew F. Lang and Andrew S. Bledsoe, eds., *Upon the Fields of Battle: Essays on the Civil War's Military History.* Baton Rouge: Louisiana State University Press, 2018.

———. *Marching Home: Union Veterans and Their Unending Civil War.* New York: Liveright, 2014.

———. "'Our Work Is Not Yet Finished': Union Veterans and Their Unending Civil War, 1865–1872." *Journal of the Civil War Era* 5, no. 4 (December 2015).

———. "The Unfortunate Colonel." *The Civil War Monitor* 6, no. 4 (Winter 2016):

———. *The War Went On: Reconsidering the Lives of Civil War Veterans.* Baton Rouge: Louisiana State University Press, 2020.

Jordan, Wayne. "The Hoskinsville Rebellion." *Ohio State Archaeological and Historical Quarterly* 47, no. 1 (January 1938).

Joyner, Charles. *Down by the Riverside: A South Carolina Slave Community.* Urbana and Chicago: University of Illinois Press, 2009.

Kamphoefner, Walter D., and Wolfgang Helbich, eds. *Germans in the Civil War: The Letters They Wrote Home.* Chapel Hill: University of North Carolina Press, 2006.

Kamphoefner, Walter D., Wolfgang Helbich, and Ulrike Sommer, eds. *News from the Land of Freedom: German Immigrants Write Home.* Ithaca, NY: Cornell University Press, 1991.

Keating, Ryan W. *Shades of Green: Irish Regiments, American Soldiers, and Local Communities in the Civil War Era.* New York: Fordham University Press, 2017.

Keller, Christian B. *Chancellorsville and the Germans: Nativism, Ethnicity, and Civil War Memory.* New York: Fordham University Press, 2007.

Kelly, Patrick. *Creating a National Home: Building the Veterans' Welfare State, 1860–1900.* Cambridge, MA: Harvard University Press, 1997.

Kesterman, Richard. "The Burnet House: A Grand Cincinnati Hotel." *Ohio Valley History* 12, no. 4 (Winter 2012).

Kirkwood, Ronald D. *"Too Much for Human Endurance": The George Spangler Farm Hospitals and the Battle of Gettysburg.* El Dorado Hills, CA: Savas Beatie, 2019.

Klement, Frank L. *The Copperheads in the Middle West.* Chicago: University of Chicago Press, 1960.

———. *The Limits of Dissent: Clement L. Vallandigham & The Civil War.* Lexington: University Press of Kentucky, 1970.

Kluskens, Claire Prechtel. "Anatomy of a Union Civil War Pension File." *NGS Newsmagazine* 34, no. 3 (July-September 2008).

———. "'A Reasonable Degree of Promptitude': Civil War Pension Claim Application Processing, 1861–1865," *Prologue* 42, no. 1 (2010).

Knepper, George. *Ohio and Its People.* Kent, OH: Kent State University Press, 1989.

Krick, Robert K. *Civil War Weather in Virginia.* Tuscaloosa: University of Alabama Press, 2007.

———. *The Smoothbore Volley That Doomed the Confederacy: The Death of Stonewall Jackson and Other Chapters on the Army of Northern Virginia.* Baton Rouge: Louisiana State University Press, 2002.

Kutzler, Evan A. *Living by Inches: The Smells, Sounds, Tastes, and Feelings of Captivity in Civil War Prisons.* Chapel Hill: University of North Carolina Press, 2019.

Landis, George. "The Society of Separatists of Zoar, Ohio." *Annual Report of the American Historical Association* (1899).

Lane, Samuel Alanson. *Fifty Years and Over of Akron and Summit County.* Akron: Beacon Job Department, 1892.

Lang, Andrew F., and Andrew S. Bledsoe, eds. *Upon the Fields of Battle: Essays on the Civil War's Military History.* Baton Rouge: Louisiana State University Press, 2018.

LaRoche, Ramona. *Georgetown County, South Carolina.* Charleston, SC: Arcadia, 2000.

Lawrence, Stratton. *Folly Beach.* Charleston, SC: Arcadia, 2013.

Legg, James B., and Steven D. Smith. *"The Best Ever Occupied . . ." Archaeological Investigations of a Civil War Encampment on Folly Island, South Carolina.* Columbia: South Carolina Institute of Archaeology and Anthropology, 1989.

Lesser, W. Hunter. *Rebels at the Gate: Lee and McClellan on the Front Line of a Nation Divided.* Naperville, IL: Sourcebooks, 2004.

Levine, Bruce. *The Spirit of 1848: German Immigrants, Labor Conflict, and the Coming of the Civil War.* Urbana and Chicago: University of Illinois Press, 1992.

Linderman, Gerald F. *Embattled Courage: The Experience of Combat in the American Civil War.* New York: Free Press, 1987.

Linenthal, Edward T. *The Unfinished Bombing: Oklahoma City in American Memory*. Oxford: Oxford University Press, 2001.

Long, David E. *The Jewel of Liberty: Abraham Lincoln's Re-election and the End of Slavery*. Mechanicsburg, PA: Stackpole Books, 1994.

Longley, Kyle. *Grunts: The American Combat Soldier in Vietnam*. New York: Routledge, 2015.

Longacre, Edward G. *The Commanders of Chancellorsville—The Gentleman versus the Rogue: The Opposing Strategies and Personalities of Lee and Hooker*. Nashville: Rutledge Hill Press, 2005.

Lowry, Thomas P. *Curmudgeons, Drunkards, & Outright Fools: Courts-Martial of Civil War Union Colonels*. Lincoln: University of Nebraska Press, 2003.

Lucas, Marion Brunson. *Sherman and the Burning of Columbia*. College Station: Texas A&M University Press, 1988.

Luebke, Peter C., ed. *The Story of a Thousand: A History of the 105th Ohio Volunteer Infantry by Albion Tourgee*. Kent, OH: Kent State University Press, 2011.

Mahin, Dean. *The Blessed Place of Freedom: Europeans in Civil War America*. Washington, DC: Brassey's, 2002.

Maizlish, Stephen E. *The Triumph of Sectionalism: The Transformation of Ohio Politics, 1844–1856*. Kent, OH: Kent State University Press, 1983.

Manning, Chandra M. *Troubled Refuge: Struggling for Freedom in the Civil War*. New York: Alfred A. Knopf, 2016.

——— . *What This Cruel War Was Over: Soldiers, Slavery, and the Civil War*. New York: Alfred A. Knopf, 2007.

Marshall, Nicholas. "The Great Exaggeration: Death and the Civil War." *Journal of the Civil War Era* 4, no. 1 (March 2014).

Marten, James A. *Sing Not War: The Lives of Union and Confederate Veterans in Gilded Age America*. Chapel Hill: University of North Carolina Press, 2011.

Marvel, William. *Burnside*. Chapel Hill: University of North Carolina Press, 1991.

——— . *Lee's Last Retreat: The Flight to Appomattox*. Chapel Hill: University of North Carolina Press, 2002.

Matsui, John H. *The First Republican Army: The Army of Virginia and the Radicalization of the Civil War*. Charlottesville: University Press of Virginia, 2016.

McFeely, William S. *Yankee Stepfather: General O. O. Howard and the Freedmen*. New York: W. W. Norton, 1968.

McPherson, James M. *Battle Cry of Freedom: The Civil War Era*. New York: Oxford University Press, 1988.

——— . *For Cause and Comrades: Why Men Fought in the Civil War*. New York: Oxford University Press, 1997.

Meier, Kathryn Shively. *Nature's Civil War: Common Soldiers and the Environment in 1862 Virginia*. Chapel Hill: University of North Carolina Press, 2013.

Middleton, Stephen. *The Black Laws: Race and the Legal Process in Early Ohio.* Athens: Ohio University Press, 2005.

Miller, Brian Craig. *Empty Sleeves: Amputation in the Civil War South.* Athens: University of Georgia Press, 2015.

Miller, Richard F., ed. *States at War.* Vol. 4: *A Reference Guide for Delaware, Maryland, and New Jersey in the Civil War.* Hanover and London: University Press of New England, 2015

———. *States at War,* Vol. 5: *A Reference Guide for Ohio in the Civil War.* Hanover and London: University Press of New England, 2015.

Mitchell, Reid. *The Vacant Chair: The Northern Soldier Leaves Home.* New York: Oxford University Press, 1993.

Moran, Daniel, and Arthur Waldron, eds. *The People in Arms: Military Myth and National Mobilization since the French Revolution.* Cambridge: Cambridge University Press, 2003.

Neely, Mark E., Jr. *Lincoln and the Democrats.* Cambridge: Cambridge University Press, 2017.

Nelson, Chris. "An Unlucky XI Corps Regiment: The 107th Ohio Volunteer Infantry." *Military Images* 22, no. 6 (May/June 2001).

Nelson, Megan Kate. *Ruin Nation: Destruction and the American Civil War.* Athens: University of Georgia Press, 2012.

Nulty, William H. *Confederate Florida: The Road to Olustee.* Tuscaloosa: University of Alabama Press, 1990.

Oakes, James. *The Scorpion's Sting: Antislavery & the Coming of the Civil War.* New York: W. W. Norton, 2013.

Ofeldt III, Frank A. *Fort Clinch.* Charleston, South Carolina: Arcadia, 2017.

Ortiz, Paul. *Emancipation Betrayed: The Hidden History of Black Organizing and White Violence in Florida from Reconstruction to the Bloody Election of 1920.* Berkeley and Los Angeles: University of California Press, 2005.

Ouchley, Kelby. *Flora and Fauna of the Civil War: An Environmental Reference Guide.* Baton Rouge: Louisiana State University Press, 2010.

Parker, Daisy. "John Milton, Governor of Florida: A Loyal Confederate." *Florida Historical Quarterly* 20 (April 1942).

Patchan, Scott C. *Second Manassas: Longstreet's Attack and the Struggle for Chinn Ridge.* Washington, DC: Potomac Books, 2011.

Pfanz, Harry W. *Gettysburg—The First Day.* Chapel Hill: University of North Carolina Press, 2001.

Phillips, Jason. "Battling Stereotypes: A Taxonomy of Common Soldiers in Civil War History." *History Compass* 6, no. 6 (2008).

Piston, William Garrett. "Cross Purposes: Longstreet, Lee, and Confederate Attack Plans for July 3 at Gettysburg," in Gary W. Gallagher, ed., *The Third Day at Gettysburg & Beyond.* Chapel Hill: University of North Carolina Press, 1994.

Poole, W. Scott. *South Carolina's Civil War: A Narrative History.* Macon, GA: Mercer University Press, 2005.

Proctor, Samuel. "Jacksonville During the Civil War." *Florida Historical Quarterly* 41, no. 4 (April 1963).

Prokopowicz, Gerald J. *All for the Regiment: The Army of the Ohio, 1861–1862.* Chapel Hill: University of North Carolina Press, 2001.

Pula, James S. *Under the Crescent Moon with the XI Corps in the Civil War,* Vol. 1: *From the Defenses of Washington to Chancellorsville, 1862–1863.* El Dorado Hills, CA: Savas Beatie, 2017.

Rable, George C. *Fredericksburg! Fredericksburg!* Chapel Hill: University of North Carolina Press, 2002.

Ramold, Steven. *Baring the Iron Hand: Discipline in the Union Army.* DeKalb: Northern Illinois University Press, 2009.

Reardon, Carol, and Tom Vossler. *A Field Guide to Gettysburg: Experiencing the Battlefield through Its History, Places, and People.* Chapel Hill: University of North Carolina Press, 2013.

Reihmann, Max. "A Gettysburg Story of Interest." *Case Shot & Canister: A Publication of the Delaware Valley Civil War Round Table* 27, no. 8 (August 2017).

Reynolds, Donald E. *Editors Make War: Southern Newspapers in the Secession Crisis.* Carbondale: Southern Illinois University Press, 2006.

Rhea, Gordon C. *The Battles for Spotsylvania Court House and the Road to Yellow Tavern, May 7–12, 1864.* Baton Rouge: Louisiana State University Press, 1997.

Rioux, Anne Boyd. *Constance Fenimore Woolson: Portrait of a Lady Novelist.* New York: W. W. Norton, 2016.

Rollins, Richard. *"The Damned Red Flags of the Rebellion": The Confederate Battle Flag at Gettysburg.* Redondo Beach, CA: Rank and File Publications, 1997.

Rose, William Ganson. *Cleveland: The Making of a City.* Kent, OH: Kent State University Press, 1990.

Roseboom, Eugene H. *The History of the State of Ohio,* Vol. 4: *The Civil War Era, 1850–1873.* Columbus: Ohio State Archaeological and Historical Society, 1944.

Rosen, Robert N. "Charleston, Siege of (1863–1865)," in Walter B. Edgar, ed., *South Carolina Encyclopedia.* Columbia: University of South Carolina Press, 2006.

Samito, Christian G. *Becoming American under Fire: Irish Americans, African Americans, and the Politics of Citizenship during the Civil War Era.* Ithaca, NY: Cornell University Press, 2011.

Sandow, Robert M., ed. *Contested Loyalty: Debates over Patriotism in the Civil War North.* New York: Fordham University Press, 2018.

Savage, Kirk. *Standing Soldiers, Kneeling Slaves: Race, War, and Monument in Nineteenth-Century America.* Princeton: Princeton University Press, 1999.

Sawyer, Franklin. *The Eighth Ohio at Gettysburg.* Washington, DC: E. J. Gray, Printer, 1889.

Schafer, Daniel L. *Thunder on the River: The Civil War in Northeast Florida.* Gainesville: University Press of Florida, 2010.

Sears, Stephen W. *Chancellorsville*. New York: Houghton Mifflin, 1996.

———. *Gettysburg*. New York: Houghton Mifflin, 2003.

Selby, John G. *Meade: The Price of Command, 1863–1865*. Kent, OH: Kent State University Press, 2018.

Shankman, Arnold. "Soldier Votes and Clement L. Vallandigham in the 1863 Ohio Gubernatorial Election." *Ohio History* 82, nos.1–2 (Winter–Spring 1973).

Sheehan-Dean, Aaron. "The Blue and Gray in Black and White: Assessing the Scholarship on Civil War Soldiers," in Sheehan-Dean, ed., *The View from the Ground: Experiences of Civil War Soldiers*. Lexington: University Press of Kentucky, 2007.

Sheriff, Carol. *The Artificial River: The Erie Canal and the Paradox of Progress*. New York: Hill and Wang, 1996.

Silber, Nina. *The Romance of Reunion: Northerners and the South, 1865–1900*. Chapel Hill: University of North Carolina Press, 1992.

Simpson, Brooks D. "Great Expectations: Ulysses S. Grant, the Northern Press, and the Opening of the Wilderness Campaign," in Gary W. Gallagher, ed., *The Wilderness Campaign*. Chapel Hill: University of North Carolina Press, 1997.

Slotkin, Richard. *The Long Road to Antietam*. New York: Liveright, 2012.

Smith, Jacob. *Camps and Campaigns of the 107th Ohio Volunteer Infantry, 1862–1865*. Reprint ed. Navarre, Ohio: Indian River Graphics, 2000.

Smith, Mark M. *The Smell of Battle, The Taste of Siege: A Sensory History of the Civil War*. New York: Oxford University Press, 2015.

Smith, Thomas H. "Crawford County 'Ez Trooly Dimecratic': A Study of Midwestern Copperheadism." *Ohio History* 76, nos. 1–2 (Winter/Spring 1967).

Smith, Timothy B. *Shiloh: Conquer or Perish*. Lawrence: University Press of Kansas, 2014.

Sodergren, Steven R. *The Army of the Potomac in the Overland and Petersburg Campaigns*. Baton Rouge: Louisiana State University Press, 2017.

Stackpole, Edward J. *Chancellorsville: Lee's Greatest Battle*. 2nd ed. Harrisburg, PA: Stackpole Books, 1988.

Starr, Stephen Z. "The Grand Old Regiment." *Wisconsin Magazine of History* 48, no. 1 (Autumn 1964).

Sternhell, Yael A. "Revisionism Reinvented? The Antiwar Turn in Civil War Scholarship." *Journal of the Civil War Era* 3, no. 2 (June 2013).

Stone, Jr., H. David. *Vital Rails: The Charleston & Savannah Railroad and the Civil War in Coastal South Carolina*. Columbia: University of South Carolina Press, 2008.

Stout, Harry S. *Upon the Altar of the Nation: A Moral History of the Civil War*. New York: Viking, 2006.

Suhrer, Andrew B. *The Flying Dutchmen*. Bloomington, IN: Author House, 2008.

Sutherland, Daniel E. *Fredericksburg & Chancellorsville: The Dare Mark Campaign*. Lincoln: University of Nebraska Press, 1998.

Swierenga, Robert. "The Settlement of the Old Northwest." *Journal of the Early Republic* 9, no. 1 (Spring 1989).

Taylor, Amy Murrell. *Embattled Freedom: Journeys through the Civil War's Slave Refugee Camps*. Chapel Hill: University of North Carolina Press, 2018.

Taylor, Robert A. *Rebel Storehouse: Florida's Contribution to the Confederacy*. Tuscaloosa: University of Alabama Press, 2003.

Teters, Kristopher. *Practical Liberators: Union Officers in the Western Theater during the Civil War*. Chapel Hill: University of North Carolina Press, 2018.

Thomas, Edison H. *John Hunt Morgan and His Raiders*. Lexington: University Press of Kentucky, 1985.

Trefousse, Hans L. *Carl Schurz: A Biography*. Knoxville: University of Tennessee Press, 1982.

Trommler, Frank, and Joseph McVeigh, eds. *America and the Germans: An Assessment of a Three-Hundred-Year History*. Philadelphia: University of Pennsylvania Press, 1985.

Trudeau, Noah Andre. *Out of the Storm: The End of the Civil War, April–June 1865*. Boston: Little, Brown and Company, 1994.

Ural, Susannah, ed. *Civil War Citizens: Race, Ethnicity, and Identity in America's Bloodiest Conflict*. New York: New York University Press, 2010.

———. *Hood's Texas Brigade: The Soldiers and Families of the Confederacy's Most Celebrated Unit*. Baton Rouge: Louisiana State University Press, 2017.

Van Tassel, David D., and John J. Grabowski, eds. *The Encyclopedia of Cleveland History*. Bloomington and Indianapolis: Indiana University Press, 1996.

Van Tassel, David Dirck, and John Vacha. *"Behind Bayonets": The Civil War in Northern Ohio*. Kent, OH: Kent State University Press, 2006.

Varon, Elizabeth R. *Appomattox: Victory, Defeat, and Freedom at the End of the Civil War*. New York: Oxford University Press, 2013.

Vignos, Cindy. "The Novelty Cutlery Company," *Oregon Knife Collectors Newsletter* (October 2000).

Walker, Mack. *Germany and the Emigration, 1816–1885*. Cambridge, MA: Harvard University Press, 1964.

Warner, Ezra J. *Generals in Blue: Lives of the Union Commanders*. Baton Rouge: Louisiana State University Press, 1964.

———. *Generals in Gray: Lives of Confederate Commanders*. Baton Rouge: Louisiana State University Press, 2006.

Waugh, John C. *Re-Electing Lincoln: The Battle for the 1864 Presidency*. New York: Da Capo, 2001.

Weber, Jennifer L. *Copperheads: The Rise and Fall of Lincoln's Opponents in the North*. New York: Oxford University Press, 2006.

Webber, Philip E. *Zoar in the Civil War*. Kent, OH: Kent State University Press, 2007.

Weeks, Jim. *Gettysburg: Memory, Market, and an American Shrine*. Princeton: Princeton University Press, 2003.

Weinstein, Leonard. "The Relationship of Battle Damage to Unit Combat Performance." Institute for Defense Analysis Paper P-1903 (April 1986): 3–5.

Welcher, Frank J. *The Union Army, 1861–1865: Organization and Operations*. Bloomington: Indiana University Press, 1989.

Wells, Cheryl. *Civil War Time: Temporality and Identity in America, 1861–1865*. Athens: University of Georgia Press, 2005.

White, Jonathan W. *Emancipation, the Union Army, and the Reelection of Abraham Lincoln*. Baton Rouge: Louisiana State University Press, 2014.

———. *Midnight in America: Darkness, Sleep, and Dreams During the Civil War*. Chapel Hill: University of North Carolina Press, 2017.

Will-Weber, Mark. *Muskets and Applejack: Spirits, Soldiers, and the Civil War*. Washington, DC: Regnery History, 2017.

Wills, Brian Steel. *Inglorious Passages: Noncombat Deaths in the American Civil War*. Lawrence: University Press of Kansas, 2017.

Wilson, Mark R. *The Business of Civil War: Military Mobilization and the State, 1861–1865*. Baltimore: Johns Hopkins University Press, 2006.

Winters, Harold, et al. *Battling the Elements: Weather and Terrain in the Conduct of War*. Baltimore: Johns Hopkins University Press, 1998.

Wise, Stephen R. *Gate of Hell: Campaign for Charleston Harbor, 1863*. Columbia: University of South Carolina Press, 1994.

Wittenberg, Eric J. *The Union Cavalry Comes of Age: Hartwood Church to Brandy Station, 1863*. Washington, DC: Brassey's, 2003.

Wittenberg, Eric J., J. David Petruzzi, and Michael F. Nugent. *One Continuous Fight: The Retreat from Gettysburg and the Pursuit of Lee's Army of Northern Virginia, July 4–14, 1863*. El Dorado Hills, CA: Savas Beatie, 2008.

Wittenberg, Eric J., and Scott L. Mingus, Sr. *The Second Battle of Winchester: The Confederate Victory That Opened the Door to Gettysburg*. El Dorado Hills, CA: Savas Beatie, 2016.

Woods, Terry K. *Ohio's Grand Canal: A Brief History of the Ohio & Erie Canal*. Kent, OH: Kent State University Press, 2008.

Wright, Robert E., and George David Smith. *Mutually Beneficial: The Guardian and Life Insurance in America*. New York and London: New York University Press, 2004.

Theses and Dissertations

Altavilla, Keith F. "Can We Call It Anything but Treason? Loyalty and Citizenship in Ohio Valley Soldiers" (PhD diss., Texas Christian University, 2013).

Coles, David James. "Far from Fields of Glory: Military Operations in Florida during the Civil War, 1864–1865" (PhD diss., Florida State University, 1996).

Elrod, Matthew. "The Impact of the Civil War on Northern Kentucky and Cincinnati, 1861–1865" (Master's thesis, Northern Kentucky University, 2006).

Frawley, Jason. "Marching Through Pennsylvania: The Story of Soldiers and Civilians in the Gettysburg Campaign" (PhD diss., Texas Christian University, 2008).

Gladwin, Jr., William J. "Men, Salt, Cattle and Battle: The Civil War in Florida, November 1860–July 1865" (Research paper, U.S. Naval War College, 1992).

Kinney, Thomas. "From Shop to Factory in the Industrial Heartland: The Industrialization of Horse-Drawn Vehicle Manufacture in the City of Cleveland" (PhD diss., Case Western Reserve University, 1998).

Shankman, Arnold. "Candidate in Exile: Clement Vallandigham and the 1863 Ohio Gubernatorial Election" (PhD diss., Emory University, 1969).

Siber White, Elizabeth. "The *Wiedergeburt* in the Religion of the Zoarites" (Master's thesis, Western Michigan University, 1985).

Spickelmier, R. K. "Training of the American Soldier During World War I and World War II" (Master's thesis, U.S. Army Command and General Staff College, 1971).

Trester, Delmer John. "The Political Career of David Tod" (PhD diss., The Ohio State University, 1950).

INDEX